Data Storytelling with Google Looker Studio

A hands-on guide to using Looker Studio for building
compelling and effective dashboards

Sireesha Pulipati

BIRMINGHAM—MUMBAI

Data Storytelling with Google Looker Studio

Copyright © 2022 Packt Publishing

Publishing Product Manager: Heramb Bhavsar
Senior Editor: Nazia Shaikh
Content Development Editor: Sean Lobo
Technical Editor: Rahul Limbachiya
Copy Editor: Safis Editing
Project Coordinator: Farheen Fathima
Proofreader: Safis Editing
Indexer: Tejal Daruwale Soni
Production Designer: Ponraj Dhandapani
Marketing Coordinators: Priyanka Mhatre and Nivedita Singh

First published: October 2022

Production reference: 2311022

Published by Packt Publishing Ltd.
Livery Place
35 Livery Street
Birmingham
B3 2PB, UK.

ISBN 978-1-80056-876-1

www.packt.com

To my father, Seshagiri Rao Pulipati, who is my north star and inspiration. To my husband, Uma Shanker Avvari, for being the anchor of my life and of everything I do and achieve.

– Sireesha Pulipati

Foreword

Some years ago, I was standing on a career precipice. I was in the middle of my first ever product launch, which was being crowd funded on KickStarter. The product was a low tech boardgame approach to creating wireframes for business dashboards; it was called the Dashboard Wireframe Kit. This was a completely new environment to me, having left the world of Big 4 analytics consulting and plunged into the foray of being an independent consultant with a heavy specialization in data visualization and driving the adoption of dashboards in enterprise.

One of the very early supporters of what I was doing was the author of this book. She was a vocal advocate for storytelling with data, though what really stood out was her practical perspective on how to go about it. She had a perspective that could only be borne out of years of working in the field and actually having to figure out what works, and what was best left as theory, from the many books out there on the topic.

I've read these books, and many of them present excellent theory. Others present thoughtful technical approaches to using certain specific tools. Rarely do you come across a work that combines the two. Yet, that is what the author has achieved here – a highly valuable distillation of data visualization best practices, with a targeted technical application to Google Looker Studio. Put down whatever else you are reading, because this book compresses a vast amount of knowledge into a potent knowledgebase that will make you a proficient in both visualization, and in applying that expertise directly in the tool. Enjoy!

Nicholas Kelly
Author | Delivering Data Analytics

Acknowledgements

Writing this book had been a joyful, challenging, and rewarding experience. Many people helped and supported me along the way. I express my deep gratitude to the Packt team for their support and guidance at every step of the process. Special thanks go to Heramb Bhavsar, for proposing the book idea and convincing me that it needed to be written. I thank my editors Nazia Sheikh and Sean Lobo, for their attention to detail that helped improve the quality of the book manyfold.

I'm grateful to Joshua Vickery for his wise counsel and for being my sounding board throughout the journey. I'm especially thankful to Remy Welch for her time, encouragement, and keen insights on the final draft. Many thanks to Corey Mc Williams and Udaya Yarasi for their feedback on some of the early drafts. A great big thank you to Nicholas Kelly for providing the foreword to the book at very short notice.

Last, but not least, I couldn't have written this book without the sacrifices made by my husband, Uma Shanker, and my two sons, Akhil and Gowtham. They held the family fort as I spent inordinate amounts of time in the writing process over several months, and cheered me on endlessly.

Contributors

About the author

Sireesha Pulipati is an experienced data analytics and data management professional. She has spent the last decade building and managing data platforms and solutions, and she is passionate about enabling users to leverage data to solve business problems. Sireesha holds a master's degree in business administration and a bachelor's degree in electrical engineering. Her work history spans multiple industries – healthcare, media, travel and hospitality, high-tech, and more. She is currently at Google as a technical lead, helping with the business intelligence and analytics strategy for the teams building and supporting the Knowledge Graph. Outside of work, Sireesha enjoys hiking and reading books. She currently resides in the San Francisco Bay Area.

About the reviewers

Ganesh is a self-motivated IT professional with extensive experience in leading and managing information technology projects in companies such as Oracle and Standard Chartered Bank. He has completed a postgraduate degree with computer science as his major at Bharathidasan University, and executive education in finance from the Indian Institute of Management, Kozhikode. As a passionate data visualization expert, he has designed beautiful eye-catching dashboards in both Google Looker Studio and Zoho Analytics for various clients. He also specializes in the development of applications using the Zoho suite of products.

I would like to thank Packt Publishing for giving me the opportunity to review this book. I thank my family, friends, and all the well-wishers for supporting me all these years.

Ralph Spandl moved to Montreal after finishing his studies at the HdK (University of Fine Arts) in Berlin, where he founded r42, which slowly became a web agency with a nice portfolio of companies, working in the financial, industrial, and leisure sectors and a few non-profit organizations. For years, Ralph had a soft spot for data visualization, which he planned to center his professional career around. Since 2018 or thereabouts, he has been doing just that, designing and coding data visualizations, and he is now working with Supermetrics on the implementation of the first commercial Looker Studio chart library, a collection of data visualizations that allow you to push the limits of Looker Studio.

Table of Contents

3

Visualizing Data Effectively   51

Part 2 – Looker Studio Features and Capabilities

4

Google Looker Studio Overview   81

5

Looker Studio Report Designer   129

6

Looker Studio Built-In Charts   179

7

Looker Studio Features, Beyond Basics   243

Part 3 – Building Data Stories with Looker Studio

8

Employee Turnover Analysis   301

Preface

Organizations and individuals are increasingly relying on data to make important decisions. Presenting data visually makes it easier to interpret and analyze. **Google Looker Studio** is an easy-to-use and collaborative tool that helps you explore your data and transform it into beautiful visualizations. With Looker Studio, you can build and share dashboards that help monitor key performance indicators, identify patterns, and generate insights that ultimately drive decisions and actions.

The goals of this book are threefold: first, provide foundational know-how on basic design and visualization principles, second, offer a practical and demystified guide on using Looker Studio for visualizing data, and third, give a walk-through of the structured dashboard building process and the various deliberations involved in it. *Data Storytelling with Google Looker Studio* begins with laying out the foundational design principles and guidelines that are essential to creating accurate, effective, and compelling data visualizations. We then delve into the features and capabilities of Looker Studio – from the basic to the advanced – and showcase their application with examples. The book then takes you through the process of building dashboards with a structured three-stage process called the **3-D approach** using real-world examples. The approach involves determining the objectives and needs of the dashboard, designing its key components and layout, and developing each element of the dashboard. These examples take you through the thought process of various design and implementation considerations.

Reports and dashboards are two forms of presenting data visuals together. They fundamentally serve different purposes and differ in terms of level of detail, interactivity, breadth and so on. However, for all practical purposes of this book, the distinction between the two doesn't matter too much. Hence, I use the terms *report* and *dashboard* interchangeably through much of this book. In cases where the distinction makes a difference to the topic discussed, I call that out specifically.

All through the writing of this book, right up to its publication, the tool we used was called "Data Studio." Google announced the rebranding of the tool as "Looker Studio" on October 11, 2022, which reflected on the tool itself as well as the associated documentation and support pages almost instantaneously, or so it seemed.

Google acquired Looker, the new-age enterprise **Business Intelligence (BI)** and data analytics platform, in 2019. With its logical semantic layer, in-database architecture, API and developer-friendly capabilities, Looker provides a powerful platform to meet enterprise business intelligence needs. Looker became part of the Google Cloud offerings, and it complemented the existing free Data Studio tool. Together, the two business intelligence tools provided flexibility and choice to the users.

The rebranding is part of a strategy to consolidate all Google Cloud's business intelligence services under the Looker brand. The Data Studio tool itself remains the same, and there is no change in its capabilities and features as a result of this. From a UI standpoint, only the logo is changed. Also, the product is still free. Google has introduced a new premium tier to Looker Studio, called Looker Studio Pro, with additional capabilities and support that cater to enterprise teams.

This book is only limited to the free Looker Studio (formerly, Data Studio) tool and does not touch upon any enterprise capabilities of the Pro version of Looker Studio or the Looker platform. While an attempt is made to use the new name - Looker Studio - as much as possible throughout the book, screenshots and images mostly reflect the old name and logo.

A big part of this strategic move by Google is the strong integration between Looker Studio and the Looker Platform. Looker enables you to create semantic models of your data by defining relationships between data sets, creating metrics, and encapsulating business logic. With the new Looker connector, you can connect to your Looker models from Looker Studio and visualize the data, without you needing to build the relationships, creating metrics, or formatting fields within Looker Studio. While the connector is free, you need a valid license and appropriate permissions to the Looker Platform to connect. Looker is in turn very deeply integrated with BigQuery. Looker by itself does not store any data. It connects to the data stored in BigQuery, and provides a logical layer on top of it to meet the data exploration, analytical, and reporting needs of the users. It thus leverages the powerful analytical capabilities of BigQuery. The Looker platform has its own visualization layer, which is complementary to Looker Studio. As a BI enthusiast, I'm very excited about this direction that Google has taken with its BI portfolio and I will closely follow its evolution - you should too.

Who this book is for

If you are a beginner or an aspiring data analyst looking to understand the core concepts of data visualization and you want to use Google Looker Studio for creating effective dashboards, this book is for you. No specific prior knowledge is required to benefit from this book.

If you are a more experienced data analyst or business intelligence developer, you will find this book useful as a detailed guide to using Looker Studio as well as a refresher of the core dashboarding concepts.

If you are a business professional looking to build reports and run analyses on your own, this book empowers you with the knowledge and skills you need to visualize data effectively using the simple and easy-to-use tool Looker Studio.

What this book covers

Chapter 1, Introduction to Data Storytelling, introduces the concept of data storytelling, its format, and its manifestation in dashboards and reports.

Chapter 2, Principles of Data Visualization, covers foundational principles and guidelines that enable the creation of effective and compelling data visualizations.

Chapter 3, Visualizing Looker Effectively, describes some common chart types and their applications along with pitfalls to avoid.

Chapter 4, Google Looker Studio Overview, gets you started with Looker Studio and describes how to work with and manage key entities such as data sources, reports, and explorerss.

Chapter 5, Looker Studio Report Designer, examines key report designer options, settings, and elements such as report theme, pages, filter controls, styling, and more that help design reports in Looker Studio.

Chapter 6, Looker Studio Built-In Charts, reviews the built-in charts provided by Looker Studio and their configurations.

Chapter 7, Looker Studio Features, Beyond Basics, covers advanced features such as calculated fields, parameters, blending, report templates, community visualizations, and report optimization.

Chapter 8, Employee Turnover Analysis, walks you through building a detailed report analyzing employee turnover for a fictious company using the 3-D approach: Determine, Design, and Develop.

Chapter 9, Mortgage Complaints Analysis, walks you through building a dashboard for monitoring mortgage-related complaints received by the **Consumer Financial Protection Bureau (CFPB)**, a US agency, using the 3-D approach.

Chapter 10, Customer Churn Analysis, walks you through building a dashboard to analyze the customer churn phenomenon for a broadband service company using the 3-D approach.

Chapter 11, Monitoring Looker Studio Report Usage, describes how to track and monitor usage of Looker Studio reports using Google Analytics.

To get the most out of this book

Looker Studio is a web-based tool. You need a Google account and a supported browser to follow along and benefit from the book. Basic SQL knowledge will help you explore a few topics, but is not mandatory. Access to a Google Cloud Platform account, either a free trial or paid, is nice to have and will help you visualize data from BigQuery public datasets. You can leverage the free BigQuery sandbox for this purpose as well.

Software/hardware covered in the book	Operating system requirements
Looker Studio (web-based)	NA
Google Cloud Platform subscription (free trial or paid) or BigQuery sandbox (free)	NA
Google Analytics (web-based)	NA

Google Cloud Platform is used to demonstrate visualizing data from BigQuery, Google's petabyte-scale cloud data warehouse. It is leveraged only in a couple of chapters in the book. No prior knowledge of BigQuery is expected. The details of how to get started with it and connect to it from Looker Studio are included in *Chapter 9, Mortgage Complaints Analysis.* Google Analytics is a free Google tool and is used to monitor the reports of Looker Studio in *Chapter 11, Monitoring Looker Studio Report Usage.*

If you are using the digital version of this book, we advise you to type the code yourself or access the code from the book's GitHub repository (a link is available in the next section). Doing so will help you avoid any potential errors related to the copying and pasting of code.

Download the example code files

You can download the example code files for this book from GitHub at `https://github.com/PacktPublishing/Data-Storytelling-with-Google-Data-Studio`. If there's an update to the code, it will be updated in the GitHub repository.

We also have other code bundles from our rich catalog of books and videos available at `https://github.com/PacktPublishing/`. Check them out!

Download the color images

We also provide a PDF file that has color images of the screenshots and diagrams used in this book. You can download it here: `https://packt.link/5u31Q`.

Conventions used

There are a number of text conventions used throughout this book.

`Code in text`: Indicates code words in text, database table names, folder names, filenames, file extensions, pathnames, dummy URLs, user input, and Twitter handles. Here is an example: "BigQuery provides this information as part of the `census_bureau_acs` public dataset."

A block of code is set as follows:

```
CREATE TABLE `datastudio-343704.data_viz.baseball_schedule`

AS

SELECT * FROM `bigquery-public-data.baseball.schedules
```

Bold: Indicates a new term, an important word, or words that you see onscreen. For instance, words in menus or dialog boxes appear in **bold**. Here is an example: "The **SETUP** tab is where you choose the appropriate data source and add different fields – dimensions and metrics that make up the chart."

> **Tips or important notes**
> Appear like this.

Get in touch

Feedback from our readers is always welcome.

General feedback: If you have questions about any aspect of this book, email us at customercare@packtpub.com and mention the book title in the subject of your message.

Errata: Although we have taken every care to ensure the accuracy of our content, mistakes do happen. If you have found a mistake in this book, we would be grateful if you would report this to us. Please visit www.packtpub.com/support/errata and fill in the form.

Piracy: If you come across any illegal copies of our works in any form on the internet, we would be grateful if you would provide us with the location address or website name. Please contact us at copyright@packt.com with a link to the material.

If you are interested in becoming an author: If there is a topic that you have expertise in and you are interested in either writing or contributing to a book, please visit authors.packtpub.com.

Share Your Thoughts

Once you've read *Data Storytelling with Google Looker Studio*, we'd love to hear your thoughts! Scan the QR code below to go straight to the Amazon review page for this book and share your feedback.

https://packt.link/r/1-800-56876-2

Your review is important to us and the tech community and will help us make sure we're delivering excellent quality content.

Part 1 – Data Storytelling Concepts

This part introduces the concept of data storytelling, its importance, and its purpose. It presents the fundamental design principles that are key to building effective visualizations. It also looks at the basic dos and don'ts of data visualization and dashboard/report design. You will gain the foundational knowledge that's needed before you begin your own data storytelling journey.

This part comprises the following chapters:

- *Chapter 1, Introduction to Data Storytelling*
- *Chapter 2, Principles of Data Visualization*
- *Chapter 3, Visualizing Data Effectively*

1
Introduction to Data Storytelling

Data storytelling makes the presentation of data compelling and persuasive. This is a book about learning how to use the **Looker Studio** tool to visualize data and build useful reports and dashboards. Before we learn how to build different visual data representations, it's important to first understand the craft of storytelling with data and its utility. It will serve us well to take a step back and understand the big picture.

This introductory chapter sets the stage for understanding the meaning of data storytelling and its importance. We will go through the components of a good data story, understand how data storytelling manifests at work, and learn the key skills required to be a good storyteller. Finally, we will learn about an approach to building effective data stories. In this chapter, we will cover the following main topics:

- Understanding data storytelling
- Building data stories – an approach

Understanding data storytelling

Simply put, data storytelling means telling a story using data. According to Brent Dykes, author of the bestselling book *Effective Data Storytelling*, data storytelling is the skillful amalgamation of data, narrative, and visuals.

Why tell a story? Stories are an integral part of our lives and are the most natural way we consume and retain information. Compared to straightforward facts and messages, stories are memorable, impressionable, relatable, and persuasive. Stories appeal to the humanness of the audience. Stories often help in communicating a complex concept or message more effectively. This is evident through the prevalence and effectiveness of parables, fables, and other forms of stories throughout human history.

Structuring a data story

Stories can be told in different ways and can have different purposes. Some have a moral or a lesson to teach, some report events, while others just entertain. In the simplest sense, a story has a beginning, a middle, and an end. This basic structure is referred to as Aristotle's arc, known to have been introduced by the ancient Greek philosopher.

Figure 1.1 – Aristotle's arc

The traditional narrative arc expands on this basic linear structure and involves building up tension through rising and falling action. German playwright Gustav Freytag's five-step paradigm, commonly known as Freytag's Pyramid, forms the basis of most modern-day stories.

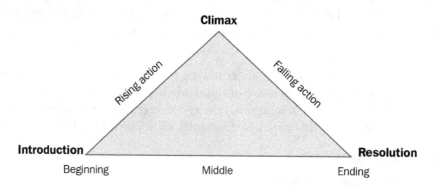

Figure 1.2 – Traditional story structure – Freytag's Pyramid

In this traditional form of narrative, the most important aspects of the story are revealed in the latter half of the story – climax through resolution. The traditional story approach when applied to data stories typically involves the following narrative flow:

1. Provide the context
2. State the problem
3. Highlight the impact
4. Share the key insight

The other major form of storytelling is news reporting. It follows an inverted pyramid format. The most important information is provided at the beginning, followed by the key supporting information, and finally, the least important details.

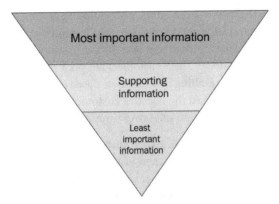

Figure 1.3 – News story structure

When a data story is created using the news story approach, it follows the following sequence of steps:

1. Share the key insight
2. Provide the context and causes
3. Details through drill-throughs/drill-downs

A data story can use either of these approaches depending on the presentation format, the audience, and the objective of the narrator – to influence a decision, to inform, to trigger an action, and so on. If you are presenting data to an executive audience with little time to spare, you might want to follow the news story approach by starting with the key insight. This will help you get their attention and then you can delve into the details as needed.

On the other hand, when you are trying to present a complex or counter-intuitive insight, you might want to follow the more traditional approach of first setting the stage with the context and evidence, then laying out the problem, drawing attention to the impact of this problem, and finally closing with one or more solution recommendations.

The purpose of a data story could either be explanatory, where we explain a phenomenon, or be actionable, where we want to elicit an action or decision through actionable insights. While data can also be used to describe a situation, the descriptive nature doesn't typically make a story by itself. Data on its own has no useful meaning. It needs to be gleaned for information and insights. And it is these insights that we are usually after.

Instances of powerful data stories that persuade action and influence decision making are ubiquitous. Consider a non-profit organization that is seeking donations for supporting cancer research. Sharing personal stories of those who suffered from cancer and those who benefitted from the research supported by the organization makes an incredible impact on the potential donors. Presenting a data story around the effectiveness of the organization, the amount of money raised, the membership growth, and the people served helps potential donors and volunteers to connect with the cause and persuade them to take action.

As another example, consider the owners of an online personalized gift store. Their sales are declining and they would like to understand what action they can take to remedy the situation. By analyzing sales and customer feedback data, they learned that over 30% of customers in the last 6 months have experienced shipping delays and damage. These customers left poor reviews on the e-commerce site and prominent social media forums, resulting in poor sales. Based on this insight, the owners decide to replace the shipping carrier. This caused the negative customer feedback to dwindle immediately and the store saw more positive feedback and sales over time.

Data storytelling is not the same thing as data visualization. While data visualization refers to the effective representation of data through graphics and visuals, data storytelling goes beyond just data visualization. Visuals are critical but are only one component of data storytelling. Data storytelling embeds data visuals in a narrative and presents a cohesive picture.

> **Note**
> Much of this book is focused on building great visualizations with Looker Studio. We will touch upon the narrative aspects of data storytelling where applicable.

When building a data story, always start with understanding your data and identifying the key insight or phenomenon you would like to share. Then create a narrative that you would like to take your users or audience through. Follow that with sketching the scenes and designing the storyboard. Only then work on building the visuals and presentation.

> **Further reading**
> For a deeper understanding of the psychology of storytelling and various aspects of data stories, read Brent Dykes' book *Effective Data Storytelling*.

Presenting data stories

Data stories can be presented either to a live audience for direct consumption or to an offline audience to consume the content indirectly. Data stories can take many forms – documents, PowerPoint presentations, videos, websites, dynamic dashboards, reports, and more. When you present directly to the audience, you are in full control of the narrative. You determine what the audience sees at any point in time. You can carefully walk them through your various story scenes in sequence, building up the necessary tension and anticipation.

In this mode, you can also employ various visual aids and tools – images, animations, video, text, charts, and more – to facilitate the narrative and make the presentation more compelling. The audience passively consumes the information you are providing. Nevertheless, it can be presented in quite an engaging way. Perhaps the best example of data storytelling comes from the Swedish physician and public speaker Hans Rosling's iconic narration of the story of the world using augmented reality animation. You can watch it on YouTube at `https://www.youtube.com/watch?v=jbkSRLYSojo`.

On the other hand, when the intent is to present to an audience or users who will consume the content later, the format can be static, such as in published reports or articles, or can be interactive, such as on dashboards, websites, and so on, allowing the audience to interact with the content and explore. In offline consumption mode, you need to be really cautious about driving the desired user behavior so that all users can interpret and understand the key insight or phenomenon consistently and with little ambiguity.

When the data is static and doesn't change over time, as the narrator or storyteller, you know exactly the insight or the message that needs to be conveyed and how best to present it. A good example of using text and visuals to narrate a story about *child mortality data* can be found at `https://vizhub.healthdata.org/child-mortality`.

With the help of simple animations, powerful visuals, and supporting text, the narrator has built a compelling narrative to highlight the problem of child mortality and how uncovering inequalities in child survival accelerates progress toward achieving the *Global Sustainable Development Goals* for child mortality (`https://data.unicef.org/topic/child-survival/child-survival-sdgs/`).

If data is not static and is updated on a regular basis, you are not in control of what the narrative will be because the insights may change over time. This is usually the case with business reports and dashboards. For this reason, it is static data that is the most amenable to creating data stories. However, you will still benefit from the data storytelling approach to develop these dashboards to create as cohesive a narrative as possible. Business dashboards are usually good at serving descriptive and explanatory purposes. However, you can also strive to help users identify any insights easily through intelligent design.

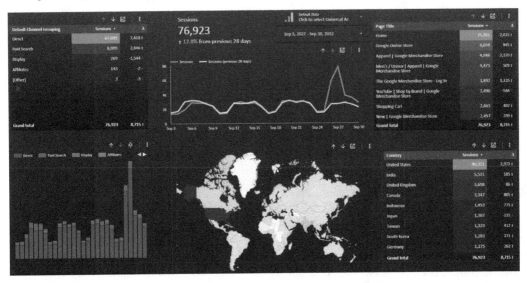

Figure 1.4 – Source: Looker Studio Report Gallery

This screenshot is an example of a well-designed dashboard. It is built using Google Analytics data and is available for use as a template from the **Looker Studio Report Gallery**.

Report versus dashboard

While I often use the terms *report* and *dashboard* together or interchangeably in this book, they actually represent two distinct forms of presenting data and generally serve different purposes. However, the concepts I discuss in this book apply to both constructs.

The following table lists some major differences between reports and dashboards:

Report	Dashboard
Usually focused on a single topic	Provides a single view of a range of related topics
Detailed and more granular	Summarized and less granular
Can span multiple pages and sections	A single page or screen
Can serve broader audience and multiple objectives	Usually serves best a single persona and objective
Can include high level of interactivity to allow users to explore the data and analyze further	Little to no interactivity required so that users can consume the information at a single glance

Table 1.1 – Differences between a report and a dashboard

> **Note**
>
> In Looker Studio, there is only a `Report` object, using which you can build either detailed reports or high-level dashboards based on the audience and the purpose at hand.

In the next section, we will discuss the role data storytelling plays in organizations.

Data storytelling at work

Being data-driven is the hallmark of all successful organizations. Thomas Davenport, the world-renowned thought leader, published his groundbreaking work *Competing on Analytics* in 2006. Ever since then, companies across industries have embraced analytics and embarked on the analytics journey to truly differentiate themselves from the competition. They achieved this by linking analytics with decision making. According to Davenport, there are five stages along the path to competing successfully in analytics:

1. Analytically impaired
2. Localized analytics
3. Analytical aspirations
4. Analytical companies
5. Analytical competitors

Irrespective of where an organization is on this journey, there are several avenues to leverage data and analytics to generate insights, persuade people, or influence and aid decision making. Analytics can help understand what is happening across different business functions viz. finance, customers, marketing, sales, and so on, and why. They can help determine the effectiveness of projects and programs across the organization to enable better decisions regarding resources. They can provide insights into optimizing people processes and allow for a data-driven approach to address human capital issues. Analytics can also be useful on a personal level – to influence your leadership or peers using data. Some examples of these different types of analytics are listed as follows:

- **Business analytics**: *F*inancial performance, customer engagement, product analytics, campaign effectiveness, sales pipelines, and so on

- **Project/program analytics**: *R*esource allocation, avoiding sunk cost fallacy, alignment with key results and objectives, and so on

- **People analytics**: *E*mployee attrition, absenteeism, **diversity, equity, and inclusion** (DEI) compliance, recruitment and hiring efficiency, employee engagement, learning and development effectiveness, and so on

- **Manage up/down**: *B*ring data and analytics that showcase your impact to the performance review conversations with your manager, tell a story backed by data to pitch your idea to peers, and so on

A critical capability that enables organizations to progress through the five stages of competitive data analytics and become truly data-driven is **data literacy**. Data literacy is the ability to read, understand, communicate, and work with data effectively. Thinking critically about the data and the insights it generates is also a core aspect of data literacy. For an organization to achieve a competitive advantage through data and analytics, its employees need to have high levels of data literacy and it has to be more prevalent across the organization. The main components of data literacy are as follows:

- **Understand**: *K*now what the data represents and the purpose it serves; understand key metrics.

- **Read**: *I*nterpret graphical and visual representations of data correctly.

- **Produce**: *W*rangle, clean, and prepare data appropriately to meet the analytical needs.

- **Communicate**: *C*onvey the insights effectively through the use of various tools and techniques.

- **Critical thinking**: *B*e curious about the data and what it can tell us and think critically about the insights it generates.

Essential skills for data storytelling

Data storytelling specifically addresses the *Communicate* aspect of data literacy. But it also embodies the other components as you cannot generate insights and communicate effectively without first understanding the data, working with the data, and thinking critically about the data. So, the key skills required to be a good data storyteller are as follows:

- **Get and prepare the data**

  - Identify the right data to address the problem at hand and obtain it. You might have to work with other teams to get access to that data. Or in the case of external data, you might have to make an API call, scrape the web, or download the data yourself.

  - Clean the data, format it, and munge it appropriately (reshaping, aggregating, filtering, and so on).

- **Analyze the data and generate insights**

  - Explore the data and understand the trends and relationships among different attributes. Create new metrics and apply analytical methods to glean insights.

- **Visualize the data**

  - Visualize the data in appropriate charts. You'll need to have the technical skill to use a specific tool – be it Google Sheets, Google Slides, MS Excel, MS PowerPoint, Looker Studio, Looker, Tableau, and so on.

- **Build a narrative**

  - Choose an appropriate narrative structure and design the storyboard.

Data storytelling is an essential skill that allows for effective communication through data. *Simplicity* can be thought of as the mantra of data storytelling so that anyone and everyone can understand the message and insight clearly and unambiguously. However, certain complex problems and phenomena might require a little more advanced representation and nuanced interpretation. A higher level of data literacy among stakeholders ensures that such data stories drive quality decision making.

At work, data storytelling usually manifests in the form of static slide decks, documents, and spreadsheets or dynamic dashboards and reports. The next section explains an approach that we can follow to build effective dynamic dashboards and reports based on the tenets of data storytelling described in the first section of this chapter.

Building data stories – an approach

Business dashboards and reports pose unique challenges in crafting a story owing to the dynamic nature of the data they support. In this section, we are going to learn about the **3-D approach** to designing and building effective dashboards. The approach consists of three main stages as shown in the following figure:

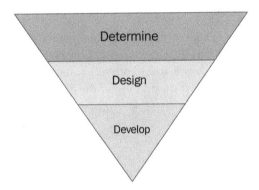

Figure 1.5 – Stages of the data storytelling approach

In the **Determine** stage, you need to work on determining the audience for the dashboard, the key business questions they need answering, and the data required to answer those questions. In the **Design** stage, you will work on the narrative, select the right visuals, and identify the required interactive controls. In the **Develop** stage, you create the visuals and implement the right colors and visual cues for a seamless user experience. In this final stage, you will choose the appropriate delivery method and accordingly deploy and share the dashboard or the report.

Let's go through each of these stages in the rest of this section.

Determine

When embarking on the journey of building a dashboard, start by determining the following:

- **Users:** Who are the primary users of the dashboard? Interview key target users to capture the key business objectives, challenges they face, and questions they need answering in their day-to-day work. Consolidate these requirements and define personas. Among other relevant information, a persona captures the following:

  - Name and role

  - Responsibilities/objectives

  - Needs and expectations

  - Challenges

Ideally, a dashboard should be built to fit only a single persona. Trying to meet the needs of multiple personas with a single dashboard is a recipe for disaster, which could leave all users less than satisfied. On the other hand, a report can accommodate the needs of multiple personas and be as comprehensive and detailed as needed.

- **Business questions**: Identify the key business questions from the identified persona(s) and define critical analytical user journeys. Have a clear understanding of the problem the dashboard is going to address and the supporting evidence required.

- **Data**: Find the data needed to address the business questions and provide additional context. Determine the appropriate level of data granularity needed. Make sure that the data can be accessed. If the right data is not available to provide complete and accurate answers to the previous business questions, adjust the purpose of the dashboard appropriately and set the right expectations with the end users.

Design

After determining the target users, well-defined business questions, and the data required to build the dashboard, the next step is to work on the design. Designing a dashboard involves the following aspects:

- **Design the right metrics**: Break down the main question into key subcomponents and define the right metrics. Determine which metric types – absolute numbers, differences, percentages, ratios, and so on – are the most appropriate. For example, ratios or percentages to enable comparisons, simple aggregations to summarize data, and so on. Identify any data preparation and manipulation needs in order to build these metrics.

- **Choose the right visualization type**: Determine the right chart types to use with different metrics and highlight appropriate relationships and associations. In the next chapter, we'll review some common chart types and general guidelines as to when each is appropriate.

- **Design the narrative**: Determine the flow of information and craft the story. Sketch the layout and organize various charts to fit the narrative. User experience studies have shown that most users consume content from top left to bottom right in a Z path. Accordingly, place the most important visuals at the top, and add supporting charts below them, creating a logical flow.

- **Design interactivity**: It is also in the design stage that you determine the interactive filters that you need to provide so that the users can make appropriate selections and view different slices of data. Provided the tool of choice offers the capability, you can also design cross-filtering capabilities between related charts to help users better understand the data. This is also an appropriate time to determine whether the users could benefit from implementing any alerts – when a metric raises above or falls below a threshold, a notification can be sent out to the users so that they are informed of the discrepancy or anomaly automatically and in a timely fashion. This enables users to take appropriate and timely action.

The outcome of this stage can be anything from a simple hand-sketch to a mockup implementation built with dummy data.

Develop

Once you have crafted the narrative, designed the layout, identified the right metrics, and chosen the appropriate visualizations, it's time to develop the dashboard by implementing the design. You start with connecting to the data and building the metrics. You then develop each individual chart and arrange them according to the layout design. In this stage, you choose the right colors, themes, text, annotations, and other visual aspects that provide a desirable user experience. Implement alerts to trigger notifications to users as needed.

Once you finish developing the dashboard, you deliver it to end users by deploying it and providing access. Users can consume the dashboard either directly by accessing the tool on which it is built or subscriptions can be set up so that they can receive the latest snapshot of the dashboard to their email inboxes at a suitable frequency. As part of this stage, you will also make sure the dashboard is refreshed with the latest data at a pre-determined frequency, which is largely dependent on the freshness of the underlying data source.

Walking through an example

Let's deepen our understanding of the **3-D data storytelling approach** to building dashboards with an example. A UK-based online retail company sells unique all-occasion gifts to its largely wholesale customer base. It caters to customers across many countries. We are going to build a dashboard in Looker Studio based on its online sales data. The data is made available by UC Irvine in its Machine Learning Repository (`http://archive.ics.uci.edu/ml/datasets/Online+Retail`). The Online Retail dataset has been donated to UCI Machine Learning repository by Dr. Daqing Chen of London South Bank University.

> **Citation**
>
> Daqing Chen, Sai Liang Sain, and Kun Guo, Data mining for the online retail industry: A case study of RFM model-based customer segmentation using data mining, Journal of Database Marketing and Customer Strategy Management, Vol. 19, No. 3, pp. 197–208, 2012 (Published online before print: 27 August 2012. doi: 10.1057/dbm.2012.17).

To build this example dashboard, I've added a new column to this data. You can access the modified dataset at `https://github.com/PacktPublishing/Data-Storytelling-with-Google-Data-Studio/blob/a31bf2de1ca10db433cf9d0ecb15c3cf4fa882d2/online_sales.zip`. This dataset is also used throughout the book to illustrate several examples.

Determine

The target audience for this dashboard is going to be the director of international business. The key objective of this persona is to improve international business by increasing revenue, the customer base, and expanding to more countries. They need to understand how sales are generated from various countries, spot trends and anomalies, and ultimately identify opportunities for expansion. The director has requested a summary dashboard to monitor the year-to-date and month-to-date sales metrics for international countries. Some of the questions that the dashboard should help answer include the following:

- What's the proportion of international business compared to the whole?
- How have international sales trended monthly and weekly this year?
- How many sales are generated from new customers versus repeat customers?
- How many sales do top products generate over time?
- What's the number of total sales generated and the number of active customers in the top countries?

In order to answer these questions, we need sales data generated from online stores at a weekly or daily granularity. We also need the country, product, and customer information in order to be able to slice and dice these attributes.

Design

Once we have determined the target audience and key business question(s) that the dashboard needs to cater to, the next step is to design the right metrics and visual representation elements. The key metrics that can serve this simple summary dashboard could be total sales amount, number of customers, average sales per customer, number of orders, and average sales per order. We then need to look at the data and determine whether any data manipulations and data preparation is required to accommodate the metrics identified. In this case, no data preparation is required before connecting the data to Looker Studio. In a real life scenario, you will almost always need to make some changes to your data in order to visualize it in the way you want.

Next, we need to identify the right visualizations based on the chosen metrics and the questions that need to be answered:

- **The proportion of international business compared to the whole**: We can use a pie or donut chart to show the proportion of an attribute value compared to the whole
- **Weekly/monthly sales trends broken down by new versus repeat customer sales**: We can use a stacked bar chart to compare sales by new versus repeat customers over time and add a line to represent the total sales so that the trend is easier to perceive

- **Top countries by sales and number of customers**: A bar chart is a great choice to compare multiple dimension values for easy comparison

- **Top products by sales**: Again, a bar chart is a great fit here

- **Sales trends of top products over time**: A simple time series is best represented by a line chart

- **Revenue distribution across different countries**: A filled map provides a single-glance view of the geographical presence and approximate ranking of different geographical regions.

Now is the time to build the narrative and create a wireframe for the dashboard. It involves designing the layout of the dashboard and placing the visuals and other components of the dashboard appropriately on the page. It could be a simple sketch on paper, whiteboard, or digital notes application. You can also use spreadsheet applications such as Google Sheets to quickly plug in some mock or sample data and build simple charts. Drawing tools within document and presentation slide applications can also be leveraged for this purpose to some extent.

For higher fidelity wireframes, you can opt for commercial tools such as Adobe Illustrator, Figma, Balsamiq and so on. The following figure shows the wireframe that's hand-drawn on a digital notes app:

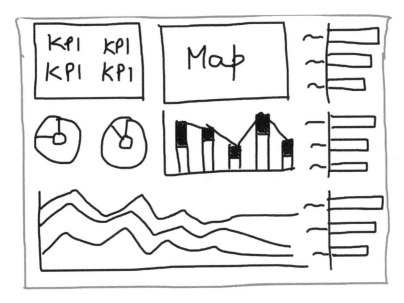

Figure 1.6 – Handdrawn sketch demonstrating the wireframe of the example sales dashboard

The narrative involves the user starting at the key high-level metrics at the top left and then looking at the year-to-date sales numbers for the top countries. Next, the user can look into the monthly and weekly sales trends, and finally, delve into top product sales and trends.

As the target audience, The Director of International Business, expects to consume most of the information at a glance, there are no explicit interactive filters that need to be designed. Given that, having a country filter to enable users to select a particular country and look at the metrics per country may be helpful. We can leverage the cross-filtering capability of the reporting tool (Looker Studio) and have the filled map chart serve as a country filter. Selecting a country from the map can filter the remaining charts on the dashboard. Also, combining the weekly and monthly trends into a single chart through drill-down functionality results in a cleaner look and better user experience.

Develop

With the key dashboard components identified and the design complete, it's time to implement the design and develop the dashboard. The first thing to do is connect the data to the report. Then we consider whether any custom fields and metrics need to be set up within the tool and create them accordingly. We implement each of the visuals as per the components identified in the design step and build out the dashboard following the layout. The UK is excluded from all the charts except the pie/donut charts depicting the proportion of international sales. Also, only the past 12 months of data need to be selected for the entire dashboard to provide the year-to-date view.

The aesthetics of the report is important. Take care to choose the minimum number of colors on the dashboard to have a cleaner look. We ensure that the same color is used to represent an attribute or metric across different charts within the dashboard as much as possible. This is important to avoid confusion. Implement other aspects such as axes, data labels, and legends with consistency throughout the dashboard. Enable cross-chart filtering for mainly the filled map so that the rest of the dashboard metrics and visuals can be filtered for a particular country. Disable it for the donut charts, where it doesn't make sense.

With all the design elements implemented, we test the dashboard for data accuracy – that metrics are showing up correctly and interactivity, cross-filtering and drill-down, and consistency. Further testing can also be done to ensure performance, data freshness, and security. Finally, publish the dashboard and share it with the users. The following figure shows what the dashboard could look like:

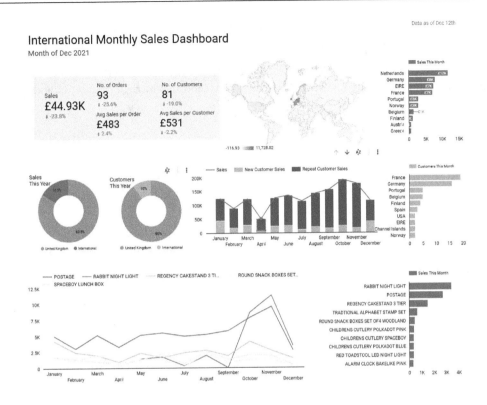

Figure 1.7 – Example sales dashboard built for a UK-based online retail company

We will be following the same approach to build effective dashboards and reports in *Part 3* of this book. There, we will go into the details of how to build various charts and implement other dashboard elements.

Summary

In this chapter, we have discussed what data storytelling is and how it's distinguished from data visualization. We have understood the core elements of a data story and how data stories differ for static and dynamic content. We have learned about the **3-D approach** to building data stories for dashboards that comprises three major stages: determine, design, and develop. In the determine stage, we determine the target users of the dashboard, the key business questions that the dashboard needs to address, and the data required to answer those questions. In the design stage, we build the narrative, define the right metrics, and choose the right visualizations and interactivity. Finally, in the develop stage, we actually build the visuals and interactions and choose the colors and other visual aspects. We also deliver the dashboard to the end users and ensure data freshness as part of this final stage.

It is really important to have a good understanding of the data storytelling elements and approach to be able to build compelling data products.

In the next chapter, we will be taking this understanding a step further and will learn about foundational principles of data storytelling, best practices of visualization, choosing the right chart types, and other design aspects.

2

Principles of Data Visualization

Data storytelling is both an art and a science. The art part refers to the story structure and narrative elements that bind data and visual components together, whereas the science part of data storytelling pertains to the foundational principles of design and visual perception and their application. This book largely concerns itself with building data stories through dashboards and reports. It primarily deals with the science aspect of data storytelling. These forms of data presentation provide limited narrative flexibility owing to the dynamic nature of the data they represent. As the data changes over time, the insights it conveys and the story it tells will change accordingly. This makes it difficult to incorporate a rigid narrative. Hence, much of the emphasis is put on design elements such as the chart types, colors, and layout, that constitute the building blocks of storytelling through data, rather than on the narrative elements.

This chapter introduces several guiding principles and key design aspects to consider while building data visualizations. We will cover foundational concepts such as the simplicity of design, principles of visual perception, organization of content, and information accuracy. These principles form the bedrock of any decent visual design. Color plays a very important role in visual design and greatly affects how visual elements are perceived. We will delve into various aspects of choosing the right color schemes based on the specific use cases and audience needs.

For a deeper and more comprehensive study of these ideas, you can peruse other resources mentioned in the *Further reading* section at the end of the chapter. Additional data visualization concepts, primarily various chart types and gotchas, are discussed in the next chapter, *Chapter 3, Visualizing Data Effectively*.

In this chapter, we are going to cover the following main topics:

- Understanding foundational design principles
- Reviewing Gestalt principles of visual perception
- Using color wisely

Understanding foundational design principles

Well-crafted and effective dashboards are built on the foundations of design and visual perception that have been explored and studied for centuries. In contemporary times, Edward Tufte and Stephen Few are recognized as pioneers and the most notable leading experts of modern-day data visualization. Through their prolific work, they have elucidated the many intricacies of visualizing data and information effectively. In this section, we are going to review the following foundational principles and guidelines that form the basis of any good dashboard:

- Simplicity of design

- Organizing the layout

- Accuracy of information presented

Simplicity of design

The single most important guiding principle to building any visual representation of data is **simplicity**. Achieving simplicity mainly involves removing all distractions away from the data to be represented. In Edward Tufte's words, it's avoiding *chart junk*. Chart junk or non-data ink is anything that doesn't represent data or information. It can take the form of redundant data, too many colors, **three-dimensional (3-D)** effects, dark gridlines, and much more. Chart junk interferes with the effective consumption of information. The rest of this section presents some common examples of *chart junk* and how they can be minimized effectively.

The following screenshot shows two variations of a bar chart depicting the average unit price for each product category. The gradient color and the textured color of the bars in the two charts respectively are distracting and do not add any information to the chart:

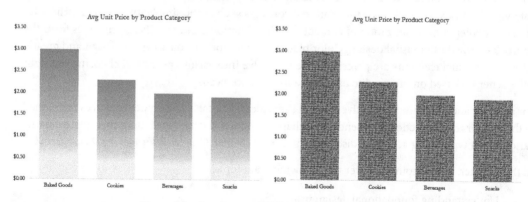

Figure 2.1 – Bar charts with distracting uses of color

Use solid colors to represent data and avoid using extraneous effects in an attempt to make a chart more visually appealing. The same applies to the background textures and patterns, as shown in the following screenshot:

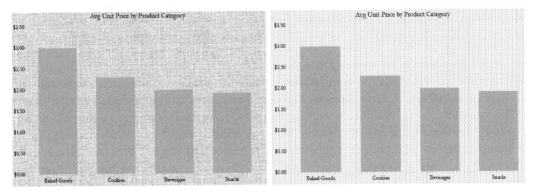

Figure 2.2 – Charts with distracting backgrounds

Background images for charts prove to be even more damaging to the eye, making it much more difficult to read and understand the data, as is the case here:

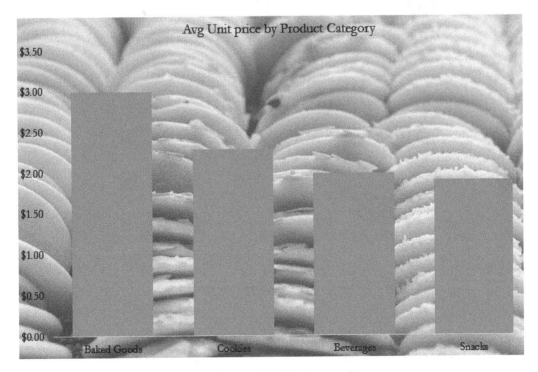

Figure 2.3 – Chart with ineffective use of images

While relevant and beautiful images usually grab the attention of users and it seems like a good idea to include them, a chart or a dashboard is not the right place for them. They distract users away from the objectives of the chart and jeopardize its utility. Use neutral solid colors as backgrounds, or none at all. This particular example showcases an especially bad case of using images, where the image doesn't add any informational value. While the chart can perhaps be improved in other ways such as better color choice, labels, and so on, images as chart backgrounds seldom add value.

That said, images can aid data storytelling when justly used. Logos are often included in dashboards for branding purposes, while meaningful and relevant icons add value by enabling easier interpretation and increasing visual appeal. Pictographs are also a good example of displaying data as images. They are effective only for a small amount of data, though. The following screenshot shows male and female image icons (sourced from `free-vectors.net` under the *Attribution 4.0 International (CC BY 4.0)* license `https://creativecommons.org/licenses/by/4.0/`) that add context to the donut charts and a pictograph depicting the performance rating with star images (image by `rawpixel.com`):

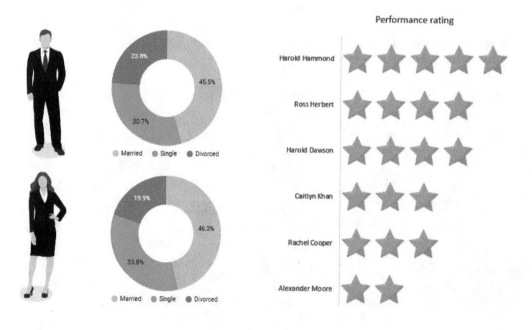

Figure 2.4 – Meaningful and appealing use of images

What about gridlines? Are they really chart junk? Judiciously placed gridlines help users to interpret charts easily. If there are too many lines or bars in a chart, adding gridlines may clutter the chart further. Dark-colored and thick gridlines are definitely noisy and considered non-data ink. Adding a large number of gridlines also contributes to chart junk. Use lighter and thin lines sparingly so as to enable the user to read the chart without difficulty while taking care not to clutter the chart. The following screenshot shows a line chart with distracting gridlines on the left and a chart with de-emphasized and useful gridlines on the right:

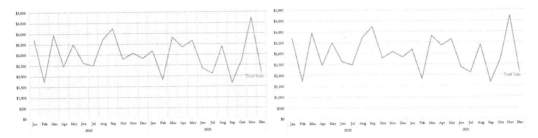

Figure 2.5 – Use gridlines in charts sparingly and in a non-interfering way

Simplicity also involves showing or encoding only enough information and nothing more. It is often tempting for a dashboard developer to incorporate all the different analyses and details that users can ever find useful into the dashboard and make it all-encompassing. Such a tendency leads to inefficiency and hinders users from achieving their objectives from the dashboard. If the users need to sift through the many visuals and details provided in the dashboard to get their basic questions answered, the dashboard is not simple enough. It is a case of **Too Much Information (TMI)**. A visual—and thereby a dashboard—should contain the right amount of detail and precision to serve the objectives of the target users. The dashboard shown in the following screenshot attempts to provide information about a lot of aspects of Google Ads—campaigns, ad types, search keywords, devices, ad channels, asset types, and more. The level of detail varies, and it has a cluttered look:

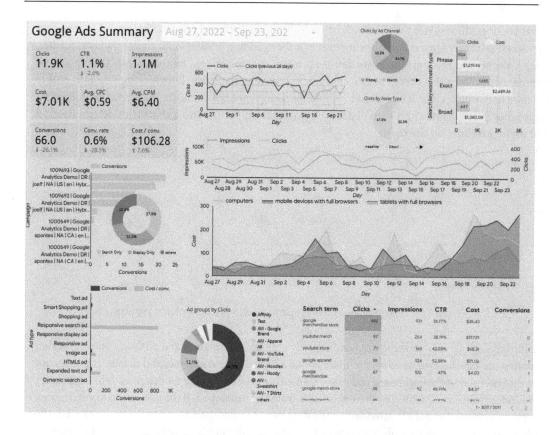

Figure 2.6 – Dashboard displaying too much information

Providing appropriate labels and context is key in making a dashboard easily readable. This includes elements such as titles, annotations, legends, units of measurement, and more. Consistency in the font style, font size, legend position, units of measurement, and numerical precision is a key enabler of simplicity in design. Having consistent elements across the dashboard puts a lower cognitive load on users as they do not have to process each element differently.

Removing, hiding, and de-emphasizing the details of less-important data is as essential as highlighting more important data elements. A dashboard where everything is highlighted is one in which nothing stands out. The way various elements in a chart or a dashboard are organized also affects how effective and meaningful the chart can be. The design should serve how we humans naturally perceive information visually.

Organizing the layout

The human eye typically follows the path of Z while consuming information visually. In this pattern, we scan content from the top left to the top right and then glance down through the content diagonally to the bottom left and continue to the bottom right. It is important to organize content in a way that supports the natural flow of eye movements. Keep this in mind while designing the layout of the dashboard so that it can meet its objectives more effectively. You should position the most important information in the top left and the least important information in the bottom right. It is more effective to place **key performance indicators** (**KPIs**) and other key metrics at the top of the dashboard, followed by relevant charts that explain these key metrics and provide the needed context to interpret the metrics appropriately.

Organizing filters in a dashboard or a report is an interesting challenge. In general, all the filter controls that apply to the entire report or page need to be displayed together in a single area. It can be toward the right of the page or on the top, but care should be taken not to obstruct users' readability of the actual data, and also not to take up too much of the dashboard's prominent real estate.

Occasionally, when a particular filter is applicable to only a specific chart or a group of charts, it can be placed near those charts and use enclosures such as borders or background shading to indicate that these filters and associated charts belong to a single group. This is one application of the Gestalt principle of enclosure. *Figure 5.26* in *Chapter 5, Looker Studio Report Designer*, illustrates this idea.

Another important aspect of designing the layout of a dashboard or a report is to place relevant charts and elements together, not just filters and associated charts, but also different charts that depict the same metric or explain the same phenomenon. Also, if the same legend applies to multiple charts, you can display it just once and place it in such a way that it can be used to interpret those multiple charts easily without having to look back and forth. This is the Gestalt principle of proximity at play. The layout is also mainly influenced by the narrative and the story being told by the dashboard or the report.

When organizing charts horizontally or vertically, make sure to align the axes to provide a consistent and clean look. This makes a comparison of different charts easier. Unrelated to the layout, using the same scale for different charts depicting the same or a similar metric enables accurate and easier comparison. In some cases, however, it may be unreasonable to have all charts set to the same scale. For example, sales revenue in Canada might range from $500k-10m, while in Japan it could be $10k-50k. Say, you are visualizing these as separate charts on the same dashboard and you do not want users to make direct comparisons. In such situations, try not to place them on the canvas close to each other to discourage direct comparison. Also, clearly label the axes and make sure the information is getting across in a visually understandable way.

Accuracy of information presented

The primary objective of a data visualization or a dashboard is to show information accurately and meaningfully. It should not mislead users to perceive information incorrectly or make inaccurate conclusions. All the design principles we have discussed in this section so far should only be leveraged to serve this ultimate purpose—for example, simplifying the dashboard shouldn't take it away from its intended meaning or clarity. Other forms of technically correct but undesirable ways of implementing these principles that impact the overall accuracy include but are not limited to the following:

- Emphasizing wrong elements, which may lead to incorrect interpretations
- Grouping inappropriate or incohesive elements, which may tell a totally different story than the one intended
- Not choosing the right type of chart, which causes users to interpret data incorrectly

The following section examines the classic principles of **Gestalt theory** and preattentive processing attributes that explain the various tendencies of human vision and how they relate to visualizing data.

Reviewing Gestalt principles of visual perception

Gestalt means **an organized whole** or **form**. This set of principles was developed by German psychologists in the 1920s to describe how humans perceive and interpret the world around them visually. These principles have since become the foundation for all design work—ranging from websites, logos, e-learning platforms, maps, advertisements, and more, to data visualizations. The following screenshot lists the key Gestalt principles that help design data visualizations that make the most intuitive sense:

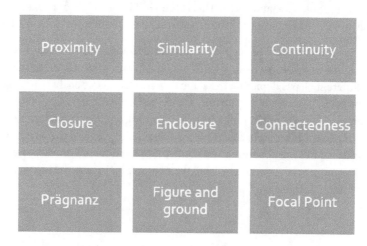

Figure 2.7 – Gestalt principles of visual perception

We will review each of these principles and how they can be applied to data visualizations, in the rest of this section.

Proximity

The principle of proximity posits that we tend to perceive elements that are placed close to each other as belonging to a single group. In the following screenshot, we can see three groups of circles based on the relative distance among the circles:

Figure 2.8 – Gestalt principle of proximity

In the case of a dashboard, the way white space is used to arrange various charts indicates which charts or elements are related. This enables users to read and interpret certain visuals together.

The proximity principle can also be used within a single visualization. We can observe three groups of data points in the scatterplot shown in the following screenshot based on their proximity or lack thereof:

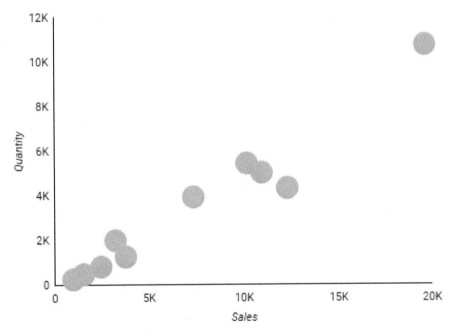

Figure 2.9 – Principle of proximity at play in a scatterplot

In the line chart shown in the following screenshot, the placement of labels close to the respective lines clearly indicates which line represents which country. This eliminates the need for a separate legend and helps reduce clutter:

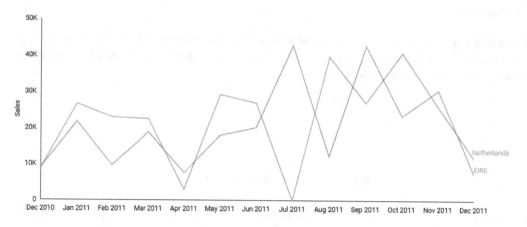

Figure 2.10 – Using the principle of proximity with labels

Another example that demonstrates the utility of the proximity principle is the clustered bar chart shown in the following screenshot. If the intention is to easily compare sales among different products for each country, clustering the countries together is not a suitable representation, as users are required to compare the bars that are spaced far from each other:

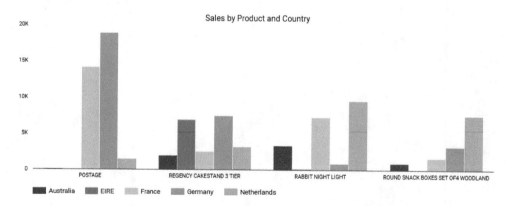

Figure 2.11 – Clustered bar chart that doesn't facilitate easier comparison
of sales among different products for each country

Instead, by clustering different quarters together as shown in the following screenshot, it becomes easier for the user to compare sales across quarters for each country. So, it's important to understand how the data needs to be interpreted and design the visual accordingly:

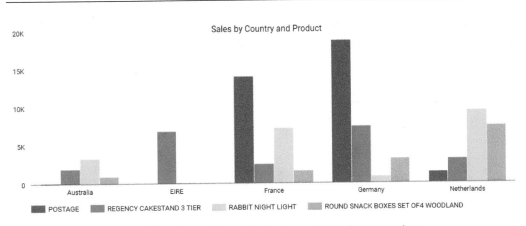

Figure 2.12 – Appropriate clustering to enable easier comparison
of sales among different products for each country

The principle of proximity encourages you to place elements that are related to each other or those meant to be interpreted together close to each other.

Similarity

We perceive visual elements that are similar to each other as related. The principle of similarity says that elements that share attributes such as color, shape, size, and so on are seen as belonging to a group. In the following screenshot, we primarily identify two groups of circles based on their color:

Figure 2.13 – Gestalt principle of similarity by color

In the same way, the following items are recognized as two different groups—circles and triangles, based on the shared shape:

Figure 2.14 – Gestalt principle of similarity by shape

The principle of similarity is crucial for representing data visually, and we rely heavily on it. One common application is the use of legends. Based on the shared color, we interpret what the elements in a chart represent. You can see an example of this here:

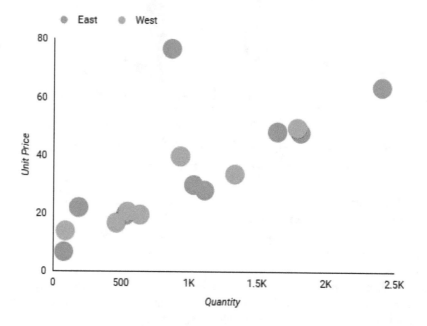

Figure 2.15 – Using color to identify related data in a scatterplot

In the preceding screenshot, the similarity principle is applied through the use of shared color in two ways: to perceive two groups of dots and to identify that the blue dots belong to the **East** region and the orange ones to the **West** region, with the help of the legend.

Continuity

The principle of continuity says that we follow continuous shapes, curves, and lines in order to make sense of the data. In the following screenshot, circles that are placed along the smooth curve are perceived as related compared to other random circles:

Figure 2.16 – Gestalt principle of continuity

In designing charts, the principle of continuity plays out in multiple ways. It enables us to view a continuous line even where there are gaps due to missing data instead of treating those two broken lines as separate. The following screenshot illustrates this phenomenon:

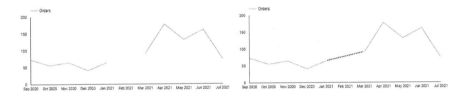

Figure 2.17 – Principle of continuity at play with missing data

Another place where we can use the principle of continuity is in bar charts. The chart on the left in the following screenshot isn't easy to interpret because the products are sorted alphabetically and the bars do not follow a smooth path. On the other hand, the chart on the right is sorted by the length of the bars, resulting in a continuous pattern and making it much more readable:

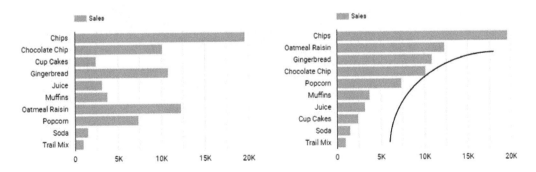

Figure 2.18 – Applying the principle of continuity to bar chart with sorting

The principle of continuity allows us to perceive elements that are arranged along a line or a curve as related to each other or part of the same group.

Closure

The principle of closure states that we tend to perceive familiar shapes and figures as a whole, even though they are broken and have gaps. In the following screenshot, we perceive the shapes as a star and a circle, even though they are not complete:

Figure 2.19 – Gestalt principle of closure

A common way we apply the principle of closure to designing graphs is by allowing users to see the two axes of the chart and perceive the complete boundary of the chart. This eliminates the need to use explicit borders and other aspects that result in a cluttered look. You can see an example of this here:

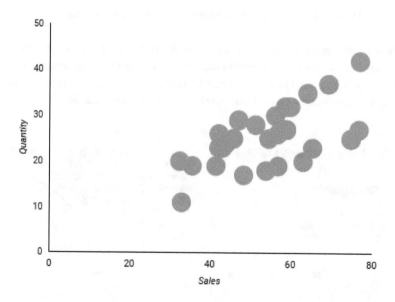

Figure 2.20 – Application of the principle of closure with open axes

The preceding screenshot shows a chart with two axes lines that allow us to discern the complete boundary of the chart, despite depicting only a partial boundary. Many visualization tools provide this behavior by default and do not enclose the chart on all sides. This helps in providing an uncluttered look.

Enclosure

The principle of enclosure says that we identify those elements enclosed by a boundary as belonging to a group. In the following screenshot, we consider the circles enclosed by the shape to be related:

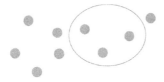

Figure 2.21 – Gestalt principle of enclosure

In the following dashboard example, the set of KPI metrics are enclosed within a gray box and are meant to be perceived as related and represent a group:

Figure 2.22 – Using the principle of enclosure in a dashboard to group related KPI metrics

Within a chart, we can enclose certain data points to have the user treat them as a group or even direct their attention to those elements, as illustrated here:

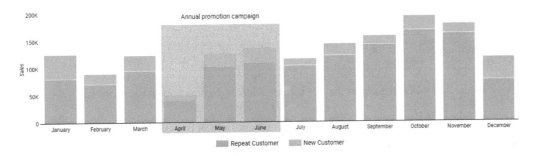

Figure 2.23 – Using the principle of enclosure within a chart

The preceding chart displays sales amount from repeat and new customers in different months of the year. A sales promotion campaign is run during the months of **April** through **June**, targeting new customers. Highlighting these months in the chart helps direct the user's attention to understand the impact of the promotion.

Connectedness

We see elements that are connected as related as opposed to elements that are disconnected. This principle of connectedness can be illustrated in the simple screenshot that follows, which shows two instances of the collection of circles where they are connected in two different ways—vertically and horizontally:

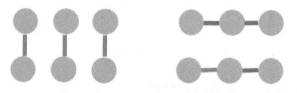

Figure 2.24 – Gestalt principle of connectedness

We see three and two groups of circles respectively, based on how they are connected. In the following screenshot, the line chart on the left showcases the law of connectedness where by virtue of the connected line, the points are interpreted as related to each other. In contrast, the data points in the scatterplot on the right do not express any connectedness:

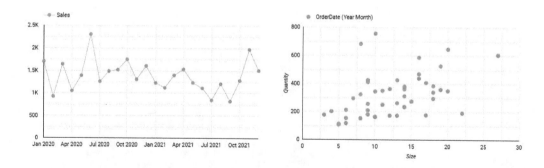

Figure 2.25 – Only the points that are connected to each other appear to be related

In the chart shown in the following screenshot, the text annotation is connected to the data point to indicate that the annotation applies to only this specific data point. This is another example of using the principle of connectedness in designing data visuals:

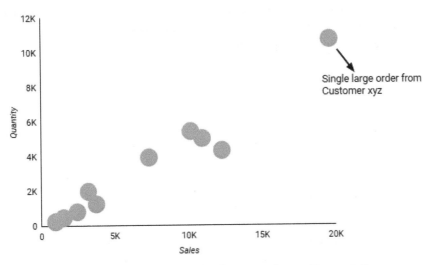

Figure 2.26 – Using the principle of connectedness with annotations

Connectedness generally exerts a greater influence on perception than proximity or similarity. It means that the elements that are connected to each other are perceived as a group, even if they are equally close to some other elements or similar in color or shape to others.

Prägnanz

We discussed the importance of simplicity while designing dashboards and visuals in the first section of the chapter. The Gestalt theory also emphasizes simplicity through the principle of prägnanz, which means pithiness or simplicity. It says that the human brain tends to see and interpret complex and ambiguous patterns and objects in the simplest form possible. We need to design things in the simplest form that can convey the information so as not to place an undue cognitive burden on the users.

In the following screenshot, we are likely to see two overlapping circles in each case, rather than a bunch of separate curves or shapes put together:

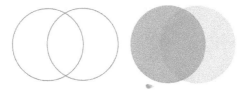

Figure 2.27 – Gestalt principle of prägnanz

In the case of data visualizations, the principle of prägnanz takes the form of sorting the bars and columns or representing timelines from left to right rather than in the reverse order, or even adding a trendline to a time-series chart to provide a simpler, intuitive, and more logical representation of information. *Figure 2.18*, under the principle of continuity, shows how an appropriately sorted bar graph is more easily readable than otherwise. In this example, both principles dictate the same representation:

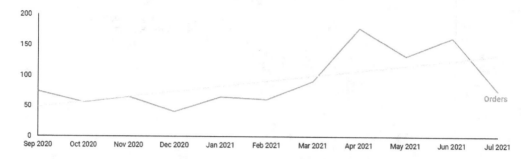

Figure 2.28 – Trend lines provide a simpler presentation of time-series data

The line chart shown in the preceding screenshot showcases the application of the principle of prägnanz through the use of trend lines and natural ordering of the time axis from left to right.

Figure and ground

The principle of figure and ground describes that we see things either as a figure in the foreground or in the background. We can use this tendency to place important and useful elements in the foreground and put less important or supporting elements in the background. This helps to guide users' attention to the key information. It is essential to create a clear distinction between the figure and the ground through enough contrast and other aspects such as focus (make things in the background out of focus by blurring, fading, or tinting), size (make elements in the foreground larger in size compared to those in the background), and so on. The classic Rubin's vase image shown in the following screenshot is an example of visual illusion that results when an element can either be a figure or a ground. While this destabilized relationship between figure and ground may have its application, forms of design where there is little distinction between the foreground and background should generally be avoided in data visualizations:

Figure 2.29 – Rubin's vase with destabilized figure-ground relationship

A good example of this principle at play in charts is a geographical bubble map with the map forming the background and the bubbles forming the foreground, as illustrated here:

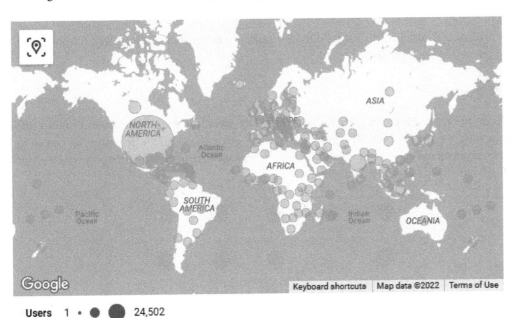

Figure 2.30 – Geographical bubble map provides an example of a stable figure-ground relationship

When using chart backgrounds or dashboard themes with non-clear backgrounds, choose colors carefully to achieve enough contrast so that foreground elements can be clearly and unambiguously identified. You can see an example of this here:

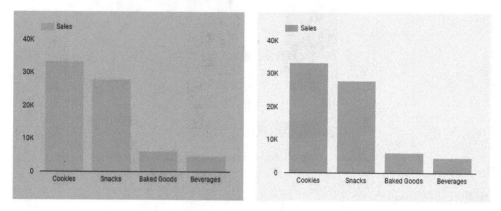

Figure 2.31 – Using the principle of figure-ground with contrast

In the preceding screenshot, the chart on the left makes a poor design choice as it results in greater eye fatigue and hence is harder to read.

Focal point

Finally, the principle of focal point states that elements that stand out from others are more noticeable than the rest. We can use distinctive properties such as color, shape, size, orientation, and so on to create focal points and capture the user's attention. In the following screenshot, two properties—color and shape—are used to create a focal point:

Figure 2.32 – Gestalt principle of focal point

This principle relies on the preattentive processing phenomenon in human vision through which information is processed by humans subconsciously and automatically. Some of the attributes that help with preattentive processing, as identified by Colin Ware in his book *Information Visualization: Perception for Design*, include hue, intensity, length, width, curvature, orientation, shape, size, added marks, spatial grouping, **two-dimensional** (**2D**) positioning, blur, enclosure, and movement (flicker or motion). You can see an illustration of these attributes here:

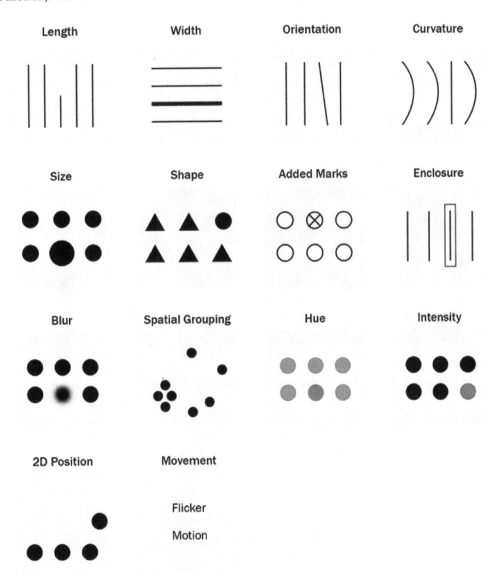

Figure 2.33 – Preattentive attributes

Of these attributes, only some—such as length and 2D position—can encode quantitative information well; some others—such as intensity, line width, size, blur, and flicker—can encode limited quantitative information, and others—such as shape, hue, and so on—do not encode any quantitative information.

Data visualization charts use various preattentive attributes to represent data. For example, a bar or column chart uses length to enable users to quickly identify the largest and smallest values. Judicial use of color helps highlight appropriate elements that users ought to pay attention to. Consider the following example where, as part of Cartier's performance evaluation report, the column chart uses a distinctive color to highlight Cartier's sales numbers. This directs users' attention immediately to their sales performance in relation to their peers:

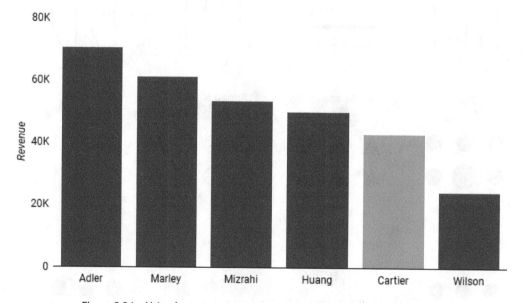

Figure 2.34 – Using hue as a preattentive processing attribute in a bar chart

In a dashboard or a chart, these preattentive attributes of color, size, position, and so on can also be used with textual elements such as annotations, KPI numbers, important updates, instructions, and more. For example, in a card visual, the current period value is shown in a bigger font size, and the comparative number against the previous period is shown in a smaller size, as follows:

MTD Sales

£44.93K

⬇ -23.8%

Figure 2.35 – Example of using preattentive attributes of color, size,
and position to direct users' attention appropriately

Displaying occasional notes regarding data quality, data latency, or other pertinent information in the dashboard using a bright hue or an icon in a prominent position makes sure users do not miss this important information. You can see an example of this here:

Figure 2.36 – Dashboard displaying an important note on the top along with an icon

The preceding screenshot depicts the top portion of a dashboard with an important note about missing or incomplete sales data. The note is accompanied by a relevant icon in a bright color to capture user attention.

Using color wisely

Color is perhaps the most important preattentive processing attribute that helps us to focus on and distinguish different elements easily. On the other hand, by choosing colors poorly, we hide or distract users from the purpose of the visual. In this section, we will go over some best practices in using color effectively.

Use fewer distinct colors

Having too many distinct colors in a visual or a dashboard can cause unnecessary strain on the eyes. Nothing really stands out in a jumble of disparate colors, and it becomes difficult to process the information. Three is a good number of colors to aim for using in a dashboard. You can include up to a couple of additional colors that are related to or in the same spectrum as the main colors. *Figure 1.7* in *Chapter 1, Introduction to Data Storytelling*, is a good example of using fewer colors on a dashboard. The same dashboard using a number of different colors looks noisy, as shown in the following screenshot:

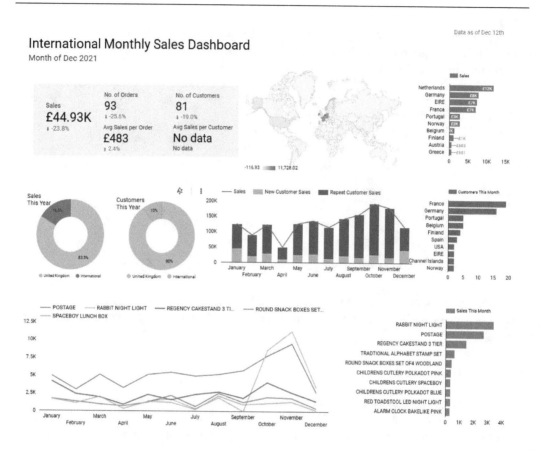

Figure 2.37 – Example dashboard using too many colors

Following the same idea, do not use color meaninglessly. In the bar chart shown in the following screenshot, different products are represented in different colors but the color doesn't provide any additional information. In fact, it is highly distracting and makes it harder for users to read the chart:

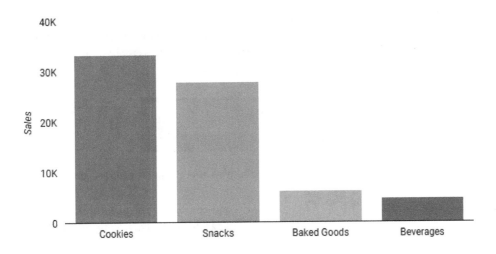

Figure 2.38 – Bar chart with a meaningless application of color

You need to be very deliberate in choosing colors for your visualizations to provide the best **user experience (UX)**.

Choose an appropriate color palette and scheme

You can choose themes and a color palette that are readily available in many visual tools or build your own based on the company logo colors, website colors, or other specific needs. A light versus dark report theme is the first choice to make. Each has its own appeal and benefits. A light background works better when there is a lot of text to display as research states that we read dark text on a light background more efficiently than vice versa (*Nielsen Norman Group*: `https://www.nngroup.com/articles/dark-mode/`). A light theme also allows you to use a wider range of colors than a dark theme. On the other hand, dark themes look more stylish and elegant. Dark backgrounds work best when the design is minimalistic. You should also consider whether your report might be printed out - in this case a light theme will save on a lot of printer ink. Whether a light or dark background, pick colors that provide good contrast. With dark themes, choose lighter and unsaturated colors for better readability. The colors used for non-data graphical elements in the dashboard such as text, shapes, and lines should be minimal, non-intrusive (unless specifically intended to draw attention), and provide enough contrast. There are several color contrast checkers available on the web that help you test the contrast of background and foreground (*Top seven free color contrast checkers and analyzers*: `https://axesslab.com/top-color-contrast-checkers/`). The rest of the section discusses the colors to be used for data.

Using a monochromatic color scheme with a range of distinct shades and tones and extending it with a single contrast color is a common and effective strategy. This not only helps reduce cognitive overload by mostly sticking to variations of a single color but also enables emphasis and highlighting with the use of the contrast color. You can see an example of this here:

Figure 2.39 – Monochromatic color scheme with an optional single contrast color

Leveraging a single bright color sparingly to highlight and emphasize the needful is a very useful design strategy that results in a cleaner and more powerful dashboard that efficiently directs the users' attention to the most prominent information.

In individual visualizations, depending on the type of data you are trying to represent, you can choose sequential, diverging, or qualitative color schemes. A sequential color scheme is usually monochromatic in nature—that is, based on a single color. It starts with the main color or origin hue and continues with decreasing intensity. You can see an example of this here:

Figure 2.40 – Sequential color to represent quantitative data

Conversely, a diverging color scheme is polychromatic. It uses two distinct colors on either end of the spectrum, transitioning from one hue to another in between at the lowest levels of intensity. An additional hue can be used in the middle of the divergent color scheme to represent three different ranges of values instead of just the two extremes, as depicted here:

Figure 2.41 – Diverging color scheme with two (on the left) and three (on the right) hues to emphasize extreme values at both ends of the continuum

Quantitative information, either discrete or continuous, is best represented by sequential or diverging schemes. A divergent palette helps emphasize extremes and should be used when there is a clear and meaningful pivot point in the metric value being represented. It can be zero for metrics such as profit (profit or loss) and rate of growth (positive growth or negative growth), or a reference point such as poverty level, target value, median, average, and so on. A divergent color scheme also allows users to see more differences in data.

A sequential palette is useful to show variation in a metric with no meaningful mid-point. Examples include metrics such as sales amount and number of users, which just range from the lowest to the highest values, and there is no well-defined central value where the change in hue is meaningful. Sequential palettes are more intuitive to read as the highest and lowest values can easily be discerned. Divergent palettes, on the other hand, often require a key for users to understand which colors represent more desirable versus less desirable values. A common application of using a divergent color scheme to represent data is a heatmap where two distinct hues are used to indicate hot and cold phenomena respectively.

To encode qualitative information such as products, categories, regions, and so on, you should use a categorical color scheme, which can span the entire spectrum of hues or just a subset of them. An example categorical palette is provided here:

Figure 2.42 – Categorical color scheme to represent unordered qualitative data

For ordinal qualitative data such as risk level (low, medium, high) or level of agreement in the Likert scale (strongly disagree to strongly agree), and so on, a monochromatic scheme such as the one shown next is a better fit. Similar to the continuous values, the lightness or darkness of the color can indicate the ordinal position of the qualitative value:

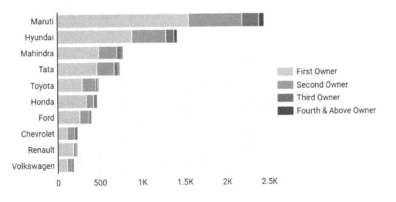

Figure 2.43 – Monochromatic color scheme to represent ordinal qualitative data

An interesting problem arises when you try to use color to represent a large number of categories. On one hand, it introduces a lot of noise to the chart. On the other hand, if the number of categories exceeds the number of distinct colors available in the palette, the colors are reused. This introduces conflict and confusion. Often, this problem can be addressed in the following different ways:

- Limit the number of categories to be depicted in the chart by filtering for only the key categories that users are interested in—for example, the top five.

- Identify three-five key dimension values and bundle all the remaining less important values into an **Other** bucket. You can apply a muted color to the **Other** bucket to de-emphasize it.

- Choose a different chart type so that the categories need not be represented by a color—for example, using a bar chart instead of a donut chart.

Use color consistently across the dashboard

Always use the same color for the same dimension or metric value throughout the dashboard. Not doing so results in a very poor UX. Using color in a consistent manner eases the burden on users and enables them to understand and interpret the charts faster. Using different colors for the same attribute in different charts requires users to decode the color encoding for each chart separately. Applying color in a conflicting way adds additional complexity and confuses the user. For example, in the chart shown in the following screenshot, the two colors blue and orange are used inconsistently for the countries **Netherlands** and **EIRE**. This is undesirable and hampers the effectiveness of the dashboard:

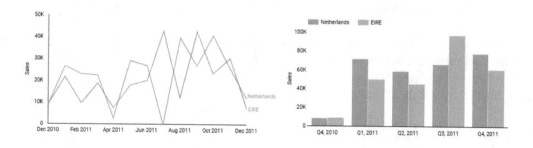

Figure 2.44 – Conflicting use of color across charts

Some colors have a natural meaning, and it bodes well for us to use them in a way that aligns with the associated meanings. Perhaps the most widely used encoding is the traffic-light colors for KPIs and other metrics: green to represent the good—a positive value or an increase, red to represent the bad—a negative value or a decrease, and— spacing optionally—yellow to represent caution for values that need to be watched out for. Using these colors in a way that defies this natural association results in a poor UX.

In the following screenshot, the card visual on the left displays the negative rate of change appropriately in red. However, the visual on the right depicts a negative rate of change in sales with a green color, which is counterintuitive:

Figure 2.45 – Using color counterintuitively

Similarly, while choosing a divergent color scheme, especially in heatmaps, choose warm and cold colors appropriately. Select warm colors such as red, orange, and yellow to represent hot phenomena such as higher user activity, higher sales, a higher number of issues, and so on, and cold colors such as blue, green, and purple to indicate cold phenomena such as lower activity, lower sales, and a lower number of issues respectively. You can see an example of this here:

Order Month / Daily quantity (vs Target)

Order Day	January	February	March	April	May	June	July	August	September	October	November	December
1	-	340	-2,880	2,374	-11,186	-4,120	-7,642	-5,053	12,829	-	1,686	11,819
2	-	-5,645	-6,505	-	-	-1,162	-	624	-4,275	-6,620	13,319	11,952
3	-	1,935	3,414	-9,340	-3,133	-7,443	-11,894	660	-	9,652	19,019	-
4	-7,061	-3,633	-1,668	-1,955	765	-	682	22,992	-4,059	3,689	18,546	-2,604
5	3,435	-	-	-237	2,331	-1,530	6,696	-2,800	8,484	31,161	-	29,119
6	7,461	-12,952	-10,011	-6,424	4,632	-5,833	4,275	-	-41	16,268	8,295	14,026
7	1,475	-6,321	-1,285	-4,644	-	3,462	3,956	-9,920	1,211	15,431	12,689	24,612
8	-	-4,799	-8,082	-5,770	-4,308	5,784	-3,319	-1,896	1,944	-	11,124	19,460
9	-6,819	-7,852	-10,542	-	-2,049	15,275	-	605	1,100	-7,725	21,238	-2,051
10	-5,986	-3,553	767	-9,474	2,719	-6,866	-10,786	-772	-	10,405	23,077	-
11	14,093	-5,169	-4,535	-1,501	1,233	-	-11	25,191	6,122	5,091	13,513	-
12	-4,867	-	-	121	21,141	-5,518	-1,240	-3,038	2,086	525	-	-
13	-4,886	-12,285	-12,259	3,100	74	-5,613	1,206	-	21,904	2,859	5,356	-
14	8,091	-1,531	1,717	2,401	-	-28,752	1,904	-11,865	-5,410	2,475	30,959	-
15	-	7,533	-6,062	-2,274	-10,102	14,978	-8,159	-4,859	14,181	-	15,221	-
16	-10,819	990	-2,417	-	-516	3,178	-	-3,787	166	-6,689	14,353	-
17	-1,655	-456	5,589	-6,819	11,886	-3,322	-3,958	8,567	-	15,214	15,779	-
18	-6,336	-6,835	-1,244	7,246	3,785	-	-634	18,122	-6,034	13,960	8,535	-
19	2,108	-	-	-617	2,783	60	11,287	-4,391	13,973	4,039	-	-
20	-6,280	9,654	-835	2,973	154	518	1,795	-	20,702	25,802	4,369	-
21	-62	6,456	-4,799	3,253	-	-7,154	4,747	-6,836	4,581	9,728	9,004	-
22	-	6,448	-116	-	-2,264	769	-4,981	387	17,263	-	20,284	-
23	-9,806	-1,378	-3,717	-	1,443	-728	-	112	6,222	-7,932	22,350	-
24	-3,090	-3,276	3,157	-	629	-5,173	2,271	14,288	-	6,514	8,743	-
25	-207	-5,112	-1,697	-	-3,161	-	457	-1,816	4,329	9,686	16,026	-
26	-4,146	-	-	665	1,192	-11,505	-1,440	2,756	-52	5,865	-	-
27	-4,026	-10,142	-10,592	2,836	1,713	-5,165	-1,141	-	6,060	17,301	-3,839	-
28	2,414	-5,120	-1,875	-1,816	-	4,642	14,700	-8,230	10,157	8,845	13,647	-
29	-	-	17,413	-	-10,916	-3,456	-3,528	-	11,265	15,511	-	-
30	-11,633	-	4,719	-	-	6,297	-	-4,818	7,009	5,062	11,482	-
31	-2,432	-	1,237	-	-3,454	-	5,873	-8,024	-	-10,074	-	-

Daily Quantity (vs Target)
-28,752   31,161

Figure 2.46 – Heatmap with warm and cold colors

The heatmap in the preceding screenshot represents hot and cold phenomena using an appropriate divergent color scheme.

A big caveat to using and relying on green versus red colors to show desirable and undesirable patterns is that not everyone can distinguish these colors from each other. This can be mitigated in one or more ways, as follows:

- Completely avoid using red and green together in visualizations. Using alternative colors will require a key or legend for users to understand what the colors mean.

- Use icons such as arrows and other visual cues in addition to or instead of color to indicate good versus bad.

- Use different intensities for red and green colors, when used together. This allows people with red-green blindness to differentiate them well, as color vision deficiency is mainly about not identifying certain hues, rather than their intensities.

Consider inclusive color schemes

Last but not least, choose color schemes that are colorblind-friendly so that they can be universally accessible. This is especially important for widely distributed content. Color blindness is much more prevalent than we think—it affects about 4.5% of the entire population. There are many different types of color blindness, the most common being red-green blindness, affecting almost 99% of the color-blind population. This type of **color vision deficiency** (**CVD**) takes several forms: those who cannot see the red color at all (protanopia), those who can identify only some shades of red (protanomaly), those who cannot see the green color at all (deuteranopia), and those who can identify only some shades of green (deuteranomaly). While we can still choose certain shades of red or green and have people with red-green CVD distinguish between the two, they don't all see those colors as red and green. Blue is generally a safe color and is widely used in data visualizations. Choose and build colorblind-safe color palettes with care. All data visualization and reporting tools provide colorblind-friendly palettes for you to choose from. There are tools available, such as the one provided by David Nichols at `https://davidmathlogic.com/colourblind/`, that can help you understand how people with CVD actually see different colors and build your own colorblind-friendly palettes. Some color contrast checkers (**Colour Contrast Analyser** (**CCA**) `https://www.tpgi.com/color-contrast-checker/`) also determine how color contrast can affect people with CVD.

Summary

Data storytelling is a skillful amalgamation of narrative and visual representation. In this chapter, we learned about the design principles that form the foundation for building effective and compelling data visualizations. These principles are rooted in the nature of human vision and perception. We reviewed the centuries-old but still very much applicable Gestalt principles of visual perception and looked at three major guiding themes for data storytelling in this chapter.

We understood that simplicity is the hallmark of a great data story. Keeping things simple and to the point and removing all noise and distractions from the design are key to a great UX. Going further, we learned that organizing the layout of the dashboard to present a cohesive picture and fit the intended narrative is important.

Above all, representing the data accurately should be the main goal. A well-designed dashboard with incorrect information will not only be ineffective but also damaging by leading to incorrect insights and decisions.

Color is an important design element that needs careful application. We examined some guidelines on how to use it appropriately in data visuals as well as across the dashboard. We learned about various color schemes and their applications. The next chapter discusses how to choose the right visualization types and common pitfalls to avoid while designing visualizations.

Further reading

To learn more about the principles and foundations of data visualization, you can refer to the following resources:

- *Tufte, Edward. The Visual Display of Quantitative Information. Graphics Press.* Second Edition. 2001.

- *Few, Stephen. Information Dashboard Design. Analytics Press.* Second Edition. 2013.

- *Knaflic, Cole Nussbaumer. Storytelling with Data. John Wiley & Sons.* 2015.

- *Wilke, Claus O. Fundamentals of Data Visualization: A Primer on Making Informative and Compelling Figures. O'Reilly Media.* 2019.

- *A detailed guide to colors in data vis style guides:* `https://blog.datawrapper.de/colors-for-data-vis-style-guides/`

3
Visualizing Data Effectively

Presenting data in the right form allows for effective interpretation. There are many types of charts that can be used to visualize data. However, certain types of charts are better suited than others to depict particular types of data or answer certain types of questions. This chapter examines some basic chart types, which are available in Looker Studio, and their appropriate use. We will also look into some data visualization pitfalls that are commonly observed and understand how to avoid or mitigate them.

In this chapter, we are going to cover the following main topics:

- Choosing the right visuals
- Avoiding common pitfalls

Choosing the right visuals

Using the right chart types to represent data is perhaps the most important design decision you need to make as a dashboard developer. In this section, we will review the most common types of charts and discuss how to use them appropriately.

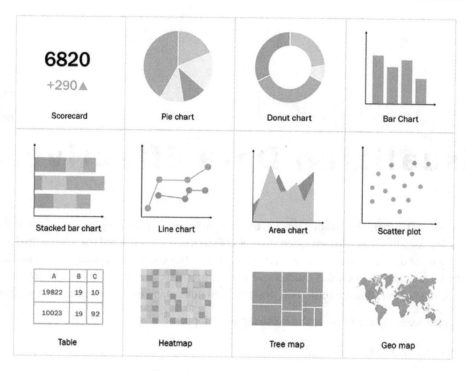

Figure 3.1 – Common chart types

> **Note**
>
> There are additional visualization types available to the ones discussed in this chapter that are used less widely. The objective here is to introduce only the most basic chart types rather than offering a comprehensive list. You can refer to the resources listed in the *Further reading* section of the chapter for broader and more in-depth coverage.

Different chart types are suitable for representing different types of data. Broadly, data can be either categorical type or numerical type. Examples of categorical data include countries, gender, education levels, and risk groups. Categorical data can be measured either on a nominal scale or an ordinal scale. Nominal values are just labels that don't have any quantitative value associated with them and thus cannot be inherently compared among themselves – for example, specific product(s) you want to purchase from a store. Ordinal values, on the other hand, have an inherent order to them. A good example is measuring risk group as low, medium, or high, where each value exists in relation to others on an ordinal scale.

Numerical data can be either discrete or continuous and is measured against a quantitative scale. A discrete value is something that cannot be further broken down, such as the number of employees. Continuous data, on the other hand, can take on any value within a range, such as employee salary.

Another aspect that dictates the right chart type to use is the objective at hand – what you want to convey through the chart. Common objectives include showing the following:

- Distributions – How data is distributed across a spectrum. Line charts, scatter charts, and histograms are the most common forms of distribution charts.

- Compositions – How different parts make up a whole. Pie, tree map, and stacked bar charts are some chart type examples to use for this purpose.

- Relationships – Show the correlation or pattern of some type among two or more attributes. Scatter charts and bubble charts help with depicting relationships.

- Comparisons – Compare different attribute values and find the higher/highest or lower/lowest data points and trends. Line charts, bar charts, geographical maps, and choropleth charts are good chart type examples to show comparisons.

Scorecards

Scorecards are a simple and very useful way to represent **Key Performance Indicator (KPI)** values, usually a single metric, as text. This allows users to monitor and keep track of the most important metric values. The card visual displays the metric value and its name, as follows.

Avg Sales per Order
£657

Figure 3.2 – A scorecard with a single KPI value

However, the value alone without any context is rarely useful. In general, KPIs are measured in the context of time – daily, weekly, monthly, yearly, and so on, and users are usually most interested in is knowing how these metrics change over time. With scorecards, users would like to understand at a glance whether the KPIs are tracking well compared to the previous period – for example, percentage change in the current month's KPI compared to the previous month's KPI value, as shown in the following figure.

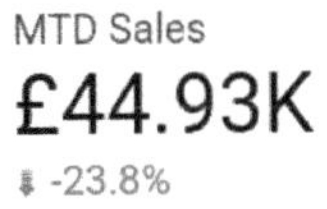

MTD Sales
£44.93K
↓ -23.8%

Figure 3.3 – A scorecard with a single KPI and rate of change compared to the previous period

Using color and icons such as green upward or red downward arrows to indicate the increasing or decreasing behavior of the concerned metric adds some much-needed context. Using a green color for desired behavior and a red color for undesired behavior is a widely applicable norm, but it poses difficulties for color-blind people when these two colors are displayed together. Using any other colors to represent the good and the bad is counterintuitive and imposes an additional cognitive load on users. One way to address this is to use different intensities – a very light green color and a very dark red color. Almost everyone can differentiate between light and dark colors. Another option is to leverage icons such as emojis to indicate whether the metric is tracking well or not.

Pie and donut charts

When you want to display a proportion of different dimension values compared to a whole, a pie or donut chart fits the bill. Pie charts are easy to understand and are appealing to look at compared to other alternatives such as bar charts. For these reasons, both designers and users prefer these charts to be part of their dashboards. However, these charts are notorious for being very ineffective in representing data.

Humans cannot interpret and compare areas and angles as well as they can do with lengths and widths. So, when values close to each other are depicted in a pie or donut chart, the human eye cannot easily distinguish different magnitudes. Also, when there are a large number of categories, the pie chart becomes really cumbersome, making it harder to understand the data. The following figure showcases both flaws.

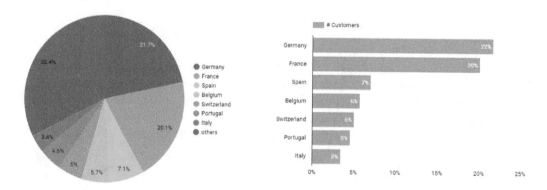

Figure 3.4 – A pie or donut chart is ineffective when used with too
many categories. Use alternatives such as bar charts

Both pie and donut charts have the same characteristics and suffer from the same drawbacks. While there are some valid scenarios where these charts do not often make a good choice, by taking care of a few aspects, you can design them to be decent enough. Bar charts provide a good alternative when there are more than a few dimension values to represent.

You can design useful pie or donut charts by keeping in mind the following:

- Use a pie or donut chart only when the intention is to compare the proportion of a category to the whole. It should not be used to compare different categories among themselves.

- Use these charts only when there are fewer categories – ideally 2 to 5.

- Always make sure the sum of all proportions equals 100%. It is easy to get this wrong if pre-computed percentages that do not sum up to 100% are plotted and displayed.

Also, labeling the data in a pie or donut chart is very critical – the proportion, the category name, and optionally, the value. It is these labels that help in actually making these charts interpretable, without which they are effectively useless. So, do not forget to add labels to the chart.

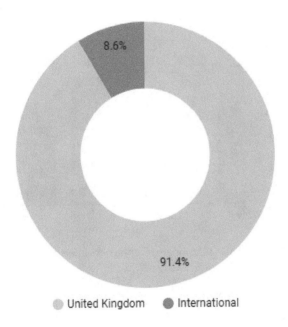

Figure 3.5 – A pie or donut chart works well with only a few categories

The preceding donut chart is a good example, which depicts just two categories. Pie/donut charts have a big advantage over bar charts in representing a few dimension values with widely varying proportions, as the former enable much easier interpretation of a composition.

Bar charts

A bar chart, whether horizontal or vertical, is one of the most fundamental and widely applicable chart types. When you want to compare different values of a dimension based on a metric, the bar chart is your friend. The dimension values can be nominal values without any inherent order, such as products, countries, and customers, or they can be discrete ordinal values, such as age groups and risk levels. The following chart compares different salespersons based on the total sales they have generated.

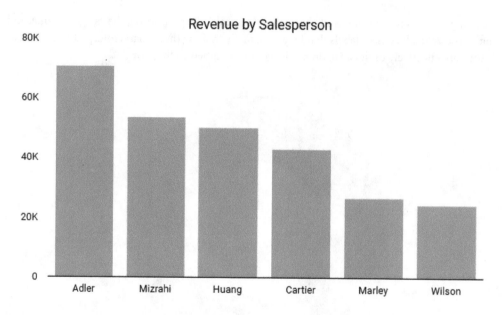

Figure 3.6 – A bar chart to compare revenue generated by salespersons

Horizontal bars are preferred in the following circumstances:

- When there are a large number of dimension values
- When the dimension values have longer names

For example, as shown in the following figure, long product names make a horizontal bar chart more suitable compared to using vertical bars.

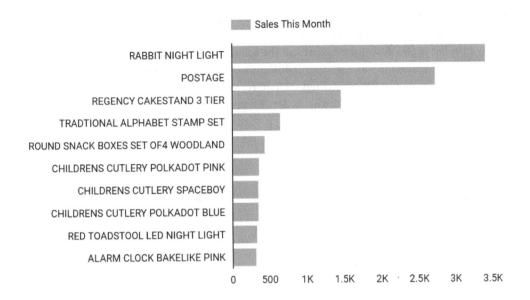

Figure 3.7 – A horizontal bar chart to accommodate long dimension names

Whether long or not, labels in horizontal bar charts are in general easier to read and process, as the layout follows our natural order of reading information. If the dimension values do not have an inherent order, the bar chart is usually sorted by the metric value. On the other hand, if the bar chart depicts a dimension with ordinal values, the bars should be sorted by the dimension values themselves. In the following chart, the bars are arranged in the increasing order of the age groups instead of the length of the bars. This allows for a more intuitive interpretation of the chart.

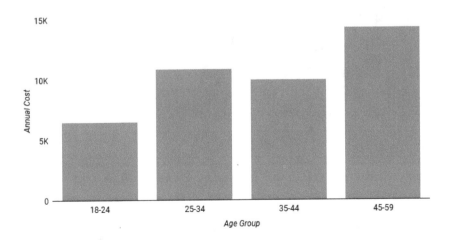

Figure 3.8 – A bar chart sorted by the ordinal values of the dimension

A key thing to note while building bar charts is that the *y* axis must start at 0 in order to provide an accurate representation of data. Starting the axis at a different positive value misleads the user because the length of the bar in this case doesn't represent the actual metric value. In the following figure, the chart on the right side with the *y* axis starting at **40K** indicates that Alder's performance is about twice that of Mizrahi's when, in fact, it's only about 40% more, as shown by the chart on the left, in which the *y* axis starts at 0 and the length of the bar is a true representation of the sales value.

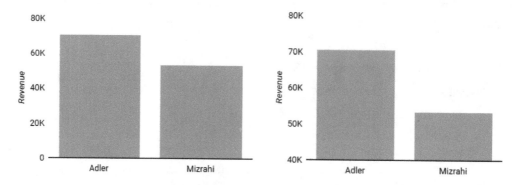

Figure 3.9 – The y axis of a bar chart should always start at 0 for accurate representation

A histogram is a special type of bar chart that depicts the frequency distribution of a numerical variable in a dataset. It groups the continuous numerical values into bins and displays them along the *x* axis. The frequency or the number of rows in the dataset that lies within each bin is represented on the *y* axis.

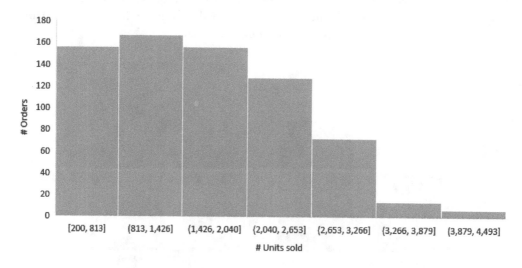

Figure 3.10 – A histogram showing the distribution of orders by units sold

A clustered bar chart, also referred to as a grouped bar chart, is a variation of the bar chart that either depicts more than one metric across a dimension or compares more than one dimension based on a single metric, as shown in the following figure.

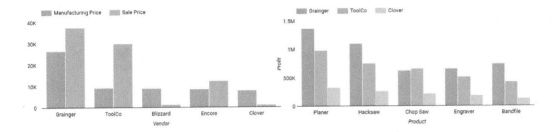

Figure 3.11 – Different ways of using a clustered bar chart

A bar chart allows you to compare the values of bars that are close to each other better than those that are far apart. Hence, following the gestalt principle of proximity, carefully choose which bars need to be clustered together versus which need to be along the axis. In the preceding example, the clustered bar chart on the right facilitates an easier comparison of profit across different vendors for each product than the other way round.

In the case of displaying multiple measures as a cluster of bars, make sure that the metrics are really comparable and can work with the same axis and scale. Use this variation when the intention is to compare the two metric values for each dimension value – for example, actual versus budget and current quarter sales versus previous quarter sales. To be most useful, make sure the clusters contain only a small number of bars, ideally no more than four.

Yet another style of bar chart is the stacked bar chart, in which each bar is broken down by a second dimension and the slices are shown as stacks within a single bar instead of as independent bars, as in the case of the clustered bar chart. The overall length of each bar indicates the total metric value of the dimension along the axis, which enables an accurate comparison of dimension values on it. When depicting a single measure by two dimensions, a clustered (grouped) bar chart and a stacked bar chart can display the same data, just in different ways. Like clustered charts, visualize only a few stacks per bar for them to be most effective.

The lengths of different stacks representing the second dimension in each bar, on the other hand, enable only an approximate interpretation of the values and comparison among themselves. Users may need to do some mental math to understand the magnitudes accurately. Also, comparing these stacks across different bars is really difficult with the exception of the bottom- or left-most stack in the case of the vertical bar chart and the horizontal bar chart respectively, owing to the fact that stacks, apart from the first one, do not offer a consistent starting point for easier comparison.

Stacked bar charts help you to compare totals and simultaneously see the composition of a metric by another dimension. They are useful when the value of the overall metric is more important than the breakdown by the second dimension. Stacked bar charts enable you to notice any marked changes at the breakdown or stack level that are likely to cause variation in the totals. The following figure shows the same data as the clustered (grouped) bar chart in the preceding figure as a stacked bar chart, showing the profit for various products broken down by vendors.

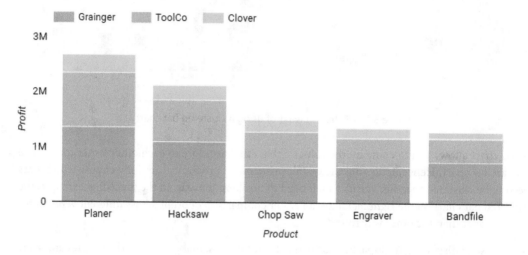

Figure 3.12 – A stacked bar chart

A 100% stacked bar chart is a closely related form of a stacked bar chart, with the length of the overall bar representing 100% of the dimension value on the axis. The stacks in the bar depict the percent contribution by each of the breakdown dimension values, as shown in the following figure.

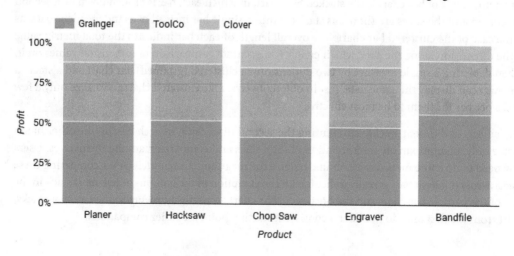

Figure 3.13 – A 100% stacked bar chart

Like the stacked bar chart, it enables only approximate comparison along the bar and is not amenable to comparing stacks across different bars. The main purpose of stacked charts is to provide a better understanding of the big picture, without much focus on little differences.

Line charts

Line charts are a natural choice to represent time-series data, where the x axis represents time and the y axis represents the metric. In general, a line chart can have any attribute that depicts continuous values with a uniform interval of measurement, not just time. Line charts provide an understanding of the overall trend and pattern of a variable depicted on the y axis along the continuous values of a variable represented on the x axis. The following figure shows a line chart that plots total monthly sales over time.

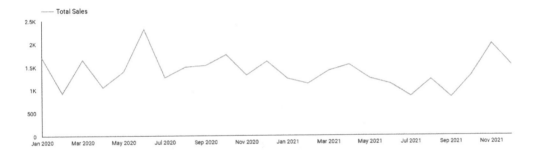

Figure 3.14 – A simple line chart

The metric can be broken down by a dimension with discrete values and represented by multiple lines. Displaying too many lines clutters the chart and makes it ineffective. General guidance says that you can show up to five lines to provide the most value.

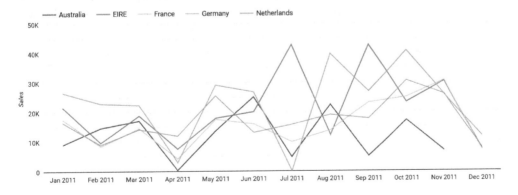

Figure 3.15 – A line chart with multiple lines depicting sales by different countries

While the data visualization community and experts generally agree that *y* axis for bar charts must start at 0, there is no consensus on whether it's mandatory for other chart types to do so too. Starting the *y* axis for a line chart at a value that makes sense for the specific dataset enables you to view the changes along the axis more clearly. A classic example is the stock market price variation over time. Starting the *y* axis at 0 for this visualization has the line appear almost flat and makes it difficult to interpret the variations. Choosing the historically lowest value as the starting point will make the visual more useful in this case. The main focus of line charts is to depict relative changes along the line rather than the actual value at any point. Hence, the actual height at which the line appears doesn't affect users' ability to understand the variation correctly, even if it dramatizes the magnitude, as illustrated in the following figure. Be sure to notice the *y*-axis scale to interpret the magnitude though.

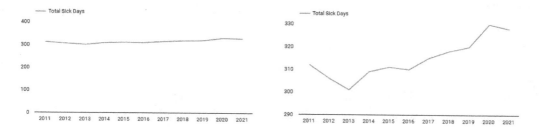

Figure 3.16 – A line chart with a y axis starting at a reasonable value
for the dataset helps better read the variation in values

Area charts are just line charts filled with color and can be thought of as a combination of a line and a bar chart. This means that in addition to a change in values along the axis, area charts help users to understand the magnitude of a value by the overall area. Accordingly, like bar charts, area charts must start their *y* axes at 0.

Area charts are commonly used with multiple lines to compare different categories. They work best when data is divergent and overlap among the lines is minimal. In the following area chart, the daily number of tickets closed by two members of the technical support team is divergent enough to provide a useful visual.

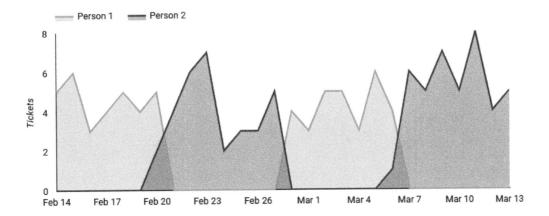

Figure 3.17 – An area chart with divergent data

When the lines overlap a lot, the overlay of colors causes confusion and makes it difficult for users to read the chart, as shown in the following figure. If the colors are not transparent, it further limits the utility of the chart as a result of occlusion or data being hidden.

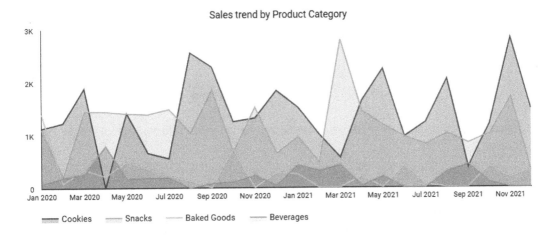

Figure 3.18 – An area chart with a highly overlapping series is confusing

Stacked area charts and 100% stacked area charts are more commonly used than regular area charts because they do not suffer from the problem of occlusion. Similar to stacked bar charts, stacked area charts are useful to depict both the overall total and composition by breakdown dimension at the same time. They allow users to understand any sharp changes at the individual series level along the horizontal axis that impact the overall total. Stacked area charts mislead users in discerning the true trends for the dimension values beyond the first one, just like the stacked bar charts.

Stacked area charts add additional complexity, as it is very difficult for users to accurately compare areas. Also, not everyone understands or interprets these charts properly. Hence, these should generally be used with caution.

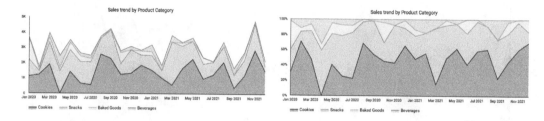

Figure 3.19 – Stacked area charts make it harder to discern the actual trends of different dimension values

Sparklines are a form of line charts that were introduced by the data visualization guru Edward Tufte. These are useful to provide the historical context for a metric. These lines neither show any axes nor any values, except the latest data point. Sparklines are space-efficient and well suited for a dashboard. But be sure to only use them when the actual values of the other points isn't relevant to your story.

Figure 3.20 – Sparklines add historical context

The preceding figure shows how a card visual can be augmented with the historical trend of the sales metric using a sparkline:

Combo charts

Combo charts allow you to represent different series with a different marker type – line, bar, area, and so on. The most common form of combo chart is the one which is composed of bars and lines, as follows.

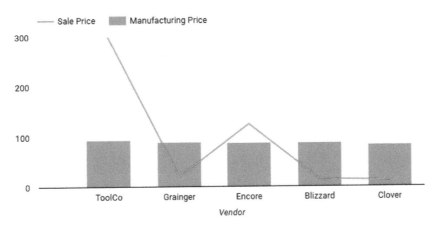

Figure 3.21 – A combination chart with a single y axis

A combination chart is helpful in augmenting a main chart with an overlay of a different set of data for comparison purposes. The secondary series can use the same axis as the main series or a different axis on the right.

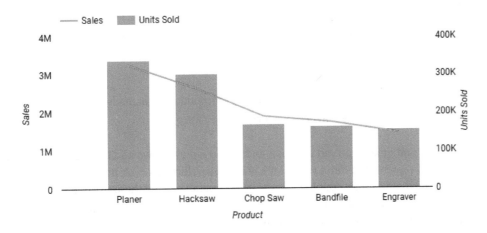

Figure 3.22 – A combination chart with dual Y axes

However, dual axes make the chart difficult to read and can lead users to interpret a series incorrectly. Hence, you should generally avoid them and consider alternative ways of presenting the data.

Scatterplot

When you are interested in understanding the correlation between two metrics, a scatterplot is the way to go. A scatterplot allows you to represent a large number of items and provides the general distribution of the items with respect to both metrics.

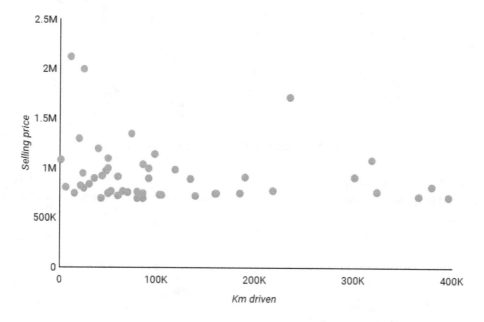

Figure 3.23 – A scatterplot depicting the distribution of car models
based on distance traveled and sales price

In addition to the *x* and *y* axes, you can use color and size to represent two additional metrics. Color can also be used to represent distinct values of a breakdown dimension. A mark type or shape is another way to display additional grouping. However, incorporating all of these attributes at the same time may clutter the chart and make it difficult to read. Take care to use these dimensions judiciously to provide a simplistic yet useful display of information.

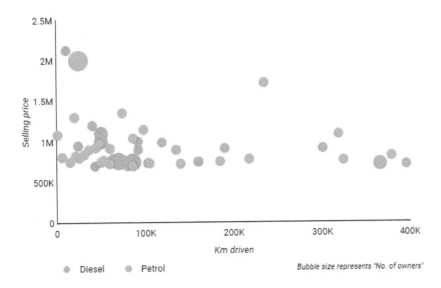

Figure 3.24 – A scatterplot using color and size to represent additional information

The scatterplot in the preceding figure depicts used cars, using color to represent a breakdown by fuel type, and size to indicate number of owners.

Tables

Tables are the best way to display detailed data. They also enable you to present several dimensions and metric values together easily. The following is an example of a table with multiple dimensions and multiple metrics. The profit values are shown as data bars instead of text.

	City ▾	Product	Units Sold	Gross Sales	Profit
1.	Seattle	Chips	1,463	$2,677	
2.	Seattle	Chocolate Chip	1,266	$2,367	
3.	Seattle	Muffins	159	$475	
4.	Seattle	Gingerbread	1,100	$2,398	
5.	Seattle	Juice	356	$577	
6.	Seattle	Popcorn	693	$1,296	
7.	Seattle	Oatmeal Raisin	530	$1,505	
8.	San Francisco	Chips	2,963	$5,422	
9.	San Francisco	Chocolate Chip	2,053	$3,839	
10.	San Francisco	Popcorn	438	$819	
11	San Francisco	Gingerbread	539	$1,175	

1 - 33 / 33   〈   〉

Figure 3.25 – A table with multiple dimensions and metrics

Tables can be part of detailed reports rather than compact dashboards. They tend to support the summary displays of metrics and allow users to investigate and understand details as needed. Tables are also commonly used in operational dashboards to help track day-to-day activities. When designing a dashboard, a user's need to see detailed data in the form of tables can be addressed by providing a drill-through report or a link to a separate view with the table display, instead of directly incorporating the table in the dashboard.

Pivot tables, as shown in the following figure, allow users to view metric values summarized against two dimensions along rows and columns respectively, and they also allow you to include associated dimension hierarchies.

			West			East		Region / City / Sales
⊟ Category	Product	Seattle	San Francisco	Total	New York	Atlanta	Total	Grand total
Snacks	Trail Mix	-	-	-	-	$966.07	$966.07	$966.07
	Popcorn	$1,295.91	$819.06	$2,114.97	$2,361.81	$2,870.45	$5,232.26	$7,347.23
	Chips	$2,677.29	$5,422.29	$8,099.58	$4,807.41	$6,701.46	$11,508.87	$19,608.45
Cookies	Oatmeal Raisin	$1,505.2	$2,871.24	$4,376.44	$2,820.12	$5,080.76	$7,900.88	$12,277.32
	Gingerbread	$2,398	$1,175.02	$3,573.02	$2,862.34	$4,423.22	$7,285.56	$10,858.58
	Chocolate Chip	$2,367.42	$3,839.11	$6,206.53	$2,169.2	$1,774.63	$3,943.83	$10,150.36
Beverages	Soda	-	-	-	-	$1,521.45	$1,521.45	$1,521.45
	Juice	$576.72	$1,053	$1,629.72	$1,322	$257.58	$1,579.58	$3,209.3
Baked Goods	Muffins	$475.41	$218.27	$693.68	$702.65	$2,368.08	$3,070.73	$3,764.41
	Cup Cakes	-	$122.59	$122.59	$74.75	$2,248.48	$2,323.23	$2,445.82
Grand total		$11,295.95	$15,520.58	$26,816.53	$17,120.28	$28,212.18	$45,332.46	$72,148.99

Figure 3.26 – A pivot table with row and column hierarchies

In short, a large amount of detailed data with suitable aggregations can be represented in pivot tables in a user-friendly way.

Heatmap (matrix)

Heatmaps use color intensity to represent metric values. Heatmaps when applied to tabular or matrix data help in comparing categories along rows and columns. You can use either a sequential color scheme or a diverging color scheme to make sense of the distribution of data along chosen dimension values. Using color to emphasize relationships among dimension values and the distribution of a depicted metric makes it easier to understand data patterns, compared to raw numbers.

| | | | | | Vendor / Profit |
Country	Blizzard	Clover	Encore	Grainger	ToolCo
Canada	194K	368K	-139K	1M	916K
France	213K	286K	-110K	960K	713K
Germany	133K	248K	-116K	927K	883K
Mexico	185K	183K	-138K	1M	764K
United States of America	221K	231K	-200K	1M	552K

Figure 3.27 – A heatmap depicting the distribution of profit by country and segment

The heatmap in the preceding figure uses a warm color to represent the lowest profit and vice versa. This chart provides a quick way to gauge problem areas quickly and also how prevalent these concerned aspects are.

Treemap

A treemap is a good way to visually represent hierarchical data primarily using area and color attributes. For example, the following chart displays the sales for each category, depicted by the first level of boxes for each category. The sales by each product that belongs to a category are represented by the second level of rectangular boxes. The area of each box is proportional to the total sales for a particular category or product. Color can be used either to depict an additional metric value or a dimension. This is a form of heatmap.

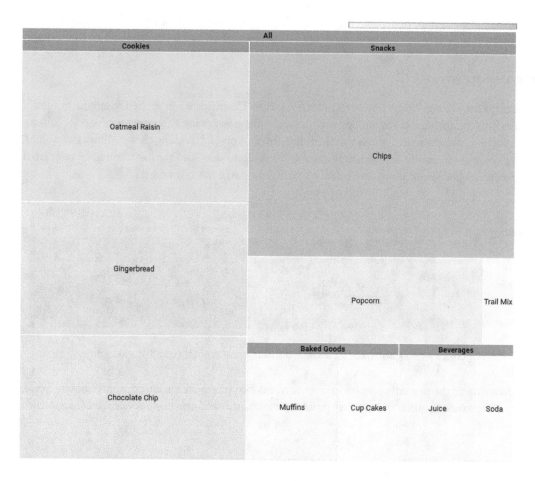

Figure 3.28 – A treemap displaying the proportion of sales across a product hierarchy

Treemaps are similar to pie charts in that they help represent the composition of data. In addition, treemaps allow you to drill down into one or more dimensions. Given that both area and color intensity provide only approximate comparisons, treemaps are useful only to present a high-level and approximate composition of dimensions and the extreme values of the metric, depicted by the color intensity.

Another limitation of the treemap is that dimension values on the lower end of the metric range would be too small and not easy to identify, especially if the range (the difference between the largest and smallest value) of the metric values is too large.

Geographical maps

Displaying location-based data on a geographical map makes the most intuitive sense. Almost all data visualization tools enable you to plot standard geographical areas, such as countries, states or provinces, cities, countries, and zip codes, out of the box. Some tools allow you to create custom areas such as regions and sales territories as well. Furthermore, some tools allow you to import or integrate advanced mapping data and capabilities directly into your dashboard.

> **Note**
> Advanced geospatial visualizations involve a fundamentally different type of data, called raster data, which is more closely related to images. This requires specialized tools such as Google Earth Engine or ArcGIS to visualize, and will not be covered in this book.

In more basic geographical charts, you present data on a map using either bubbles or a filled color. In the bubble geographical map, you can also use color in addition to the bubble size to represent an additional metric or a non-geographical dimension value for grouping, as shown in the following figure.

Figure 3.29 – A bubble geographical map chart, using bubble size to represent
the metric and color to represent the metric breakdown by dimension

The filled map fills the entire geographical area with the corresponding color, based on a single chosen metric. It provides an overview of the distribution across geographical locations and displays spatial patterns and relationships effectively. These filled maps are also called choropleth maps.

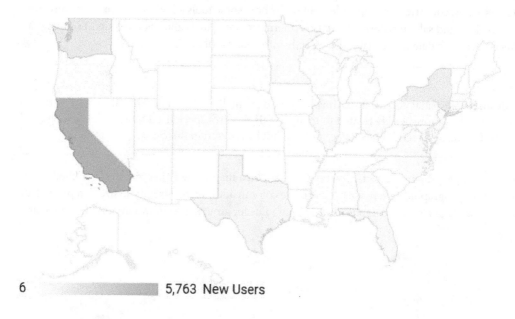

6   5,763 New Users

Figure 3.30 – A filled geographical map displaying sales across different countries

Both bubble and filled map charts are great at providing high-level regional patterns but are not suitable for identifying subtle differences.

Others

There is a plethora of other chart types out there that could be beneficial additions to your data visualization arsenal, but we cannot cover them all here. A good reference for additional chart types is https://flowingdata.com/chart-types/. However, the principles and guidelines we have discussed in this chapter should help you to evaluate those varied chart types and make the right decision for your data and your dashboard.

Avoiding common pitfalls

In this final section of the chapter, we will go through some of the common pitfalls and gotchas to watch out for while designing dashboards and visuals. You will see that these usually involve either inadequate application of the design principles we have discussed in this chapter or a complete lack of adherence to them.

Overloading a dashboard

A dashboard that tries to convey too much is an overloaded dashboard. It is tempting for dashboard developers to respond to users' relentless demands for additional information by adding more and more visuals and information to an existing dashboard. This tendency will only result in a cluttered dashboard that will be cumbersome to use and understand.

Also, trying to address the needs of different groups of users with the same dashboard is a bad idea. Limit the scope of the dashboard and align it with a single major objective and persona. Provide additional details to the users through separate dashboards and enable seamless navigation to facilitate users' analytical journeys. Create separate dashboards to serve different teams and objectives.

Understand the distinction between a dashboard and a report, and avoid or include details accordingly. Reports by definition tend to be elaborate, may contain multiple pages, and can cater to the needs of multiple personas. Also, do not clutter a dashboard or a report with too much non-data link.

Designing a poor or incohesive layout

By not thinking about the narrative and not having an understanding of the way humans consume visual data, you are likely to create a poor layout that isn't optimized for the quickest and easiest interpretation of information. Placing unrelated visuals together results in an incohesive layout that hurts the user experience and makes a dashboard really ineffective. You should spend time on the intended narrative you want to present to users and work deliberately to organize content on the dashboard to provide a cohesive picture.

Not emphasizing key information and a message

Use preattentive attributes such as color, intensity, size, length, and orientation to your advantage, and emphasize key information that needs attention. Also, a chart or a dashboard where everything is highlighted is one where nothing stands out. Use these attributes judiciously and sparingly to alert users to problematic or undesired behavior that needs attention.

Using color excessively or inappropriately

Do not use too many colors in a dashboard or a chart. Excessive color strains the human eye and makes it more difficult to process information. Also, do not use color to represent data when it doesn't add any meaning to it.

Using dual axes in charts without caution

Using dual axes to present two different metrics in a single chart can lead to incorrect insights, especially about the relationship between the two data series. The dual axes can be implemented in different ways:

- Each axis represents a different metric in the same units but on a closely related scale (most confusing).

- Each axis represents completely different metrics and units of measure. This is a more appropriate use of dual axes with less confusion, but care should be taken when comparing the rate of change or absolute values of the two series.

- Both axes represent the same metric but at different occurrences. This is the most effective application of dual axes.

In the following figure, the chart on the right, which represents the total sales and percentage sales from new customers on either axis, may be acceptable. The one on the left though is misleading and confusing, giving the impression that both the product categories – **Apparel** and **Shoes** – are generating sales from new customers at a similar rate.

Figure 3.31 – Use dual axes with extreme caution

Using separate charts to present two metrics is the simplest alternative to using a complicated combo chart that is ineffective. Using a single axis, made possible either by plotting series with closely related scales and the same units of measurement or by plotting indexed values of both metrics, is another alternative.

Inappropriate manipulation of axes

Bar charts whose axis don't start at 0 are plain wrong and present a very incorrect view of data. This pitfall must be avoided like the plague. The comparisons among the bars will be distorted when the bars do not start at 0. Always start the axis for the bar chart at 0. *Figure 2.58* shows how such charts mislead users.

On the same note, for a line chart, you need to pick the scale that best brings out the trend that users are interested in. For example, the left chart in the following figure is not really useful, as the change in data over time is not depicted well, with the *y* axis ranging from 0% to 40%. The company sales have been growing a mere 2% to 4%, and defining the *y*-axis scale around these values represents the trend better, as shown in the chart on the right.

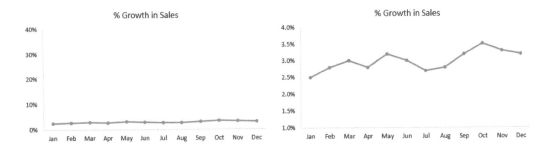

Figure 3.32 – An appropriate scale for the line chart to depict the trend well

Another aspect of axis design is "scale." If you want to compare a metric across multiple charts, make sure the axis scales for those charts are the same. Using different scales for a metric in different charts leads to inaccurate comparisons and insights.

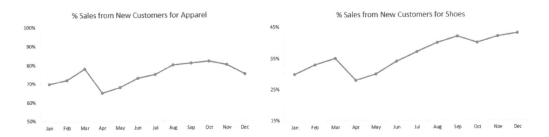

Figure 3.33 – Dissimilar axis scales lead to inaccurate comparisons

The preceding figure shows the percentage sales obtained from new customers for two product categories – **Apparel** and **Shoes** – in side-by-side line charts. At first glance, both categories seem to be acquiring customers at the same rate and the **Shoes** category is probably doing better, given the increasing trend. However, upon closer inspection, you can see that the two charts use different scales on their *y* axes. You realize that it is the **Apparel** category that is actually doing better.

Using inappropriate or complex chart types

Of course, using the most appropriate chart to represent the information is of paramount importance. In cases where multiple chart types are suitable, choose the simplest one. Do not use hard-to-read or complex chart types for the sake of novelty. In cases where the complexity of the data warrants a sophisticated chart, which requires greater efficacy from the users, include it in a dashboard only after making sure users are comfortable with it and can use it effectively. Provide helpful instructions and explanatory notes within the dashboard to aid users as needed. Alternatively, you can plan to convey the same information through a collection of simpler charts.

For example, consider the following radar chart. It shows the performance rating of different employees along six attributes.

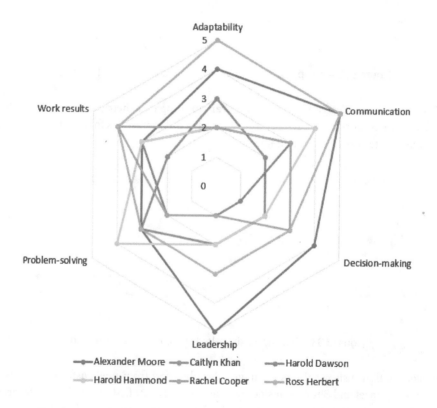

Figure 3.34 – A radar chart depicting employee performance scores along multiple attributes

Radar chart

A radar or spider chart can visualize one or more series of data over multiple quantitative variables. For example, you can easily compare the performance of different students across different courses. Given that it depicts variables in a circular fashion, it is especially suitable for comparing a series along different time periods, such as quarterly or monthly.

However, radar charts can be quite complex to read, especially when more than a few series are plotted. Also, filling the polygons with color results in occlusion – where the top polygon covers all the other polygons underneath it.

In this chart, the area of the polygon represents the overall performance of an employee. The intention is to be able to compare the performance of multiple employees among themselves. There are multiple things that make radar charts hard to read:

- The circular shape requires a conscious effort to compare values across the attributes and there is no implicit ordering.

- You cannot accurately compare the areas of different series visually. Also, the differences in the metric appear inflated as the resulting area of the polygon changes exponentially.

Alternatively, this data can be represented in a much simpler and more effective way using a bar chart. A clustered bar chart works best when there are only a few series, (i.e., employees, in this example) to compare.

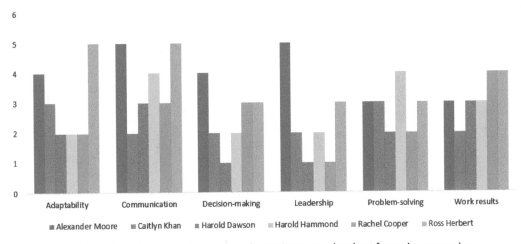

Figure 3.35 – A clustered bar chart is one alternative to a radar chart for easier comparison

You can use small multiples – a number of separate bar charts, one for each series (i.e., employee), each depicting the metric (i.e., performance rating) on the same scale – when there are more than a few series.

Summary

Using the right chart type to display information is of paramount importance. In this chapter, we reviewed a selection of common chart types to help you make the right choice for your needs. We discussed some of the common pitfalls and gotchas in visualizing data and how to avoid them.

This marks the end of part one of the book, which focused on the concepts of data storytelling and guiding principles. In part two of the book, we will explore Google's data visualization tool Looker Studio and its features and capabilities. The next chapter introduces the tool and examines its major components.

Further reading

To learn more about visualizing data effectively, you can refer to the following resources:

- Knaflic, Cole Nussbaumer. *Storytelling with data*. John Wiley & Sons. 2015.
- Berinato, Scott. *Good charts*. Harvard Business Review Press. 2016.
- Jones, Ben. *Avoiding data pitfalls*. Wiley. 2019.
- *Chart Types. FlowingData.* `https://flowingdata.com/chart-types/`.
- *The Data Visualization Catalogue.* `https://datavizcatalogue.com/`.

Part 2 – Looker Studio Features and Capabilities

Part 2 provides an overview of the various components of Looker Studio and describes related terminology and concepts. It delves into how to work with data sources, reports, charts, explorers, and more. You will gain a good understanding of the platform and its many features and capabilities.

This part comprises the following chapters:

- *Chapter 4, Google Looker Studio Overview*
- *Chapter 5, Looker Studio Report Designer*
- *Chapter 6, Looker Studio Built-In Charts*
- *Chapter 7, Looker Studio Features, Beyond Basics*

4

Google Looker Studio Overview

Google Looker Studio is a data visualization tool from Google that enables you to create data stories through interactive dashboards. It is a completely online (that is, web-based) tool that facilitates seamless collaboration. It has a simple drag-and-drop interface that enables both non-technical and technical users to easily build visuals and reports. At the time of writing, Looker Studio is provided by Google for free.

It was first introduced in 2016 as Looker Studio 360, which is a premium reporting platform for large enterprises and part of Google Analytics Suite 360. The free version of Looker Studio, targeted at individuals and smaller teams, was announced almost immediately. The product had been in beta status for a couple of years and in 2018, it became generally available. Google Looker Studio is tightly integrated with Google Marketing Platform, which is the expanded and rebranded version of Google Analytics 360 Suite, and Google Cloud Platform. It supports hundreds of non-Google data sources as well.

In a move to consolidate the multiple business intelligence offerings of Google Cloud under one umbrella, Google rebranded Data Studio as Looker Studio in October, 2022. Looker Studio is part of the Looker brand, which primarily comprises three offerings: Looker Studio, Looker Studio Pro, and Looker platform. This book only concerns itself with the free Looker Studio tool and its capabilities. Looker Studio Pro is the premium version of Looker Studio, which provides some enhanced enterprise capabilities, such as better asset management and team collaboration, and technical support on top of the free version.

This introductory chapter to Looker Studio will get you started with Looker Studio and provide an overview of its major entities – data sources, reports, and explorers. To leverage Looker Studio effectively, it is essential to understand the purpose of each entity and how these entities are related to each other. This chapter will walk you through performing several operations on these entities. You will learn how to work with and manage these entities, such as creating, sharing, copying, and publishing them.

In addition to building standard reports, Looker Studio allows you to explore data in an ad hoc manner through explorers. Explorer is still an experimental feature at the time of writing and is expected to go through major changes and improvements. Note that the Explorer tool within Looker Studio may look and behave in a very different way by the time you are reading this book. In fact, given the web-based nature of Looker Studio, the whole application undergoes frequent and rapid changes multiple times a month to offer new and expanded capabilities. Leverage and engage with Looker Studio's vast community, Report Gallery, official help pages, and support forums to keep up to date, receive tips and recommendations, and more. All in all, Looker Studio is a flexible and simple tool that addresses the evolving needs of users.

In this chapter, you will create a simple report that visualizes call center data in Looker Studio. You will do this incrementally over the next few chapters, building upon what you've learned throughout. To start, you will create the data source and enrich it. All the chapters in this part of the book focus mainly on providing you with the tool know-how and include limited data storytelling insights. You will see a lot of these concepts coming together and applied to practical examples and walkthroughs in the later chapters, primarily from *Chapter 8* onwards and to some extent in *Chapter 6* and *Chapter 7*.

In this chapter, we are going to cover the following topics:

- Getting started with Google Looker Studio
- Working with data sources
- Working with reports
- Working with Explorer
- Leveraging Looker Studio Gallery
- Getting help with Looker Studio
- Building your first Looker Studio report – creating the data source

Technical requirements

To follow the implementation steps for the various operations described in this chapter, you will need to have a Google account so that you can create reports with Looker Studio. It is recommended that you use Chrome, Safari, or Firefox as your browser. Finally, make sure Looker Studio is supported in your country (`https://support.google.com/looker-studio/answer/765767 9?hl=en#zippy=%2Clist-of-unsupported-countries`).

Getting started with Google Looker Studio

Google Looker Studio can be used by both individuals and organizations for their data exploration, visualization, and reporting needs. Whether you are a part of an organization or acting as an individual, you need a Google account to access and work with Looker Studio.

Organizations can leverage Google Cloud Identity directly to provision and manage Google accounts for its members. They can also synchronize users from other identity providers to Google Cloud Identity so that organizational users can access Google products and services. If the organization also uses Workspace (formerly called G Suite), a collection of collaboration and productivity tools, the administrators need to enable Looker Studio for the organization's users.

As an individual, you can use your Google account (either a Gmail address or any non-Gmail address mapped to your Google account).

To get started, log into your Google account and navigate to `datastudio.google.com`. You will be taken to the home page of the tool, as shown in the following screenshot:

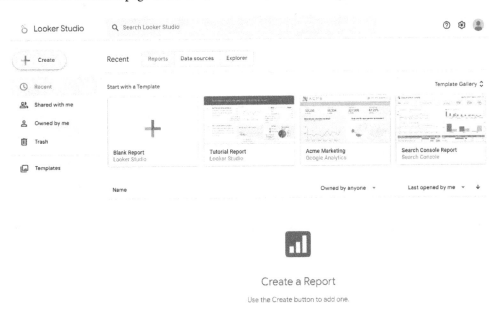

Figure 4.1 – Google Looker Studio home page

Like most Google products, the home page has a search bar on the top that lets you search the Looker Studio content that you have access to. You can search based on the name of the content, owner name or email, who you shared the content with, or who shared the content with you.

You can generate three types of content or files in Looker Studio – **Reports**, **Data sources**, and **Explorers**. These are arranged under the corresponding tabs under the search bar. You can switch between these views easily. By default, the home page displays the **Reports** tab, which shows the list of reports that you have recently accessed. The **Reports** tab also displays a template gallery widget at the top so that you can start creating a report easily by either using a template or starting from a blank report. The **Create** button at the top left allows you to create a report, a data source, or an explorer.

The left navigation panel allows you to filter the content to show recently accessed files, files owned by you, files shared with you, or files or content that have been deleted and are in the **Trash** area.

Before you can start creating content in Looker Studio for the first time, you need to choose the country you are in and accept the **Looker Studio Terms of Service** and **Google Ads Data Processing Terms** policies, as shown in the following screenshot:

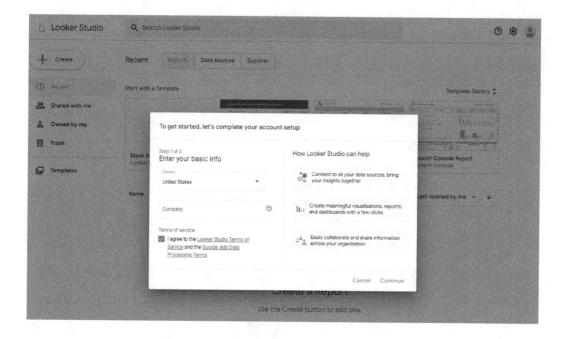

Figure 4.2 – Looker Studio account setup completion

Choose your email preferences regarding which updates you would like to receive on the next screen and complete your account setup.

> **Note**
>
> In the case of organizations, Cloud Identity or Workspace administrators can accept the terms of service on behalf of the organization so that the organization users or members don't need to accept or sign the terms individually.

How it works

The four major entities in Looker Studio include a dataset, a connector, a data source, and a report. They are linked to each other as shown, in the following diagram:

Figure 4.3 – Major entities of Looker Studio and their relationship

A **dataset** is the physical data source in the form of files, database tables, Google Analytics views, and more that exists outside of Looker Studio. On the other hand, a **Data source** is the logical construct that manifests within Looker Studio based on the underlying dataset. It is the **Connector** entity that makes the connection between the two possible. The connector functions as the pipeline between the physical dataset and logical data source. Looker Studio offers over 500 connectors for a wide variety of data stores. A **Report** is a physical object in Looker Studio that you can use to create either a single-screen dashboard or a multi-page report. A report is built on top of the data source, and its fields and metrics are used to display information. A single report can use multiple data sources. Likewise, a single data source can be used to build several reports.

An Explorer is a relatively newer entity and is generated by the Looker Studio Explorer tool, which has been available as an experimental feature since 2018. Like reports, Explorers are built on top of a data source. Explorer allows you to explore the data in an ad hoc manner. The relationship diagram with Explorer added looks as follows:

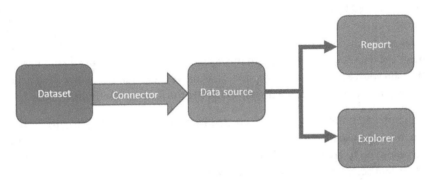

Figure 4.4 – The Explorer entity is the newest addition to Looker Studio

The user who creates an entity – be it a data source, report, or explorer – is deemed the owner of that object and has full control over it, including setting up sharing options, deleting the object, and more. It is possible to transfer ownership of the reports and data sources you create to a different user through sharing options. Once the transfer is complete, you will retain edit access to those assets until the new owner updates your permissions. Organizational users using Google Workspace or Cloud Identity can only transfer ownership within their domain, whereas individual users can do so with any other Google account.

We will discuss these Looker Studio entities and how to work with them in a little more detail throughout this chapter.

Working with data sources

A data source is a foundational element in Looker Studio that lets you explore data and build reports. It is the logical representation of the physical data that resides in external systems such as files, databases, data warehouses, applications, and so on. It defines the schema of the fields sourced from the underlying dataset. It allows you to rename as well as update the data types and formats of the fields. You can also add calculated fields and metrics to enrich the dataset. All this results in a logical data model that facilitates analysis and reporting. Data sources in Looker Studio enable you to create a consistent definition of metrics and representation of data across reports.

Creating a data source

A data source in Looker Studio can be created in two ways: from within a report or directly from the home page. When the data source is created while creating or editing a report, it is scoped for just that report and is referred to as an **embedded data source**. An embedded data source is not available for use or editing outside the report it was created in. While collaborating with others on building a report, an embedded data source provides the greatest flexibility because all the report editors can edit and manage the data source as needed. In this scenario, the report authors do not have to worry about how the data source impacts other reports. Sharing a report that uses embedded data sources with others shares both the report and the data sources embedded in it with those users.

On the other hand, when the data source is created from the home page using the **Create | Data source** option, it can be used by multiple reports and is termed a **reusable data source**. A reusable data source enables you to create and use a consistent data model across the organization. You can share a reusable data source with others with appropriate permissions for them to be able to view, use, or edit the data source. After creating an embedded data source, it is possible to convert it into a reusable data source, if needed, to make it available outside the context of the associated report. A report can use both embedded and reusable data sources together.

Connectors to various data stores, systems, and platforms allow data sources to connect to the dataset and access the data. Google provides several free connectors for you to leverage. This includes connectors to Google products such as Google Sheets, Google Analytics, Google Ads, Search Console, Google Cloud Storage, Google Surveys, Google Marketing Platform, and more, as well as connectors to common database systems such as Google BigQuery, Amazon Redshift, Google Cloud SQL, Google Cloud Spanner, Microsoft SQL Server, MySQL, PostgreSQL, and more. Google also provides a File Upload connector to let users upload CSV data.

Beyond these types of connectors provided by Google, a large number of connectors that support a wide variety of data platforms, applications, and systems are offered by Looker Studio partners. Google enables anyone to create a custom connector through the Looker Studio Community Connectors Program, which is an open source project.

In the rest of this section, we will go through the steps to create these two types of data sources.

Creating an embedded data source

Create a new report by clicking on the **Blank Report** tile on the home page or by selecting the **Report** option after clicking the **Create** button above the left navigation panel, as highlighted in the following screenshot:

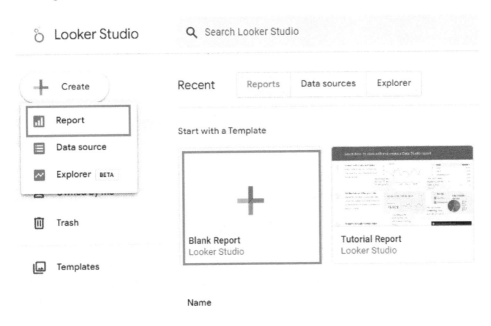

Figure 4.5 – Creating a new report

This creates a blank report and immediately displays the **Add data to report** screen, as shown in the following screenshot. Browse and search through the plethora of connectors made available by Google and Looker Studio partners. Choose an appropriate one to read the data from the source. For illustration purposes, choose the **Google Sheets** connector to create a data source from the data stored in a Google spreadsheet:

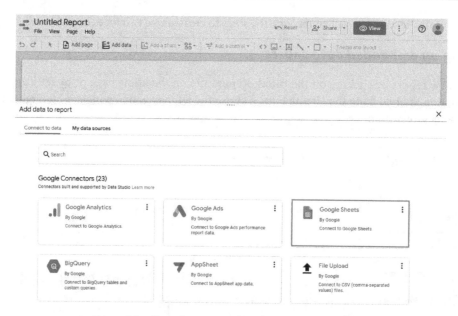

Figure 4.6 – Choosing a connector from the list available

By default, Looker Studio connects to Google Sheets under the same Google account you are using with Looker Studio. When you are adding data from Google Sheets for the first time, you need to authorize Looker Studio to make the connection. This is generally true for any type of connector you are using for the first time. Then, you must select the appropriate spreadsheet and the worksheet that contains the needed data. Under **Options**, you can confirm if the first row contains column headers and whether to consider any hidden or filtered cells. You can also choose a range of cells from the worksheet as the dataset. The options provided vary, depending on the connector type. Click the **Add** button and accept any confirmatory message to finish creating the data source:

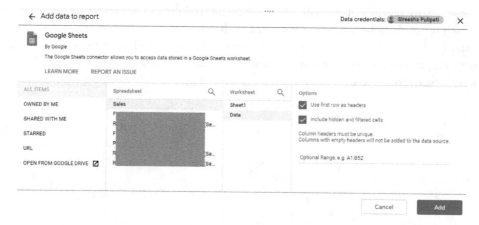

Figure 4.7 – Choosing the dataset – Google Sheets connector options

Follow these steps to create an embedded data source while creating a new report:

1. Click on **Create | Report** or the **Blank Report** tile on the home page.

2. Choose the connector from the **Add data to report** screen.

3. Provide the connection details and authorize Looker Studio to connect to the dataset.

4. Select the tables, files, and so on and click **Add**.

You can add a new embedded data source to an existing report by selecting the **Add data** icon from the toolbar. This brings up the same **Add data to report** screen as mentioned earlier. Here, you can proceed with the same steps of choosing a connector and selecting the source file, dataset, table, and so on:

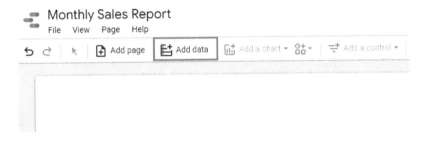

Figure 4.8 – Adding a data source to an existing report

Another place where you can add an embedded data source to a report is from the data sources section of the report. This can be accessed by choosing the **Manage added data sources** option from the **Resource** menu:

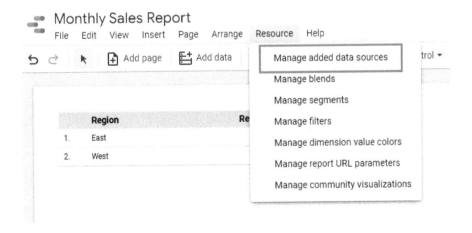

Figure 4.9 – Navigating the list of data sources that were added to the report

From the **Data sources** pane within the report, click on **ADD A DATA SOURCE** to add new data to the report:

Figure 4.10 – Adding a data source from the "Data sources" section in the report

Follow these steps to create an embedded data source from an existing report:

1.   Click on **Add data** from the toolbar OR choose **Resources | Manage added data sources** from the menu and click on **Add a Data Source** from the **Report data sources** screen.

2.   Choose the connector from the **Add data to report** screen.

3.   Provide the connection details and authorize Looker Studio to connect to the dataset.

4.   Select the tables, files, and so on and click **Add**.

You can also add data to the report from the **Data** panel on the right and the **SETUP** tab of the chart configuration.

Figure 4.11 – Adding data to the report from the Data panel and SETUP tab

Looker Studio offers this flexibility to make the experience of working with the tool seamless.

Creating a reusable data source

A reusable data source can be created from the home page by clicking the **Create** button and choosing the **Data source** option. This brings up the **Connectors** page, as shown in the following screenshot, where you can find and select the appropriate connector. You can provide a name for the data source in the header:

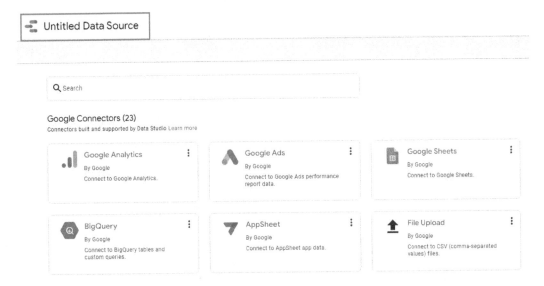

Figure 4.12 – Creating a reusable data source

Follow these steps to create a reusable data source:

1. Click on **Create | Data source** on the home page.

2. Choose the connector from the **Add data to report** screen and proceed with authorization, choosing the dataset steps:

Figure 4.13 – Converting an embedded data source into a reusable data source

You can also convert an embedded data source into a reusable one. However, this is only possible when you own the data credentials that were used for the embedded data source.

Follow these steps to convert an embedded data source into a reusable data source:

1. From the report designer, select **Manage added data sources** from the **Resource** menu to view the data sources that have been added to the report.

2. Click on the **Make reusable** link to make the data source available to be used with other reports:

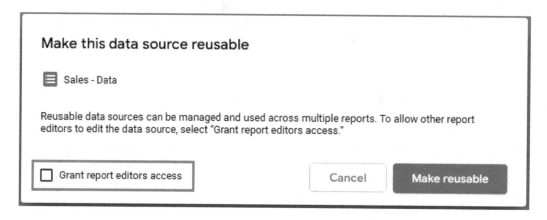

Make this data source reusable

⊟ Sales - Data

Reusable data sources can be managed and used across multiple reports. To allow other report editors to edit the data source, select "Grant report editors access."

☐ Grant report editors access   Cancel   **Make reusable**

Figure 4.14 – Restricting the level of access to the reusable data source

While the other editors of the report can edit and change the newly converted reusable data source by default, you can uncheck the option to make it read-only for other report editors.

Managing data freshness

Almost always, data sources do not import data into Looker Studio but rather maintain a live connection to the underlying dataset. This is very beneficial in cases when the underlying dataset is huge or is getting frequently updated. Having a live connection ensures that the latest data updates are surfaced in the data sources and reports automatically. The one exception where the data is imported into Looker Studio is when connecting to CSV files.

The underlying dataset is queried separately for individual charts and components in the report. This means that Looker Studio pushes the aggregations and other computations back to the more powerful underlying data platforms whenever possible. However, retrieving the data from the underlying dataset every time can be slow and there is no value in running the same queries and computations again and again, especially when the underlying data doesn't change. For these reasons, the query results are usually stored in a temporary cache within Looker Studio to provide better performance while exploring the data, building the visuals, or interacting with the reports.

The cache is refreshed automatically periodically. The refresh frequency options available vary, depending on the data source connection and the underlying data platform. For example, the default refresh rate for a Google Sheets data source is 15 minutes, with the other options being every hour, every 4 hours, and every 12 hours. A data source connected to Big Query, however, has a default refresh rate of 12 hours and provides more granular data freshness options, and can be set in increments of minutes and hours ranging from 1 to 12 hours. The appropriate data freshness frequency is generally guided by one or more of the following aspects:

- To match the update frequency of the underlying dataset
- To optimize the query cost of underlying paid data services
- To improve the performance of the Looker Studio reports

The last point implies that there is usually a performance impact on a report while its data source refresh is happening. Depending on the size of the report and the number of queries generated, the refresh may take a while. It's important to set the data refresh rate that balances the data freshness needed, the performance of the report, and the cost incurred by the underlying platform, if applicable. You can view and choose the frequency of data freshness for a data source from its **Edit** screen:

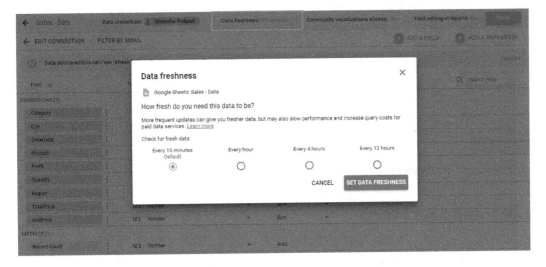

Figure 4.15 – Choosing the appropriate data freshness for the data source

One exception to the live connection is the **File upload** connector. If you have your data stored in local CSV files, it is not possible to make an online connection to the files. You need to upload the files to Looker Studio to create a data source for this dataset. Looker Studio stores these files in Google Cloud Storage, which is the object storage service provided by Google Cloud. There are certain restrictions as to the format of the files and limitations concerning the size and number of files that can be uploaded by a user.

At the time of writing, there is a 100 MB file size limit per dataset. Also, an individual user can only use 2 GB of storage in total across all such data sources. You can refer to the official Looker Studio documentation to learn more about these limitations.

If your dataset is split across multiple CSV files with the same structure – that is, the same fields are in the same order – Looker Studio allows you to upload these files together to form a single data source:

Figure 4.16 – Creating a data source from multiple files using the File Upload connector

Controlling data access

While creating a data source, you make the connection to the underlying dataset by providing your own data credentials. These are referred to as **Owner's credentials**. When you share this data source or a report with others using this data source, they will be able to view the data, even if they do not have access to the underlying dataset. You can have a data source use **Viewer's credentials** instead, which requires anyone who is using this data source to have their own credentials to access the data. You can change the type of credentials while editing the data source, as shown in the following screenshot:

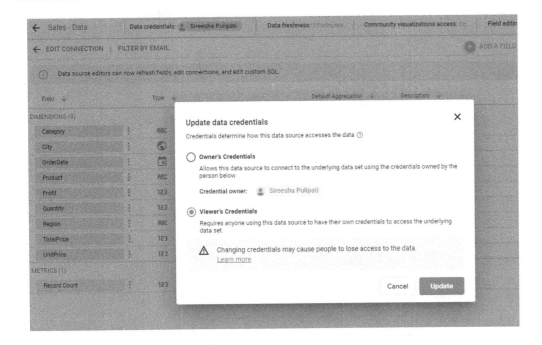

Figure 4.17 – Updating the data credentials for the data source

Using **Viewer's credentials** with the data source provides better data security and ensures that unauthorized users cannot see the data, even if they could access the report itself.

Sometimes, you may want to restrict access to a subset of data in the data source based on who views the report. A common scenario is where different salespeople need to see different records of the sales data based on the territories they belong to. One approach is to build different data sources and corresponding reports pre-filtered for each territory or salesperson. But this would be a very inefficient and unwieldy approach resulting in a large number of data sources and reports to maintain. The best way to handle this is to define a single data source and filter the underlying dataset dynamically based on who is logged in. You can implement the email filtering feature for the data source, which lets you choose a field in the dataset that contains the email of the user who can see each row of data.

Follow these steps to enable email filtering for a data source:

1. Select **Resource | Manage added data sources** from the menu and click the pencil icon for the concerned data source. This opens the **Data source edit** screen.

2. Click **Filter by Email** at the top.

3. Check the box for **Filter data by viewer email** and click **Select email field** to choose the field that contains the email address of the users to filter by. It is essential that this field contains the full email address and also that the text matches the case of the user account exactly. Any case mismatches will result in a filter mismatch:

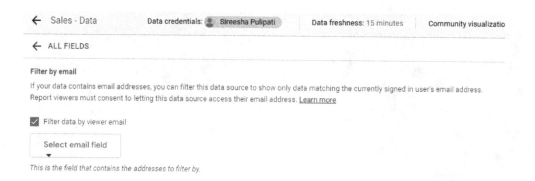

Figure 4.18 – Filtering the data based on the email of the user accessing the report

Generally, when a Looker Studio report is made publicly accessible, anyone will be able to view the report without requiring them to use a Google account. However, when the **Filter by Email** feature is enabled for a data source, report viewers must sign in to view the related reports and consent to allow their email address to be used by the data source to show them the relevant data:

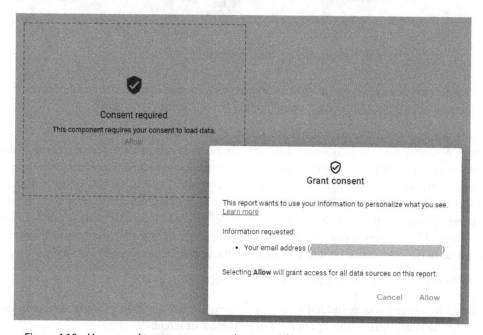

Figure 4.19 – Users need to grant consent when email filtering is enabled for a data source

Email filtering applies to report editors as well. They will only be able to view the data that is mapped against their email ID. A user only needs to grant consent once per data source within a report. At any time, users can revoke their consent to stop providing their email addresses to the reports from Looker Studio's **Settings** area, as follows:

1. From the Looker Studio home page, click **Settings** (gear icon) at the top right.

2. Select the **Revoke Consent** tab from the left panel and click the **Revoke all** button. This prevents all the reports and data sources from using their email addresses to filter the data:

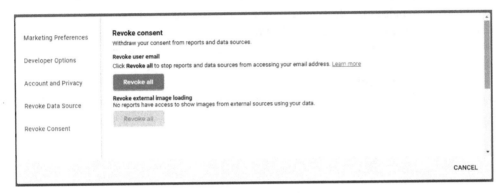

Figure 4.20 – Revoking consent to allow reports and data sources
to use your email address to filter the data

At the time of writing, it is not possible to revoke consent for individual data sources and reports. Once the consent is revoked for all content, the user can explicitly allow only specific reports and data sources to use their email address.

This is a simple example where each row in the data source can be viewed by only one user, with the email address field in the dataset storing only a single address. Often, you may want to allow multiple users to look at the same set of data. This can be achieved in Looker Studio using data blending, which we will cover in *Chapter 7, Looker Studio Features – Beyond Basics*.

Editing a data source schema

When you open a reusable data source or choose to edit an embedded one, you will find that all the fields from the dataset are listed under the **Dimensions** group. A default metric called **Record Count** is also added under the **Metrics** group. While the dimension field contains a value for each row of the dataset, a metric is a summary field that is computed across multiple rows of data on the fly when used in the charts. Dimension fields are typically used to group the data in charts and the metrics are aggregated for the selected dimensions. Dimension fields can be added as metrics in the chart configuration, which applies the Count Distinct aggregation to the non-numerical fields and the defined default aggregation method for the numerical dimension fields.

Looker Studio detects the data type of the fields automatically based on the underlying dataset. While Looker Studio does a decent job recognizing the appropriate data types, you may want to adjust them in the data source settings to meet your analytical and reporting needs. For example, defining the right geo dimension type is key to visualizing the data in maps. You can also set numerical fields as percentages or in terms of duration in seconds to allow the data to be represented appropriately in the charts.

For each field, you can define a default aggregation method in the data source. Default aggregation is the method of aggregation – that is, sum, average, median, and so on – and is computed in a visual by default when a field is added to it. By default, Looker Studio sets the default aggregation to **None** for all non-numerical dimension fields, **Sum** for all numerical dimension fields, and **Auto** for all metrics. The **Auto** method implies that the metric is already an aggregation and cannot be further aggregated. For numeric dimension fields, you can define the appropriate aggregation method. For example, you can change the default aggregation method for percentage or ratio fields to average or median. You can also rename the fields to be more user-friendly just by typing in the new name over the old one:

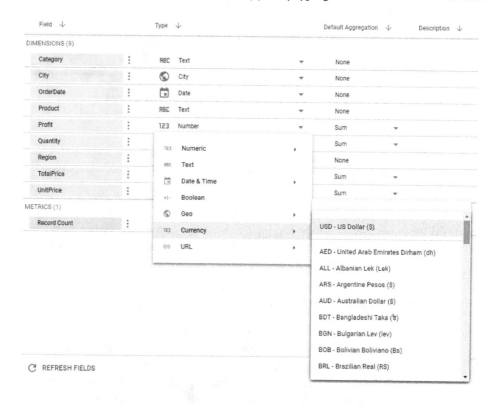

Figure 4.21 – Editing the data types of the data source fields

It is possible to change the aggregation method, data type, and format from the default choice to something else as needed in each of the charts while building a report. Making this change at the data source level, however, ensures that the right aggregations and data formats are used consistently across different visuals by default:

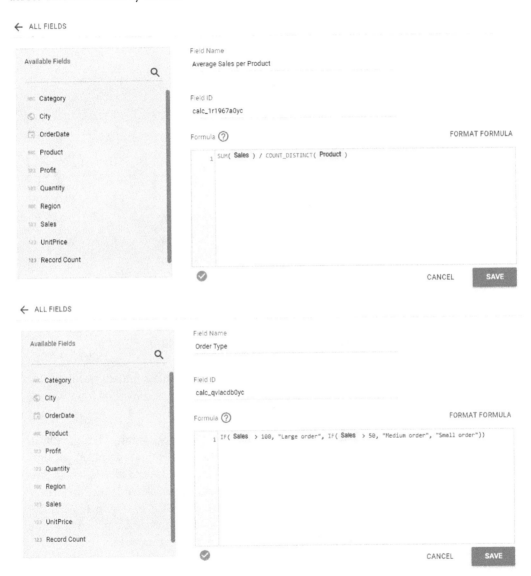

Figure 4.22 – Creating calculated fields

You can enrich the data source by adding new calculated fields derived from the native fields by applying business or conditional logic, performing arithmetic operations, and manipulating text fields. A calculated field can be a dimension or a metric. The preceding screenshot shows both examples.

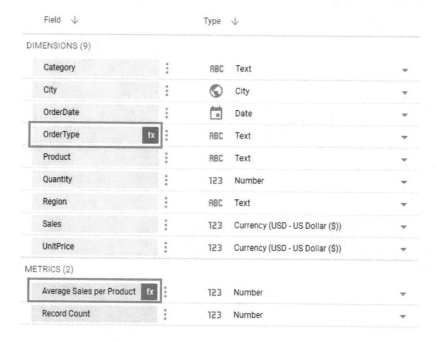

Figure 4.23 – Calculated fields in the data source field list

The calculated fields are denoted with "fx" in the fields list to differentiate them from the regular fields. We will go through some common functions and the calculated fields you can create from them in *Chapter 7*, Looker *Studio Features – Beyond Basics*.

You can hide any data source fields that you do not want to expose to report editors. Click the ellipsis for the field and choose the **Hide** option. The hidden fields are grayed out on the data source's page and do not appear under **Available Fields** in the report designer. Exposing only derived fields and hiding the corresponding regular fields is a common scenario. For example, you can hide the "first name" and "last name" fields and show only the concatenated full name derived field. Another example is when you want to prevent report editors from changing the method of aggregation for any field. You can create a calculated field with the desired aggregation and hide the original field.

Report editors can change field definitions while configuring charts and controls. They can change the display name, data type, output format, and aggregation for any visible data source fields. By default, **Field editing in reports** is enabled for all new data sources. It can be disabled, if desired, from the top of the data source editor page. It helps you, as the data source editor, to completely control how the fields are displayed and used in reports.

Other common data source operations

Beyond editing the schema and managing data freshness and access, a few other common things that you can do with a data source include duplicating or copying the data source, sharing the data source, and more.

Copying a data source

You may want to copy a data source to make it easier for you to create different customized versions of the same dataset. When you create a data source copy, you may have to reconnect to the underlying dataset to confirm your access. The data source copy typically has the same list of fields, including the calculated fields, the same data types, aggregations, and more. If the reconnected dataset in the copied data source differs from the original dataset, you can see the changed fields and update any dependent calculated fields accordingly. If you are not the owner of the data source that you are copying, you can update the credentials for the copy with your own.

Copying an embedded data source creates another embedded data source within the same report. Copying a reusable data source from the home page will result in a reusable data source:

Figure 4.24 – Copying a reusable data source from the home page

However, when you duplicate a reusable data source from within a report, it results in an embedded data source. Be mindful not to create copies of data sources thoughtlessly if they do not serve any distinguished purpose as this proliferation can quickly become unmanageable and confusing.

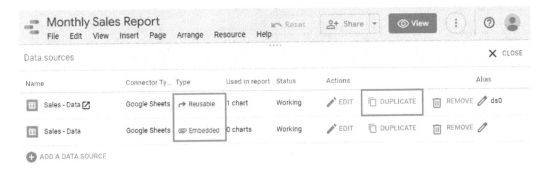

Figure 4.25 – Duplicating a data source from within a report

Sharing a data source

An embedded data source is part of the report it is created from and is shared through the report itself. You can share a reusable data source with others by selecting the **Share** option and providing the user's emails and level of access (view versus edit). While sharing, you can manage access through controls such as disabling copying for viewers, preventing editors to add new people, and so on.

Follow these steps to share a data source with others:

1. Open the data source and click on the **Share** button at the top right of the data source. Alternatively, from the home page, select **Share** from the options under the ellipsis on the right for the listed data source:

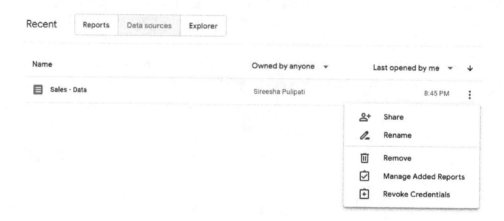

Figure 4.26 – Sharing a reusable data source

2. Add the user's emails and choose the appropriate access – that is, **Can view** or **Can edit**:

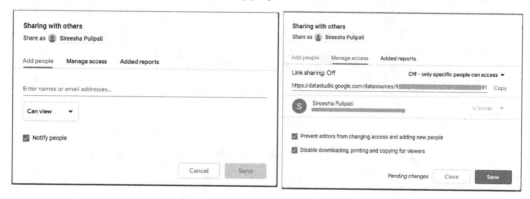

Figure 4.27 – The sharing options for a reusable data source

3. Under **Manage access**, you can enable sharing through the data source link. You can choose to have the link work for anyone or only for those to whom you have explicitly given access.

The sharing dialog box also allows you to view the list of reports that have been added to this data source and remove the association for any, as needed:

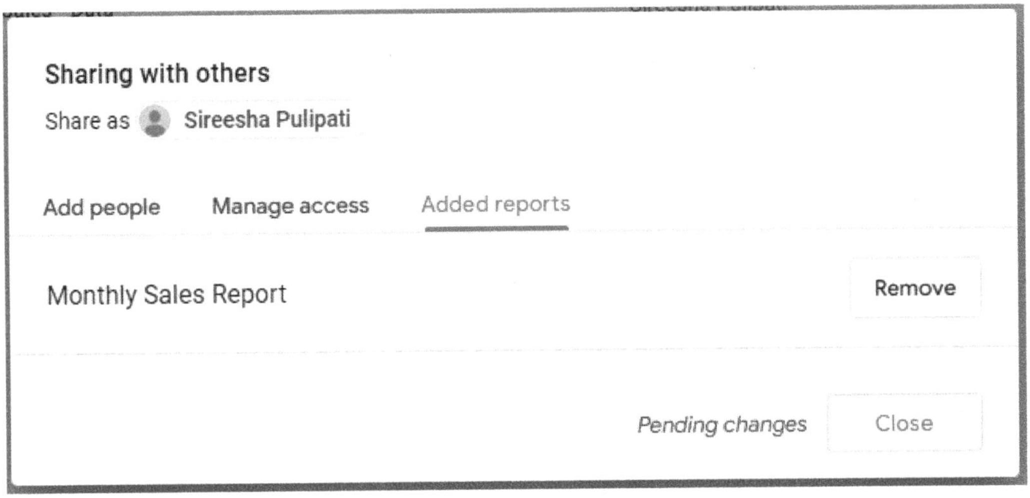

Figure 4.28 – View reports added to the data source

Transferring ownership

Any data source that you create is owned by you by default. An asset can only have a single user account as an owner at a time. You can transfer ownership to a different user through sharing settings. You can only transfer the ownership of assets that you own. One caveat is that it is not possible to transfer the ownership of a File Upload data source.:

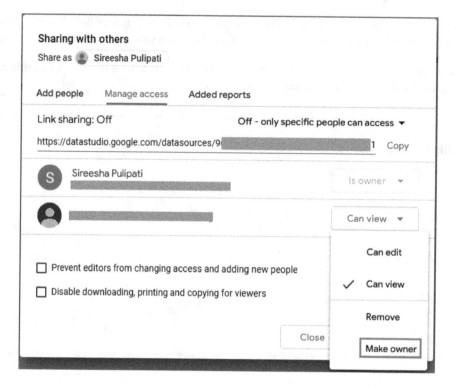

Figure 4.29 – Making a different user the owner of the data source

The steps for this are as follows:

1. Open the **Sharing with others** dialog box from the top of the report.

2. From the **Manage access** tab, make sure that the data source is shared with the new intended owner, either as a viewer or an editor. If not, add them from the **Add people** tab, click **OK**, and reopen the sharing options.

3. From the **Manage access** tab, expand the dropdown beside the user and choose **Make owner**. Click **Yes** in the confirmation dialog box:

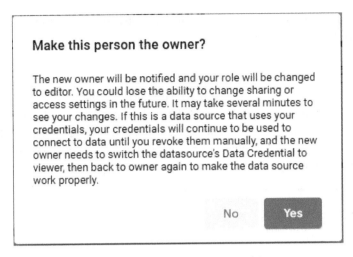

Figure 4.30 – Transferring ownership

The credentials that are used for the data source are retained post the ownership transfer until the new owner updates them. You can manually revoke your credentials post the transfer from the home page. Follow these steps:

1. From the Looker Studio home page, select the **Data sources** tab.

2. Find the data source in the list or search for it at the top.

3. Expand the ellipsis and select **Revoke credentials**:

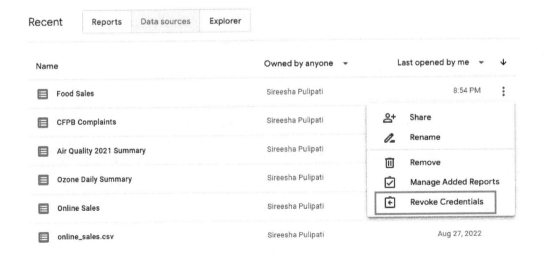

Figure 4.31 – Revoking data source credentials post ownership transfer

Once you revoke your credentials, the data source will not be able to connect to the underlying dataset until the data source credentials are updated.

Others

Apart from the operations we've discussed so far, you can also edit the connection details for a data source, refresh the fields, rename the data source, delete the data source, and more. For a reusable data source, you can view the list of all the reports using it and manage them using the **Manage added reports** option that's available from the ellipsis menu on the home page. This allows you to see whether the data source has been set up properly for a report or detach a report from the data source:

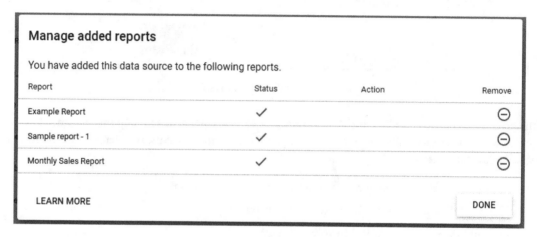

Figure 4.32 – Managing the added reports for a data source

You can also revoke the credentials that are used for a data source, which prevents the data source from connecting to the underlying dataset until the credentials are updated.

Working with reports

A report in Looker Studio is an asset or entity that enables you to build data stories in the form of dashboards and reports. Conceptually, a dashboard is a centralized tool that provides an at-a-glance view of key performance metrics. It is usually limited to a single page or screen and displays information at a summary level. On the other hand, a data report is an organized representation of data in visuals and text with enough detail. A report usually spans multiple pages to provide a comprehensive analysis of the concerned topic. A more detailed list of the differences between the two forms of data presentation was provided in *Chapter 1, Introduction to Data Storytelling*.

Creating a report

You can create a new report either from the home page or from within another report. The first step when creating a report is to add a data source to it. While creating the report, you can either create an embedded data source specific to that report or select an existing reusable data source.

Follow these steps to create a report from the home page:

1. Go to the home page.

2. Click on **Create** | **Report** OR click on the **Blank Report** template.

3. Create a new data source or choose an existing reusable data source from the **Add data to report** screen:

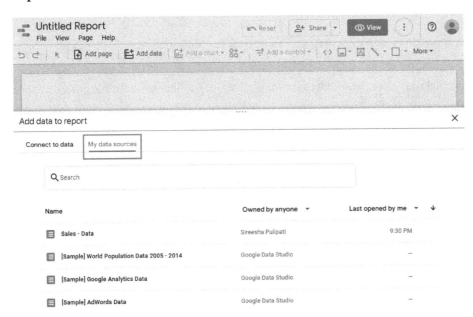

Figure 4.33 – Adding an existing reusable data source to the report

Now, you must create a new report from within another report:

1. Make sure you have the report open in edit mode.

2. From the menu, choose **File** | **New Report**.

You can also create a report directly from a reusable data source:

- Open the data source from the home page.

- Click on **Create Report** button at the top right.

A new report will open in a separate browser tab:

Figure 4.34 – Creating a report from the reusable data source

A report has two different modes that you can interact in – **Edit** mode and **View** mode.

When you have just created a new report, the report is opened in **Edit** mode. In this mode, you can design and build your report by adding and editing charts, pages, filter controls, and other components. You can preview the report by switching to the "read-only" **View** mode. **View** mode enables you to see and interact with the report as the end users would. Historically, **Edit** mode didn't allow for much interactivity and required report editors to switch to **View** mode to understand how the visualizations change based on user interaction with filters and other controls. This has changed since November 2021 when interactivity was added to **Edit** mode, greatly improving the report-building experience:

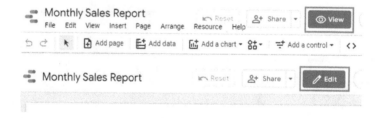

Figure 4.35 – Toggling between the Edit and View modes

As a report owner or editor, you can switch between **Edit** and **View** mode by clicking on the toggle button at the top. Users with only view access to the report will not see the **Edit** toggle.

Creating a report from a template

A report template allows you to look at your data quickly and provides a ready-to-use finished product. It also serves as a great starting point when you need a customized report. The template gallery on the Looker Studio home page provides several report templates created by Google using datasets with a standard schema such as Google Analytics, Firebase application analytics, Ads, and so on using publicly available data.

A larger number of templates are available in the Report Gallery available at `https://datastudio.google.com/gallery` that have been submitted by partners and the community.

Report templates from **Gallery** come with data controls added at the top for each of the data source used in the template. Data controls allow you to quickly replace the default data with your data sources so that you can see how the template looks with your data. Alternately, a template can also just come with a data source that has been shared with you, in which case you can just make a copy by clicking **Edit and Share** and work with the report as needed. From the template's data controls, select **Use my own data** and click **Replace data** to choose your data sources:

Figure 4.36 – Adding data to a template in place to understand how it looks with your data

The list of fields and metrics available in your data source schema should match those in the data source that was used to build the report template. If any fields are missing or if there's a mismatched data type, the charts and controls in the template may be broken. You cannot edit a template until you convert it into a report by clicking the **Edit and share** button. This creates a copy of the template as a report, which you can then edit to add data, modify charts, and so on just like any other report.

If you copy the template as a report without replacing the original data sources using **Replace data**, the report will contain errors if you have only view access to the data sources used with the template.

Follow these steps to create a report from a report template:

1. Click on a template from the featured list on the home page. Alternatively, go to **Template Gallery** (from the left navigation panel or the top-right link on the **Reports** home page) to view the full list of templates available and click on the one you want to use. This opens the template.

2. Select **Use my own data** from the top of the template and click **Replace data** to choose your data for each of the data sources

3. Click the **Edit and share** button at the top right to turn the template into a report.

Publishing a report

By default, any changes made to the report are automatically shown to the report viewers. Often, when you are making substantial or time-consuming changes to a report that has already been shared with others, you may not want the viewers to see the work-in-progress state. The **Report publishing** feature allows you to control when the viewers can see the changes. You need to explicitly enable this feature for a report.

Follow these steps to enable **Report publishing**:

1. Open a report in **Edit** mode.

2. From the menu, choose **File | Publishing settings**.

3. Toggle the manual **Report publishing** button on and click **Save**:

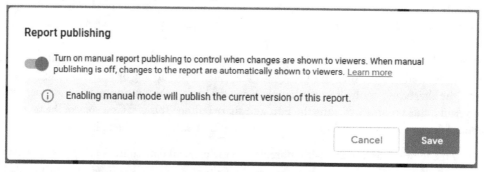

Figure 4.37 – Turning on manual report publishing

When **Report publishing** is turned on, the report designer displays a **Publish** button to allow report editors to manually publish the changes when appropriate. As a report editor, you can switch between the work-in-progress **Draft version** and **Published version** to view the differences and understand the changes:

Figure 4.38 – Report features with publishing turned on

Sharing a report

You can share a report with others in different ways:

- Inviting people
- Scheduling email delivery
- Sharing the report link
- Embedding the report
- Downloading the report

As with data sources, you can share Looker Studio reports by providing the names or email addresses of the users and choosing the appropriate level of access.

Follow these steps to share a report with others by inviting them:

1. Click on the **Share** button at top of the report or choose **File | Share** from the menu. This will open the **Sharing with others** dialog box.

2. Under the **Add people** table, provide the names or email addresses of the people you want to add.

3. Choose whether to give those people **View** or **Edit** access.

There are additional controls under the **Manage access** tab on the **Sharing with others** screen that affect what people with access can do with the report and how they can find and share the report:

- You can prevent report editors from sharing the report with more people or changing the access of the existing users.

- You can disable downloading, printing, and copying operations for report viewers.

- You can enable broader sharing of the report through a web link by turning on the **Link sharing** feature. This also allows you to restrict the level of access for users who have the report link:

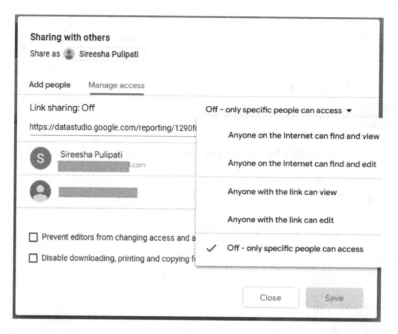

Figure 4.39 – Managing the access of the people that the report is shared with

You can also obtain the link to the report directly by selecting the **Get report link** option from the dropdown attached to the **Share** button.

Follow these steps to share a report using its link:

1. You can get the report link in two ways:

    A. Expand the sharing options by clicking on the drop-down icon beside the **Share** button at the top of the report. Then, select **Get report link**.

    B. Click on the **Share** button at top of the report or choose **File | Share** from the menu. This will open the **Sharing with others** dialog box. Switch to the **Manage access** tab and find the link under the **Link sharing** section.

2. Copy the link and share the link with the users through other means – email, chat, and so on.

Please note that whether the people who have the link can access the report depends on the **Link sharing** options you have set up, as shown in the following screenshot:

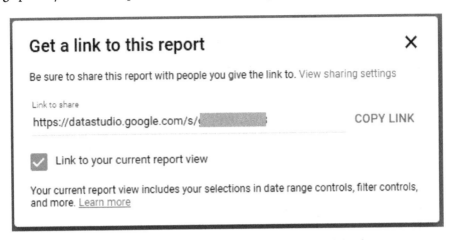

Figure 4.40 – Getting a link to the report for sharing with others

Another way to share a report is to email a snapshot of the report to the users on a scheduled basis.

Follow these steps to share the report via scheduled email delivery:

1. Expand the sharing options by clicking on the dropdown icon beside the **Share** button at the top of the report. Then, select **Schedule email delivery**.

2. Provide the email addresses of the recipients.

3. Optionally, customize the email subject and message.

4. Set the start date and time to begin the schedule. The time zone is set to that of your operating system.

5. Choose the frequency of the email delivery – daily, weekly, monthly, every weekday, or define a custom frequency:

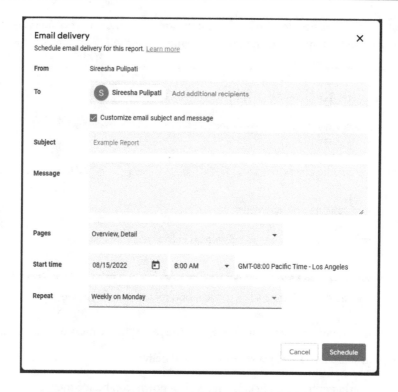

Figure 4.41 – Setting up scheduled email delivery of the report

Each recipient will receive an email with an attached PDF of the report. The email body includes a preview of the report and a link to it. One prerequisite for successful delivery is that the report PDF needs to be generated successfully. You will be notified by email if your scheduled email report fails to go out.

> **Note**
> Do not share a report that has email filtering enabled using scheduled email delivery. This is because the report PDF will be generated based on the access of the user creating the schedule rather than that of the recipient of the report. Always share such reports by sending the report link directly.

It is possible to embed Looker Studio reports in your applications, which enables you to distribute your report broadly and does not require viewers to visit the Looker Studio site. Looker Studio provides you with the embed code or URL that you can add to your applications. You can either embed the report as an iFrame using code or using the oEmbed format with the embed URL.

Follow these steps to embed a Looker Studio report:

1. Expand the sharing options by clicking on the dropdown icon beside the **Share** button at the top of the report. Then select **Embed report**. Alternatively, choose **File | Embed report** from the menu.

2. Select **Enable embedding** for the report, if you haven't done so already.

3. Choose either the **Embed code** or **Embed URL** option. You can set the iFrame size with the **Embed code** option.

4. Choose **COPY TO CLIPBOARD** and add it to your application.

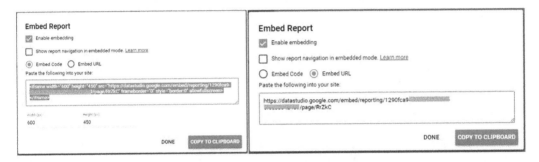

Figure 4.42 – Embedding a report

An embedded report is fully functional and the viewers can interact with the report components and navigate around just like they can when they view it on the Looker Studio site. The security and access controls you have set for the report are reflected in the embedded reports as well. If you have made your report publicly accessible, anyone viewing your application or website can view the report. On the other hand, if you have restricted access for the report to only specific users or groups, only those users can see the embedded report in your application. These users need to be logged into their Google accounts to be able to see the report. The same applies to the reports enabled with email filtering.

You can also download a snapshot of the report as a PDF, which can then be shared via other means. Downloading large, complex, multi-page reports may lead to network timeout issues and cause the download to fail or download only a partial report. You can try to download at a different time or consider downloading only a subset of the report pages. Keep in mind that once a report is exported and downloaded, any access restrictions that were put in place in Looker Studio no longer apply to that copy.

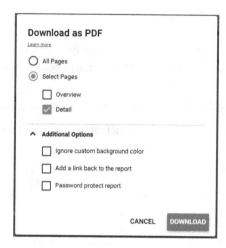

Figure 4.43 – Downloading a report as a PDF

Follow these steps to download a report:

1. Expand the sharing options by clicking on the dropdown icon beside the **Share** button at the top of the report. Then, select **Download report**. Alternatively, choose **File | Download report as | PDF** from the menu.

2. Choose to download all pages or specific pages only

3. Optionally, choose one or more of the following options:

    A. Ignore custom background color

    B. Add a link back to the report

    C. Password protect report

4. Click **Download**.

Transferring ownership

You can transfer the ownership of a report that you own to another user from the **Sharing** settings. Any user who can access the report can be made the owner by choosing **Make owner** from the permission options. Any data sources that the report uses will continue to use the previous credentials post-transfer. The new report owner can edit and update the connection settings and credentials for data sources embedded within the report. However, reusable data sources used within the report cannot be edited by the new report owner and need to be transferred separately.

You can transfer reports that use File Upload data sources. The new report owner will be able to view the data and, in the case of an embedding data source, edit the connection settings and refresh the data source.

Other common report operations

A couple more useful operations that you can perform on a report include creating a copy of the report and refreshing all the data within a report. Let's take a look.

Copying a report

You can copy any report that you have view access to unless it is specifically disabled for viewers. Report editors and owners can always copy a report. Duplicating a report enables you to use and modify a report that you do not own. Making copies of a report also helps you easily create different variations of it without the need to build them from scratch.

Copying a report copies all the report components and controls. However, this operation does not copy the data source. While copying a report, you need to choose a data source to use with the copied report.

Follow these steps to copy a report:

- Select the **Make a copy** option from the ellipsis at the top of the report. Alternatively, in **Edit** mode, choose **File | Make a copy** from the menu.
- Select the new data source(s) to use with the copy. They can be the same as the original data sources or different.
- Click **Copy Report**.

If you do not have access to the original data source, it will be displayed as **unknown** in the **Copy** dialog box. Here, you must select a new data source that you have access to or create a new one that can support the report elements.

Refreshing the report data

The data displayed in a report could be served by directly querying the underlying dataset or serving it from the cache. The cache is automatically refreshed based on the Data Freshness frequency set for each of the associated data sources. However, report editors can refresh the data for a report on-demand by selecting the **Refresh data** option, as shown here:

Figure 4.44 – Manually refreshing the report data

This updates the cache for all the data sources used in the report. If any schema changes are made in the underlying dataset, such as adding additional columns or modifying data types, those changes can only be reflected within the report by reconnecting to the data source. This requires edit access to the data source.

Working with Explorer

Looker Studio Explorer is an exploration tool that enables you to quickly examine the data and obtain insights faster. It provides you with a temporary scratch area where you can easily explore the data and perform ad hoc analysis. Within an Explorer, you create explorations in one or more tabs. Any work you do in an explorer is not saved automatically, unlike reports and data sources. However, you can save your exploration if you wish for later use. Even though Explorer has been available to users for a while, it is still an experimental feature at the time of writing. What this means is that the functionality may change at any time and swiftly, potentially in a disruptive manner.

You can either explore a data source or a chart in a report. Having a separate place to explore the data means that you do not have to create and manage a report if all you need to do is look at the data and understand it. Likewise, you can explore any chart in a report and perform ad hoc analysis on it without having to edit the report.

The Explorer interface provides the same chart controls and design elements that are available for reporting. You can add any charts you build in Explorer to a new or existing report:

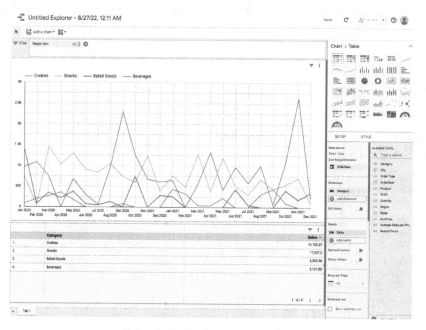

Figure 4.45 – Explorer user interface

While explorations are and look different from reports in many ways, they differ in a couple of significant ways:

Report	Exploration
Reports and their changes are automatically saved	Explorations and their changes are not automatically saved unless explicitly saved by you
Can be shared with others	Cannot be shared with others; you need to export visuals to a report and share the report

Table 4.1 – Differences between a report and an exploration

> **Note**
> Given the experimental nature of the Explorer feature, it is very likely that the functionality described in this section may differ drastically by the time you read this. However, it is the expectation that the basic premise of "an exploration" as a temporary, private space for quick and dirty data exploration will still hold.

Creating an Explorer

You can create an explorer in one of three ways:

- Directly from the home page
- From the data source
- From a chart in a report

Follow these steps to create an explorer from the home page:

1. Click on the **Create | Explorer** option at the top left.
2. Select an existing data source or create a new one:

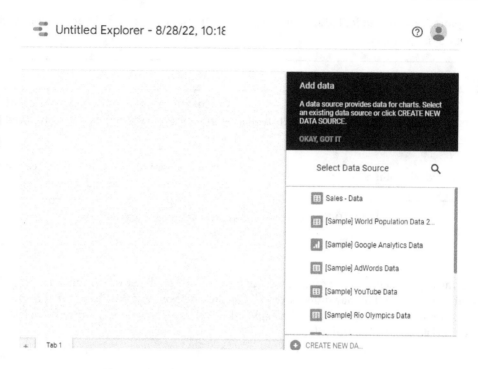

Figure 4.46 – Creating an explorer from the home page

You can only explore a reusable data source.

Follow these steps to create an explorer from a data source:

1. Open the data source in Edit mode (from the home page or the report's data sources screen).

2. Click **EXPLORE** at the top right:

Figure 4.47 – Creating an explorer from a data source

Follow these steps to create an explorer from a report:

1. Open the report

2. Right-click on a chart in the report and choose **Explore**.

3. The chart will open in Explorer with the appropriate fields and filter selections:

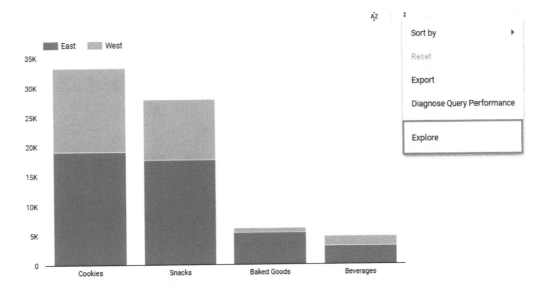

Figure 4.48 – Creating an explorer from a report

Two conditions need to be met for exploring a report:

- The data source used for the chart should be reusable

- You need view access to the data source

You do not need to have edit access to the report itself.

Exporting from Explorer

You can export from Explorer either to a new report or an existing report. Since you cannot share an exploration with others, exporting it to a report is the only way to do so. Hence, exporting options are available as sharing options in Explorer. First, you need to save the exploration before you can share or export. Sharing only affects the components on the current tab of the exploration:

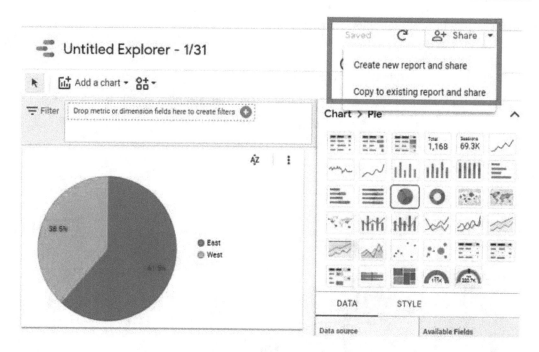

Figure 4.49 – Exporting from Explorer

Exporting a new report involves creating a new report connected to the data source used for exploration. On the other hand, exporting to an existing report involves the components on the current tab of the exploration being copied to the clipboard, which you can then paste into an existing report. The reusable data source that's used with the exploration is added to the report if it's not already present.

Using Explorer in an analyst workflow

An example workflow of an analyst starting from a data source may look like this:

1. Say that a business analyst needs to find answers to some key questions around business performance and gets access to a Looker Studio data source that represents the relevant data.

2. The analyst explores the data visually in Explorer and performs some analyses.

3. The analyst finds the answers they are looking for and leaves Explorer without saving. Alternatively, they may save the exploration to revisit it at a later time:

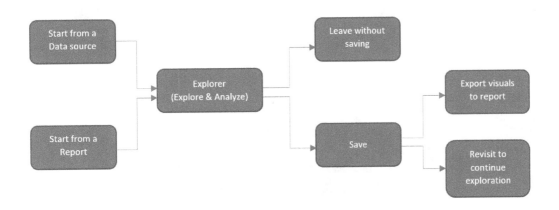

Figure 4.50 – Workflow of an analyst using Explorer

An example workflow of an analyst exploring a chart from a report may look as follows:

1.   An analyst is perusing a report and would like to explore a particular visual further by modifying or expanding it to find new insights.

2.   The analyst explores the visual in Explorer and draws new insights.

3.   The analyst saves the exploration and exports the visuals to a new report for sharing.

Leveraging Looker Studio Gallery

Looker Studio provides a gallery of reports showcasing various report templates and custom visualizations. These are created and published by the community using the developer tools that Google has provided for Looker Studio. You can access Report Gallery at `https://lookerstudio.google.com/gallery`.

Report Gallery is also a place where Looker Studio users can share their work with the larger community:

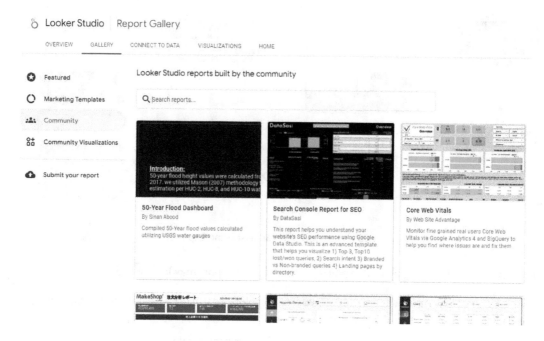

Figure 4.51 – Report Gallery with templates, reports, and community visualizations

Any report templates submitted by the community can also be found in Report Gallery. All submissions will be vetted by Google and made available in the gallery upon approval.

Getting help with Looker Studio

Looker Studio has a vibrant and active help community (`https://support.google.com/looker-studio/community?hl=en`) that enables users to find help, have discussions, provide and receive tips, and more. Google employees and Looker Studio experts around the world provide answers and engage enthusiastically. You will also find product announcements in this forum.

The official product documentation (`https://support.google.com/datastudio/?hl=en`) is a great resource to get help on how to work with Looker Studio.

Building your first Looker Studio report – creating the data source

As you learn about Looker Studio and explore its various capabilities, you will build a simple report in Looker Studio in an incremental manner. You will do this in this chapter to *Chapter 6, Looker Studio Built-in Charts*. You will work with the call center dataset of a fictional company that provides meal subscription services to customers in the United States.

The objective of this report is to visualize customer call trends and patterns concerning key factors such as call topics, customer attributes, and so on and also to monitor performance metrics such as **Call Abandonment Rate** and **Average Speed of Answer**. The dataset contains 6 months of customer call details from January to June 2022.

As the first step, you must create a reusable data source. The dataset is a CSV file that can be accessed at `https://github.com/PacktPublishing/Data-Storytelling-with-Google-Data-Studio/blob/master/Call%20Center%20Data.csv`. Download the file to your local machine. Make sure that you save it in UTF-8 compatible CSV format. Use the File Upload connector to create the data source, as follows:

1. Click on **Create | Data source** from the home page.
2. Choose the **File Upload** connector from the **Add data to report** screen and choose the file to upload. Please note that if the file is not saved as a *CSV UTF-8* file, the upload may fail.
3. Once the file is uploaded, set the data source name as **Call Center** and click **CONNECT**.

Now, review the available fields and update the schema. The dataset includes call details such as call time, duration, and topic, as well as information about the customer making the call, such as location and customer tier. The following screenshot shows the enriched data source that facilitates visualizing this data:

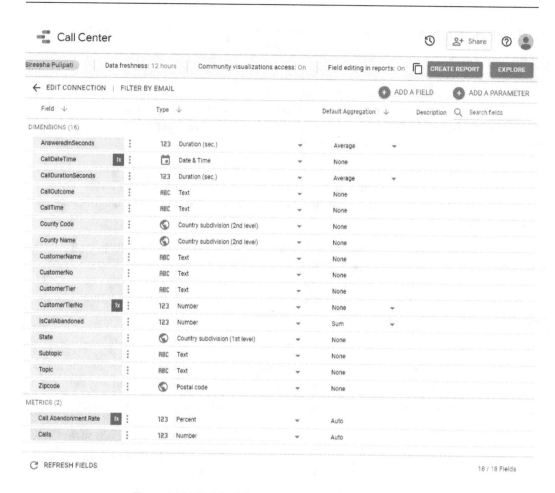

Figure 4.52 – Enriched data source of the call center dataset

Update the data source as follows:

1. Modify the following field data types:

    -   **AnsweredInSeconds: Numeric - Duration (sec.)**

    -   **CallDurationSeconds: Numeric - Duration (sec.)**

    -   **County Code: Geo - Country subdivision (2nd level)**

- **County Name: Geo - Country subdivision (2nd level)**

- **State: Geo - Country subdivision (1st level)**

- **Zipcode: Geo - Postal code**

2. Change the default method of aggregation for the two duration fields – **AnsweredInSeconds** and **CallDurationSeconds** – to **Average**.

3. Each row in this dataset represents an individual call received by the call center. Hence, rename the **Record Count** default metric field to **Calls** by clicking on the field name to make it editable and provide the desired name.

4. You will notice that the **CallTime** field, which represents the date and time the call was made, is interpreted as the **Text** type. Create the calculated field, **CallDateTime**, to parse these values as the **Date & Time** type. Use the following formula:

```
PARSE_DATETIME("%Y-%m-%d %H:%M:%S", CallTime)
```

5. The call abandonment rate is an important performance metric for a call center. A high call abandonment rate is undesirable and implies that callers get frustrated and hang up before their problem can be fixed over the call. It is calculated as the percentage of abandoned calls out of total calls. Create the calculated field – **Call Abandonment Rate** – as follows and set its data type as **Numeric → Percent**:

```
SUM(IsCallAbandoned) / Calls
```

6. The **CustomerTier** field represents the customer segment based on the lifetime value of the customer and includes four tiers – Bronze, Silver, Gold, and Platinum. To be able to sort these tiers in the increasing order of their value and importance, create a derived numerical field – **CustomerTierNo** – as follows:

```
CASE CustomerTier
  WHEN 'Bronze' THEN 1
 WHEN 'Silver' THEN 2
  WHEN 'Gold' THEN 3
  WHEN 'Platinum' THEN 4
END
```

In the next chapter, you will create a report and add this data source to it.

Summary

In this chapter, you learned how to access Looker Studio and understood its basic components. Looker Studio comprises four major entities – data sources, connectors, reports, and explorers. You use a connector to connect to the underlying dataset, be it Google Sheets, CSV files, Google Analytics, or anything else from the 500+ supported data platforms and systems. The connector creates a data source in Looker Studio, which is the logical representation of the underlying schema of the dataset. You can enrich the data source by modifying the data types, creating derived fields, and so on.

Reports are built using data from one or more data sources. You can explore data in a temporary environment called Explorer, which gets discarded at the end of your session by default. Explorers are private to you. You can choose to add your explorations to a report for sharing purposes. We reviewed how to create and work with data sources, reports, and explorers. We briefly touched upon the Looker Studio Report Gallery and ways to get help with using the tool.

In the next chapter, we will focus on the report designer and how to design and style various report components.

5

Looker Studio Report Designer

A report is the core element of Google Looker Studio and allows you to build data stories through visual components. It is a collection of visuals that enables you to monitor key performance metrics, describe trends and relationships, and explain relevant phenomena. In the previous chapter, you learned how to access Looker Studio and gained an understanding of its major entities – data sources, connectors, reports, and explorers. Now, you are ready to use it to build reports. Whether it is creating a view-at-a-glance dashboard depicting the overall performance of a business or a detailed report on a specific function or problem, the Looker Studio Report Designer provides a flexible, feature-rich, and easy-to-use interface.

This chapter lays out various components of the Report Designer and how you can use its key capabilities. By the end of this chapter, you will have gained an understanding of the major components of Looker Studio's Report Designer and learned about configuring elements such as dimensions, metrics, filters, non-data graphics, external content, and more. This chapter does not discuss these features concerning any specific chart type, but rather provides a general understanding of them. You will continue building your first Looker Studio report by creating a new report using the Call Center data source that we set up in the previous chapter. You will add data visualizations to this report in the next chapter, where you will learn about building and configuring various chart types. Similar to the previous chapter, this chapter is mainly about honing into the many useful features of Looker Studio. Interesting applications and related insights will be shared in the future chapters.

In this chapter, we are going to cover the following topics:

- Report designer overview
- Working with data for charts
- Implementing filters
- Adding design components

- Embedding external content
- Styling report components
- Building your first Looker Studio report – creating a report from the data source

Technical requirements

To follow the implementation steps for the various operations described in this chapter, you need to have a Google account so that you can create reports with Looker Studio. It is recommended that you use Chrome, Safari, or Firefox as your browser. Finally, make sure Looker Studio is supported in your country (`https://support.google.com/looker-studio/answer/7657679?hl=en#zippy=%2Clist-of-unsupported-countries`).

Report Designer overview

You can develop a dashboard or a report using Looker Studio's **Report Designer**. As an author and editor of a report, you spend almost all your time in the Report Designer. It allows you to add data to your report, build and configure charts, and add text, images, and other controls. Here, you can define filters, add pages, manage navigation, and choose color themes. The following screenshot highlights the major sections of the designer, all of which we will be reviewing in detail in the rest of this chapter:

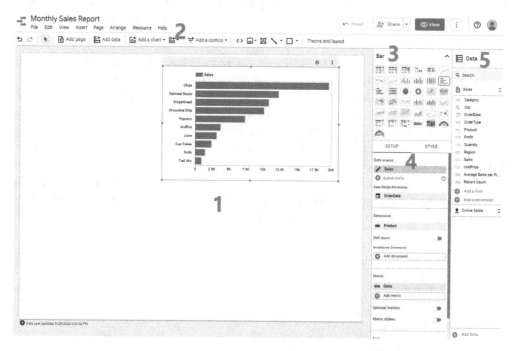

Figure 5.1 – Major sections of the Report Designer

Let's look at each of these components, which have been numbered, in detail:

1. **Canvas:** In the center is the canvas, which is where you place visuals and other elements.

2. **Toolbar and menu:** At the top is the toolbar, which provides shortcuts to some common operations and controls, as well as more comprehensive menu options.

3. **Chart picker:** You can easily switch between different chart types from the chart picker at the top right. This section only appears when a visual is selected on the canvas and it can be collapsed and expanded as needed.

4. **Chart configurations – SETUP and STYLE:** Below the chart picker are the **SETUP** and **STYLE** properties panels for the selected chart. The **SETUP** tab is where you choose the appropriate data source and add different fields – dimensions and metrics that make up the chart. You also define sorting, date ranges, filters, and more from here. The **STYLE** tab provides you with options and settings that determine how the chart looks – colors, axes, legends, gridlines, and so on.

5. **Data panel:** A report can include multiple data sources and the **Data** panel on the right displays all the data sources that have been added to the report. You can view the list of available fields for each of these data sources, which you can drag and drop either on the canvas directly or in the **SETUP** tab to configure charts. This panel allows you to search for fields across data sources, which makes it easy to discover and use the right data fields, especially when there are more than a few data sources. You can also make the experience more manageable by expanding and collapsing the data sources as needed.

Other sections and panels appear on the right when appropriate selections are made, such as page navigation, themes, page settings, report settings, and so on.

Adding charts to the canvas

When you create a new report, the first step is adding a data source to it. Next, you must add charts and other components to the canvas to start building your dashboard. You can add a chart to the canvas in one of three ways:

*   Dragging the fields from the **Data** panel to the canvas. This creates a table visual, which you can then change by selecting the appropriate chart type from the chart picker on the right.

*   Clicking **Add a chart** from the toolbar, selecting the required chart type, and placing it on the canvas. Then, you can add the appropriate dimension and metric fields to the **SETUP** tab for this chart.

*   Choosing **Insert | Chart type** from the menu and dropping it on the canvas. Then, you can choose the dimension and metric fields to be represented in the chart in the **SETUP** tab.

The canvas is a free-form area in which you can move different components around and arrange them as needed. The grid lines on the canvas allow you to align the visuals appropriately. The smart guides help you with this alignment. You can adjust the grid properties such as size, padding, offsets, and more from the options provided under the **View** menu. Using *Shift* and the appropriate arrow key allows you to move the components in smaller steps, giving you more control in adjusting the positioning. The **Arrange** menu's options assist you further in organizing content on the canvas by grouping visuals and associated components, aligning and distributing components properly, and more.

Adding additional data sources

Often, your dashboard may need to represent data from different datasets and you may need to add additional data sources to your report to complete your analysis or data story. There are multiple ways in which you can add data to an existing report:

- Select **Add data** either from the toolbar at the top or from the **Data** panel on the right to view the **Add data to report** screen and add either a new embedded data source or an existing reusable data source.

- You can add any reusable data source accessible to you directly from the **SETUP** panel. Click on the current data source's name to expand the dropdown of the list of data sources available to you. Choose the one you need and add it to the report. You can also add an embedded data source by clicking on the **ADD DATA** option at the bottom, as shown in the following screenshot:

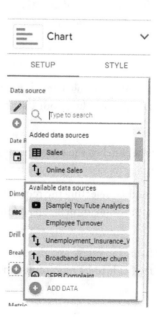

Figure 5.2 – Adding another data source from the SETUP tab

- You can also add new data from the report data sources screen by going to **Resource | Manage added data sources** from the menu.

In the next section, let's learn how to add and manage pages.

Adding and managing pages

A Looker Studio report can span multiple pages. This allows you to build detailed reports while organizing different sections on different pages. You can add a page to the report by selecting the **Add page** option from the toolbar. You can also add a new page from the **Page** menu. Having more than one page in a report changes the **Add page** icon to the page navigation control.

The **Report Pages** panel can be opened either by selecting the page navigation control on the toolbar or by choosing **Page | Manage pages** from the menu. The **Report Pages** panel is a one-stop place to create, rename, delete, copy, and hide pages, among other things. You can add expandable sections, dividers, and headers to organize the pages effectively. Sections help create tiered, multi-level groupings of pages. Icons can be added to the pages, as well as other top-level organization elements.

Looker Studio offers three ways to display report page navigation:

- On the left, listing the pages and top-level content holders vertically (as shown in the following screenshot)
- As tabs at the top that are laid out horizontally side by side
- At the top left, enabling you to navigate through the pages sequentially (next, previous)

The **Left** navigation type provides the most complete support for all content elements – that is, sections, headers, and dividers. You can collapse and expand the pane as needed. Adding icons to page elements is especially useful with the **Left** navigation type. When collapsed, icons are still displayed in the pane, enabling easier navigation. **Navigation type** is set from the **Theme and layout** panel's **LAYOUT** tab. The **Left** and **Tab** layouts are visible in **Edit** mode by default, in addition to **View** mode. You can turn off this setting from the **View** menu by unchecking **Show navigation in edit mode**:

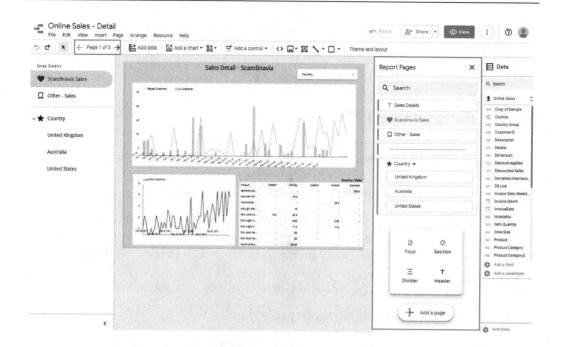

Figure 5.3 – Managing report pages

You can have different charts on a report page to visualize data from different data sources. However, you can set a default data source to use at the page level. This ensures that when there are multiple data sources attached to your report, any visuals you add to the page use the desired data source by default. This can be done by using the **Current Page Settings** panel that appears on the right by choosing **Page | Current page settings** from the menu:

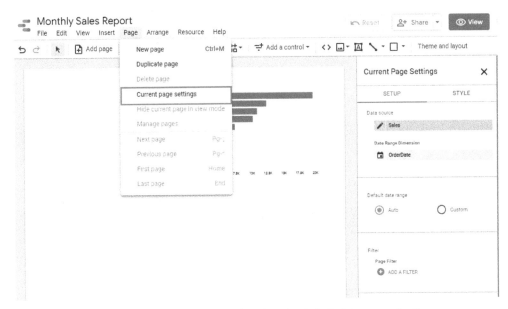

Figure 5.4 – Current page settings – choosing the default data source for the page

The **STYLE** tab under the **Current Page Settings** panel allows you to set background color and canvas size properties for this page. The ability to define these properties at the page level allows you to be consistent across the page, as well as to customize each page of the report differently. For example, you may want to display wide tables on a particular page and adjust the canvas size accordingly.

The **Page** menu provides additional options such as navigation, duplicating the current page, deleting the current page, and so on. You can also choose to hide the current page in **View** mode, either from the menu or via page options from the **Report Pages** panel.

Choosing a report theme and layout

You can customize the look and feel of the entire report using the **Theme and layout** options. A report theme configures default settings such as chart palette, background, font styling, and so on for the report and its components. Looker Studio provides a list of built-in themes for you to choose from. These built-in themes offer a good range of options – light versus dark background, monochromatic versus polychromatic color scheme, muted versus bright hues, and more. If none of them meet your needs or suit your taste exactly, you can customize a given theme and adjust the settings appropriately. Click on **Theme and layout** from the toolbar to make the panel appear on the right, as shown in the following screenshot:

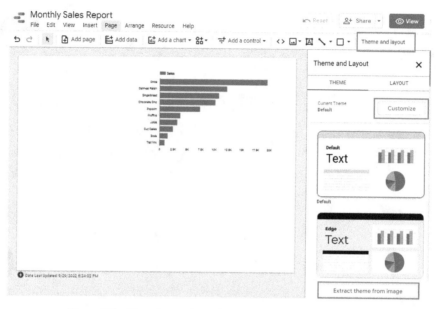

Figure 5.5 – Choosing and customizing a theme for the report

Looker Studio also allows you to generate a theme based on an image, such as a logo or any other relevant image. I've provided the image of the Packt logo (displayed on the left in the following screenshot), and Looker Studio has generated three themes that I can choose from based on the logo colors, as shown on the right of the following screenshot:

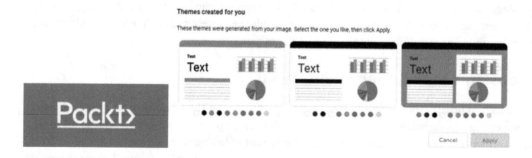

Figure 5.6 – Generating themes from an image

Several layout properties can be set for the entire report that determine how the report and its components look and are arranged by default. Some key layout settings you can define consistently across the report include the following:

- Canvas size
- Grid properties

- Page navigation position
- Header visibility for the charts

The report theme and layout determine the default settings for the report components, which can be changed and customized for individual components later.

Defining Report Settings

Similar to **Page Settings**, you can define certain properties at the report level. This makes it easy for you, as a report editor, to apply consistent settings throughout the report. You can access **Report Settings** by choosing **File | Report Settings** from the menu. This displays the appropriate panel on the right, as shown in the following screenshot:

Figure 5.7 – Report Settings

First and foremost, you can set a default data source for the entire report, which you can override at any page or visual level as needed. You can also provide your **Google Analytics measurement ID** and **Google Maps API key** under the **Report Settings** area. The former helps you track the report usage using Google Analytics, while the latter enables you to use a greater number of Google Maps loads in the report than the free quota allowed by Google.

You can apply data filters at the report level as well. An example scenario where this is useful can be where you are creating an employee absenteeism dashboard for a particular department, such as finance. Your data source includes data from other business units as well and you do not want to expose any non-finance employee data in the dashboard. You can define a report filter on the department field, which then applies to all charts within the report.

Date Range Dimension is another setting we can define at the report level to achieve consistency. This field determines the timeframe of the data that can be shown for a component. For example, if we always want the report to show only the current quarter orders, we can set **Date Range Dimension** to **Order Date** at the report level and choose the range as **This quarter**.

As report viewers view and interact with the report, Looker Studio preserves any filter changes and goes back to default values when it's reset. Viewers can save the links to specific filtered views as bookmarks when we enable this capability at the report level under the **Custom bookmark links** setting. Filter settings are then automatically added by Looker Studio to the report URL as encoded JSON strings. These links can then be shared with others or bookmarked for later reference. Report editors cannot generate such encodings within Looker Studio at the time of writing.

Current report view

Another way to obtain a report view link that reflects all current filter selections is by using the **Get report link** property via the report's **Share** options. This shortened URL can then be shared with others or bookmarked as needed.

Working with data for charts

This section will help you understand the major data configurations for charts and controls and how to use them. When a component is selected on the canvas, the **SETUP** and **STYLE** panels display the chart data and style formatting configurations, respectively. The **SETUP** tab allows you to choose the right data source and appropriate fields for the dimensions and metrics for the selected chart. The **Data** panel displays the list of fields that are available from the chosen data source. You can also set other properties such as sorting, filters, and so on. *Figure 5.8* shows the options for the table chart type.

Adding dimensions

A dimension is a field that represents the value for each row of the dataset. They are usually descriptive attributes of your data. You can drag and drop the fields from the **Data** panel onto the appropriate position under the **Dimension** section. Alternatively, you can click on the **Add dimension** button to select the field from the dropdown that appears, as shown in the following screenshot:

Figure 5.8 – Adding a dimension in the SETUP panel

You can change the data type and format of the dimension to be used for this specific chart by clicking on the left of the dimension name, which displays the default data type defined in the data source. You may want to change the data types for the chart fields in the **SETUP** tab in two situations:

- The default data types are not set properly at the data source level and you do not have access to edit the data source

- You need to present the data within the chart using a different format than the rest of the page or report

A common example of when you will want to do this is when you're changing the format of the date field to a less granular one such as **Year Month** or **Year Quarter**, where the timestamp is **Hour**. Depending on the default data type of the field, only those types and formats applicable are enabled for selection. For example, you cannot set the data type for a date field to **Boolean** or change the text data type to **Number**. The following screenshot shows the format options available for the **Order Month** field:

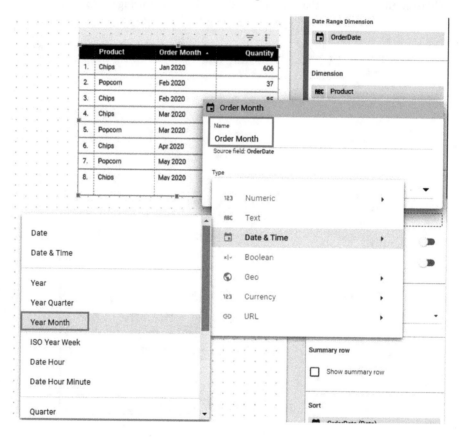

Figure 5.9 – Changing data type and format of a dimension

You can also provide a more user-friendly name to be displayed in the chart for a field. In the preceding example, the **Order Date** field is set to use the **Year Month** format and has been renamed **Order Month**. It is this name that is displayed in the chart – in table headers, legends, axes labels, and so on.

In addition to the available fields from the selected source, you can create a new custom field as a dimension within the **SETUP** panel. Just like in the data source, you can choose any of the existing fields and built-in functions to derive a new field. Examples could be concatenating or splitting two fields and extracting a substring. However, this field is only available within the context of the associated chart. Hence, it cannot be reused across multiple charts.

> **Note**
>
> As a best practice, refrain from creating calculated fields within the charts and the reports as much as possible and instead implement them in either the underlying dataset or in Looker Studio's data source. That way, you do not need to keep making the same transformations over and over again in different charts and reports.

Date Range Dimension

Looker Studio provides the option to choose a **date range dimension** at different levels – chart, page, and report. It defines the timeframe for the data depicted in the chart, page, and report, respectively. Looker Studio automatically chooses the first date column in the field list as the date range dimension. You can change this selection to a more appropriate date field as applicable. You can also manually choose a field if Looker Studio cannot identify a date field from the data source.

An exception to this behavior is for components built using a Google Analytics data source, in which case the date range dimension is automatically set based on the properties defined in Google Analytics and cannot be changed in Looker Studio:

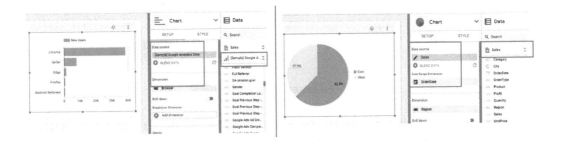

Figure 5.10 – The Date Range Dimension configuration option is not available for Google Analytics data sources (screenshot on the left). Chart configuration using a Google Sheets data source is displayed on the right for comparison

You can define the default date range for the chosen date range dimension. You can find this section a little further down in the **SETUP** tab. There is the **Auto** range option, which is different for different data sources based on the settings defined in the connector. For example, the auto date range for Google Analytics is **Last 28 days**, while for Google Sheets, it's all the data in the sheet. You can customize the default date range applicable to the chart by selecting **Custom** and choosing the appropriate range from the options available:

- **Fixed**: This allows you to define a fixed start date and end date for your chart
- **Pre-defined ranges**: For example, **Today, Last n days, This week, This month to date**, and more
- **Advanced**: This allows you to define flexible rolling date ranges

The following screenshot shows a custom date range setting that includes only the past 3 completed months:

Figure 5.11 – Advanced date range settings

Some chart types such as tables, scorecards, time series, and others in Looker Studio allow you to compare data for the current date range against a past date range. For example, if you have defined your default range as **Last 7 days**, you can choose to compare it against the 7 days before that. There are different options to define your comparison date range, similar to the default date range:

- **Fixed**: Define a specific period in the past with a fixed start date and end date
- **Previous period**: Matching timeframe before the default date range
- **Previous year**: Same timeframe as the previous year
- **Advanced**: Flexible rolling range

For the example depicted in the preceding screenshot, where the default date range is defined as the most recent 3 completed months – Noember 2021 to January 2022 – the comparison date range is set to the same 3 months exactly 1 year ago – from November 200 to January 2021 – when the **Previous year** option is selected.

Adding metrics

Similar to the dimensions, you can add metrics from the list of available fields. Metrics represent summarized values aggregated over multiple rows of data. Metrics can be predefined in the data source to facilitate consistent and easy use by different report editors. It is possible to add either a metric field or a dimension field from the list as a **metric** for the chart. When a dimension field is chosen as a chart metric, the values are aggregated. However, you can only choose a dimension field as a **dimension** for the chart.

Methods of aggregation

When a dimension field is selected as a metric, it is suitably aggregated for the dimensions defined for the chart. The method of aggregation typically defaults to **Sum** if the field is a numerical or Boolean field and **Count Distinct** for string and other fields. You define these default aggregation methods for the fields within the data source. You can choose a different method of aggregation for a chart in the **SETUP** panel. Click on the left of the field name that shows the aggregation type to view the options available. Looker Studio provides the following aggregation methods:

- **Sum**
- **Average**
- **Count**
- **Count Distinct**
- **Min**
- **Max**
- **Standard Deviation**
- **Variance**

These options vary based on the data type of the field. The following figure shows the methods of aggregation that are possible with numeric, date, and text fields (from left to right):

Figure 5.12 – Methods of aggregation for a metric

Similar to dimensions, you can provide an appropriate and user-friendly name for the metric to be displayed in the chart. The default is the actual field name from the data source. For example, when you are visualizing the first order date in a chart, change the aggregation for **Order Date** to **Min** and name it **First Order Date**, as shown in the following figure:

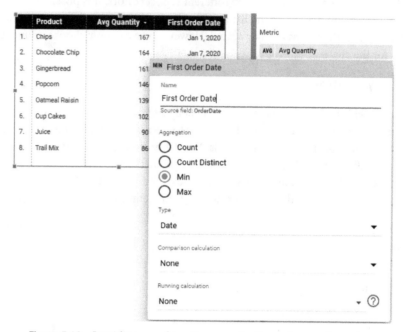

Figure 5.13 – Providing user-friendly names to dimensions and metrics

You can change the format of the value that's displayed in the chart under **Type**. For a numeric metric, it could be a plain number, a percentage, the time duration in seconds, or any of the currencies. For a date metric, you can choose to display it as any part of the date, such as quarter, month, day of the month, week, hour, minute, and so on.

You may find yourself in a situation where you want to display the actual values of a metric, rather than some aggregation. You can achieve this by adding the most granular dimension to the chart. For example, to display the sales amount of each order, add OrderID as dimension and Sales as metric. A metric is always aggregated even if it's against a single row. In the prior example, the Sales metric can be aggregated as Sum, Average, Median, Min, or Max because all these provide the same result as the unaggregated order sales amount. Keep in mind that the purpose of a dashboard is to summarize and display insights from your data, not to display it outright. Accordingly, metrics are usually aggregated to some degree over multiple rows.

Comparison metrics

Many analyses involve metrics that compare two different aggregations of a metric. An example could be the percent of total sales generated by each product, where the sales of each product are compared to the total sales. Looker Studio allows you to compare metric values in a chart to the corresponding total or max values. The options available include the following:

- Percent of total

- Difference from total

- Percent difference from total

- Percent of max

- Difference from max

- Percent difference from max

The following screenshot shows a table chart that displays different comparison metrics for product sales. You need to add multiple instances of the **Sales** field under the **Metrics** section and choose different comparison calculations for each to display all these metrics together in the table:

	Product	Sales ▾	% Total Sales	% Diff from Total Sales	% Max Sales	% Diff from Max Sales
1.	Chips	$19,608.45	27.18%	-72.82%	100%	0%
2.	Oatmeal Raisin	$12,277.32	17.02%	-82.98%	62.61%	-37.39%
3.	Gingerbread	$10,858.58	15.05%	-84.95%	55.38%	-44.62%
4.	Chocolate Chip	$10,150.36	14.07%	-85.93%	51.77%	-48.23%
5.	Popcorn	$7,347.23	10.18%	-89.82%	37.47%	-62.53%
6.	Muffins	$3,764.41	5.22%	-94.78%	19.2%	-80.8%
7.	Juice	$3,209.3	4.45%	-95.55%	16.37%	-83.63%
8.	Cup Cakes	$2,445.82	3.39%	-96.61%	12.47%	-87.53%
9.	Soda	$1,521.45	2.11%	-97.89%	7.76%	-92.24%
10.	Trail Mix	$966.07	1.34%	-98.66%	4.93%	-95.07%

Figure 5.14 – Table chart displaying comparison sales metrics

When you define a comparison date range for your chart, you can compare current period data with past period data. In such scenarios, you can choose the comparison metric (the total or max value you are comparing the actual metric value to) for the past data to be either the one that corresponds to the current data or the past data. The two options are available for each of the comparison calculations, as shown in the following screenshot:

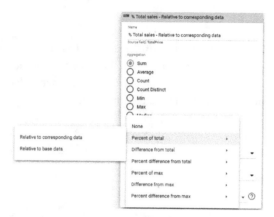

Figure 5.15 – Comparison metric options when using the comparison date range

This functionality can be better understood using an example. Consider a situation where, for a monthly time series chart, you have defined the year 2021 as the current date range and the previous year (that is, 2020) as the comparison date range. When you want to use a comparison metric such as the percent of total yearly sales, you can compare the 2020 monthly sales value to the total sales of either 2020 or 2021. Choosing the **Relative to corresponding data** option calculates the percent total sales for each month in 2020 against 2020's yearly total sales. On the other hand, selecting the **Relative to base data** option compares 2020's monthly sales against the total sales for the default date range, which is 2021. Remember that this choice only affects the comparison calculation for the comparison date range (for example, past data) and not the default date range (for example, the current data):

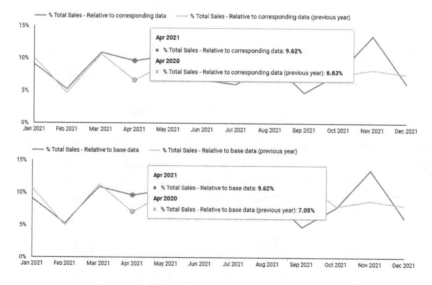

Figure 5.16 – % Total Sales for the comparison date range (2020)

The preceding screenshot shows two instances of the time series chart, each calculating the **% Total Sales** value for 2020 against different baselines.

Running calculations

Looker Studio allows you to compute and visualize running aggregations for a metric within a chart. For example, you can calculate running totals, running differences, running averages, and more. The available options are as follows:

- Running sum
- Running average
- Running min
- Running max
- Running delta
- Running count

By definition, these metric values vary based on how the data in the chart is sorted. These cumulative calculations have multiple applications. They are especially useful when you are interested in not only the final metric value but also the granular data leading toward it. This includes tracking progress toward meeting sales targets, calculating the number of users acquired, determining the bank account balance, and more.

Optional metrics

You can provide end users with the flexibility to choose one or more metrics to be displayed in a single chart by enabling optional metrics in the **SETUP** panel and selecting additional metrics. This helps in two ways:

- It declutters a chart that is displaying multiple metrics simultaneously by allowing the end users to choose only one or more metrics at a time
- It optimizes the real estate on the dashboard and reduces redundancy by having a single chart to present multiple metrics sliced by the same dimension, which the end users can interactively choose one or more from

The following bar chart enables report viewers to interactively choose which of the three metrics they would like to see in the chart at a time:

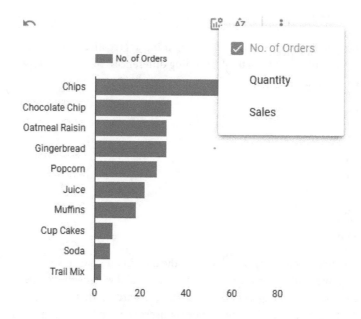

Figure 5.17 – Optional metrics enabled for the bar chart

Some chart types do not provide the ability to use optional metrics – that is, scatterplots and maps.

Sorting data in the charts

Often, you will want to sort the chart data in a specific way to make the visual most effective and easy to read. Say, for example, you created a table chart displaying a long list of salespeople, their targets, and actual sales, and you want to see salespeople with the highest actual sales value at the top of the table. Or maybe you have a bar chart depicting the quantity sold by product. It makes sense to order the products by the highest quantity sold. The sorting options in the **SETUP** tab enable you to set the order in which data in a chart is displayed. You can define how to sort the data visualized in the chart – column values in a table or dimension values on an axis – by any of the chart fields, a new derived field, comparison calculations, and running calculations, as well as other available fields in the data source. Looker Studio allows you to sort the chart data using up to two fields, as shown in the following screenshot:

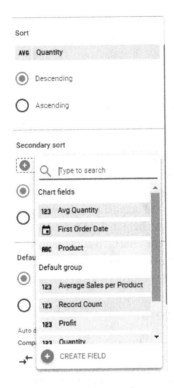

Figure 5.18 – Primary and secondary sort options

For certain chart types, such as bar charts, line charts, and pie charts, you can allow report viewers to change sorting interactively using the chart configuration. To do so, you can choose **Change sorting** from the **SETUP** tab.

Figure 5.19 – Change sorting from the chart header

This setting is usually enabled by default. Report users can change the sorting order as well as chart dimensions to sort by from the chart header options.

Implementing filters

Depending on your objective and the data story you are going to tell, you may want to represent only a subset or slice of data in your report. You can visualize just a subset of data from the data source by defining filters. As a report editor, you can define and apply filters to one or more charts, a page, or the entire report. These filters, referred to as editor filters, are not visible to the report viewers, so they cannot be manipulated by them. Editor filters are used to visualize certain subsets or slices of data in the chart to answer specific questions. For example, you want to display sales from only the new customers over time to compare against their cost of acquisition. Or, you want to look at the top products sold in the United Kingdom. Editor filters also help in tightly controlling the user interpretation of data by limiting the data they can view within the chart. To allow report viewers to slice and dice the data in the visuals interactively without them needing to edit the report, you add interactive filter controls to the report canvas. We will discuss these controls later in this section. First, let's review editor filters.

Understanding editor filters

Filters are reusable elements in a Looker Studio report. You can define a filter on any data source available to the report. You can create them from the **SETUP** properties panel for a chart, **Current Page Settings** for a page, or the **Report Settings** pane for the report. When a filter is created from any of these locations, the filter is automatically applied to the corresponding chart. By doing this, the filter can be reused for any other charts using the same data source. Let's say that you created a **Region** filter for a bar chart from the **SETUP** panel and filtered for **West Region**, as shown at the top of the following figure. This filter is then available for you in the **Filter picker** area to apply to any other charts, controls, or pages across the report. This can be seen at the bottom of the following figure:

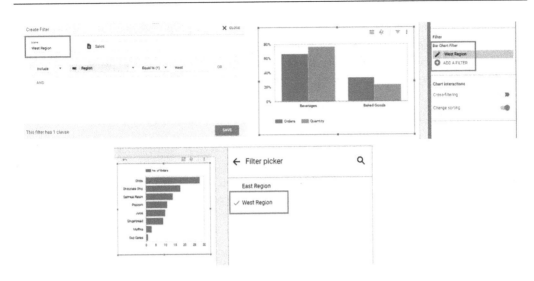

Figure 5.20 – Creating filters once and reusing them across the report

You can also create and manage a filter independently from the menu. Select **Manage filters** from the **Resource** menu to view the **Filters** page:

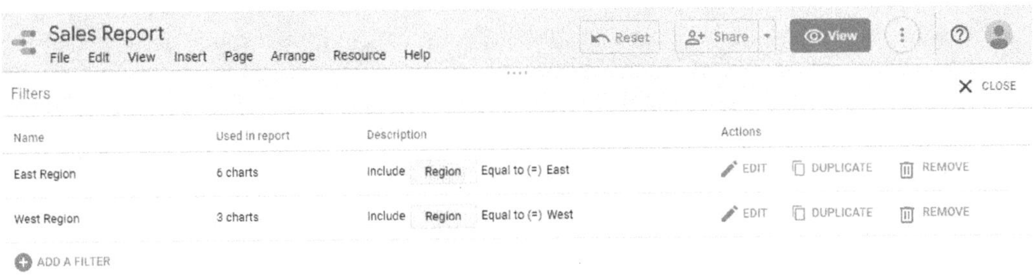

Name	Used in report	Description				Actions			
East Region	6 charts	Include	Region	Equal to (=) East		EDIT	DUPLICATE	REMOVE
West Region	3 charts	Include	Region	Equal to (=) West		EDIT	DUPLICATE	REMOVE

Figure 5.21 – The Filters page

From the **Filters** page, you can edit, duplicate, or remove existing filters. You can also edit the applied filters directly from the **SETUP** tab, page settings, or report settings. However, you cannot duplicate or delete filters from there. Removing filters from anywhere other than the **Manage filters** pane will only detach the filter from the corresponding element – that is, the chart, page, or report. The filter itself remains available for use within the report.

From the **Manage filters** page, you can create filters on any data source that was added to the report. Whereas, when creating the filter from report settings, page settings, or chart **SETUP** panel, the data source is automatically set to the one configured for the report, page, or chart, respectively. You cannot change the filter data source in these cases.

Adding an editor filter

To create a filter at the chart level, select the chart on the report canvas and select **ADD A FILTER** from the **SETUP** panel. If it's the first filter you are defining in the report, this directly opens the **Create Filter** pane at the bottom. Otherwise, the **Filter picker** area will appear with the available filters to use. Then, you can select **CREATE A FILTER** to create a new one. Optionally, you can specify a name for the filter. Providing appropriate names for filters enables you to easily reuse them across your report. The data source that's used by the chart is set as the filter data source. Then, you can specify the conditions:

- **Include or Exclude: Include** retrieves the data rows that match the filter condition, while the **Exclude** option retrieves all the rows that don't match the criteria specified.

- **Field from the data source**: This can be either a dimension or a metric.

- **Operator:** The options available differ based on the data type of the field selected. For string fields, you can choose from options such as **Contains**, **Starts with**, **RegExp Match**, **RegExp Contains**, **In**, and so on. For numeric and date fields, the options include comparison operators such as **Greater than**, **Less than**, **Between**, and more.

- **Value:** The value that is operated upon and being compared to.

The filters can be simple with just one condition clause. They can also be complex, allowing you to combine different conditions using OR and AND logic:

Figure 5.22 – Filtering with multiple condition clauses

In the preceding screenshot, the filter is defined with three clauses: one to retrieve orders from all cities except New York and New Jersey (identified by the **Starts with New** condition) and the other two to define small orders – conditions on sales amount and quantity, either of which qualifies as a small order.

You can also add a filter to a group of charts on a page. First, group the charts by selecting them and choosing the **Group** option from the **Arrange** menu, using the right-click context menu, or using the *Ctrl + G* keyboard shortcut. Select the group by clicking on any of the component charts; you will see the **Group Properties** pane on the right, as shown in the following screenshot. You can add a filter to the group from here:

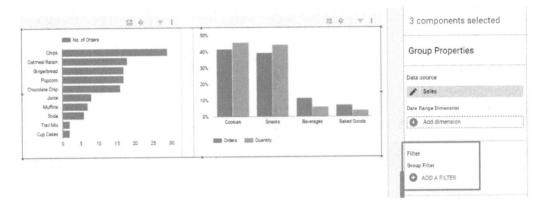

Figure 5.23 – Adding filters to a group of charts

Similarly, you can add a filter to a page from the **Page Settings** pane, which appears upon selecting **Page | Current page settings** from the menu. Select the appropriate data source from the **SETUP** tab and then select **ADD A FILTER**. You can either choose from the available filters in the **Field picker** area or create a new one. The filter data source for the new filter is set to the chosen data source for the page. Adding a filter at the report level also works the same way. You can get to the **Report settings** pane by choosing **File | Report settings** from the menu.

All these filters are part of the report design and are completely transparent to end users. Providing report viewers with the ability to filter the data presented in the report by one or more fields empowers them to look at different slices of data and generate insights. Interactive filter controls serve this purpose.

Interactive filter controls

Interactive filter controls are report components that you add to your report, along with the visuals on the canvas. Looker Studio offers the following controls to use as interactive filters:

- Drop-down list

- Fixed-size list

- Input box

- Advanced filter

- Slider

- Checkbox

- Date range control

All these controls enable you to create end user filters based on dimension fields from the data source. You can add a control to the canvas from the toolbar, as shown in the following screenshot:

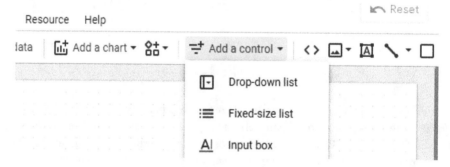

Figure 5.24 – Adding a control to the report canvas

Once you add a filter control of a specific type to the report, you can change it to another type from the control drawer at the top of the **Properties** panel. Choosing a different control type retains the relevant properties of the existing type. This makes it easier for you, as a report editor, to switch between various types while building the report without having to build the control from scratch every time:

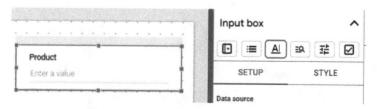

Figure 5.25 – Changing the control type easily from the control drawer

When you add a filter control to the canvas, it affects all the charts on the page that use the same data source as the control. They also filter charts based on different data sources that use the same fixed schema connector, such as Google Analytics, Google Ads, and others. This is because those datasets share the same internal identifiers for the fields.

It is possible to make a filter control applicable to the entire report across multiple pages. Select **Arrange | Make report-level** from the menu to make the control appear on every page of the report automatically in the same position on the canvas. This allows the user to interact with the filter from any page and affects the entire report. You can revert this by choosing **Arrange | Make page-level** from the menu:

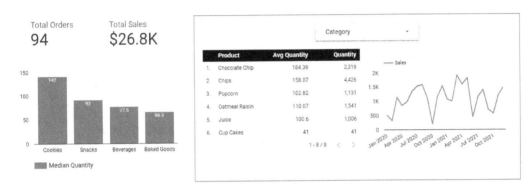

Figure 5.26 – Applying a filter control to a subset of charts on the page

You can limit the scope of the control by grouping one or more charts along with the control. This allows the user to filter only a subset of components on the report page using the control. It is good practice to highlight this group visibly in some way – enclosed by a shape, common background color, proximity, and so on – so that report viewers can easily understand that they are related. Otherwise, it leaves the users confused as to what data is impacted based on their filter selections. The preceding screenshot shows an example report page where the **Category** filter is only applied to the table and line charts on the right.

Drop-down list

The **Drop-down list** control enables the report viewer to choose one or more values of the chosen dimension field. The field can be of any data type – string, numeric, date, and so on. This control just lists all the distinct values of the field. As the report editor, you can provide default selection values to filter on. When you specify nothing, all the values are selected by default. First, choose the appropriate data source for the control and then pick the control field to use as the filter.

Optionally, the **Drop-down list** control allows you to display a metric for each of the dimension values. Just like adding a metric to a chart, you can choose existing metrics from the data source or generate one from the dimension fields by choosing the appropriate method of aggregation. You can also create a custom metric. The following screenshot shows a **Category** drop-down list control with **Cookies** and **Baked Goods** as the default selections and displays **Quantity** as the metric:

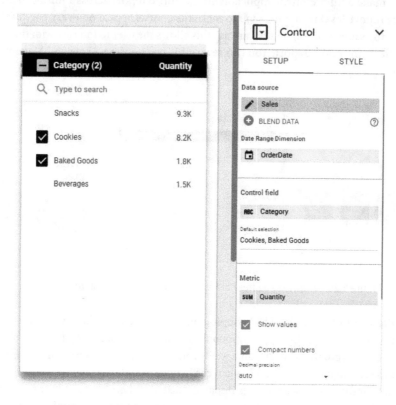

Figure 5.27 – Drop-down list control

You can sort the list values either by the chosen metric or by the dimension values themselves. You can hide the metric from the control by unchecking **Show values**. It is not necessary to show the metric values in the control to sort the dimension values by the metric. You can define the number of dimension values to make available in this control. The default is 5,000. However, you can choose from the options available. This can be as low as 1 up to 50,000 values:

Figure 5.28 – Important style options for the drop-down list control

By default, the control allows you to select multiple values. You can change this behavior and make it a single selection from the **STYLE** tab. You can also determine whether to include the search box in the control. While having the ability to search for the dimension values is helpful for longer lists, it might be a distraction if the dimension only has a few distinct values to choose from.

Fixed-size list

The **Fixed-size list** control has the same properties and behaves the same as the drop-down list control except that it displays all the values in a fixed-size box that you set as the report editor:

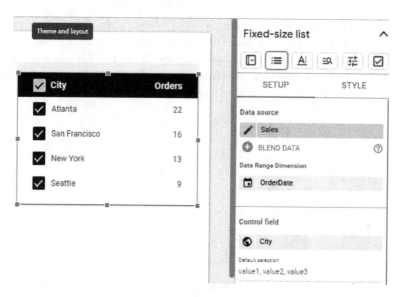

Figure 5.29 – Fixed-size list control

To configure the control, you must select the data source, specify the control field, provide any default selection values, add a metric, sort the values, and so on, as shown in the preceding screenshot.

Input box

The **Input box** control enables the user to type in specific dimension values to filter on for the associated charts. While this is not a user-friendly and commonly used filter control, it can be useful in scenarios where there are too many dimension values and the users know exactly what they are looking for. The **Input box** control matches the user input value against the chosen dimension and filters the chart data. By default, it checks for an exact match. However, you can make it easier for the users by determining how the matching happens. You can choose the appropriate search operator from the options available in the **STYLE** tab:

- **Equals** (default)
- **Contains**
- **Starts with**
- **RegExp**
- **In** (comma-separated values):

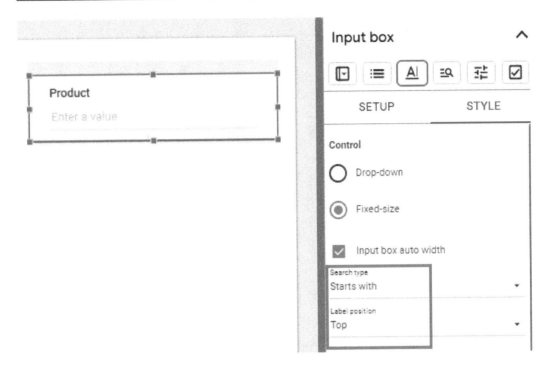

Figure 5.30 – Setting the search type for the Input box control

Note that searching in Looker Studio is case-sensitive by default, though it can vary based on the connector.

Advanced filter

The **Advanced filter** control is similar to the **Input box** control except that it allows the report viewers to interactively choose the search type to use. In the case of the **Input box** control, once the search type is set by the report editor, it cannot be changed by the report viewer. It may also not be evident to the end user as to how the matching happens with the **Input box** control without the editor leaving explicit instructions:

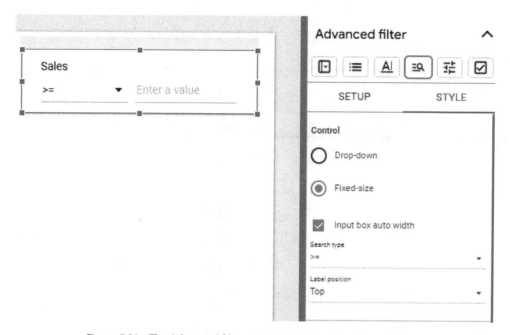

Figure 5.31 – The Advanced filter control with the default search type

The **Advanced filter** control takes this ambiguity away and empowers report viewers to choose the appropriate search type to suit their needs. You can set the default search type to be displayed in the control from the **STYLE** tab.

Slider

The **Slider** control allows the user to filter data by a numerical field. If you choose a field of any other data type, an error is displayed in the control. You cannot use a metric (which is an aggregation over multiple rows of the data source) field, such as average price, total gross margin percentage, and others, though. It has to be a dimension field. You can define the minimum and maximum values that the slider represents from the **STYLE** tab. By default, the full range of field values is included. However, you can choose a custom range for the end users to interact with. There are four slider modes to choose from:

- **Range**: The user can set both the minimum and maximum value of the field
- **Single value**: This lets the user select a single value of the field
- **Locked min**: The user can only adjust the max end of the slider range
- **Locked max**: The user can only adjust the lowest end of the slider range:

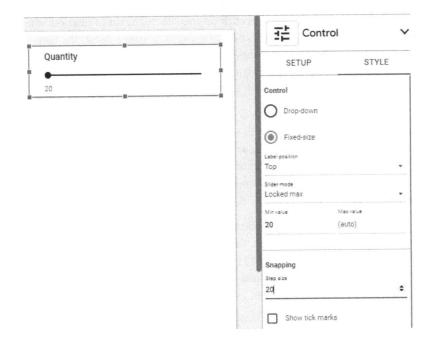

Figure 5.32 – The Slider control's style options

Another useful style property is **Step size**. You can define how much the values should increment as the user interacts with the slider. The preceding screenshot shows the various important style properties for the **Slider** control.

Checkbox

Checkbox is another data type-specific control. It can only be used with Boolean fields. This control allows you to filter the data in the charts for either true or false values, but not both. So, use this control carefully. This control just displays the name of the Boolean field and the user can click on the name to check it, which represents the true value, and filter the charts accordingly:

Figure 5.33 – The Checkbox control with a Boolean field when unselected (left) and selected (right)

This control acts as a toggle and the user can click on the control again to uncheck it and reverse the filter condition to match the false value. The preceding screenshot shows the two states of the **Checkbox** control. Selecting the checkbox causes the affecting charts to display only small orders, whereas unselecting the checkbox displays only non-small orders.

Date range control

The **Date range** control allows the end users to set the timeframe for the chart data without editing the report. It provides a calendar widget with several pre-built date ranges to choose from, such as last week, last year, this month, and so on. Report viewers can also define custom date ranges as per their needs. These are the same features and options that are available to report editors in the chart **SETUP** panel while configuring the report.

The **Date range** control requires you to just choose a default date range to apply. The specific date field in the data source that gets filtered is set for each component separately. The **Date Range Dimension** option can be set at any level – chart (in the **SETUP** tab), page (**Current Page Settings**), or the entire report (**Report settings**). For a chart, the first data field (alphabetically by field name) from the associated data source is automatically chosen as the date range dimension. You can change it to an appropriate date field as needed:

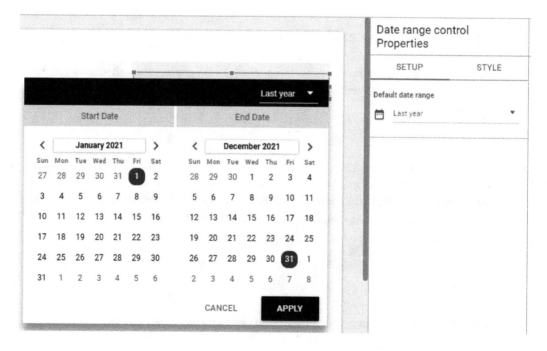

Figure 5.34 – Date range control options

The **Date range** control is the only one where you do not choose the control field in its properties. The generic nature of this control enables you to leverage just a single control to filter different date fields as applicable to various charts. Beware that if the **Date range dimension** property is not set for any chart, the **Date range control** will not filter the data in the chart even if the chart uses a date field as regular dimension.

Metric sliders

Metric sliders are another interactive filter option available for end users to determine what data is displayed in a visual. However, this filter only applies to metrics. This filter is built into the chart and you must enable it from the **SETUP** panel for the specific chart. Metric sliders allow the report viewer to filter the chart by metric value. By default, the full range of metric values is included. The end user can choose to view only a subset of data based on the aggregated metric value. If multiple metrics are depicted in a chart, sliders are provided for each, as shown in the following screenshot:

Figure 5.35 – Metric sliders to filter the chart by metric values

You can enable the **Metric sliders** option from the **SETUP** tab. At the time of writing, you can enable either the **Optional metrics** or **Metric sliders** option for a chart, but not both.

Cross-filtering

Cross-filtering allows you to use a chart to filter all the other charts in a group or on the report page. It provides an intuitive way of filtering and drilling through different dimensions by directly interacting with the charts. You can select one or more dimension values from any chart, including specific date ranges in time series charts to filter other charts accordingly. The following screenshot shows an example of Google Search Console data analysis, in which the time series chart and donut chart serve as filters for each other, as well as the remaining clustered bar chart.

It represents the application of cross-filtering to depict the distribution of **clicks and click through rate** for the top 10 countries based on search traffic originating from **Desktop** devices between April 10 and April 17:

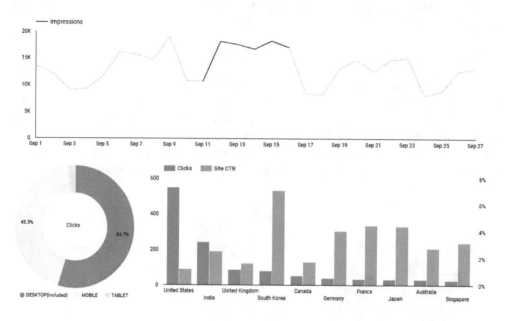

Figure 5.36 – Filtering charts interactively through cross-filtering

In many cases, cross-filtering eliminates the need to have explicit filter controls and helps save space in the dashboard. Filter controls are still useful for providing greater flexibility in selecting values, such as choosing built-in and custom date ranges, using sliders, and so on. Sometimes, explicit filter controls can also be a design choice based on end user preferences.

You can enable or disable cross-filtering for each chart in its configuration. Using cross-filtering may heavily slow down the report. So, limit cross-filtering by enabling it for only a few charts, if appropriate.

Adding design components

Besides the charts, which we will explore in the next chapter, and the interactive controls, there are other components that you can add to the report canvas that aid in designing the report. They are as follows:

- Images
- Text
- Lines
- Shapes

Static images, such as logos, can be displayed in the report as a separate component. Alternatively, you can use an image as a background for a chart or page by increasing the transparency of the image and overlaying the charts on top of the image, not that it's a good practice. You can either upload the image or provide a URL to add the image to the report.

The text component is useful to add anything from the report header to chart titles to annotations and more. It allows you to insert hyperlinks as well. You can link to relevant external content or a different page within the same report, thereby creating your own desired page navigation. Text is perhaps the most helpful design component while creating data stories with Looker Studio. Lines help connect various report elements or to separate them. This basic element is something you want to have in your design arsenal.

A common way to use the rectangular and circular shapes is to enclose data or report elements to visually group related components, as shown in *Figure 5.22*. Shapes can also be leveraged to highlight certain data points in the charts, as shown in *Figure 5.23*.

Embedding external content

Apart from the aforementioned design components, you can also embed external content into your Looker Studio report. You can embed any content that is accessible via a URL, so long as embedding is allowed on the content by its provider. Examples include YouTube videos, Google Drive documents (Docs, Sheets, Slides, Forms, and so on), Google Calendar, and other web content, including non-Google sites.

You can even embed a Looker Studio report within another report. Just enable embedding for the Looker Studio report that you want to embed from its **report settings**. Report users need to have access to the embedded content to be able to view and interact with it appropriately.

To embed external content in the report, select the **URL Embed** icon from the toolbar and provide the content URL in the properties pane. The embedded content is displayed within the embed component and the users can interact with it as if they are doing so in the content's native environment. This capability enables you to create a better user experience for your report by bringing together all the relevant pieces of information and content in one place. A useful scenario is where you can embed a Google Sheet with the glossary of terms relevant to the report on a separate page, as shown in the following screenshot:

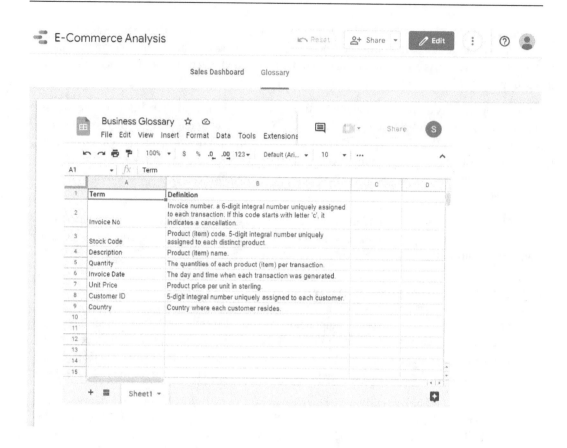

Figure 5.37 – Embedding Google Sheets in the Looker Studio report

This enables report users to look up metric definitions in the glossary and get the needed context to understand and interpret the report, all without leaving Looker Studio:

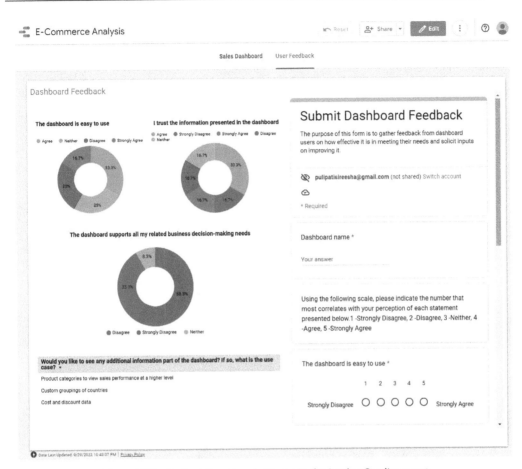

Figure 5.38 – Embedding Google Forms in the Looker Studio report

Another use case is where you can collect feedback from report users through an embedded Google Form. You can choose to visualize the aggregated responses in the same Looker Studio report, as shown in the preceding screenshot.

Styling report components

For any component you add to the report canvas, there are style properties that define how the component looks. Some properties are unique to a component type, while some others are common across different types of components. Some properties affect the structure or functionality of the component beyond just appearance. Examples include **Search type** for the **Input box** and **Advanced filter** controls, the number of bars in a bar chart, and so on. In this section, we will only focus on some general appearance-based style properties. Style properties that alter the functionality of a component are described in the respective sections throughout this book (for example, the *Charts* section in *Chapter 6, Looker Studio Built-in Charts*).

Background and Border

This is the one style property that applies to all report components – be it a shape, control, or chart. The only exception is the line element. You can set the following properties under this style:

- Background color

- Opacity/transparency

- Border line properties – color, weights, line type, and rounded corners

- Border shadow:

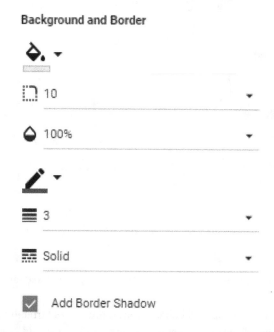

Figure 5.39 – Background and Border style properties

The preceding screenshot shows an example selection of these properties.

Text styles

Text appears in several forms in report components – data labels, axis labels, headers, and so on. Some components have more text elements than others. For example, a scorecard chart type only has a data label property, a drop-down box list control has header and data label properties, and a bar chart has text properties for axis labels and legend labels. General font-based properties you can configure include the following:

- Font color

- Font size

- Font type

The **Text box**, **Table**, and **Scorecard** components are purely text-based and provide additional properties to customize the appearance, such as text padding and text alignment, among others. Choose the appropriate values for these properties to elevate the report's look and feel. The following screenshot shows the label and padding properties for the scorecard chart:

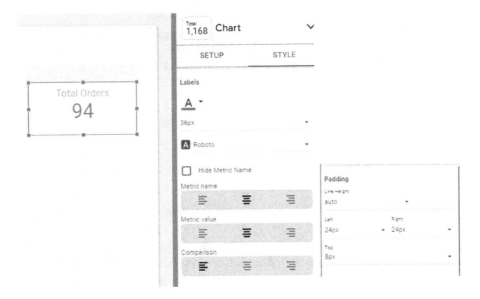

Figure 5.40 – Label style properties for a scorecard chart

Text and labeling are important elements of dashboards that should be focused on as much as the charts themselves.

Common chart style properties

For chart components, you can style common elements such as axes, grid lines, legends, and chart headers. These elements apply to most chart types.

Axes

First of all, you can choose to not display axes in your charts. This might be helpful when you would like to have a cleaner look and the axes lines do not contribute to the message intended. The following bar chart is an example. Here, text labels are used to indicate each category. The objective of this chart is to communicate the popularity ranking of different products based on quantity sold and the scale or metric values are not relevant. At the time of writing, it is not possible to hide only one axis in Looker Studio:

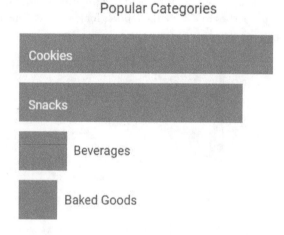

Figure 5.41 – Chart with axes hidden

When you display axes, you can choose to show or hide axis titles. You may not want to show axis titles if the dimensions and metrics represented are indicated via chart titles or other means. You can also reverse the direction of the axes – either the *x axis, y a*xis, or both – if it aligns better with the dashboard's and audience's needs:

Figure 5.42 – Axes properties for a bar chart

When the axis represents a metric, you can configure the minimum, maximum, and custom tick interval values for the axis. You can use a shorter axis range to display only a subset of data, exclude outliers, and more. You can also make the axis logarithmic. This is useful when you are representing a metric with a very large range of values on the axis. Be careful not to place a chart with a logarithmic scale, and a chart with a standard scale too close to each other without making the difference in scales clear. Their proximity will encourage comparison, and the user may not notice the different scales and may draw incorrect conclusions. The preceding screenshot shows the style properties available for its axes.

Grid

The grid properties allow you to configure several aspects of the chart:

- Axis font properties – color, size, and type
- Data label font size
- Gridlines color
- Chart area border and background

The following screenshot shows a scatterplot with custom grid configurations. Note that the color selection for the axis applies to the legend labels as well by default. However, you can set the legend label color separately under the **Legend** properties. You can remove gridlines from the chart by choosing **Transparent** from the color palette. At the time of writing, Looker Studio does not provide an option to customize horizontal and vertical gridlines separately:

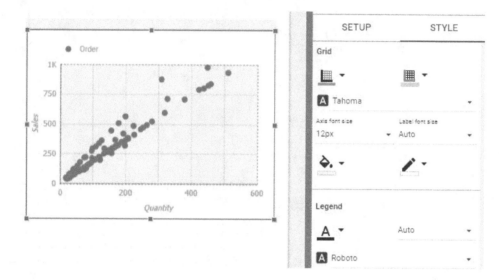

Figure 5.43 – Grid options allow you to configure axis labels, gridlines, and the chart area

Legend

Legend properties enable you to define the display position of the legend concerning the chart area – top, bottom, or to the right. You can also choose not to show the legend by selecting the **None** position. You can set the font properties for the legend labels – that is, color, size, and type. You can determine the proper alignment of the legend corresponding to its display position – left, right, or center when displayed on the top or bottom of the chart and top, middle, or bottom when displayed on the right.

When there are more than a few series that need to be represented in the legend and they do not all fit within the chart area, those labels are shown in multiple lines that can be accessed using navigational arrows:

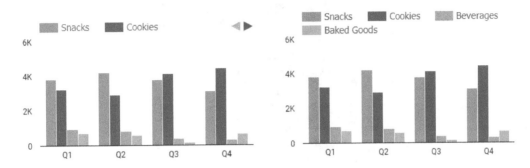

Figure 5.44 – Styling chart legends (Max Lines=1 on the left, Max Lines=2 on the right)

When you choose to display the legend at the top of the chart, you can define the maximum number of lines that a legend can use to show the labels instead of displaying them in a single line with navigational controls to scroll through all the values. The preceding screenshot depicts two instances of the same bar chart with different max lines settings for the legend.

Chart headers

Chart headers enable report viewers to interact with the chart and perform the following actions:

- Sort by different chart fields
- Export chart data to CSV or Google Sheets
- Drill up and down – available when drill down is enabled for the chart
- Explore the chart – opens the chart in Looker Studio Explorer
- Choose from optional metrics – available when optional metrics are enabled

In the following screenshot, the chart header is set to **Always show** to let users readily choose optional metrics from the header:

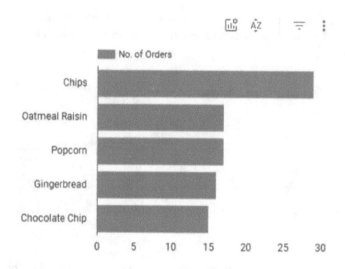

Figure 5.45 – The chart header can be set to "Always show" and displayed in any desired color

The default setting for the chart header is to show on hover. This is an ideal choice that provides full functionality and at the same time does not clutter the report page. However, you can choose to always show it, if needed. The other option available is not to show it at all. When you do not show the chart header, the end users can still access all actions except optional metrics and metric sliders from the contextual menu upon right-clicking. Optionally, you can customize the color of the chart header icons so that they match the chart and report colors.

Configuring style properties in report themes

You can set default style properties for various aspects of components across the whole report through report themes. You choose a theme from the list of built-in themes, create new ones by customizing existing themes, or generate a new theme based on an image. Report themes allow you to apply consistent styles across the entire report. Key style properties that can be set in a report theme include the following:

- **Background**: For the report pages and separately for the components
- **Text style**: The default font properties for all forms of text – text boxes, data labels, legend labels, and so on
- **Chart palette and other colors**: For series, dimension values, grids, chart headers, and more

The theme settings can be overridden for any individual component. These customizations stay put even when you switch to a different theme. You can always revert a component to the theme settings if you do not like your changes.

Building your first Looker Studio report – creating a report from the data source

In the previous chapter, *Chapter 4, Google Looker Studio Overview*, you created and set up the data source using the call center dataset available at `https://github.com/PacktPublishing/Data-Storytelling-with-Google-Data-Studio/blob/master/Call%20Center%20Data.csv`. In this section, you will create a report from that data source, configure some settings, and add a couple of components. Follow these steps:

1. Open the **Call Center** data source from the Looker Studio home page.

2. Click the **CREATE REPORT** button at the top to create a new report and confirm this to add this data to the report.

3. Rename the report **Call Center Analysis**

4. Open the **Report Settings** pane by selecting the appropriate option from the **File** menu. Set **Call Center** for **Data Source** and add **CallDateTime** for **Date Range Dimension**.

5. From the **File** menu, select the **Current page settings** option to open the pane on the right. Make sure that **Data source** is set to **Call Center**. Choose **CallDateTime** for **Date Range Dimension**. Keep **Default date range** set to **Auto**:

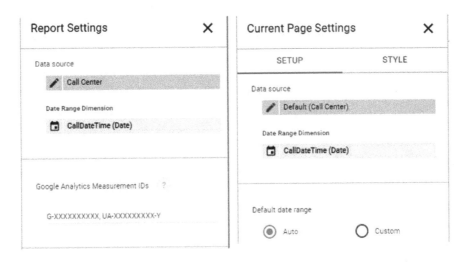

Figure 5.46 – Data source and Date Range Dimension configuration at the report and page level

6. Switch to the **STYLE** tab in the **Current Page Settings** pane and increase the canvas size to **1000px** or as needed.

7. From the toolbar, select **Theme and layout** and choose the **Groovy** built-in theme or anything else that you wish to use.

8. Delete the table chart that gets added to the canvas by default.

9. Add a text box to the canvas by selecting the respective icon from the toolbar. Place it at the top of the canvas and give the report a title – for example, **Call Center Analysis Dashboard**. With the component still selected, configure the text alignment, font size, and any other desired formatting from the **Text Properties** pane. Increase the font size to **40px** and center align the text:

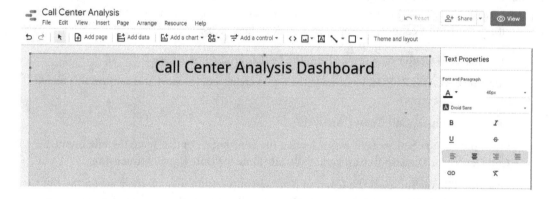

Figure 5.47 – Adding a title to the page using the Text control and configuring the properties

10. Add a date range control to the page by selecting the appropriate option from the **Add a control toolbar** dropdown. Place it in the top-right corner. From the **STYLE** tab for this control, make the background color **Transparent**:

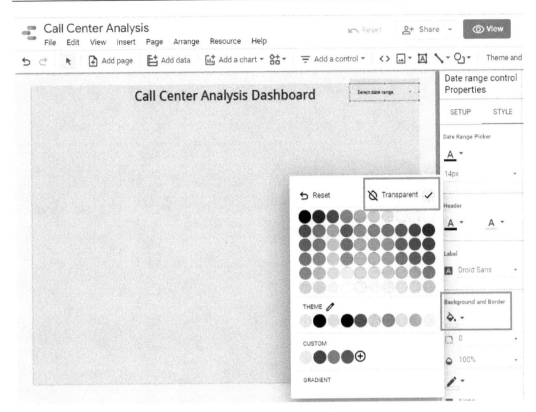

Figure 5.48 – Date range control style properties

You will add charts to this report in the next chapter.

Summary

As a report editor, you will spend most of your time working in the report designer, adding and configuring charts and controls. In this chapter, we explored various elements of the Report Designer. At the report level, you can add additional data sources, manage report pages, and choose report themes and other settings. We also looked at ways to add charts and additional data sources.

Designing a report component usually involves setting the appropriate data and style properties. You can define the data format, sorting, and aggregations for data fields that are represented in the component. You can add interactive filter controls to the report to enable report viewers to slice and dice the data without needing to edit the report configuration. There are some non-data components such as lines, shapes, and images that you can use to enhance the look and utility of your report.

In the next chapter, we will look into various chart types and how to configure them.

6
Looker Studio Built-In Charts

Data can be visualized using many different types of charts. Depending on the type of data to be represented and the insight to be gained, a specific chart type could be better suited than others. You looked at some common visualization types and their appropriate use in *Chapter 3, Visualizing Data Effectively*. Looker Studio offers a set of built-in chart types that you can use to create beautiful and meaningful dashboards. This chapter examines each of the built-in chart types using the call center dataset that we have worked with in the previous two chapters and explores how to configure them.

In this chapter, we are going to cover Looker Studio's built-in chart types grouped under different sections. In the end, we will add some of the relevant charts to the report we have been building since *Chapter 4, Google Looker Studio Overview*, to create a coherent dashboard. The primary objective is to understand each built-in chart and its configuration, irrespective of whether the final dashboard requires it or not.

In this chapter, we will cover the following topics:

- Charts in Looker Studio – an overview
- Configuring tables and pivot tables
- Configuring bar charts
- Configuring time series, line, and area charts
- Configuring scatter charts
- Configuring pie and donut charts
- Configuring geographical charts
- Configuring scorecards
- Configuring other chart types
- Building your first Looker Studio report – adding charts

Technical requirements

To follow the example chart implementations in this chapter, you need to have a Google account so that you can create reports with Looker Studio. It is recommended that you use Chrome, Safari, or Firefox as your browser. Finally, make sure Looker Studio is supported in your country (`https://support.google.com/looker-studio/answer/7657679?hl=en#zippy=%2Clist-of-unsupported-countries`).

You can access the Looker Studio report that includes all the built-in charts that will be explored in this chapter at `https://lookerstudio.google.com/reporting/6d1bddb7-9c1f-4869-bafe-499e4d05d411/preview`, which you can copy and make your own. The completed "first Looker Studio report" that presents a simple dashboard depicting key call center metrics and patterns can be found at `https://lookerstudio.google.com/reporting/b198dfb0-2b0b-43fc-9da4-19fc1e7362c5/preview`.

Charts in Looker Studio – an overview

Looker Studio offers different chart types to visualize data. Built-in charts are components that Looker Studio provides as part of the tool, which you can configure to visualize data. At the time of writing, there are 36 built-in chart types and variations available in Looker Studio under the categories of **Table**, **Scorecard**, **Time series**, **Bar**, **Pie**, **Google Maps**, **Geo chart**, **Line**, **Area**, **Scatter**, **Pivot table**, **Bullet**, **Treemap**, and **Gauge**.

Collectively, these chart types address most data visualization needs. If your use case requires a chart type beyond these built-in types, Looker Studio allows you to create custom visualizations using JavaScript libraries. Such custom chart types are called community visualizations. You can also use custom visualizations created by others and made available to all through Looker Studio's Report Gallery (`https://lookerstudio.google.com/gallery?category=visualization`). We will explore community visualizations in *Chapter 7, Looker Studio Features, Beyond the Basics*:

Figure 6.1 – The chart picker displays all the available built-in chart types

Report users may occasionally want to download data from an individual chart so that they can analyze this specific subset of data further on their own or create a snapshot of the chart data for future comparisons. From **View** mode, report users can export data from a chart to a CSV file or Google Sheets, so long as the report owner hasn't restricted the operation in the report sharing settings. The **Export** option is available from the chart header and the right-click menu (only for the built-in chart types). The exported data reflects all the filters and date range selections that are currently applied to the chart and only includes the fields available in the chart.

The data source that we will use in this chapter to explore all the built-in charts is based on the call center dataset available at `https://github.com/PacktPublishing/Data-Storytelling-with-Google-Data-Studio/blob/master/Call%20Center%20Data.csv`. Refer to *Chapter 4, Google Looker Studio Overview*, for instructions for setting up the data source. Alternatively, you can use the enriched data source made available to you at `https://lookerstudio.google.com/datasources/ebf4f00c-2cf3-41a4-95a4-97e698af9594`. To follow along, create a new report from the data source by following these steps:

1. Open the data source from the preceding link. If you are using your own data source, open it from the **Data sources** tab of the Looker Studio home page.

2. Click the **CREATE REPORT** button at the top right to create a new report. Confirm this to add the data source to this report.

The defined data source includes some modifications that are useful for creating the example charts in this chapter. You may perform further modifications such as providing consistent and business-friendly naming conventions, adding additional calculated fields, and so on to configure the charts more easily and to help with further analysis of data.

In the following sections, we will delve into each chart category. For each chart type, we will cover the most relevant and important configurations using the **Call Center** data source. For complete and the most up-to-date chart references, please refer to the official Looker Studio support page at `https://support.google.com/lookingstudio/topic/7059081?hl=en&ref_topic=9207420`.

Configuring tables and pivot tables

Tables are the most basic form of representing data. They provide flexibility to display any number of data fields together. A table chart is best suited when you want to show the most granular data, a large number of fields, or multiple metrics with very different units and scales aggregated for one or more dimension fields. Table and pivot table charts in Looker Studio allow you to display metrics in three ways:

*   Numbers
*   Bars
*   Heatmap

In this section, you will create a few tables and pivot tables using the **Call Center** data source and explore various configuration settings.

Table with numbers

The **Call Center** data source includes details of the calls made by customers from various states of the United States of America. Let's add a table chart to the report to display multiple metrics for each state, as shown in the following screenshot:

	State	Calls	Call Abandonment Rate ❶ ▾	Avg Call Duration ❷ ▾	% Diff from Max Avg Duration	Avg Speed of Answer	Most Recent Call Time
1.	Maine	7	28.6%	00:20:13	92.4%	00:00:26	Jun 2, 2022, 10:50:25 AM
2.	North Dakota	8	25.0%	00:21:52	99.93%	00:00:39	Jun 18, 2022, 1:27:19 PM
3.	Indiana	21	23.8%	00:16:51	77%	00:00:48	Jun 30, 2022, 1:01:28 PM
4.	Colorado	56	23.2%	00:16:34	75.72%	00:00:42	Jun 27, 2022, 4:13:31 PM
5.	Wyoming	9	22.2%	00:15:37	71.4%	00:00:41	Jun 28, 2022, 9:21:22 AM
6.	Michigan	88	20.5%	00:16:31	75.47%	00:00:40	Jun 28, 2022, 4:20:03 PM
7.	North Carolina	118	20.3%	00:17:50	81.53%	00:00:40	Jun 29, 2022, 1:26:06 PM
8.	Kansas	35	20.0%	00:16:46	76.62%	00:00:37	Jun 28, 2022, 3:51:51 PM
9.	Massachusetts	41	19.5%	00:17:13	78.64%	00:00:42	Jun 30, 2022, 1:58:39 PM
10.	Connecticut	39	17.9%	00:17:59	82.15%	00:00:39	Jun 29, 2022, 1:01:46 PM
	Grand total	3,859	15.0%	00:17:20	79.19%	00:00:39	Jun 30, 2022, 4:38:05 PM

1 - 10 / 50   < >

Figure 6.2 – Table chart to visualize detailed data or several metrics together

In the report designer, make sure the **Call Center** data source is selected from the **Data** panel. Click on **Add a chart** from the toolbar and select **Table** from the list. Configure the following properties in the **SETUP** tab for the chart:

- *Dimensions and Metrics*:

  - Add **State** under **Dimension**. You can drag and drop the field from the **Data** panel into the **SETUP** pane or directly onto the table. Remove the dimension that is shown by default by clicking the **X** icon when you hover over the field in the **SETUP** pane. You can also select the data source field by clicking on the **Add dimension** pill under the **Dimension** section and choosing the data source from the drop-down that displays the available fields from the data source. These methods apply to adding chart metrics as well.

  - Add the following as **Metrics**. The default method of aggregation that's selected for each metric is based on the corresponding setting in the data source. Remove the metric that's displayed by default in the table by clicking the X icon, if it's not one of the following:

    - **Calls**: This is the default **Record Count** metric renamed in the data source and represents the number of calls as each record in the dataset represents a unique call.

    - **Call Abandonment Rate**: This is a calculated field defined in the data source that computes the percentage of abandoned calls.

    - **CallDurationSeconds**: Click on the pencil icon for this field and set the display name to **Avg Call Duration**. From the same edit pane, change the **Aggregation** method to **Average**, if it's not already selected:

Figure 6.3 – Renaming a chart field from the edit pane. This can be accessed by clicking on the pencil icon on the left portion of the field in the SETUP tab

- Add **CallDurationSeconds** a second time by dragging and dropping the field from the **Data** panel or by selecting the field from the **Add metric** pill. Hover over the left of the added field and click the pencil icon that appears to open the edit pane. Then, set **Comparison calculation** to **Percent difference from max**. It doesn't matter which of the two relative options – **Relative to corresponding data** or **Relative to base data** – you choose for this example as it only displays the data that applies to the comparison date range configured for the chart and we haven't done so. You can find a detailed explanation of these options in *Chapter 5, Looker Studio Report Designer*. Set its name to **% Diff from Max Avg Duration**.

- **AnsweredInSeconds**: Click on the pencil icon for this field and set the display name to **Avg Speed of Answer**. From the same edit pane, change the **Aggregation** method to **Average**, if it's not already selected.

- **CallDateTime**: This is the calculated field and can be derived from the original **CallTime** field of the dataset by parsing it to the **Date & Time** type. Click the pencil icon to open the edit pane, set the **Aggregation** method to **Max**, and rename the display name `Most Recent Call Time`.

> **Note**
> The most recent call time for each state may not be very useful information to see. It is included in the current example with the sole purpose of showing that a table chart allows you to display metrics of different data types and aggregations.

- *Sorting*:

  Table charts allow you to sort the data by two fields. You can sort by **Call Abandonment Rate** in descending order to view the states with the highest proportion of calls where customers hang up before the customer service agents could resolve their issue at the top of the table. You can add a secondary sort field to break any ties in the primary sort field. For this example, choose **Avg Call Duration** as the secondary sort field. It is possible to sort the table by fields that are not displayed in the chart. This configuration defines the default sorting of data in the table. The report viewers can change the sort order by clicking on the column header. They can also sort the table on any column other than the configured primary and secondary sort columns. Resetting the report restores the default sorting configured by the report editor.

- *Filtering*:

  You can restrict the data that gets displayed in a chart by adding a filter under the **Filter** section in the **SETUP** tab. For example, to look at only the call metrics from Platinum customers, you can add a filter, like so:

  I.   In the **Filter** section, click **Add a Filter**.

  II. In the **Filter** pane, define an **Include** condition where **CustomerTier** is **Platinum** and name it `Platinum customers`, as shown in the following screenshot:

Figure 6.4 – Defining a filter to include only calls from Platinum customers

A summary row for the table will help us get a sense of the metrics for the overall data being visualized. Just check the box to show summary data. The summary value is computed using the method of aggregation chosen for the field in the chart.

Another key configuration that is important for table design is limiting the number of rows to display per page. By default, it is 100. A vertical scrollbar lets users read through all the rows on a single table page. The pagination controls at the bottom right allow users to browse through a large number of rows spanning multiple pages. For this example, set the row limit to 10.

Using the configurations from the **STYLE** tab, you can define the look and feel of the chart. The preceding table uses the following style configurations:

1. Select the **Wrap Text** option under **Table Header** and **Table Body**.

2. Update **Table Colors** as desired – for the header background (yellow) and odd row color (light gray). Displaying alternate rows with a different background color increases readability, especially when the table shows a lot of text.

3. For each of the columns in the table, you can choose a proper alignment. In the case of metrics, you can set appropriate decimal precision and visual presentation – be it a number, a bar, or a heatmap. This example displays all the metrics as only numbers. For **Column #2** and **Column #4**, which represent the **Call Abandonment Rate** and **% Diff from Max Avg Duration** metrics, respectively, set **Decimal precision** to **1**.

Adjust the width of the table and columns appropriately by resizing the chart on the canvas. You can use the **Resize columns** option from the right-click (or ellipses) menu of the chart. It provides two options:

*   Fit to data

*   Distribute evenly

You can enable horizontal scrolling in the **STYLE** properties to scroll through a large number of columns. In this example, all the fields fit well within the table width, so we do not need any horizontal scrolling.

Table with bars

Table charts in Looker Studio are versatile. In addition to displaying metrics as numbers, you can also visualize them as data bars and heatmaps. The following table chart shows two metrics – **Calls** and **Call Abandonment Rate** – for the top 10 states by call volume as bars:

	State	Calls ▾	Call Abandonment Rate
1.	Texas	3,037	14.6%
2.	New York	2,583	14.7%
3.	California	2,354	13.5%
4.	Florida	2,324	14.7%
5.	Pennsylvania	1,569	14.8%
6.	Illinois	1,355	13.7%
7.	Washington	1,314	14.3%
8.	Georgia	1,149	14.7%
9.	New Jersey	1,055	14.0%
10.	Ohio	1,054	16.2%

Figure 6.5 – Table with metrics shown as bars

The chart configurations for this chart are as follows:

- In the **SETUP** tab, do the following:

    I.   Select **Call Center** as the data source.

    II.   Choose **State** as the dimension field and **Calls** and **Call Abandonment Rate** as metrics.

    III.   Limit **Rows per Page** to 10.

    IV.   Sort using the **Calls** field in **Descending** order.

- In the **STYLE** tab, configure the following:

    V.   Unselect **Show pagination** under **Table Footer properties**

    VI.   For each metric column, select **Show number** to see the metric value beside the data bars

Out of these configurations, there are three options, when combined, that enable the table to display only the top 10 states by call volume. These are as follows:

- Sorting the table by the number of calls
- Limiting the number of rows per page to 10
- Disabling pagination

When you display the metrics as horizontal bars, you can also specify a target value to show a target line across the bars, as shown in the following screenshot:

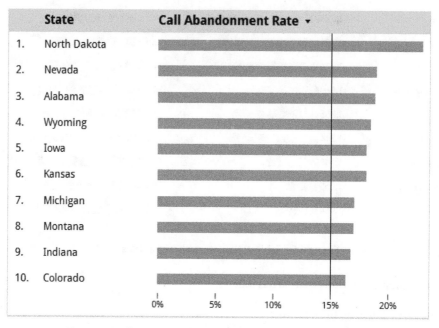

Figure 6.6 – Showing the target line for the data bars in a table

The preceding table also displays the axis to aid the interpretation of the metric values without explicitly showing each number beside the bar. You can find these configurations under the **Metric** settings in the **STYLE** tab.

Table with drill down

Drill down allows you to visualize different granularities of data in the same chart. It enables you to go from a more general view of data to a more specific view and vice versa with a single mouse-click. This provides an intuitive way to gain a more in-depth insight into data. By adding multiple dimensions to a table and enabling **Drill down** in the **SETUP** tab, you can look at data at different levels of detail – one level at a time. *Figure 6.7* depicts the call abandonment rate by each state and county. The report viewer can use the up and down arrows in the chart header to drill down to **County** and drill up to **State** as needed.

The configurations for this table chart are as follows:

- From the **SETUP** tab, configure the following:

  - Select **Call Center** as the data source.

  - Add **State** and **County Name** as dimension fields. Set the display name for the latter as **County** from the edit pane by clicking the pencil icon for the field.

  - Toggle the **Drill down** option.

  - Add **Call Abandonment Rate** as the metric:

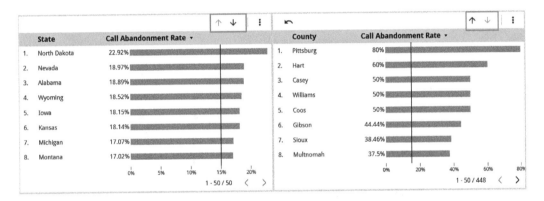

Figure 6.7 – Drill down and up dimensions

The **STYLE** configurations include the following:

- In the **Metrics** section, select **Bar** to display the metric as a bar.

- Select **Show number** and **Show target**. Set **Target value** to **0.15**. This displays the target line at 15%.

- Check **Show axis**:

Figure 6.8 – Key STYLE settings for the metric of the table

It is also possible to drill down only for a selected dimension value. For example, if you want to only look at the counties of **Alabama**, select the row and choose **Drill down** from the right-click context menu:

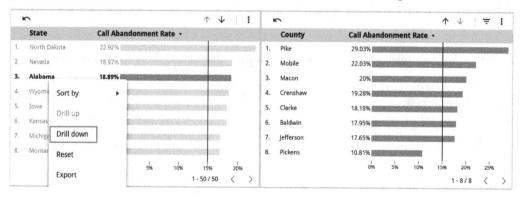

Figure 6.9 – Drill down dimension value

Drill down is a functionality that is available for several other chart types in addition to tables. Pivot tables have expand-collapse capability instead of drill-down, which we will cover in the next section.

Pivot tables

Pivot tables allow you to visualize data in a matrix or cross-tab form. You can summarize one or more metrics by dimension values along rows and columns. Just like regular tables, pivot tables allow you to present metrics as numbers, data bars, and heatmaps. Let's say that you would like to understand how high or low the call abandonment rate is at different times of the day on each weekday. A pivot table with a heatmap provides an effective way to present this information, as shown here:

Day of Week	8 AM	9 AM	10 AM	11 AM	12 PM	1 PM	2 PM	3 PM	4 PM	Grand total
Monday	14.5%	17.4%	15.4%	16.4%	14.2%	14.4%	16.4%	14.4%	16.5%	15.5%
Tuesday	16.1%	14.0%	16.5%	12.5%	17.2%	13.8%	15.8%	14.1%	17.6%	15.3%
Wednesday	14.0%	16.2%	15.4%	14.0%	12.9%	13.7%	14.2%	16.5%	16.2%	14.8%
Thursday	15.3%	13.4%	13.7%	14.2%	12.8%	15.4%	14.6%	11.8%	15.5%	14.1%
Friday	16.8%	14.8%	14.7%	16.9%	16.0%	15.5%	12.5%	12.2%	12.8%	14.7%
Saturday	13.7%	15.1%	14.3%	14.7%	14.2%	14.8%	14.7%	15.4%	11.6%	14.3%
Grand total	15.1%	15.2%	15.0%	14.8%	14.5%	14.6%	14.7%	14.1%	15.1%	14.8%

Hour / Call Abandonment Rate

Figure 6.10 – Pivot table with a heatmap

While there is no significant pattern that emerges out of this data, we can see that the call abandonment rate is generally higher at the end of the day on most days of the week.

In addition to the breakdown of the metric for each hour and day of the week, you can also see the aggregated value for each hour and each weekday, respectively, by turning on the **Show grand total** option for both **Rows** and **Columns**.

Create the preceding pivot table chart as follows:

- Click on **Add a chart** and select **Pivot table**. You can either select the basic **Pivot table** chart type first and configure it to show a heatmap or directly choose **Pivot table with heatmap** from the menu.

- From the **SETUP** tab, configure the following:

  - Make sure **Call Center** is selected as **Data source**.

  - Add **CallDateTime** under **Row dimension** and change the data type to **Date & Time | Day of Week**. Set the display name to **Day of Week** in the edit pane by clicking the pencil icon for the field.

  - Add **CallDateTime** as **Column dimension** and change the data type to **Date & Time | Hour**. Set the display name as **Hour** in the edit pane by clicking the pencil icon for the field.

  - Choose **Call Abandonment Rate** as a **Metric**. Make sure the aggregation is **AVG**. If not, open the edit pane by clicking the pencil icon that appears when you hover over the left-hand side of the added field and select **Average** under **Aggregation**.

- Check **Show grand total** for both **Rows** and **Columns**.

- Sort **Row #1** by **Day of Week | Ascending** and **Column #1** by **Hour | Ascending**.

- From the **STYLE** tab, make the following changes:

  - Select **Heatmap** for **Metric #1** and change the color as needed

  - Set **Decimal precision** to **1**

Switching rows and columns

After adding dimensions as rows and columns, if you would like to switch rows and columns, you need to manually move these dimensions to columns and rows, respectively. Looker Studio does not offer a "switch rows and columns" option that can automatically do this for you.

You can depict multiple metrics in a pivot table. It is also possible to add multiple dimensions to rows and columns to break down metrics in a hierarchical manner. The following example shows two metrics – **Call Abandonment Rate** and **Avg Speed of Answer**. These metrics are broken by call topics on columns and states on rows. States are further broken down by county:

		Billing		Cancellation		Dissatisfaction	
State	County	Call Abandonment Rate	Avg Speed of Answer	Call Abandonment Rate	Avg Speed of Answer	Call Abandonment Rate	Avg Speed of Answer
North Dakota	McLean	-	-	0.0%	63	-	-
	Sargent	50.0%	61	0.0%	87	-	-
	Cass	-	-	100.0%	62	-	-
	Williams	50.0%	50	0.0%	54	-	-
	Kidder	0.0%	93	25.0%	44	0.0%	29
	Sioux	66.7%	57	0.0%	37	50.0%	49
	Pembina	0.0%	67	-	-	0.0%	11
	Grant	0.0%	22	-	-	0.0%	23
	Dickey	-	-	-	-	-	-
	Total	38.5%	53	18.2%	50	14.3%	30
Nevada	Eureka	20.0%	51	22.2%	51	12.5%	42
	Clark	40.0%	36	33.3%	37	22.2%	58
	Washoe	23.3%	36	16.7%	42	41.2%	40
	White Pine	10.8%	35	15.4%	34	4.5%	36
Grand total		14.6%	39	15.3%	39	14.6%	39

Figure 6.11 – Pivot table with multiple metrics and dimension hierarchies

You can expand and collapse dimensions on rows by enabling the respective option and choosing the default expand level in the **SETUP** tab. This provides users with the flexibility to look at aggregated metric values at the top level of the row dimension hierarchy and drill down as needed to lower-level details or vice versa. This behavior is different from the drill-down functionality available with other chart types. With **Drill down**, it is possible to drill into a single dimension value separately in addition to all the values of the top-level dimension. In the case of the pivot table's expand-collapse capability, it is only possible to expand all the values of the higher-level dimension in the hierarchy and vice versa.

The chart configurations for the preceding pivot table chart are as follows:

- Click on **Add a chart** and select a **Pivot table**.

- From the **SETUP** tab, configure the following:

  - Choose **Call Center** as the data source.

  - Add **State** and **County Name** under the **Row** dimensions and update the display name for the latter as **County** by clicking the pencil icon on the corresponding field.

  - Toggle the **Expand-collapse** button and set **Default expand level** to **County**.

  - Add **Topic** as the **Column** dimension.

  - Choose **Call Abandonment Rate** and **AnsweredInSeconds** as **Metric** types. Click the pencil icon for the latter and set **Name** to **Avg Speed of Answer**. Also, change **Type** to **Numeric | Number** to display just the number of seconds.

  - Under **Totals**, select **Show subtotals**. This will show the row subtotals for **State** when expanded to the **County** dimension. Also, select **Show grand total** for **Rows**.

  - Sort **Row #1** by **Call Abandonment Rate | Descending**, **Row #2** by **Avg Speed of Answer | Descending**, and **Column #1** by **Topic | Ascending**.

- In the **STYLE** tab, do the following:

  - Select **Bar** for **Metric #1** and **Heatmap** for **Metric #2**. Set the colors as desired.

  - Select the **Show "-"** option for **Missing Data**.

Looker Studio provides a useful configuration for tables (as well as pivot tables, scorecards, and gauges) to display missing data in one of five different ways:

- 0

- -

- null

- (blank)

- No data

Make sure the chosen dimensions on the rows follow a hierarchy from the most general to the most specific. Otherwise, the metrics may show incorrect values in the cells when the hierarchy is expanded. There is no pagination in a pivot table chart. Horizontal and vertical scroll bars allow you to read through the entire table. A pivot table chart expects to have at least one **Row dimension** field since this is mandatory, while there can be no **Column dimension** fields at all.

In the next section, we will explore various forms of bar charts and their configurations.

Configuring bar charts

Bar charts are useful for representing one or a few metrics against one or two dimensions. Looker Studio offers different variations of bar charts, including horizontal bars, vertical bars, clustered bars, stacked bars, and 100% stacked bars. You can start with any specific variation and configure the chart appropriately to transform it into a different variation. In this section, you will learn how to configure various types of bar charts using the **Call Center** data source.

Columnar bar chart

In a columnar bar chart, the dimensional values are displayed along the X-axis and the metric values are displayed on the Y-axis. The following chart shows the call volume for different call topic categories. The topics are displayed in the decreasing order of corresponding call volumes:

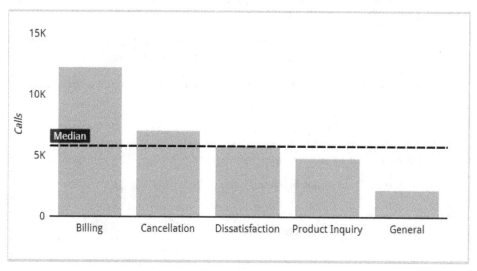

Figure 6.12 – Bar chart showing call topic categories in the decreasing order of call volumes

Showing the states as vertical bars is appropriate here because the topic names are short enough to be displayed clearly on the X-axis. By default, Looker Studio limits the number of bars to be displayed to 10. You can increase or decrease this number as per your needs from the **STYLE** tab. Here, there are only five call topic categories in the dataset and we want to display them all. So, we don't need to adjust this limit.

A reference line is added to the chart to indicate the overall median call volume. A reference line can be added using a constant value, a metric, or a parameter. You can provide any constant value to compare the bars against the reference line. You can also base a reference line on any metric used in the chart. You can choose the appropriate aggregation type for the metric selected. The aggregation can be one of the following types:

- Average
- Median
- Percentile
- Min
- Max
- Total

We will discuss parameters in the next chapter. It is possible to add multiple reference lines to a chart.

The chart configurations for the preceding bar chart are as follows:

- Click on **Add a chart** and select the columnar bar chart type.
- From the **SETUP** tab, configure the following:
  - Choose **Call Center** as the data source
  - Add **Topic** as a **Dimension**.
  - Toggle the **Drill down** option and make sure **Default expand level** is set to **Topic**.
  - Add **Subtopic** as another **Dimension**.
  - Add **Calls** as a **Metric**.
  - Sort by **Calls | Descending**. This displays the bars in the decreasing order of their height, as represented by the metric.
- In the **STYLE** tab, configure the following:
  - Choose an appropriate color for the bars.
  - Click **Add a reference line** and choose **Type** as a **Metric**. Select **Median** for **Calculation**. You can also format the properties of the line, including its weight, type (solid, dotted, dashed, and so on), and color.

In this chart, I've chosen to show the Y-axis title, hide the legend, and make the gridlines transparent.

The preceding chart doesn't display any data labels. Here, showing data labels can be optional as the Y-axis scale helps you interpret the values. Users can always view metric values in the tooltip by hovering over the chart. That said, displaying data labels on the chart can be useful when understanding the exact values is necessary without requiring additional action from users . However, excessive use of data labels can make charts and, thereby, dashboard look cluttered. So, enable them sparingly and with deliberation:

Horizontal bar chart

When the dimension values are too long or there are too many, a horizontal bar chart might be a better fit. The following chart shows the top 10 call reasons based on the number of calls received by the call center:

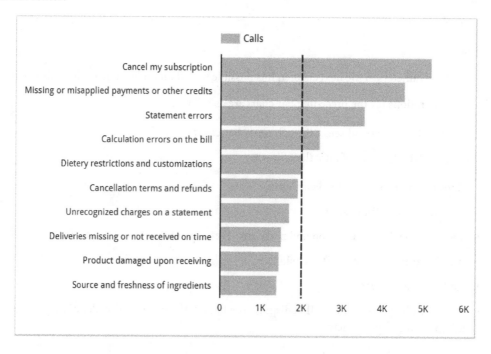

Figure 6.13 – Horizontal bar chart with long dimension values

You can adjust the width of the Y-axis to fit the labels. To do this, select the chart and hover over the Y-axis. The cursor will change to a slider, which you can move left or right as needed.

> **Tip**
>
> You can adjust any of the chart area boundaries – both axes and non-axes – on the canvas. Select the chart and align the cursor on the chart boundary to change the cursor to a slider. Then, move the slider up and down or left and right to get the desired fit and appearance. While the default positioning often works, this flexibility enables you to better fit longer axis labels and create additional space for legends, annotations, and more.

To build this chart, follow these steps:

1. Click **Add a chart** from the toolbar and select either the horizontal bar chart type directly or can select the columnar chart type and change the orientation in the **STYLE** tab.

2. Configure the following in the **SETUP** tab:

   - Add **Subtopic** as a **Dimension** and **Calls** as a **Metric**.

   - Make sure the sorting is by the added metric in descending order in the **Sort** section

3. Configure the following properties from the **STYLE** tab:

   - Choose an appropriate color under **Color by**.

   - Add a reference line of the **Constant value** type and provide **2000** as **Value**. Uncheck **Show label** to hide the reference line label.

   - Make the gridlines transparent.

By default, you can only show the bars in a single color, representing the metric being depicted. However, you can display individual bars in different colors based on a breakdown dimension. For example, the preceding bar chart can be modified to display the bars in different colors based on the higher-level topic that each subtopic falls under. Add the following configurations:

- The **SETUP** tab:

  - Add **Topic** as a breakdown dimension

- The **Style** tab:

  - Select **Stacked Bars** under **Bar chart**

  - Select **Dimension values** under **Color by**

  - Select **Show axis title** for **Bottom X-Axis**:

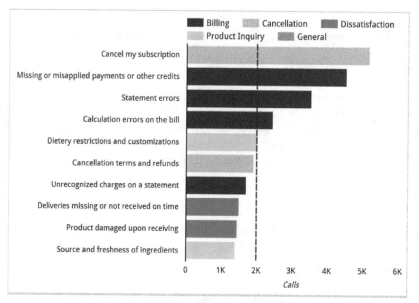

Figure 6.14 – Bar chart with multiple colors

When you use the primary dimension field as the breakdown dimension, then each bar will be colored based on the primary dimension, as shown in the following screenshot:

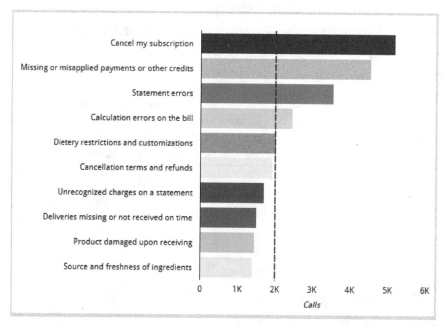

Figure 6.15 – Bar chart with the primary dimension values displayed in different colors

This is not that helpful because the call subtopics are already represented by the bars. Using different colors to represent the same will not provide any additional value. This manner of applying color to data adds noise to the chart and should be avoided.

Clustered bar chart

When a breakdown dimension is added to the chart's **SETUP** tab, you can create a clustered bar chart or a stacked bar chart. For the clustered bar chart, make sure the **Stacked bars** option is unchecked in the **STYLE** tab. You can select the regular vertical or horizontal bar chart type from the chart picker or the **Add a chart** list and configure it appropriately or directly add the clustered bar variation. In the case of a clustered bar chart, the values of the secondary dimension are represented as individual bars clustered for each of the primary dimension values.

The following screenshot shows a clustered bar chart that shows the number of calls made by customers from different tiers under each topic category:

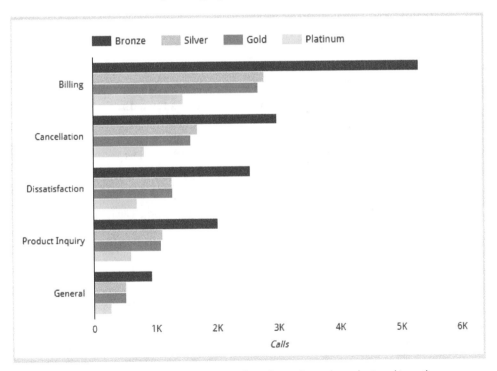

Figure 6.16 – Bar chart with the secondary dimension values clustered together

This chart displays the five topic categories as indicated by individual clusters. Customer tiers within each cluster represent different series. Similar to the number of bars, you can limit the number of series from the **STYLE** tab to show fewer bars within each cluster.

An important aspect of any chart is choosing the right colors. For any clustered or stacked bar chart, Looker Studio provides three ways to apply colors to the bars:

- **Single color**: Monochromatic shades of a single color.

- **Bar order**: Manually choose a color for each bar in the order they appear. If the bars are sorted differently, the chosen colors may represent different dimension values based on their position along the axis.

- **Dimension values**: Select colors for each dimension value. These colors apply to all charts using the same data source within a report and enable consistency.

In the preceding example, specific colors are assigned to different customer tiers, rather than the order in which they appear within the chart. This ensures that all charts where customer tiers are depicted use the same color for each tier.

The chart configurations for the preceding clustered bar chart are as follows:

- Click **Add a chart** and select the **Horizontal bar chart** type.

- From the **SETUP** tab, configure the following:

  - Select **Call Center** as the data source.

  - Add **Topic** as a **Dimension** and **CustomerTier** as a **Breakdown dimension**.

  - Add **Calls** as a **Metric**.

  - Sort by **Calls | Descending**. As a secondary sort, select **CustomerTierNo** in **Ascending** order.

- From the **STYLE** tab, do the following:

  - Choose the **Dimension values** option under the **Color by** section. Click **Manage dimension value colors** to set the appropriate colors for each of the customer tier values – Bronze, Silver, Gold, and Platinum.

  - Select **Show axis title** for **Bottom X-axis** and make the gridlines transparent.

The preceding chart includes all four customer tiers. To display only the call volumes for Gold and Platinum customers, use the following settings:

- In the **SETUP** tab, choose **CustomerTierNo** (numerical representation of customer tiers) as the **Secondary sort** field and select **Descending**. This will arrange the bars within each cluster from Platinum to Bronze.

- In the **STYLE** tab, set the **Series** option to **2**.

The resulting chart is as follows:

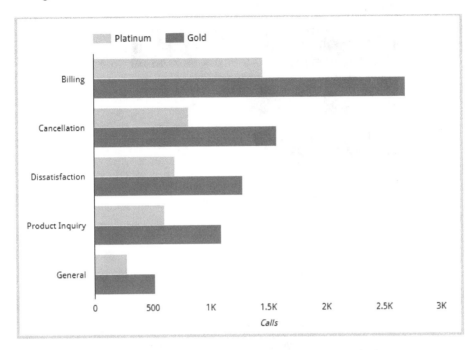

Figure 6.17 – Clustered bar chart with limited series in each cluster

Clustered bar charts provide an accurate representation of the metric value for each combination of the two dimensions – for example, the number of cancellation-related calls made by Platinum customers. However, they do not readily provide a sense of the total metric value for the dimension along the axis – for example, the total number of cancellation calls across all customer tiers.

Stacked bar chart

Instead of clusters of bars, you can display the breakdown dimension values as stacks. Stacked bar chart does not enable accurate comparison of stacks (different sections within the bar) across multiple bars as they have different starting points, all except the bottom-most one, in the case of column bar chart, and the left-most one, in the case of horizontal bar chart. However, they are helpful to understand general patterns and approximate values. The following chart presents the same data that's shown in *Figure 6.17*, but with customer tiers as stacks:

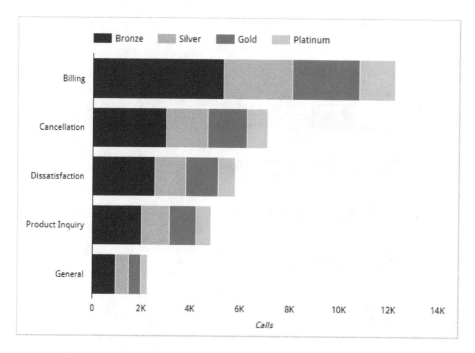

Figure 6.18 – Stacked bar chart showing the number of calls by different
topic categories made by customers from different tiers

You can choose colors by a single color, bar order, or dimension values. Using dimension-specific colors provides consistent use of color in a report. However, when there are too many dimension values across many fields being depicted, managing colors for different dimension values might become cumbersome. Also, you may want to minimize the number of distinct colors used in a report for a cleaner look and to achieve design simplicity. For these reasons, the other options are useful.

Unlike clustered bar charts, stacked bar charts provide information on the total metric value for each dimension value along the axis. From the preceding stacked bar chart, you can easily tell how many calls were made under each topic category. However, they only provide an approximate sense of the metric value for the breakdown dimension values.

100% stacked bar charts depict the percentage distribution of the breakdown dimension values for each of the dimension values along the axis. This is useful when you are interested in the distribution rather than the absolute values:

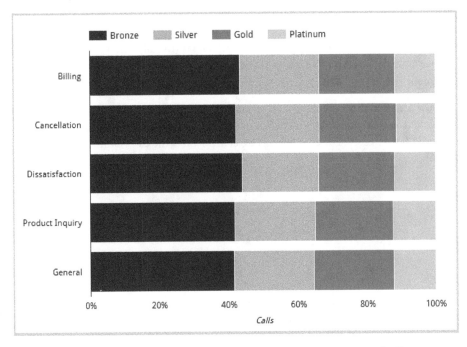

Figure 6.19 – 100% stacked bar chart depicting the distribution of calls
made by customers of different tiers for various call topics

For both a stacked bar chart and a 100% stacked bar chart, you can display the total metric value for the primary dimension in the tooltip. For example, the total number of cancellation-related calls is shown as 7,084 when you hover over the corresponding bar in the preceding chart. Enable this by selecting the **Show Total Card** option under the **Bar chart** properties in the **STYLE** tab.

In this next section, you will learn how to configure, time series charts, line charts, and area charts.

Configuring time series, line, and area charts

When you have ordinal data with continuous scales and want to accentuate the relationship of one value to the next, you can use a line chart, a time series chart, or an area chart. However, these three chart types are not always interchangeable. Each chart type has its particular utility and advantages. While a line chart can represent any dimension on the X-axis, a time series chart can only show a date or date and time dimension on its axis. In general, area charts support any dimension on the X-axis. However, in Looker Studio, they can only be plotted with a time-based dimension. Area charts and stacked area charts are usually used with a **Breakdown** dimension to represent different areas, whereas line and time series charts are effective even with a single line. In this section, we will look into each of these chart types and configure them using the **Call Center** data source.

Line chart

A line chart plots a line for a variable represented on the *Y*-axis (usually a metric) for the continuous values of the variable depicted on the *X*-axis. Line charts emphasize the trend and comparison of metric values along the ordinal axis.

While line charts are used most commonly with time on the *X*-axis, any dimension with an ordinal scale can be plotted as well – for example, the number of days since first purchase, version numbers of a software product, and so on. The following line chart depicts the call volume by the speed of the answer in seconds:

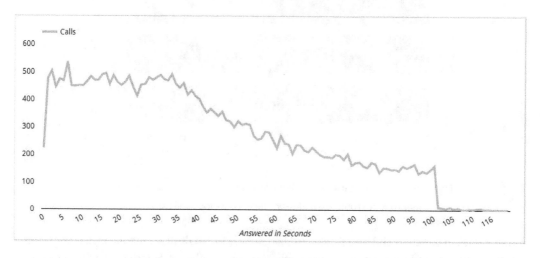

Figure 6.20 – Line chart with a numerical dimension on the X-axis

Note that the *X*-axis is just a number and not time. To achieve this representation, change the **Type** value of the **AnsweredInSeconds** dimension from **Duration (sec)** to **Number** in the **SETUP** tab, as shown in the following screenshot:

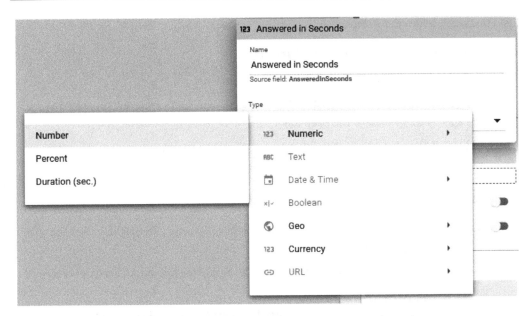

Figure 6.21 – Modifying the field type in the chart's configuration

The following screenshot shows another line chart that depicts the week when the calls were made and the number of abandoned calls on the *Y*-axis. It shows the line with smooth curves, which can be configured from the **STYLE** tab by selecting the **Smooth** property under the **General** section. Also, the data plotted in the chart is restricted to only the first 12 weeks of the year, which was done by limiting the number of points to display. By default, a line chart represents 500 points. You can decrease or increase this number to show the desired data range. In this example, **Number of Points** is set to **12**. This is similar to limiting the number of bars and series in the case bar charts. The resultant data that is displayed is primarily dependent on how the data is sorted within the chart. These configurations serve as an alternative to using chart filter conditions to restrict the data displayed in a chart:

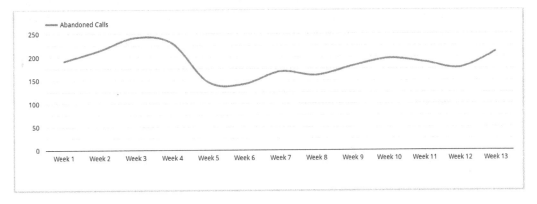

Figure 6.22 – Line chart with the date (ISO Week) on the X-axis

To build this chart, follow these steps:

1. Click **Add a chart** and select the **Line chart** type.

2. In the **SETUP** tab, configure the following:

    - Add **CallDateTime** as a **Dimension** and change the format to **Date & Time | ISO Week**. This aggregates the data at the week level.

    - Add **IsCallAbandoned** as a **Metric**.

    - Sort by **CallDateTime (ISO Week)** in **Ascending** order.

3. In the **STYLE** tab, configure the following:

    - Under the **Series #1** properties, choose an appropriate line color and weight. In this example, I've set the line weight to **4**.

    - Under the **General** properties, select **Smooth**. This makes the line smooth and curvy instead of straight-edged.

    - Limit **Number of points** to **12**. This causes the chart to show data only until **Week 12** of the year. Note that the dataset contains 6 months of data from January 1 to June 30, 2022.

    - Optionally, make the gridlines lighter by choosing a lighter shade of gray.

> **Tip**
>
> When using the **Line chart** type to visualize time series data, always configure the **Sort** property so that it uses the dimension on the X-axis in ascending order. The default sort order is usually by the metric used in the chart, which is not desirable while representing date/time or any other ordinal scale on the X-axis.

You can add multiple series (metrics) to a line chart and represent each series either as a line or bar. Let's say that you have two series and that you have configured one of them to be displayed as bars. This will result in a combo chart. You can determine if you want to use a second axis (**Right Y-axis**) and define which series is represented on which axis. The following screenshot shows a combination chart created with two metrics – **Calls** and **Call Abandonment Rate** – depicted by bars and lines, respectively. We can see that the call abandonment rate stayed roughly the same, despite the variance in the overall of calls received by the call center:

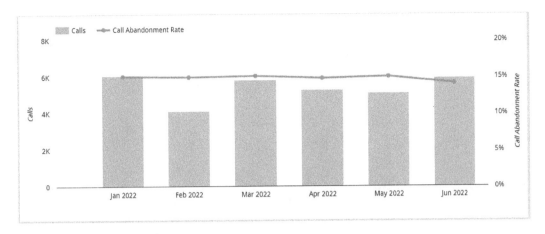

Figure 6.23 – Combination chart with lines and bars

The configurations for the preceding combination chart are as follows:

- Click **Add a chart** and select a regular line chart type. You can also choose the combination chart type directly from the list.

- In the **SETUP** tab, configure the following:

  - Select **Call Center** as the data source.

  - Add **CallDateTime** as a **Dimension** and change the format to **Date & Time | Year Month**. This aggregates the data at the month level.

  - Add **Calls** as a **Metric**.

  - Add **Call Abandonment Rate** as another **Metric** and make sure the aggregation is **Average**.

  - Sort by **Call Month (Year Month)** in **Ascending** order.

- In the **STYLE** tab, configure the following:

  - Under the **Series #1** properties, select **Bars** and choose an appropriate line color and weight.

  - Under the **Series #2** properties, choose an appropriate line color and weight. Set **Axis** to **Right** to let the **Call Abandonment Rate** series use the right axis. Select **Show Points**.

  - Show both the **Left Y-axis** and **Right Y-axis** titles.

  - Make the gridlines transparent.

You can add additional metrics to the chart and choose to display each as either a line or bars. The following chart depicts three metrics, where two of them are presented as clustered bars:

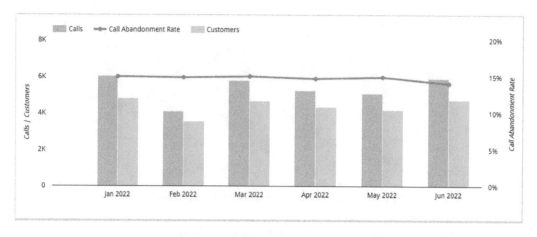

Figure 6.24 – Combination chart with a line and grouped bars

Add the **CustomerNo** field as an additional metric to the previous chart. Rename it **Customers** in the field's edit pane, which you can access by clicking the pencil icon. Configure the new series to use bars and choose an appropriate color. You can stack the bars by selecting **Stacked Bars** in the **General** section when it makes sense for the metrics being displayed – that is, when the total value of the two metrics represents something meaningful. For instance, if we have the number of inbound calls and outbound calls as separate metrics, stacking these values will provide the total number of calls. For this example, stacking the number of calls and number of customers is not meaningful.

You can use a breakdown dimension with a line chart to visualize the metric as a separate line for each of the dimension values, as shown in the following screenshot. This chart shows the number of weekly calls made by customers of different tiers.

When a breakdown dimension is used, you can only visualize one metric in the line chart:

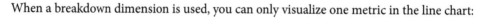
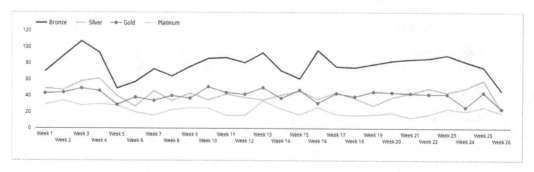

Figure 6.25 – Line chart using a breakdown dimension

If your breakdown dimension has a large number of values, you can limit the number of lines displayed by setting the **Number of Series** to the desired number. The default is 10. You can style each data series or line separately – choosing different colors and weights, enabling data labels and points, and so on. In this example, I've selected **Show Points** for **Series #3**, which represents the **Gold** customer tier. **ISO Week** starts on a Sunday, so add a chart filter to exclude January 1 as it represents partial **Week 52** from the year before.

Time series chart

Looker Studio offers a specific chart type, called **Timeseries**, that you can use with time series data. This chart type only accepts a date or datetime dimension on the X-axis. Even if you can use a line chart type to visualize a time series, the **Timeseries** chart type offers certain advantages over the line chart, as follows:

- The **Timeseries** chart provides a continuous timeline on the X-axis, even if certain dates and times are missing from the data. The **Line** chart, on the other hand, only displays the dates and times that are present in the data and does not fill in any gaps.

- **Timeseries** charts allow you to display trendlines, while **Line** charts do not.

- A **Timeseries** chart shows all the data for the entire date range selected in the **SETUP** tab, whereas a **Line** chart allows you to limit the number of data points to plot.

- In a **Timeseries** chart, the X-axis is sorted in the increasing order of time by default. In a **Line** chart, you need to explicitly sort the axis appropriately.

All the configurations and options available for line charts are also available for time series charts, except for **Number of Points**. Similar to line charts, you can create combination charts with multiple metrics, use breakdown dimensions to show a time series for each dimension value, and so on with time series charts.

A trendline that you add to your time series chart can be one of three types:

- **Linear**: Best suited to describe data with a continuous increase or decrease over time in a steady manner

- **Exponential**: Best suited to describe data that rises or falls over time at an increasing rate

- **Polynomial**: Best suited to describe large volumes of data with oscillating values that have more than one rise and fall

Choose the one that best fits your data. The following time series chart displays a polynomial trendline for **Call Abandonment Rate** that more accurately represents the slight increase between the end of March and the beginning of April and a significant dip toward the end of June. In contrast, a linear trendline will just show a line with a negative slope to depict the overall decrease in the metric value for the date range and does not represent the increase of value in between.

An exponential trendline is not applicable for this data as the rate of change is minimal and steady rather than exponential:

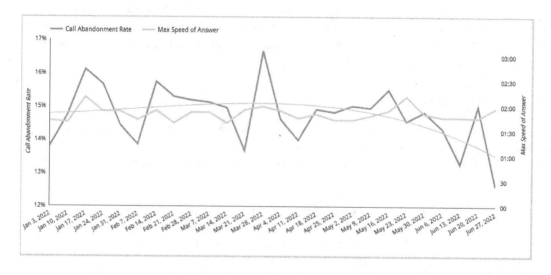

Figure 6.26 – A time series chart with a trendline and multiple series

The preceding chart depicts two series on dual axes with a trendline configured for one of the series. The configurations for this chart are as follows:

- Click **Add a chart** and select the **Timeseries** chart type.

- In the **SETUP** tab, configure the following:

  - Select **Call Center** as the data source.

  - Add **CallDateTime** as a **Dimension** and change the format to **Date & Time | ISO Year Week**. This aggregates the data at the week level.

  - Add the **Call Abandonment Rate** and **AnsweredInSeconds** fields as **Metric** types. For the latter metric, open the edit pane by clicking the pencil icon and set **Aggregation** to **Max** to plot the maximum taken to answer a call for a given week. Provide a display name of Max Speed of Answer.

  - Add a filter to exclude January 1 to remove the partial week.

Figure 6.27 – Chart filter to exclude calls made before January 2nd

- In the **STYLE** tab, configure the following:

  - Under the **Series #1** properties, choose the appropriate line color and width for the **Call Abandonment Rate** metric.

  - Set **Polynomial** to **Trendline** and adjust line color and width as desired. This example uses a line weight of **4** for the main series and **2** for the trendline.

  - Under the **Series #2** properties, choose the desired line color and weight. Set **Axis** to **Right**.

  - Show the axis titles for both Y-axes.

  - For the **Right Y-axis** option, set **Axis Max value** to **200**. At the time of writing, leaving the axis limits to **Auto** for a metric of the **Duration (sec)** data type does not show any axis labels other than **0**. As a workaround, setting the axis max value displayed, the axis ticks at 30-second intervals, which works for our data.

  - Make the gridlines transparent. Displaying gridlines with dual axes may create a mishmash of lines and add clutter.

A useful and important configuration for a time series chart is how to represent missing data. The time series chart displays a continuous scale for the entire date range without any breaks, whether or not there is data for all the intermediate periods. You can choose to represent missing data in one of three ways from the **General** properties in the **STYLE** tab:

- **Line to Zero**
- **Line Breaks**
- **Linear Interpolation**

The following figure shows three charts – the leftmost is a line chart, while the other two are time series charts. All the charts are depicting the number of abandoned calls for each month. I've introduced missing data by adding a chart filter to exclude data between Mar 1, 2022, and Apr 30, 2022:

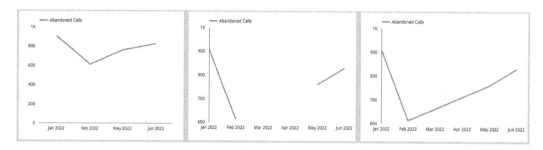

Figure 6.28 – Handling missing data for a time series

As you can see from the preceding charts, the axis on the line chart doesn't display the missing months at all and shows a continuous line. The time series chart in the middle is configured to show line breaks for missing data, while the rightmost time series chart uses linear interpolation for the missing quarters.

For all the three chart types – **Line**, **Timeseries**, and **Area** – you can show cumulative sum values of the metric along the *X*-axis by selecting the **Cumulative** option for the series from the **STYLE** tab. The following time series chart shows the cumulative number of abandoned calls throughout June:

> **Note**
>
> The **Cumulative** option, when enabled, only computes the running sum of the metric values and does not provide an option to choose a different method of aggregation. This configuration only makes sense for additive metrics and using it for any non-additive metrics such as ratios, percentages, and so on will only result in meaningless data.

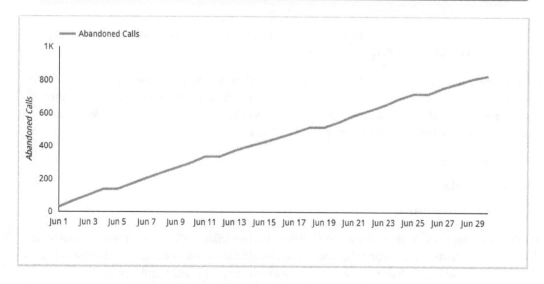

Figure 6.29 – Time series chart showing cumulative values

A time series chart without any axes displayed is called a sparkline chart. Typically, sparklines are tiny and compact. Their main purpose is to provide a general trend of the recent historical values for a metric and are almost always used along with other charts to provide historical context for a metric displayed on a scorecard, for example.

You can create a sparkline chart either by creating a regular time series chart and hiding the axes or by directly selecting the specific variation from the list:

Figure 6.30 – A sparkline chart with a scorecard

In the preceding screenshot, the sparkline chart, which displays the monthly trend of the **Call Abandonment Rate** metric, is placed on top of the scorecard depicting the year-to-date aggregation of the same metric. Use the **Arrange** menu or right-click context menu to order the components from front and back as needed.

You can choose to enable data labels on a sparkline, but this usually results in a very cluttered look due to the small size of the chart. At the time of writing, Looker Studio doesn't provide the option to display only certain data labels such as min, max, starting value, ending value, and so on. Even though a sparkline doesn't provide any contextual or value information at a glance, hovering over the data points will show the period and metric values in the tooltip.

Area chart

An area chart in Looker Studio is similar to a time series chart, but with a shaded area under the line. Similar to a time series chart, you can only use date or time on the X-axis. The following screenshot shows the number of weekly abandoned calls by customers in the Bronze, Silver, Gold, and Platinum tiers:

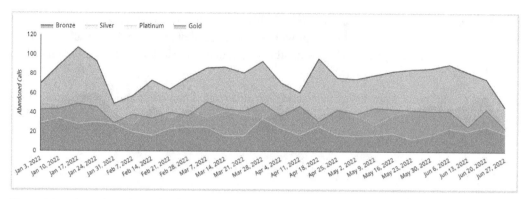

Figure 6.31 – Area chart depicting the number of abandoned calls over time for each of the customer tiers

In the case of multiple series, the entire area from the *X*-axis to each series line is shaded in different colors, resulting in overlapped colors. The shaded area in the area chart accentuates the difference in values between the series better than just lines. However, since different colors are overlaid on each other, it becomes difficult to interpret the chart correctly when there are more than a few series plotted.

The preceding area chart can be configured as follows:

- Click **Add a chart** and select the **Area** chart type.
- In the **SETUP** tab, configure the following:
  - Select **Call Center** as the data source.
  - Add **CallDateTime** as a **Dimension** and change the format to **Date & Time | ISO Year Week**. This aggregates the data at the month level.
  - Add **CustomerTier** as a **Breakdown dimension**.
  - Add **IsAbandonedCalls** as a **Metric** and rename it **Abandoned Calls**.
  - Sort **Breakdown dimension** based on **CustomerTierNo** in ascending order. The X-axis is automatically sorted for the date range, just like in a time series chart.
  - Add a filter to exclude January 1 (**CallDateTime < 01/02/2022 12:00:00 AM**).

- In the **STYLE** tab, configure the following:

  - By default, 10 series can be displayed. Since we have only four customer tiers, we don't need to adjust this number.

  - You can color the series based on either series order or by setting specific colors for the dimension values (customer tiers, in this case).

  - Set **Show axis title** to **Left Y-Axis**.

  - Make the gridlines transparent.

Similar to a time series chart, you can choose to represent missing data in one of three ways: **Line to Zero**, **Line Breaks**, and **Linear Interpolation**. With Looker Studio's area chart, you can only visualize one metric. You can add multiple metrics when the **Optional metrics** option is enabled. However, you can only choose one metric at a time.

> **Note**
>
> Area charts in general are based on line charts and can depict any dimension on the *X*-axis. In Looker Studio, the area chart is modeled like a time series chart, which means it has all the cool features of the time series chart when visualizing data over time. However, it lacks the flexibility that line charts provide for representing other forms of ordinal and continuous data. Area charts in Looker Studio also visualize only one metric at a time. Given the difficulty of interpreting area charts, these limitations can be perceived as good design choices by Google as Looker Studio doesn't allow users to create overly complex and thereby ineffective and misleading area charts.

You can convert a simple area chart into a stacked area chart by enabling the **Show stack** option from the **STYLE** tab. In a stacked area chart, the series are stacked on top of each other and the shaded areas do not overlap, as shown in the following screenshot:

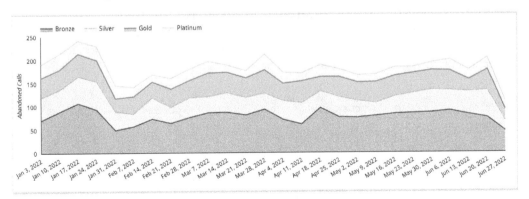

Figure 6.32 – Stacked area chart with absolute values of the metric

A 100% stacked area chart represents the percentage distribution of different series over time. Choose the **100% stacked area chart** type directly from the list or modify a simple area chart by turning on the **Show Stack** and **100% Stacking** options in the **STYLE** tab. As shown in the following screenshot, a 100% stacked area chart presents a different view from the preceding charts for the same data and tells you that the distribution of different customer tiers is pretty uniform across time:

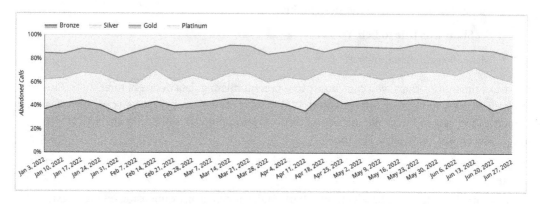

Figure 6.33 – 100% stacked area chart depicting the distribution
of abandoned calls across different customer tiers

Use stacked area charts with caution as the actual difference between two series is not based on the height of the lines but rather on the area between the two lines. It is more difficult for the human eye to perceive areas accurately compared to the length of the lines.

In the next section, we will look at scatter charts and how to configure them.

Configuring scatter charts

A scatter chart enables you to visualize a large number of data points and understand the relationship between two metrics on the X and Y axes. The points in a scatter plot represent the dimension values chosen. The coordinates of each point in the chart indicate the values of the two metrics on the axes. In this section, we will explore the key configurations of the scatter chart type using the **Call Center** data source.

The following scatter chart plots customer zip codes against **Avg Speed of Answer** and **Avg Call Duration**:

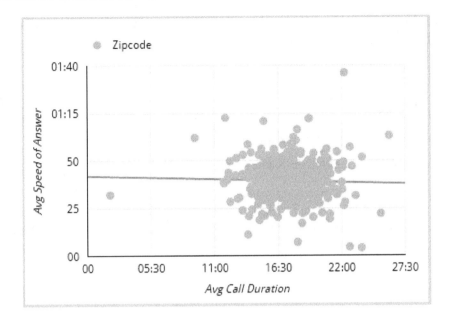

Figure 6.34 – Scatter chart with a trendline

You can add a trendline to the scatter chart to indicate the type and direction of the relationship between the two metrics on the axes. You can add a linear, exponential, or polynomial type of trendline based on your data.

By default, you can plot up to 1,000 points in a scatter chart. You can increase or decrease this number from the **STYLE** tab as per your needs. For example, you may want to decrease this number to only see the top *N* data points.

The preceding scatter chart can be configured as follows:

- Click **Add a chart** and select scatter chart type.
- Configure the following in the **SETUP** tab:

  - Select **Call Center** as the data source.
  - Add the **Zipcode** field as a **Dimension**.
  - Add **CallDurationSeconds** as **Metric X**, make sure the method of aggregation is **Average**, and set the display name to **Avg Call Duration**.

- Add **AnsweredInSeconds** as **Metric Y**, make sure the method of aggregation is **Average**, and set the display name to **Avg Speed of Answer**.

- Configure the following in the **STYLE** tab:

  - Select the desired color under **Color by**. Leave the **Bubble Color** setting to **None**. The **Bubble Color** setting allows you to color the bubble based on a dimension added to the chart.

  - Choose the **Linear** type for **Trendline** and select the appropriate line color.

  - Show the axis title for both the X and Y axes.

When an additional metric is depicted in a scatter chart by the size of the point, the chart is called a bubble chart. In the following screenshot, each point represents four dimensions – X and Y coordinates, the size of the bubble, and the color of the bubble. Looker Studio allows you to choose a dimension field to color the points or bubbles:

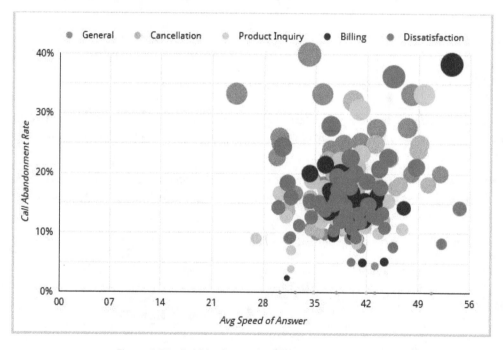

Figure 6.35 – Bubble chart colored by dimension values

Each bubble in the preceding chart represents a combination of the state that the calling customer belongs to and the call topic. The chart configurations are as follows:

- Configure the following in the **SETUP** tab:

  - Select **Call Center** as the data source.

  - Add **State** as the **Dimension** field. Also, add **Topic** as the second dimension. Like with other chart types, you can add multiple dimension fields to drill down and up from one level to another. In this example, we are not enabling the **Drill down** option. We are adding the second dimension to display the data at the granularity of **State** and **Topic**. We can use the **Topic** dimension to color the bubbles in the **STYLE** tab.

  - Add **AnsweredInSeconds** as **Metric X** and rename it **Avg Speed of Answer**. Make sure **Average** is selected as the method of aggregation.

  - Add **Call Abandonment Rate** as **Metric Y**.

  - Add **IsCallAbandoned** as **Bubble Size Metric** to represent the number of abandoned calls for each customer state and call topic. Set the display name to **Abandoned Calls**. It will show up in the tooltip.

- Configure the following in the **STYLE** tab:

  - Under the **Scatter Chart** properties, move the slider to adjust the scale of the bubble size and set the **Topic** dimension to **Bubble Color**.

  - You can set the colors of the bubbles for each value of the chosen dimension either based on the bubble order or by defining colors for specific dimension values.

  - Show the axis titles for both the X and Y axes and make the gridlines lighter.

> **Note**
> When a dimension is used to color the bubbles, Looker Studio does not provide the trendline option in the **STYLE** tab for the scatter chart.

In the next section, we will configure pie and donut charts.

Configuring pie and donut charts

Pie charts enable you to visualize data as parts of the whole. They are a good choice for depicting a few categories with largely varying proportions. In this section, we will learn how to configure pie charts and donut charts using the **Call Center** data source.

Looker Studio allows you to visualize up to 20 slices. However, depicting more than five slices usually wouldn't be very useful or effective. Consider the pie chart on the left in the following figure. It represents the proportion of calls by the top 10 call reasons. The pie chart on the right provides a much better representation with fewer slices:

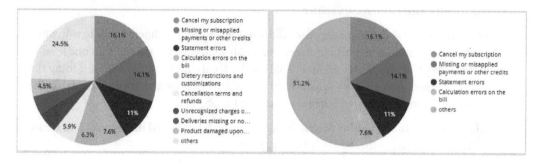

Figure 6.36 – A pie chart with too many slices (on the left) and a pie chart with an optimal number of slices (on the right)

The slices are automatically sorted by the decreasing order of the chart metric. If the number of dimension values is more than the number of slices configured, Looker Studio automatically groups the last values into the **others** category, as shown in the preceding figure. This chart can be configured as follows:

- Configure the following in the **SETUP** tab:

  - Select **Call Center** as the data source

  - Add **Subtopic** as a **Dimension** and **Calls** as a **Metric**

  - Make sure the **Sort** field is set to **Calls** and that the order is **Descending**

- Configure the following from the **STYLE** tab:

  - Under the **Pie Chart** properties, set the number of slices to **5**.

  - Color the slices based on a single color, slice order, or dimension value. In this example, I've used the **Slice order** option and selected the desired colors.

  - Adjust the legend position, if needed.

For a pie chart, **Percentage** data labels are displayed by default. Under the **Label** properties in the **STYLE** tab, you can choose one of the following options:

- **None**

- **Percentage**

- **Label** (dimension)
- **Value**

It's always advisable to display data labels, which are mostly percentage values on pie charts, since no scale can help us interpret the proportions. You can also format the font style for these labels as per your preference.

Text Contrast is a property that determines the color of the font for the labels based on the level of contrast required against the slice colors. In the preceding figure, you can see that the label is white for the brown-colored **Statement errors** slice, while the other labels are black.

Donut charts are just a variation of pie charts and have the same characteristics. Just move the donut slider from the **STYLE** tab to adjust the diameter of the donut hole. So, you can think of a donut chart as just a pie chart with a hole in its center:

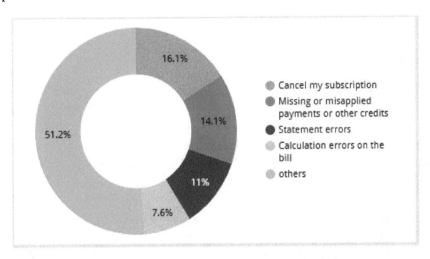

Figure 6.37 – A donut chart is a pie chart with a hole

Similar to other chart variations, you can create a donut chart directly by choosing the variation from the **Add a chart** list. You can also convert a pie chart into a donut chart and vice versa easily by selecting the appropriate chart type from the chart picker.

The next section delves into geographical charts and their configurations.

Configuring geographical charts

Geographical charts are used to visualize location data. In this section, we will learn how to use and configure the two types of charts that Looker Studio offers to represent geographical data – **Geo** and **Google Maps**.

The geographic dimensions allowed by Looker Studio include the following:

- **Continent** (for example, Europe).

- **Subcontinent** (for example, Eastern Europe).

- **Country**.

- **Country subdivision (1st level)**: States, provinces, and so on. Available only for a small number of countries (for example, the US, Canada, France, Spain, and Japan).

- **Country subdivision (2nd level)**: US counties, French departments, Italian provinces, and so on. Available only for some countries.

- **Designated Market Area**: Represents media markets. Only available for the United States (for example, Seattle-Tacoma).

- **City**.

- **Postal Code**.

- **Address** (need to be complete for accuracy).

- **Latitude, Longitude**.

> **Note**
>
> The **Subcontinent** and **Designated Market Area** geo dimensions are only available to Google Analytics data sources for geo charts. You cannot use this data type for other data sources when using the geo chart type.

Apart from these geo types, Looker Studio also accepts geospatial data types from data sources such as BigQuery, where the data is represented as polygons and points. Only Google Map charts support BigQuery's **GEOGRAPHY** data type (it's recognized as a geospatial data type in Looker Studio).

> **Note**
>
> Looker Studio offers only a handful of geo specific functions compared to BigQuery, mainly that return the name of the Geo based on its code. On the other hand, BigQuery provides many functions that allow you to transform your geospatial data in more useful ways.

Geo chart

The classic geo chart type allows you to depict a single metric for a geographical dimension. There is no option to specifically choose to use a filled color or bubbles to represent the metric in a geo chart. It is automatically set based on the geo dimension level used. The metric is represented with a filled color with higher levels such as continent, subcontinent, country, state/province (**Country subdivision – 1st level**), and designated market area. Such filled maps are also called choropleth maps. For **County** (**Country subdivision – 2nd level**), **City**, and **Latitude, Longitude**, the metric is represented by markers.

> **Note**
>
> The **Country subdivision (2nd level)**, **Postal Code**, and **Address** geo dimensions can only be used with the Google Maps chart type. These cannot be used with a geo chart.

The following figure displays the number of calls made by customers from different states and counties in the United States as a geo chart:

Figure 6.38 – Geo chart displaying the number of calls made by customer
location, state-wide on the left and county-wide on the right

Geo charts allow you to drill down into lower levels of geo dimensions. In the chart depicted in the preceding figure, you can drill down from state level to county and vice versa.

An important property for a geo chart is **Zoom area**. You can have the map zoom into one of the following geo levels based on the geo dimension(s) you are depicting in the chart:

- **World**
- **Continent**
- **Subcontinent**
- **Country**

- **Region** (state, province, and so on within a country)

The configurations for the preceding chart are as follows:

- Click on **Add a chart** and select the **Geo** chart type.

- In the **SETUP** tab, configure the following:

  - Select **Call Center** as **Data source**.

  - Add **State** as a **Dimension**.

  - Toggle the **Drill down** option and make sure **Default expand level** is set to **State**.

  - Add **County Name** as another **Dimension**.

  - Add **Calls** as a **Metric**.

  - Set **Zoom area** to **United States**.

- In the **STYLE** tab, configure the following:

  - Choose appropriate colors for the **Max**, **Mid**, and **Min** values. You can also determine which color to use for an area when no data is available for it.

  - Select **Show legend**. This legend does not display any title, so add a custom text label with the metric name using the text control and place it over the chart.

A geo chart can only visualize up to 5,000 data points. Looker Studio chooses the top 5,000 data points by the decreasing order of the metric. This sorting is not configurable. Geo charts do not represent negative metric values well. Use a Google Maps chart type instead if you would like to depict negative values.

Google Maps chart

Looker Studio allows you to visualize and explore geographical data in a Google Maps environment using the Google Maps chart. You can interactively zoom in, zoom out, move the map around, and so on, just like in the Google Maps application. Any valid and supported geo dimensions can be used with this chart. Three variations of the Google Maps chart are available:

- Bubble maps

- Filled maps

- Heatmaps

Unlike in the case of a geo chart, with a Google Maps chart, you can choose whether to represent a metric of any geo dimension level as bubbles or map areas filled with a shaded color or as a heatmap with a color gradient. The only caveats are the **Address** and **Latitude, Longitude** geo dimensions, which can be represented only as bubbles. The following Google Maps chart shows the number of calls by the customer's state using the filled map layer:

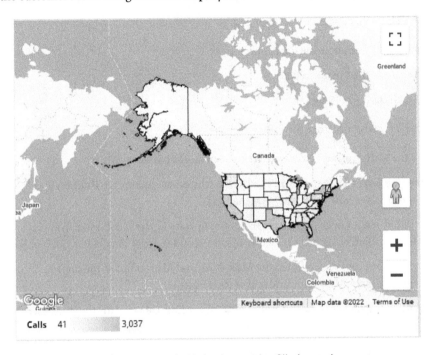

Figure 6.39 – Google Maps chart with a filled areas layer

Based on the geo dimension field used with the chart, the map zooms into the corresponding area by default. There is no specific **Zoom area** configuration for a Google Maps chart like there is in a Geo chart. The default view is often not user-friendly and requires the users to manually zoom into the desired area by using the map controls or just double-clicking on the map.

A useful setting for a Google Maps chart is the **Tooltip** dimension, which enables you to show the value of a dimension other than the default location field in the tooltip. You just have to make sure that this dimension has exactly one value for each location plotted. Otherwise, Looker Studio will return an error. This is helpful when the location field is a non-user-friendly code or ID and you want to show the location name to the user instead.

Google Map charts offer greater choice in terms of map styling options. You can choose either a **Map** (as shown in the preceding screenshot) or a **Satellite** view and select different background styles such as silver, standard, and dark. You can also set the map style to JSON and import your changes if you want something very fancy and custom.

You can even adjust the level of background details for roads, landmarks, and labels. By default, the most detailed maps are available to you, but you can set the right level of detail for your needs.

The preceding chart uses the default settings for most of the properties. You can build it as follows:

- Click on **Add a chart** and select the **Google Maps – Filled Map** chart type.

- In the **SETUP** tab, configure the following:

  - Choose **Call Center** as the data source

  - Add **State** as the **Location** field

  - Add **Calls** as a **Color metric**

- In the **STYLE** tab, configure the following:

  - Keep the **Background Layer** type set to **Map** and set **Style** to **Silver**.

  - Make sure **Layer Type** is set to **Filled areas** (the other options are **Bubbles** and **Heatmap**). This determines how the metric is visualized.

  - The **Filled Area Layer** property defines the opacity of the filled areas. You can adjust the border color and weight. Increase the opacity to 100% from the default value of 50%.

  - Choose an appropriate color for the **Max**, **Mid**, and **Min** values of the metric. This example uses green for the **Max** value and leaves the rest as-is.

  - **Legend** is displayed by default in the bottom position, along with the title. You can adjust the font and number format options as well.

The **STYLE** tab also allows you to enable or disable several map controls. By default, the following are enabled:

- Allow pan and zoom

- Show zoom control

- Show Street View control

- Show fullscreen control

The **fullscreen** control enables you to view the map enlarged to the entire screen. This provides a better experience for the users to explore. This also allows you to fit the chart in a small space on the dashboard, knowing that the users can expand it to full screen when needed. There are two more map controls that you can choose to show on the chart:

- **Show map type control**: This allows the user to switch between the map and satellite views

- **Show scale control**: This displays the map scale in miles or kilometers

The following Google Maps chart depicts the number of calls from the customers across different US counties. This chart is just a variation of the preceding chart, with the following configuration changes:

- Select the chart, and choose Bubble map from the chart picker on the top-right. Or from the **STYLE** tab, change the **Layer Type** from **Filled areas** to **Bubbles**

- In the **SETUP** tab, make the following changes:

  - Choose **County Code** as the **Location** field

  - Select **County Name** as the **Tooltip** field

  - Make sure **Calls** is added under **Size**

  - Add **Call Abandonment Rate** as a **Color metric**

- In the **STYLE** tab, make the following changes:

  - Set the **Background Layer** map style to **Standard.**

  - Reduce the level of detail for **Roads** and **Landmarks.**

  - Under the **Bubble Layer** properties, adjust the size slider appropriately, and set the bubble's opacity to 50%.

  - Choose the appropriate colors for the **Max** and **Min** values.

  - Unselect **Show Street View control** and select **Show map type control options** under **Map Controls.**

  - There are separate styling options for the **Size Legend** and **Color Legend**. This example retains the default settings for these properties:

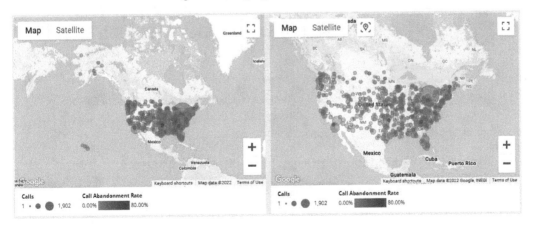

Figure 6.40 – Bubble map using a standard map layer. The default view is on the left. Manually zoom in to achieve the view of the right

Notice that the map does not zero in exactly on the specific region we filtered for. So, it becomes important to always allow the zoom and pan capabilities so that the user can explore the map as needed. There is a reset icon in the top-left corner, using which the user can reset the map to its original state after they've finished exploring.

The final variation of a Google Maps chart is a heatmap, as shown in the following figure. This displays the number of calls made by the customers from the state of California per zip code. Heatmaps plot each location as a point and draw circles around the points based on a radius property value. When these circles overlap, the values of the closest points are aggregated as either sum or weighted averages. You can provide a metric field to determine the corresponding weights of different locations:

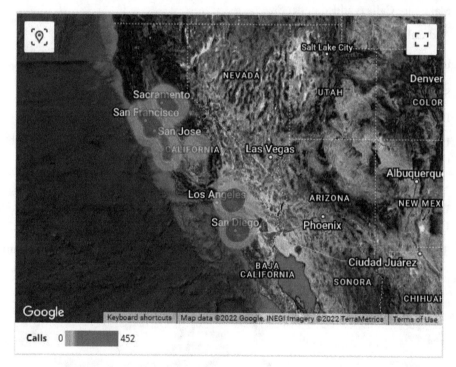

Figure 6.41 – A heatmap of the number of calls made by customers from the state of California

The configurations of this chart are as follows:

- Click on **Add a chart** and select the **Google Maps – Heatmap** chart type.
- In the **SETUP** tab, configure the following:
  - Choose **Call Center** as the data source
  - Add **Zipcode** as the **Location** field

- Add **Calls** as the **Weight** metric

- Under the **Filters** section, click on **ADD A FILTER** and create one with the **Include** condition set to **State Equal to (=) California**

- In the **STYLE** tab, configure the following:

  - Select **Satellite** as **Background Layer Type** and choose **Standard Style**.

  - Reduce the level of detail for **Roads**, **Landmarks**, and **Labels**.

  - Under the **Heatmap layer** properties, set **Heatmap aggregation** to **Sum** (which computes the weighted average based on the metric chosen) and make sure the opacity is 70%. Increase the intensity a little bit to adjust the range of colors toward the high end.

    - You can choose any colors you wish for the **Max**, **Mid**, and **Min** values. This example retains the default colors.

    - Uncheck the **Show zoom control** and **Show Street View control** options.

- Double-click on the map and pan it to zoom in as needed.

Google Maps charts do not allow you to drill down into additional levels of geo dimensions. You can only visualize a single geographical dimension and in the cases of filled areas and heatmaps, only one metric. You can depict up to two metrics with a bubble map. Requiring the drill-down capability is one use case where a geo chart is a better fit.

At the time of writing, Google Maps charts don't allow **Optional Metrics**. Geo charts, on the other hand, do support optional metrics. You can choose any one metric at a time to be visualized in the chart. In addition to the interactive map interface and allowing exploration, Google Map charts can plot a higher number of data points for the **Latitude, Longitude** field, the limit of which is up to 1 million bubbles. However, the limit for other geo dimensions is only 3,500, which is less than the 5,000-point limit for the geo chart. So, it's a tradeoff that you need to make based on the volume of data to be displayed. More importantly, the greater the number of data points plotted, the longer it takes the Google Map chart to load. Consider both the advantages and disadvantages of the two categories of geographical charts while choosing between them.

In the next section, we will learn about configuring scorecard charts, which help present key performance metrics.

Configuring scorecards

With scorecard charts, you can show a single metric value as text. They are useful to display key performance metrics. In this section, we will configure a scorecard to display the **Call Abandonment Rate** metric. The following screenshot shows the metric value for the second quarter of 2022:

Figure 6.42 – Scorecard displaying the Call Abandonment Rate metric

You can build this scorecard as follows:

- Click on **Add a chart** and select the **Scorecard** chart type.
- In the **SETUP** tab, configure the following:

  - Choose **Call Center** as the data source.

  - Add **Call Abandonment Rate** as a **Metric**. Set the display name to Q2 Call Abandonment Rate.

  - Set **Default date range** to a fixed duration of April 1, 2022, to June 30, 2022. Select the **Fixed** option from the top drop-down and select a **Start Date** and **End Date**. Our dataset only has the data for 6 months of 2022. For any up-to-date data source, you can choose other options such as **This Quarter**, **This Month**, and so on.

- In the **STYLE** tab, do the following:

  - Add two conditional formatting rules to show the value text in green when the value is less than 0.1 and in red otherwise. You can choose to set the background color for the card based on this condition as well:

Figure 6.43 – Conditional formatting rules for the scorecard

- Set **Decimal precision** to 1 under **Primary Metric**.

From the **STYLE** tab, you can configure other properties such as the text style and alignment, card background and border, padding, and so on. I've updated the **Line Height** option under the **Padding** section to **48px**.

Most metrics provide greater utility when compared against another timeframe. The following is an enhanced scorecard example that shows a comparison of the call abandonment rate for Q2 against the previous period value – that is, Q1, 2022 – below the primary metric number:

Figure 6.44 – Scorecard showing the comparison metric

You can modify the previous scorecard configurations to achieve the chart shown in the preceding screenshot using the following configurations. You can resize the chart on the canvas appropriately to fit the labels:

- In the **SETUP** tab, make the following changes:

  Set **Comparison date range** to **Previous period** to provide the change in **Call Abandonment Rate** compared to the previous quarter. The period considered by the **Previous period** option is based on the period specified in the default date range. Since we have selected the default date range as a fixed date range of 91 days, **Previous period** is set to 91 days before that, which is Q1.

  When you choose the default date range in terms of past quarters based on the current date, the previous period label is displayed as **previous quarter**. At the time of writing, I've set the default date range as follows to display the metric for Q2 (directly choosing **Last quarter** would have also worked):

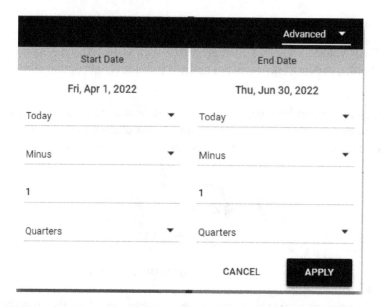

Figure 6.45 – Choosing a default date range relative to today

This changes the comparison label accordingly, as shown in the following screenshot:

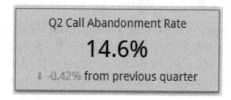

Figure 6.46 – Scorecard using relative time as the default date range

- In the **STYLE** tab, do the following:

  - Change the conditional formatting rules to set the background to red when the value is greater than 0.1 and green otherwise.

  - Under the **Comparison Metric** options, select red for a positive change and green for a negative change.

- Check the **Show Absolute Change** option. We want to show the comparison metric as an absolute change instead of a percentage change.

- Uncheck **Hide Comparison Label**. This shows some text stating **from previous quarter** beside the comparison metric value.

- Under **Labels**, center-align **Metric name**, **Metric value**, and **Comparison**.

- Select a light gray for the border line and check **Add Border Shadow** under the **Background and Border** properties.

- Make sure the **Line Height** property is set to **48px** under **Padding**. This property adjusts the space between the metric name, metric value, and comparison value.

Scorecards allow you to configure what to display when data is missing for the chosen date range. By default, **No data** is displayed. However, you can choose to show 0, a dash, blank, or "null" text.

In the next section, we will explore the remaining built-in chart types – the **Treemap** chart, **Buller** chart, and **Gauge** chart.

Configuring other chart types

In this section, we will look at the last three types of built-in charts that Looker Studio offers. These are the **Treemap** chart, **Bullet** chart, and **Gauge** chart. Both the bullet and gauge chart types represent a single metric against an optional target value. On the other hand, a treemap chart depicts hierarchical dimension data using nested rectangles.

Treemap

A treemap chart enables you to represent a single metric for one or more dimensions. It is especially useful for displaying hierarchical data. Each dimension value is a branch represented by a rectangle whose size or area is based on the metric chosen. This rectangle or branch is further divided into multiple rectangles representing the next level dimension values and so on. Only the name of the lowest level dimension is displayed as a label in each rectangle. You can display the name of the parent dimension as the branch header by enabling this option from the **STYLE** tab.

You can configure how many levels of data you want to see at a time. You can also use the **Drill down** function to add many levels of detail to the chart. Let's say that you have four dimension fields that form a hierarchy, where you have added them to the chart and enabled the **Drill down** option. When you set the **Levels to show** property to **1**, you can only see one dimension at a time as you drill up and down through the dimension hierarchy. Configuring the **Levels to show** property to **2** allows you to see **Dimension 1** and **Dimension 2** at the top of the drill hierarchy, **Dimension 2** and **Dimension 3** when you drill down once, **Dimension 3** and **Dimension 4** when you drill down once more, and finally only **Dimension 4** when you reach the bottom of the hierarchy.

The following treemap shows the number of calls by topic and subtopic. It displays two levels of dimensions at a time and also enables you to drill down through the dimension hierarchy. In this example, when you drill down to **Subtopic**, you will see only one level of data even, though the **Levels to show** property is set to **2**. This is because no child dimensions have been added after **Subtopic** in the **SETUP** tab:

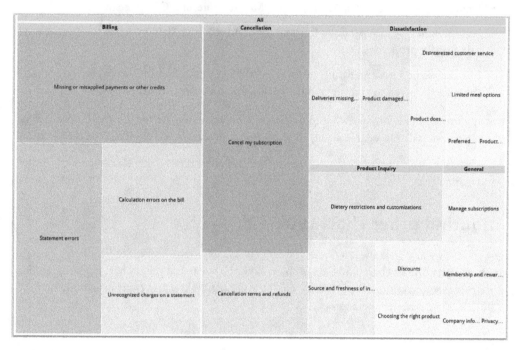

Figure 6.47 – Treemap displaying the number of police incidents by category and subcategory

By default, a treemap in Looker Studio shows 500 rows of aggregated data for the chosen dimensions. You can adjust this number from 5 to 5,000. In this chart type, both the size and the color of the rectangle are based on a single metric.

> **Note**
>
> If the metric has negative values for any rows, those values are not represented in the treemap and are excluded.

The treemap chart is automatically sorted by the decreasing order of the metric value chosen and displays the corresponding branches from the top left to the bottom right. At the time of writing, there is no explicit sort option to change this default behavior.

The preceding treemap can be built as follows:

- Click on **Add a chart** and select **Treemap** from the list.
- In the **SETUP** tab, configure the following:
  - Choose **Call Center** as the data source.
  - Add **Topic** and **Subtopic** as dimensions. Enable **Drill down**.
  - Keep **Levels to show** set to **2**.
  - Add **Calls** as a **Metric**.
- In the **STYLE** tab, configure the following:
  - Choose the appropriate colors for the **Max, Mid,** and **Min** values of the metric
  - Enable **Show branch header** and choose the desired background color for this header

Treemaps are good at showing the relative sizes of data categories at multiple levels, especially depicting the long-tailed distributions of data. They should not be used when the data is not hierarchical or when the metric values are close to each other for various dimensions.

Bullet chart

Bullet charts provide a simple way to display a single metric and benchmark it against target values. These charts are a popular choice to represent **key performance indicators** (**KPIs**). The following screenshot shows a bullet chart with a bar representing the overall **Call Abandonment Rate** of 14.8% for the first 6 months of the year 2022 against the target score of 10%. It also shows different thresholds to understand how good or bad the metric value is:

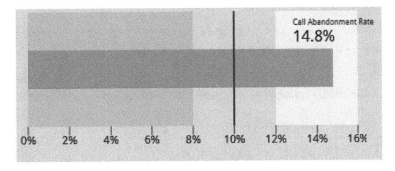

Figure 6.48 – Bullet chart depicting a metric value against the target benchmark

In this chart, three thresholds are defined at 8%, 12%, and 16%, respectively. Additionally, the target score is specified as 10%. A **Call Abandonment Rate** of 8% or less is considered very good. Anything between 8% and 12% is considered OK or average. A rate of more than 12% is considered poor.

You can only define up to three ranges – **Range 1**, **Range 2**, and **Range 3** – for a bullet chart. You can set the value of a range to 0 to remove it. If you don't want to use any ranges, set the same value that is large enough to display the metric for all range limits.

The preceding bullet chart can be built as follows:

- Click **Add a chart** and select the **Bullet** chart type.
- In the **SETUP** tab, configure the following:
  - Choose **Call Center** as the data source
  - Add **Call Abandonment Rate** as a **Metric**
  - Add the following **Range Limits**:
    - **Range 1**: `0.08`
    - **Range 2**: `0.12`
    - **Range 3**: `0.16`
  - Make sure **Show Target** is enabled and provide a value of `0.1`
- Configure the following In the **STYLE** tab:
  - Choose an appropriate color for the bar to represent the metric.
  - Select the desired color to represent the threshold ranges. The ranges are displayed in varying shades of the single color selected.
  - Make sure that you select **Show Axis** and adjust any font or number properties as desired. This example just uses the default values.

At the time of writing, Looker Studio's bullet chart displays neither the data label for the metric nor the metric name on the chart. So, a separate scorecard chart is created and overlaid on the bullet chart to display them.

Gauge chart

Similar to a bullet chart, a gauge chart also displays a single metric against a target goal. Gauge charts provide a car dashboard-like look for monitoring performance metrics. These charts provide greater flexibility than bullet charts. The key differences between them are listed in the following table:

Gauge chart	Bullet chart
The target line and ranges are not displayed by default. These properties are available from the **STYLE** tab.	The target line and ranges are configured by default. These options are available from the **Data** tab.
Up to five ranges can be defined.	Up to three ranges can be defined.
Displays the metric name and value by default and provides options to hide them.	Does not display nor provide the option to display the metric's name or value.
A comparison metric can be added.	Not applicable.
The axis min and max values can be configured. The axis is not displayed by default, but it can be enabled.	The axis always starts at 0 and the upper limit is set by the **Range 3** value. The axis is shown by default, but it can be hidden.

Table 6.1 – Key differences between a gauge chart and a bullet chart in Looker Studio

The following gauge chart displays the **Call Abandonment Rate** metric for Q2. The absolute change in the rate from the previous quarter is also shown. The black line displayed is the value of the metric for the comparison date range, which is Q1. This example doesn't represent any target goal or range:

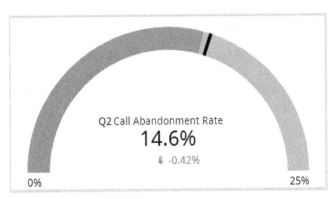

Figure 6.49 – Gauge chart with the comparison metric

This chart can be built as follows:

- Click **Add a chart** and select the **Gauge** chart type.

- In the **SETUP** tab, configure the following:

  - Select **Call Center** as the data source

  - Add **Call Abandonment Rate** as a Metric.

  - Choose a **Fixed** range of April 1st, 2022, to June 30th, 2022, as **Default date range**.

  - Set **Comparison date range** to **Previous period** to provide the change in the metric compared to the previous quarter.

- In the **STYLE** tab, configure the following:

  - Choose the appropriate colors for the bar and the range

  - Select **Show Absolute Change** to view the actual change in the metric value compared to the previous quarter rather than the default percentage change

  - Under **Comparison Metric**, choose a red color for positive change and a green color for negative change

  - Select **Show Axis** and set **Axis Max** to **0.25**

- Add a text control to add a prefix of **Q2** to the metric label. We do not want to change the display name of the field to reflect this as the same name is shown in the tooltip for the black line representing the previous period metric value.

When you add ranges and a target to the preceding chart, it looks as follows. The chart now displays two black lines – one for the target value and another for the metric value for the comparison date range. The two lines look alike and it is not possible to understand which is which without hovering over the lines to see the tooltips:

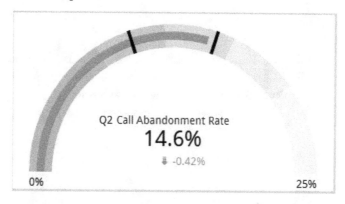

Figure 6.50 – Gauge chart with the target and ranges defined

Add the following configurations in the **STYLE** tab:

- Define four ranges as 0.08, 0.12, 0.16, and 0.2, respectively
- Select **Show Target** and set **Target Value** to 0.1

Gauge charts are often used in executive dashboards and reports for their appealing look. They are user-friendly and easily interpretable.

Building your first Looker Studio report – adding charts

You created the **Call Center** data source in *Chapter 4, Google Looker Studio Overview,* and set up a report with a title and a date range control in *Chapter 5, Looker Studio Report Designer.* Now, it's time to add visualizations to the report. I've composed the dashboard as follows using some of the charts we configured in this chapter:

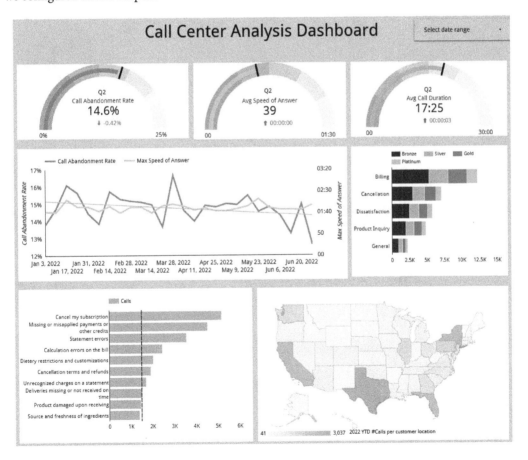

Figure 6.51–Dashboard using some of the charts we configured in this chapter

Build your report by adding a different set of charts or configurations, if you like, using what you've learned from this chapter.

Summary

Looker Studio offers several commonly needed visualization types as built-in charts. In this chapter, we examined each of the built-in charts available in Looker Studio at the time of writing and their key configurations. You understood the purpose and use of different data and style properties to build effective visualizations using a few public datasets.

In the next chapter, we will learn about some advanced features and concepts such as data blending, parameters, creating report templates, using calculated fields, and more.

7

Looker Studio Features, Beyond Basics

In the previous three chapters of this book, you have learned about how to get started with Looker Studio and explored its major entities. You understood how to use the many fundamental features of the tool to build effective data visualizations and reports. This chapter explores some additional capabilities that will allow you to create truly powerful and insightful data stories.

We will learn about **calculated fields**, which allow you to create new data values based on the existing data and support effective analytics and data representation. We will look into **parameters** that let you dynamically change the output of calculated fields or data source connection settings based on the user input. We will also learn about **data blending**, which helps create charts and controls based on multiple data sources within a report by combining those data sources through blending. Data blending has many interesting applications. A gallery of community visualizations equips you with new chart types and custom functionality that helps build more potent reports and dashboards. **Report templates** provide ready-to-use analyses for standard schema data sources and offer a great starting point for any custom report development. These reports are optimized to be highly responsive and fast-loading, resulting in a rich user experience. In this chapter, these topics are covered in the following main sections:

- Leveraging calculated fields
- Using parameters
- Blending data
- Adding community visualizations
- Creating report templates
- Optimizing reports for performance

Technical requirements

To follow the example implementations in this chapter, you need to have a Google account that allows you to create reports with Looker Studio. Use one of the recommended browsers – Chrome, Safari, or Firefox. Make sure Looker Studio is supported in your country (`https://support.google.com/looker-studio/answer/7657679?hl=en#zippy=%2Clist-of-unsupported-countries`).

This chapter uses BigQuery, Google Cloud's serverless data warehouse platform, as a data source in a couple of examples. If you do not already have a Google Cloud account with access to BigQuery, you can create a trial account (`https://cloud.google.com/free`), which provides $300 of credit for you to use on any Google Cloud resources. You need a valid credit card to enroll in the trial, but you will not be charged. Create a Google Cloud project to start using any resources.

BigQuery charges for the amount of data processed by the queries as well as for the storage of data. It has a free tier, which allows you to query up to 1 TB of data per month for free. You will be charged (or will use up the credits) only beyond this limit. Some examples in this chapter leverage data from BigQuery public datasets, which are available to anyone with a Google Cloud account. To understand using parameters with the BigQuery connector better, some familiarity with **Structured Query Language (SQL)** is expected.

Several datasets are used in this chapter to illustrate the various features and capabilities most appropriately. You can follow along by connecting to these datasets from Looker Studio. The details are as follows:

- *Online Sales*: The sales data of a UK-based retail company. The dataset is available at `https://github.com/PacktPublishing/Data-Storytelling-with-Google-Data-Studio/blob/a31bf2de1ca10db433cf9d0ecb15c3cf4fa882d2/online_sales.zip`. Unzip it and save the CSV file to your local machine. Use the File Upload connector to create the data source in Looker Studio. To ensure the upload is successful, make sure to save the file in a UTF-8 compatible format. This dataset is taken from the UCI Machine Learning Repository. This dataset is used to demonstrate calculated fields, parameters, and blending. The enriched Looker Studio data source is accessible at `https://lookerstudio.google.com/datasources/68a943df-886d-4c34-96bc-33eadde983c2`.

- *Product info*: This contains the unit cost information for the products sold by the aforementioned UK-based retail company. This can be used together with the preceding *Online Sales* dataset. This is available in Google Sheets at `https://tinyurl.com/ukprodinfo`. You can also access it as a CSV file at `https://github.com/PacktPublishing/Data-Storytelling-with-Google-Data-Studio/blob/master/Product%20Info.csv`.

- *Book Recommendation*: This dataset is available from Kaggle (`https://www.kaggle.com/datasets/arashnic/book-recommendation-dataset`). Only the `Books.csv` file is required for the current purpose. A community connector exists to allow you to connect directly to Kaggle. You can refer to the connector's GitHub page (`https://github.com/googledatastudio/community-connectors/tree/master/kaggle`) for instructions. However, this connector is not verified or reviewed and so should be used with caution – you can expect some issues. Alternatively, you can also download the dataset on your local machine and upload it to Looker Studio to set it up as a data source to follow along. As always, make sure to save the CSV file in a UTF-8 compatible format to be able to successfully upload it to Looker Studio. The dataset includes an image field and is used to create image-based calculated fields.

- *Air Quality* data is available as a public dataset in Google BigQuery. Google sourced this data from U.S. Environmental Protection Agency's internet database (`https://www.epa.gov/airdata`). A step-by-step walkthrough for creating a BigQuery data source is provided in *Part 3* of this book, as part of *Chapter 9, Mortgage Complaints Analysis*.

You can review the examples explained in this chapter using the following Looker Studio reports:

- Online Sales: `https://lookerstudio.google.com/reporting/9771fb7c-ee72-4887-903e-3211674010a9/preview`

- Book Recommendation: `https://lookerstudio.google.com/reporting/d6d2f65d-4904-42ef-b464-47fbd819b017/preview`

Make these reports your own by connecting to your own data sources and exploring the features further.

Leveraging calculated fields

Calculated fields are custom fields that you can add to data sources and charts. These fields are derived from existing fields in the data source, including other calculated fields. A calculated field can be either a dimension or a metric.

Looker Studio provides several functions grouped under six categories to help create useful calculated fields. These include the following:

- Arithmetic
- Conditional
- Date
- Geo
- Text
- Aggregation
- Miscellaneous

Calculated fields serve many purposes. They enable you to implement business logic, create user-friendly representations of data, and create complex metrics beyond simple aggregations.

Arithmetic functions enable you to perform mathematical operations such as computing logarithms, exponentials, trigonometric values, or nearest integers on numeric data. You can also do simple math using regular operators for addition, subtraction, division, and multiplication. With date functions, you can parse and format dates, extract date and time parts, and perform simple date arithmetic. Text functions allow you to work with textual data – concatenate different values, remove extraneous white space, find, extract, and replace specific pieces of text. Regular expressions enable you to match specific sequences of characters and provide greater flexibility in finding and filtering data. Looker Studio provides four regular expression functions to use with text data.

Looker Studio functions under the geo category return the names of the specified geo-location codes, for countries, regions, cities, continents, and subcontinents. With conditional functions, you can handle null values and apply branching logic using conditional expressions. Looker Studio offers different forms of conditional functions and statements such as IF, CASE, NULLIF, and COALESCE. These functions are extremely useful and have many different applications. We will see some of them throughout this chapter. You can create hyperlinks and image fields and perform explicit data type conversions using the functions provided under the miscellaneous category.

You can use aggregation functions, such as SUM, AVERAGE, and PERCENTILE, to create metric fields. By definition, an aggregation is calculated across different rows and hence the resultant calculated field is always a metric. All the other functions work on a single row of the data source and result in a dimension field. It is possible to use multiple functions in appropriate ways within a calculation so that you can apply non-aggregate functions to an aggregated output and vice versa – for example, CEIL(AVG(Score)) or AVG(CEIL(Score)). Both expressions result in a metric field, as aggregation is involved. The former formula first computes the average score for all the relevant rows of data and then returns the closest integer greater than the average value. On the other hand, the latter calculation gets the closest larger integer for each score first and then calculates the average of all the integers.

Calculated fields can be created at the data source level or for a specific chart. Those created from the **SETUP** tab for a chart are specific to that chart and are not available for use with other charts and controls. As a general practice, we should minimize creating chart-specific calculations and lean towards defining calculated fields in the data source. This enables you to reuse calculations as well as manage them easily from a central place. Data source calculated fields can include other calculated fields in their formula. However, while creating chart-specific fields, you cannot use other chart-specific fields in the calculation, even those defined within the same chart.

There are certain specific cases where chart-level calculated fields make sense or are the only choice, particularly when using blended data sources. We will explore data blending in a later section in this chapter. You may also need to create a chart-specific calculated field when you do not have edit access to the data source being used.

At the data source level, you can create a calculated field either from the **Edit** screen of the data source or from the **DATA** panel in the report designer. Click on **ADD A FIELD** and provide the following values:

- **Field Name** – Provide a name unique to the data source.

- **Field ID** (optional) – You can accept the default unique ID that Looker Studio generates or provide your own. You cannot change the **Field ID** once the calculated field is saved.

- **Formula** – Type in the formula to perform the calculation. The editor has a code complete feature, which shows helpful information on how to use a particular function. You can view and add the existing fields from the **Available Fields** section. You can also easily format the formula, no matter how complex, just by clicking the **FORMAT FORMULA** button.

Looker Studio displays a green check at the bottom to indicate that the formula is valid. Any errors associated with an invalid formula specification are displayed in red. The errors could be field-related, related to the incorrect use of functions, or something else. The data type of a calculated field is determined based on the component fields and the functions involved in the formula. You can change its data type from the data source editor or in the **New Field** pane for chart-specific calculated fields:

Figure 7.1 – Creating and editing a calculated field at the data source level

Looker Studio uses field IDs to allow you to filter data across multiple unconnected data sources. Say your report is based on multiple data sources with one or more common columns. By specifying the same **Field ID** for a particular field in all the data sources, you can create a filter control based on the field from one of the data sources and have it filter relevant charts based on all the data sources automatically. Since you cannot change the **Field ID** of an existing field, you will have to create calculated fields based on the existing fields and then specify the same desired **Field ID** in all the data sources.

Consider a scenario where you have created a report using two separate data sources: *Online sales* and *Product info*. Let's say the two data sources have the following fields:

- Online sales:

  - Country
  - CustomerID
  - StockCode
  - Description
  - InvoiceDate
  - Quantity
  - UnitPrice

- Product info:

  - ProductCode
  - ProductName
  - UnitCost

The report includes separate visualizations based on each of these two data sources. The Description field in the *Online sales* data source maps to the ProductName field in the *Product info* data source. If you would like to filter the report by product, you can easily do so using a common field ID without having to blend or join the data together. As noted earlier, the field IDs of any existing fields cannot be changed. So, create new calculated fields in each of the data sources with the following configuration:

- **Field Name**: Product (you can provide the same name in both the data sources or different names)

- **Field ID**: field_product (you must provide the same value for both the calculated fields). Take care to provide the value before clicking the **SAVE** button

- **Formula**: Drag and drop the **Description** and **ProductName** fields from the **Available fields** section for the two data sources respectivel

Click **SAVE**:

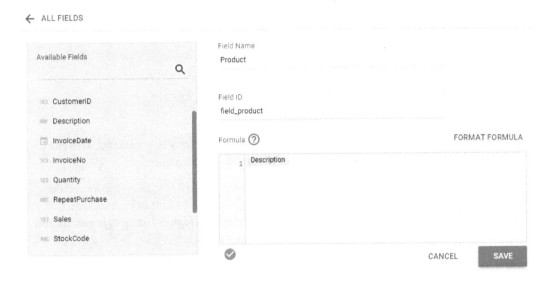

Figure 7.2 – Creating and editing a calculated field at the data source level

Now, you add a single filter control using either of the newly calculated fields. The selection will filter the entire report.

In the rest of this section, we will go through some useful and interesting applications of calculated fields in Looker Studio with some examples. Most of the examples in this section use the Online Sales dataset, which you can access at `https://github.com/PacktPublishing/Data-Storytelling-with-Google-Data-Studio/blob/a31bf2de1ca10db433cf9d0ecb15c3cf4fa882d2/online_sales.zip`. The underlying dataset is obtained from UC Irvine's Machine Learning Repository and the File Upload connector is used to create the data source from the CSV file. Make sure the file is saved in a UTF-8 compatible CSV before uploading it to Looker Studio.

Organizing dimension values into custom groups

A CASE statement provides the greatest flexibility for creating fields with conditional logic. It can be used to match a field to a single value or multiple values. You can either compare against literal values or expressions using other functions and fields. You can nest multiple case statements and also use logical operators to combine different conditions. A common application of a CASE statement is to group a dimension field's values into different categories to facilitate key analyses.

There are a couple of different ways in which you can use the CASE statement. In the simplest form, you can match a field to a literal value to derive a new field as follows:

```
CASE WEEKDAY(InvoiceDate)
   WHEN 0 THEN 'Weekend'
   WHEN 6 THEN 'Weekend'
   ELSE 'Weekday'
END
```

This calculated field indicates whether the invoice date falls on a weekday or a weekend. This allows you to understand the invoice processing needs over the weekend, for example.

Another use case is to categorize order size based on the quantity ordered. The following formula uses a slightly different syntax that enables you to specify the comparison condition on the Quantity field. This syntax is powerful and allows you to implement complex logic by using expressions and combining different conditions:

```
CASE
   WHEN Quantity <= 5 THEN 'Small Order'
   WHEN Quantity <= 10 THEN "Medium Order"
   ELSE "Large Order"
END
```

For text fields, you can compare multiple values in a single condition using the IN operator as shown in the following example. This is a more compact way of writing the formula compared to making individual matches in separate WHEN clauses.

```
CASE
   WHEN Country IN ('Iceland', 'Norway', 'Sweden', 'Finland',
'Denmark') THEN 'Scandinavia'
   ELSE Country
END
```

The IF function can also be used to create custom groupings or other conditional-derived fields. However, it may become unwieldy and difficult to read with multiple nested levels or complex conditions. Let's say you want to analyze two random samples of orders. You can denote a subset of individual orders as Sample 1 or Sample 2 using the IF function as follows:

```
IF(RIGHT_TEXT(CustomerID, 1) = '3', CONCAT('Sample' , '1'),
IF(RIGHT_TEXT(CustomerID, 1) = LEFT_TEXT(InvoiceNo,1),
'Sample2', ''))
```

This calculated field indicates whether an order belongs to `Sample 1`, `Sample 2`, or neither. The conditional logic used here is just an attempt to introduce some randomness into the sample selection. This example illustrates that you can use expressions and functions in a condition clause or result. The same calculation can be achieved using the `CASE` statement as follows:

```
CASE RIGHT_TEXT(CustomerID, 1)
    WHEN '3' THEN CONCAT('Sample' , '1')
    WHEN LEFT_TEXT(InvoiceNo, 1) THEN 'Sample2'
END
```

As a general guideline, use an `IF` function when the conditional expression has binary outcomes and a `CASE` statement when there are multiple conditions or multiple outcomes.

Manipulating text with regular expressions

Regular expressions (**regex**) enable you to match patterns of text in data. These patterns can be as specific or as general as needed. Looker Studio uses the RE2 syntax. The complete syntax reference can be found at `https://github.com/google/re2/wiki/Syntax`. Regex has universal utility and is used across applications. While regex is powerful, it can be quite complex and has a steep learning curve. The current objective is not to make you well-versed with using regex syntax, but rather, to provide a glimpse into its versatility and potential to create calculated fields within Looker Studio.

A very brief introduction to regex

At the most basic level, a regex pattern can be the exact characters to match. For example, the `data` pattern matches the text "data". However, the `data` pattern does not because regex patterns are case-sensitive by default. You can make a pattern match case insensitive by using a flag (`?i`) as follows:

```
"(?i)data"
```

The power of regex is not matching exact characters though. You can use character classes and metacharacters to define a generic pattern that can match a wide range of values. **Character classes** indicate specific characters or a range of characters. Examples include `[a-z]` for the entire lower-case alphabet, `[0-9]` for the digits, or `[abc]` for the specific letters a, b, or c.

To match whether a given text starts with the alphabet (in any case), use the pattern `"[a-zA-Z].*"`. This is equivalent to `"(?i)[a-z].*"`. In these expressions, `[a-zA-Z]` and `[a-z]` are called character classes that represent the alphabet. "`.`" And "`*`" are the metacharacters. "`.`" represents any character, whereas "`*`" means "zero or more occurrences of the preceding character." So the `"[a-zA-z].*"` pattern matches any string that starts with a letter followed by zero or more of any character.

A few example strings that the pattern matches include the following:

- Abacus

- C

- Price = $12.99

Similarly, to match text that ends with a letter, use the `".*[a-zA-Z]"` pattern.

To check for one or more occurrences of a character, use the "+" **metacharacter**. For example, the `".*[0-9]+"` pattern matches any text that ends with one or more digits such as "`sample12`" or "`Test 4`". You can also reverse the selection using the "^" **negation** metacharacter. To match text that doesn't contain any letters, use the `"[^a-zA-Z]+"` pattern. It returns `true` for the text "$12.99," as it does not contain one or more letters (so, any). Any metacharacters can be matched as literal characters by escaping them using the "\" character. The `"\\$[0-9]+\\.[0-9][0-9]"` pattern matches any text that starts with a dollar sign, followed by a number with one or more digits before the decimal point and exactly two digits after the decimal point such as "$12.99," "$3.02," or "$245.50." You can see that you need to use two backlashes each to escape the metacharacters "$" and ".". You can use the raw string literal prefix, R, instead to just use one backslash as follows:

```
R"\$[0-9]+\.[0-9][0-9]"
```

More examples can be found on the Looker Studio help page at `https://support.google.com/datastudio/answer/10496674`. Regular expressions enable you to match more complex patterns and the syntax provides a robust set of options to represent any pattern.

> **Note**
>
> If you're new to regex, it can be overwhelming to understand. Websites like regex101.com provide a regex translation tool that can help you generate the regex syntax for the transformation you're trying to accomplish. Looker Studio uses the "re2" flavor of regex. It's denoted as the Golang flavor in regex101.com. Make sure to choose this flavor to generate expressions that you can use within Looker Studio.

Regex functions in Looker Studio

Currently, Looker Studio offers four regex functions to use with text data. You can check whether a field or expression contains a specific pattern using the REGEXP_CONTAINS function. This is similar to the CONTAINS_TEXT function, which identifies whether a text field or expression contains a specified substring. As with any text matches in Looker Studio, CONTAINS_TEXT is case sensitive. The regex function enables you to perform case-insensitive matches more easily due to its nature of allowing broader patterns.

In the Online Sales data source, the **Description** field provides the product name associated with the orders, mainly in uppercase. Let's convert this into a more readable proper case first using Looker Studio's text functions as follows. This formula separates the first character of the field value using the LEFT_TEXT function. The rest of the product name is obtained using the SUBSTR and LENGTH functions, which is then converted to lowercase using the LOWER function. Any trailing spaces are removed using the TRIM function. These two pieces are finally concatenated using the CONCAT function to form the complete product name.

Create the field named **Product** as follows:

```
CONCAT(LEFT_TEXT(Description, 1),
TRIM(LOWER(SUBSTR(Description, 2, LENGTH(Description) - 1))))
```

The **Product Type** field can be derived from the preceding **Product** field using REGEXP_CONTAINS as follows:

```
CASE
    WHEN STARTS_WITH(Product, 'Set') OR REGEXP_CONTAINS(Product,
'(?i)(cases)') THEN 'Set/Case'
    WHEN ENDS_WITH(Product, 'bag') THEN 'Bag'
    ELSE 'Other'
END
```

The derived field groups products into three categories:

- Products with names that either start with Set or that contain the text (cases) as Set/Case. The regex pattern matches the text (cases) in the **Product** field whether it is uppercase or lowercase.

- Products with names that end with bag as Bag.

- The rest as Other.

The preceding formula also demonstrates the use of the STARTS_WITH and ENDS_WITH text functions to match the start and end of the product name respectively to the corresponding substrings.

Product Type can be derived using CONTAINS_TEXT instead as follows, which involves converting the product name into lowercase or uppercase using the LOWER or UPPER functions to make the comparison:

```
CASE
    WHEN STARTS_WITH(Product, 'Set') OR CONTAINS_
TEXT(LOWER(Product), 'cases') THEN 'Set/Case'
    WHEN ENDS_WITH(Product, 'bag') THEN 'Bag'
    ELSE 'Other'
END
```

While `REGEXP_CONTAINS` enables you to match substrings in a text field based on a pattern, `REGEXP_MATCH` allows you to match the entire field value against the specified pattern. In the current example, `REGEXP_MATCH` can be used instead of `REGEXP_CONTAINS` as follows:

```
REGEXP_MATCH(Product, '.*(?i)(cases).*')
```

`REGEXP_MATCH` provides greater flexibility and helps match standard formats such as IP addresses and email addresses.

With `REGEXP_EXTRACT`, you can extract substrings from a text field or expression that matches a given pattern. The following formula creates a field that represents the number of items in each product by extracting the number included in the product name:

```
IFNULL(CAST(REGEXP_EXTRACT(Product, '([0-9]+)') AS NUMBER ), 1
)
```

The function returns the first number it encounters in the product name. When no match is found, `NULL` is returned. When the product name doesn't include any number, it implies that the product comprises a single item. This is handled using the `IFULL` function.

`REGEXP_REPLACE` allows you to replace all the occurrences of a pattern with the given text. For example, you can retrieve the first and last words in the product name using `REGEXP_REPLACE` as follows:

```
REGEXP_REPLACE(Product, '\\s.+\\s', ' ')
```

The regex in the preceding formula represents text that appears between the first and last words of the product name, as indicated by the text that lies in between two spaces, including the spaces. For example, for a product name of `Pink knitted egg cosy`, the pattern matches the text "`knitted egg`", which is then replaced by a single white space by the function. The function returns "`Pink cosy`" for this product. `REGEXP_REPLACE` has varied applications and is commonly used to remove parameters from an URL field.

Using MAX and MIN across multiple fields or expressions

The `MAX` and `MIN` functions allow you to find the maximum or minimum value respectively of a single field or expression. They generate a metric field, which represents an aggregated value. However, in scenarios where you want to find the maximum or minimum value across multiple dimension fields or expressions, `NARY_MAX` and `NARY_MIN` functions come in handy. These functions compute the result for each row of the data source and return unaggregated dimension fields.

These functions are especially useful when the data is in a pivot or crosstab form. Let's say the data source has sales for each Scandinavian country as separate columns for each invoice month and you want to find the maximum sales amount across all countries and months. First, create the following NARY dimension fields to find the maximum and minimum sales value for each month across all countries:

- **Max Scandinavian Sales**:

  ```
  NARY_MAX(Denmark, Finland, Iceland, Norway, Sweden)
  ```

- **Min Scandinavian Sales**:

  ```
  NARY_MIN(Denmark, Finland, Iceland, Norway, Sweden)
  ```

The data looks as follows:

	Invoice Month...	Denmark	Finland	Iceland	Norway	Sweden	Min Scandinavian Sales	Max Scandinavian Sales
1.	Dec 2010	183.6	240	70.8	101.76	1,188	70.8	1,188
2.	Jan 2011	null	244.08	38.25	null	374.4	38.25	374.4
3.	Feb 2011	47.7	40	null	40	114.45	40	114.45
4.	Mar 2011	428.4	551.2	null	376.5	499.2	376.5	551.2
5.	Apr 2011	null	270	249.6	null	120	120	270
6.	May 2011	70.8	null	null	null	374.4	70.8	374.4
7.	Jun 2011	162	69.6	53.1	700	80	53.1	700
8.	Jul 2011	49.8	320	null	120	475.2	49.8	475.2
9.	Aug 2011	34.8	120	106.2	280	518.4	34.8	518.4
10.	Sep 2011	367.2	150	null	270	792	150	792
11.	Oct 2011	266.24	270	106.2	320	475.2	106.2	475.2
12.	Nov 2011	99.84	270	null	320	277.44	99.84	320
13.	Dec 2011	23.4	270	42.96	203.52	238	23.4	270

1 - 13 / 13   < >

Figure 7.3 – Using the NARY_MAX and NARY_MIN functions

Now, to find the lowest monthly sales amount across all countries, you can apply the MIN aggregation to the **Min Scandinavian Sales** field. Similarly, for the highest monthly sales across all Scandinavian countries, apply the MAX aggregation to the **Max Scandinavian Sales** field.

Highest monthly sales among Scandinavian countries	Lowest monthly sales among Scandinavian countries
£1,188	£23

Figure 7.4 – An application of NARY functions

The NARY functions take at least two arguments, which can be literal values, fields, or expressions. At least one argument should use a data source field. Let's say in the preceding example, you want to set an upper limit for the minimum sales across countries to be 100. The formula will look as follows:

```
NARY_MIN(Denmark, Finland, Iceland, Norway, Sweden, 100)
```

You can use NARY functions to determine the highest and lowest among multiple aggregated values or metrics as well:

```
NARY_MAX(AVG(Sales), MEDIAN(Sales))
```

Displaying images and hyperlinks

With IMAGE and HYPERLINK functions, you can make your tables more interesting and useful by displaying hyperlinks and images. To illustrate these functions, let's use the *Book recommendation* dataset from Kaggle (https://www.kaggle.com/datasets/arashnic/book-recommendation-dataset). Use the Books.csv file for this example.

The dataset includes URL fields for the book cover images in addition to the book attributes such as title, author, and ISBN. Let's say we want to display the list of Agatha Christie's books along with the book cover images and appropriate hyperlinks. To achieve this, we need to create the image- and hyperlink-derived fields in the data source.

Image fields can be created using the IMAGE function by providing an image URL and optionally, alternative text. The image URL can be an existing field or an expression resulting in a valid URL. The following formula creates an image field with Image-URL-S as the image URL field and Book-Title as an alternative text field:

```
IMAGE(Image-URL-S, Book-Title)
```

Adding this field to the table displays static images in the column. To make the images clickable and open in a separate tab, we need to create a hyperlink field. The HYPERLINK function allows you to create a hyperlink based on a URL field or expression. You also need to provide a field or expression to the function to represent the link label. You add a hyperlink to an image field by specifying the image as the link label as follows:

```
Book Cover = HYPERLINK(Image-URL-S, IMAGE(Image-URL-S, Book-Title)
```

In the following figure, **Book Title** is also shown as a hyperlink, created using a custom-generated link to Google Books based on ISBN with the following formula:

```
HYPERLINK(CONCAT('http://books.google.com/books?vid=',CAST(ISBN AS TEXT)), Book-Title)
```

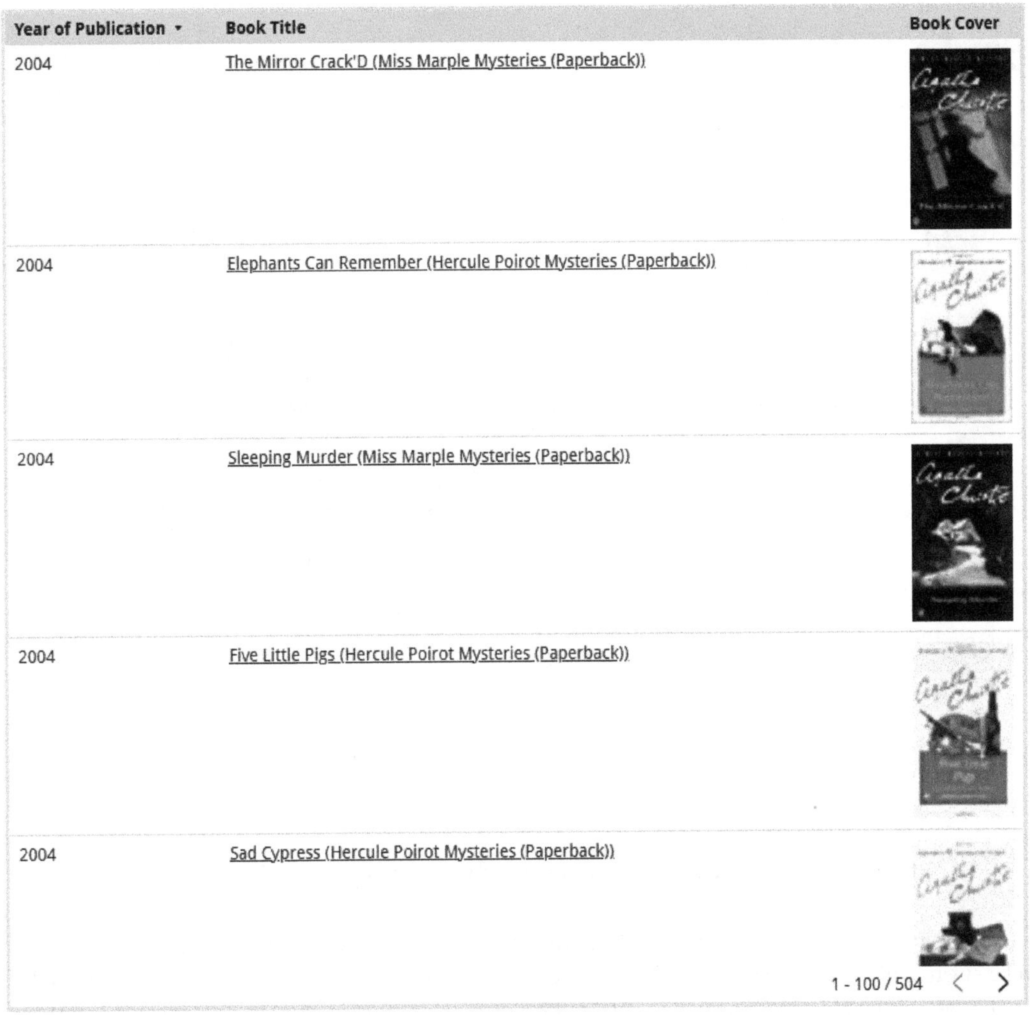

Year of Publication ▾	Book Title	Book Cover
2004	The Mirror Crack'D (Miss Marple Mysteries (Paperback))	
2004	Elephants Can Remember (Hercule Poirot Mysteries (Paperback))	
2004	Sleeping Murder (Miss Marple Mysteries (Paperback))	
2004	Five Little Pigs (Hercule Poirot Mysteries (Paperback))	
2004	Sad Cypress (Hercule Poirot Mysteries (Paperback))	

1 - 100 / 504 < >

Figure 7.5 – Images and hyperlinks in a table

Any web-accessible URL can be used to create images and hyperlinks. One caveat is that images from untrusted sources will not be displayed in Looker Studio.

Another example of leveraging hyperlink functionality is to implement drill-through capability by linking to relevant detailed Looker Studio reports or report pages from a summary report. The following image shows a sample sales summary report based on the *Online Sales* data source. The **Details** column in the table chart provides hyperlinks to individual detailed Looker Studio report pages corresponding to each **Region**:

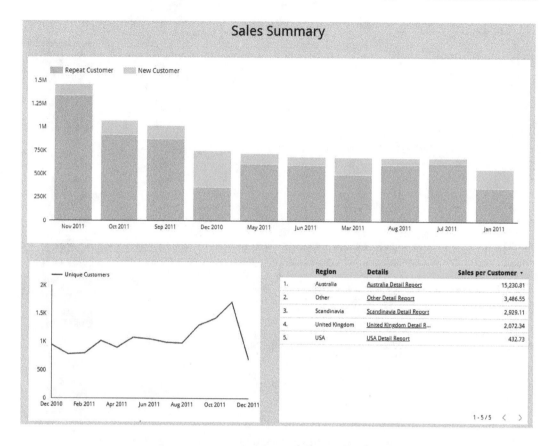

Figure 7.6 – Hyperlinking other Looker Studio reports to achieve drill-through

Create individual detail reports for each **Region**. They can be different pages of a single report or can be entirely different Looker Studio reports. Use page-level or report-level filters on the detailed report(s) as applicable. Construct the URL in the summary report as the **DS URL** field using the following calculation:

```
CONCAT('https://datastudio.google.com/u/0/reporting/xxxxxxxx-
xxxx-xxxx-xxxx-xxxxxxxxxxxx/page/',
  CASE Region
    WHEN 'Scandinavia' THEN 'xxxxx'
    WHEN 'United States' THEN 'p_xxxxxxxxxx'
    WHEN 'United Kingdom' THEN 'p_ xxxxxxxxyy'
    WHEN 'Australia' THEN 'p_ xxxxxxxxzz'
    ELSE 'p_ xxxxxxxyz'
  END )
```

Now, create the hyperlink field – **Details** – as follows:

```
HYPERLINK(DS URL, CONCAT(Region, ' Detail Report'))
```

The following image shows the detailed report that is linked to the preceding summary report using the **Details** field:

Figure 7.7 – An example detailed report for Australia

These individual reports are managed and shared independently. You can add hyperlinks in the detailed reports back to the summary report using the **Text** control. From the **STYLE** tab of the Text control, select the **Insert link** icon and provide the display text and URL, as depicted in the following screenshot:

Insert link

Display text
Back to Summary

Paste a link, or select a page
https://datastudio.google.com/u/0/reporting/7a7d876e-2956-4ff4-a155-1c807(⊗

☐ Open link in new tab

Cancel   Apply

Figure 7.8 – Inserting a link in a Text control

Through hyperlinks, you can enable navigation across different Looker Studio reports as desired.

Using parameters

Parameters in Looker Studio allow both report editors and viewers to input data values to use with calculated fields and connectors. Parameters enable you to create more dynamic reports. There are three ways in which you can use parameters in Looker Studio:

- In a calculated field, to show the results based on the parameter value set by the report editor or chosen by the report viewer
- To pass query parameters to a custom SQL query for the BigQuery connector
- To pass values to community connector parameters

The parameter values can be set and modified in multiple ways:

- The default value in the parameter configuration (by the data source editor).
- Report components – at the chart level, page level, and report level (by the report editor).
- Interactive controls in the report (by report users).
- In the report link by passing the parameter names and values as URL-encoded JSON strings. This allows advanced users to configure reports programmatically.

To pass the parameter values via a report link, the parameters need to be explicitly allowed to do so. This can be done from the **Manage report URL parameters** page, available from the **Resource** menu.

Parameters and calculated fields

Parameters for use in calculated fields are created within a data source, either from the data source editor or the **DATA** panel in the report designer by clicking the **ADD A PARAMETER** button. There are four properties you need to set to define a parameter:

- **Parameter name** – The name that is displayed in the data source and used to refer to calculated fields.
- **Data type** – This can be number, text, or boolean.
- **Permitted values** – In the case of numeric or text parameters, you can allow a specific list of values or any value. You can also define an allowed range of values for numeric parameters.
- **Default value** – The starting value that gets applied by default unless changed.

The next step is to create a calculated field that uses the parameter in its formula. Such dynamic calculated fields have many applications. Continuing with the Online sales dataset, let's say you want to determine the discount applied based on whether the customer is a new or a repeat customer. You also want to see how the sales amount varies at different values of discount percentage. To accomplish this, let's first create the **Max Discount Applied** parameter as shown in the following image. It is defined as a numeric data type that can take decimal numbers. An appropriate allowed range and default value are also provided:

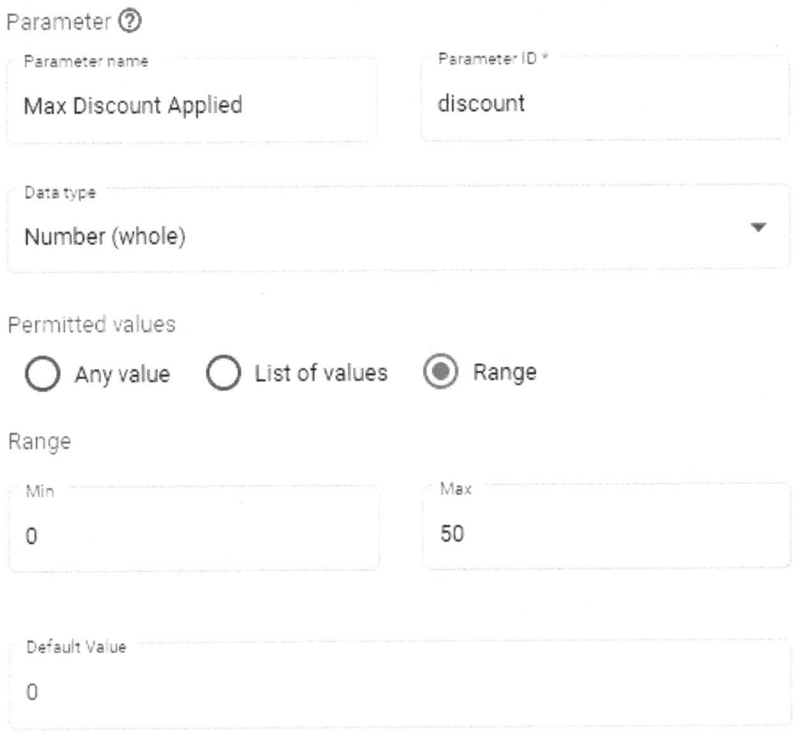

Parameter ⑦

Parameter name

Max Discount Applied

Parameter ID *

discount

Data type

Number (whole)   ▼

Permitted values

◯ Any value   ◯ List of values   ⦿ Range

Range

Min

0

Max

50

Default Value

0

Figure 7.9 – Creating and configuring a parameter

Parameters show up in purple in the data source. This **Max Discount Applied** parameter is then used in a **Discount Applied** calculated field as follows:

```
CASE RepeatPurchase
   WHEN 'Repeat Customer' THEN Max Discount Applied
   ELSE Max Discount Applied * 0.6
END
```

The **Discounted Sales** field is then calculated as the following:

```
Sales * (1 - Discount applied / 100)
```

As the report editor, you can set parameter values at the individual chart level, page level, or report level. Make sure the appropriate data source is set for the page or report to configure the associated parameters.

The parameter value can be changed from the default value to a different one for a particular chart by the report editor as part of the chart configuration. All the parameters of the data source are displayed at the bottom of the **SETUP** tab, where you can set specific values to apply to the chart as desired. The three charts in the following image display the **Discounted Sales** metric with the **Max Discount Applied** parameter configured as **50**, **10**, and **0** respectively:

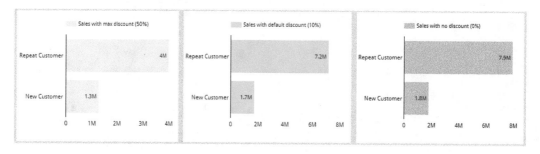

Figure 7.10 – Setting the parameter values in the report through chart configuration

You can allow report viewers to change the parameter values interactively using filter controls. In the following dashboard, a slider control is used to allow users to interactively set the discount value. Just choose the parameter as the control field:

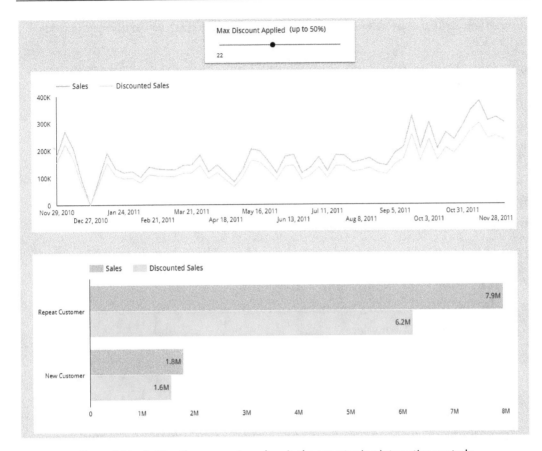

Figure 7.11 – Setting the parameter values in the report using interactive controls

One more example of using parameters with calculated fields is when calculating percentiles. Let's say, for example, you want to visualize sales at different percentiles such as the 50th (the median), 80th, or 90th in different charts. Instead of creating separate fields to calculate each percentile, you can leverage parameters using the following steps:

1. Create a parameter named **Percentile** and set it to a **Number (whole)** type. Provide a range of **1** to **99**. The default value is **50**.

2. Create a field named **Percentile Sales** with the following formula:

    ```
    PERCENTILE(Sales, Percentile)
    ```

3. For each chart displaying the **Percentile Sales** metric, configure the appropriate value for the **Percentile** parameter in the **SETUP** tab.

Note that if you desire to show different percentiles within the same chart, you must create individual fields for each.

Another application of using parameters in calculated fields is for allowing users to interactively choose the fields that make up one or more charts in the report. In the following example, the user can select the row dimension and the metric to be depicted in the pivot table.

Looker Studio offers a simpler way using the **Optional Metrics** feature, which enables report viewers to dynamically choose the metrics for a chart. However, this configuration is not available for all chart types and, of course, is limited to Metrics. And, as it is configured per individual chart, it requires the user to make the selection for one chart at a time. In contrast, the parametric approach is more generic and the selection can be applied to multiple charts at a time.

Two parameters used in this example are created as follows:

Dimension:

- **Parameter name**: Dimension
- **Data type**: Text
- **Permitted values**: List of values

  - Country

  - Product

  - Product Category

- **Default Value**: Country

Metric:

- **Parameter name**: Metric
- **Data type**: Text
- **Permitted values**: List of values

  - Sales

  - Sales with Discount

  - Quantity

- **Default Value**: Sales

You need to create two calculated fields corresponding to the two parameters defined:

- **Dimension**:

```
CASE Dimension
   WHEN 'Country' THEN Country
   WHEN 'Product' THEN Product
   WHEN 'Product Category' THEN Product Category
END
```

- **Metric**:

```
CASE Metric
   WHEN 'Sales' THEN SUM(Sales)
   WHEN 'Sales with Discount' THEN SUM(Sales with
Discount)
   WHEN 'Quantity' THEN SUM(Quantity)
END
```

Sales with Discount is calculated based on `OrderSize` and is defined with the formula:

```
CASE OrderSize
   WHEN 'Large Order' THEN Sales * (1 - Max Discount Applied /
100)
   WHEN 'Medium Order' THEN Sales * (1 - (0.7 * Max Discount
Applied) / 100)
   ELSE Sales * (1 - (0.5 * Max Discount Applied) / 100)
END
```

The following image shows the pivot table, the row dimension and the metric of which can be changed by report users dynamically using the parameter-driven controls:

| Dimension: Country | | | | Metric: Sales with Discount | | | | |

Dimension	Dec 2010	Jan 2011	Feb 2011	Mar 2011	Apr 2011	May 2011	Jun 2011	Jul 2011	Aug 2011
Australia	1,005	9,018	14,627	17,055	333	13,629	25,165	4,768	22,489
Austria	257	.	518	1,708	681	1,249	-24	1,192	1,516
Bahrain	206	-206	.	.	.	548	.	.	.
Belgium	1,810	1,154	2,161	3,334	1,954	2,727	4,273	2,474	3,536
Brazil	.	.	.	.	1,144	.	.	.	.
Canada	.	.	.	141	.	534	1,171	1,769	52
Channel Isla...	364	645	1,785	3,509	293	904	2,060	.	4,893
Cyprus	1,591	548	4,014	938	-36	.	1,109	.	.
Czech Republic	.	.	549	.	-58	.	.	.	.
Denmark	1,282	.	399	3,979	.	516	3,261	376	79
EIRE	9,030	21,657	9,674	18,783	7,570	17,921	20,060	42,741	12,157
European Co...	.	.	.	.	191	.	424	677	.
Finland	893	889	205	5,925	1,627	.	330	2,997	1,372
France	9,575	17,503	8,439	14,517	4,195	17,527	15,992	9,889	13,789
Germany	14,563	16,451	8,969	14,170	11,963	25,571	13,081	15,722	19,024
Greece		2,661	.	387	610	.		371	.

InvoiceDate (Year Month) / Metric

Figure 7.12 – Using parameters to dynamically choose the fields to visualize

Using parameters within calculated fields in this manner makes reports more interactive and dynamic. Next, you will see how parameters can be used to control the data that the report visualizes from the underlying dataset.

Parameters and connectors

When used with data source connectors, parameters are generally leveraged to retrieve the appropriate data from the underlying dataset based on the values passed. Looker Studio provides a set of official connectors that allows you to connect to data from sources such as SQL databases, Google Sheets, and Google Marketing Platform products. The BigQuery connector enables you to connect to data that is stored on BigQuery, Google's cloud data warehouse. You can build a custom connector to connect to any web-based data using AppScript. Connectors that are built this way by third parties and made available to all users of Looker Studio (some free and some paid) are called partner connectors. There are hundreds of such connectors available.

The BigQuery connector

BigQuery is Google's petabyte-scale, serverless data warehouse platform. It's easy to use and offers powerful capabilities to run analytics and turn data into insights. We will cover BigQuery in some detail in *Chapter 9, Mortgage Complaints Analysis*, which walks you through the dashboard building process and builds a data story based on the data sourced from BigQuery.

With BigQuery, you can define the data source by choosing a specific table or by providing a custom SQL query. As part of this SQL query, you can pass query parameters as substitutes for arbitrary expressions. Query parameters are commonly used in the WHERE clause of the SELECT statement. They cannot be used to pass values for identifiers, column names, or table names.

Looker Studio offers the following standard parameters, which you can enable to use in the query:

- **Date range start** with the SQL identifier as @DS_START_DATE

- **Date range end** with the SQL identifier as @DS_END_DATE

- **Viewer email address** with the SQL identifier as @DS_USER_EMAIL

The date range parameter values can be passed by report viewers using a date range control to fetch data for the desired time frame into the report. The following query uses the date range parameters to filter the *Ozone Daily Summary* table from the BigQuery public dataset, *EPA Historical Air Quality*. This data is provided by the United States **Environmental Protection Agency (EPA)** through its **Air Quality System (AQS)** database, which BigQuery makes available for the public to analyze using SQL:

```
SELECT
    state_name,
    county_name,
    date_local,
    MAX(first_max_value) AS first_max_value,
    AVG(arithmetic_mean) AS avg_value
FROM
    `bigquery-public-data.epa_historical_air_quality.o3_daily_
summary`
WHERE
    date_local BETWEEN PARSE_DATE('%Y-%m-%d', @DS_START_DATE)
    AND PARSE_DATE('%Y-%m-%d', @DS_END_DATE)
GROUP BY
    state_name,
    county_name,
    date_local;
```

Notice that the parameters are parsed as dates in the query. This is because, irrespective of the parameter data type, all parameter values are passed as strings in the SQL query. The appropriate conversion functions need to be used to handle different data types.

The email parameter is used to provide row-level access to the data. The viewer's email ID is captured in this parameter automatically, which is then used to filter the data in the SQL query. Users, when prompted, need to grant access and allow Looker Studio to pass their email addresses to the underlying dataset.

In addition to these standard parameters, you can also create custom parameters from the connection page to use in the query. For example, a custom parameter can be created as follows to be used in the query to filter the ozone quality data further on a minimum number of observations made per day:

- **Parameter name:** `Observation Count`
- **Data type:** `Number (whole)`
- **Permitted values:** `Range`
  - Min: `1`
  - Max: `17`
- **Default value:** `10`

The following screenshot shows the connection settings page for the BigQuery connector, which uses a custom query with parameters:

Figure 7.13 – Enabling standard parameters and creating custom
parameters in the BigQuery connection settings

The query used is as follows:

```
SELECT
    state_name,
    county_name,
    date_local,
    MAX(first_max_value) AS first_max_value,
    AVG(arithmetic_mean) AS avg_value
FROM
    `bigquery-public-data.epa_historical_air_quality.o3_daily_
summary`
WHERE
    date_local BETWEEN PARSE_DATE('%Y%m%d', @DS_START_DATE)
    AND PARSE_DATE('%Y%m%d', @DS_END_DATE)
    AND observation_count >= CAST(@observation_count AS INT64)
GROUP BY
    state_name,
    county_name,
    date_local;
```

When you create a custom parameter of a Text data type allowing a list of specific values, you will notice that there is an additional option called **Cardinality**. The cardinality configuration of the parameter determines the mode of selection in the corresponding control – that is, **Single-select** versus **Multi-select**. The following image shows the configuration of such a parameter and its use in the custom query. This example uses the *Air Quality Annual Summary* table, which includes pollutant measurements for various pollutants:

Figure 7.14 – Defining and using custom parameters with multi-select cardinality

The query used is as follows:

```
SELECT
    state_name,
    county_name,
    parameter_name,
    MAX(first_max_value) AS first_max_value,
    AVG(arithmetic_mean) AS avg_value
FROM
    `bigquery-public-data.epa_historical_air_quality.air_quality_
annual_summary`
WHERE
    year = 2021
    AND parameter_name IN UNNEST (@pollutant_name)
GROUP BY
    state_name,
    county_name,
    parameter_name;
```

Since the **Pollutant name** parameter is configured as multi-select and can hold multiple values, the SQL type is set as an array of strings. This requires that the UNNEST function be used in the query to extract the individual values of the parameter and allow comparison.

> **Cardinality of parameters**
>
> For parameters created within the data source and used in calculated fields, you can only set one value at a time to the parameter. There is no cardinality configuration for these parameters. Only the custom parameters created in the BigQuery connection settings have the option to hold multiple values at a time. It is possible to configure multi-select parameters while building a community, also known as a custom connector. Google provides developer resources for anyone to build custom connectors (`https://developers.google.com/lookerstudio/connector`). Partner connectors are just community connectors that meet certain requirements and have been published in the Looker Studio connector gallery. Hence, certain partner connectors may provide multi-select parameters as well.

You can hide these parameters in the data source editor page to prevent report editors from changing the values. By default, the parameters are visible and report editors can set their values for report components. They can be made available to report viewers using control fields.

Partner connectors

On the other hand, partner connectors provide certain connection parameters that can be configured by the data source owner or editor in **Connection Settings**. These parameters allow users to connect to their own data or specific datasets from the associated platform. For example, the Twitter Public Data connector by Supermetrics allows you to configure whether to query user data or tweets based on keywords and users. The Facebook Ads connector lets you select your ad accounts or choose a conversion window.

The developers of these connectors can make some of the parameters overridable. This means the values for such parameters can be modified in reports by the report editors and viewers. This allows report users to interactively query and visualize different datasets on demand. The data source editor can decide whether to make these overridable parameters available to the report users or not. Let's examine how to use parameters with partner connectors by walking through the Twitter Public Data connector example.

Select **Create | Data source** from the home page and search for the **Twitter Public Data** connector. Choose the one provided by Supermetrics. It's not a free connector but it offers a 14-day free trial. When using the connector for the first time, you begin by authorizing Looker Studio to use the connector by confirming the Google account used with Looker Studio. Then, you need to authorize the connector to connect to your data by clicking the corresponding **Authorize** button, as shown in the following image:

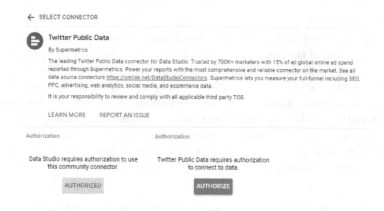

Figure 7.15 – Setting up the connector for the first time

You are then prompted to sign in to your Twitter account and authorize the connector app to access your account as follows:

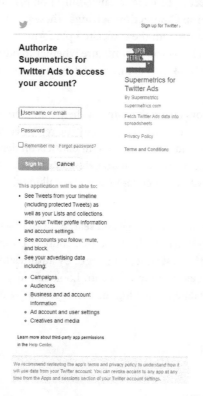

Figure 7.16 – Authorizing the connector to connect to your Twitter account

Once all the authorizations are completed, you can see the connection settings page with the licensing, Twitter account, and other pertinent information. If you are using a trial version, you may be asked to fill out a form with your contact details at this point before the connection options are displayed:

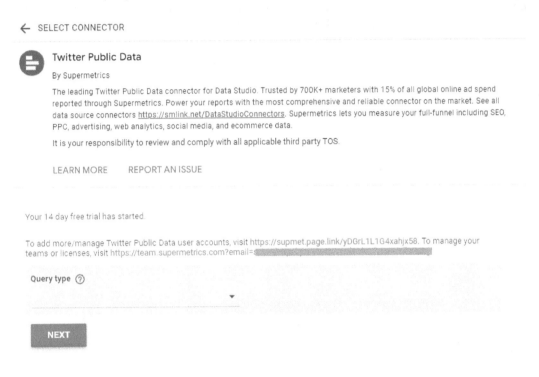

Figure 7.17 – Twitter Public Data connection options

Choose **Query type** before proceeding to the next options. This connector provides three query types that enable you to connect to different types of Twitter data:

- Twitter tweets by keyword
- Twitter user data
- Twitter user tweets

Depending on the query type chosen, the appropriate connection options are then displayed on the next screen as seen in the following image. Overridable parameters are those that have the **Allow to be modified in reports** option. When the corresponding checkboxes are selected, these parameters are available to report users to change their values interactively and request additional or different data. Click the **Connect** button and confirm the **Allow parameter sharing?** prompt to complete the creation of the data source:

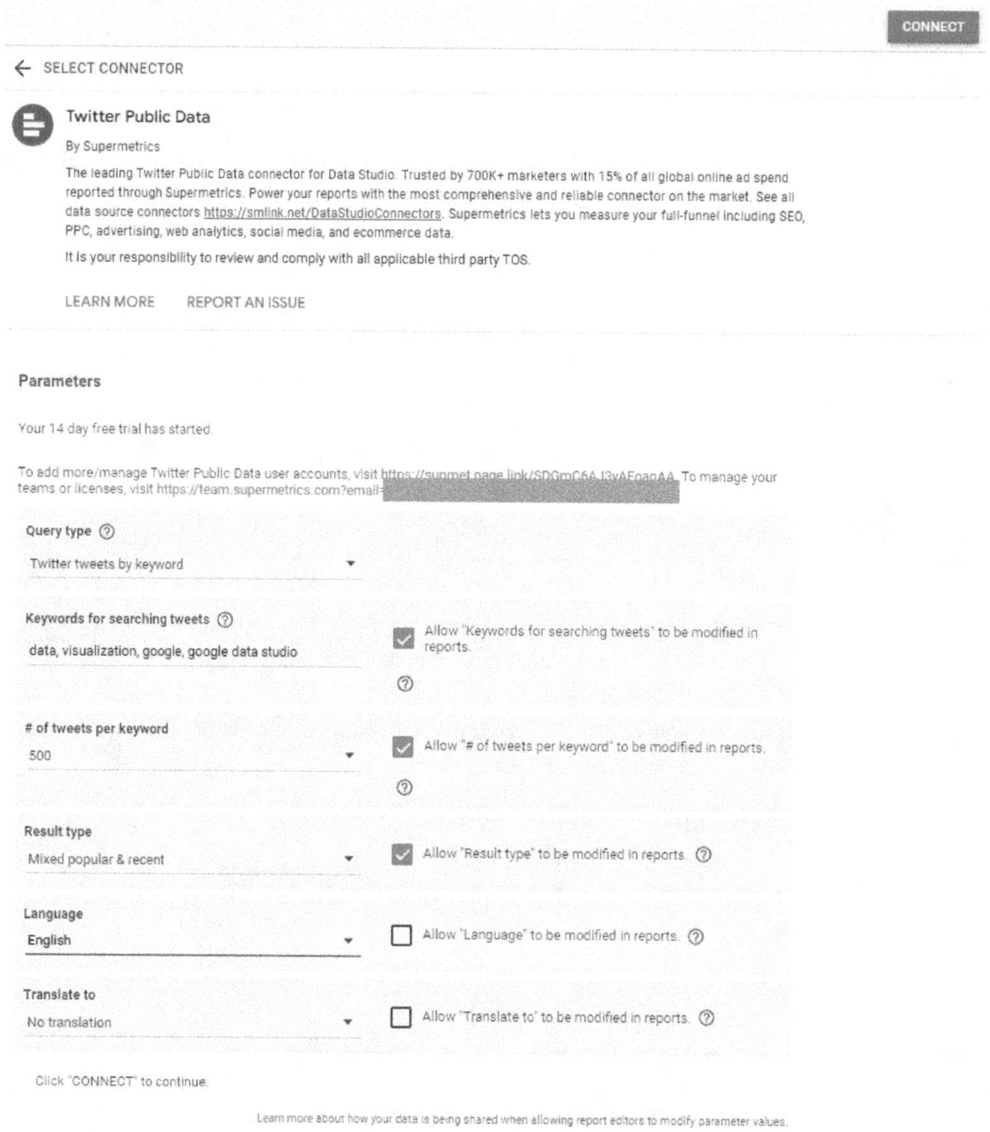

Figure 7.18 – Configuring the overridable parameters in the connection settings

You can toggle to show or hide any of these connector parameters from the data source editor page to prevent the report users from configuring these values from the report designer:

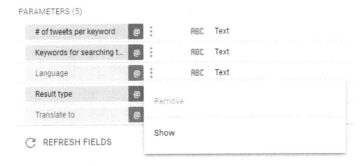

Figure 7.19 – Hiding/showing parameters from the data source editor page

Create a report using this data source and add controls for each of these parameters to allow users to interactively pull a higher or lower number of tweets based on different keywords and different types:

Tweet	Likes	Retweets ▾
1.	A ledger stone has been installed at the King George VI Memorial Chapel, following ...	103,012	8,781
2.	The period of Royal Mourning following the death of Her Majesty Queen Elizabeth ...	111,748	6,480
3.	Spare a thought for the new Trade Secretary Kemi Badenoch on board HMS Queen ...	16,313	2,619
4.	We are proud to unveil the first official coin portrait of King Charles III which has b...	11,764	1,757
5.	The official coin effigy of His Majesty The King has been revealed by the @RoyalMin...	13,790	1,439
6.	After 70 years of the cypher 'EIIR' for Queen Elizabeth II... King Charles' new cypher...	9,392	1,210
7.	I'm incandescent! 😡 Ruling there's no room in Trafalgar Square for a statue of as's ...	4,010	1,207
8.	Sadiq Khan rejects calls for statue of Queen Elizabeth to be placed on empty 4th pli...	3,146	816
9.	Glad to hear the Mayor of London made a U-turn and now "stands ready to suppor...	2,251	656
10.	The King's effigy has been created by sculptor Martin Jennings, and has been perso...	5,872	560

Keywords for searching tweets: Queen Elizabeth

# of tweets per keyword: 50

Result type: Popular

1 - 45 / 45 < >

Figure 7.20 – Setting values to connector parameters from the report

The preceding image depicts an example in which the three controls are used to fetch 50 popular trending tweets about Queen Elizabeth.

Blending data

Data blending is the process of combining data from multiple data sources. The resultant resource is called a **blend**. Blends are useful in two primary ways:

- To bring additional information into your visualizations and controls from disparate data sources
- To perform reaggregations, that is, aggregating an already aggregated metric such as calculating the average of averages or the maximum of distinct counts

Often, you may want to analyze data that resides in multiple underlying datasets together. While you can easily visualize this data in separate charts powered by the respective data sources in the report, the challenge is when you want to represent information from these different data sources together in a single component. Blends come to the rescue in such scenarios. Blends incorporate fields from constituent data sources, called tables, and can serve as a source for charts and controls. Through blending, Looker Studio makes it easy for you to combine data from different sources with a completely no-code approach.

Blends can only be created within a report and hence are embedded in it. There are three ways to create a blend:

- From the **SETUP** tab for a selected chart. Click **BLEND DATA** under the data source to join additional data sources.
- From the **Manage blends** page accessed from the **Resource** menu.
- Select multiple charts and click **Blend data** in the right-click menu.

The rest of this section explores how to create, manage, and use blends with some examples.

Blending disparate data sources

The Online Sales dataset contains the *Unit Price* data for various products. It would be interesting to look at the unit price for the products along with their unit cost to understand the profitability of various products. Since the unit cost information is available in a separate dataset, you can create a blend to visualize these different metrics together. The steps are as follows:

1. Add the two data sources to the report. Use the enriched *Online Sales* data source, which contains the `Product` calculated field, with the cleaned-up product names. Alternatively, add the *Online Sales* dataset using the File Upload connector and create the `Product` calculated field with the following formula:

    ```
    CONCAT(LEFT_TEXT(Description, 1),
    TRIM(LOWER(SUBSTR(Description, 2, LENGTH(Description) -
    1))))
    ```

    Add the *Product Info* dataset using the Google Sheets connector.

2. Build a bar chart using the **Product** and **UnitPrice** fields from the Online Sales data source. Select the method of aggregation for the metric as **MIN**. It displays the top 10 products with the highest unit price.

3. Keep the chart selected and click **BLEND DATA** in the **SETUP** tab:

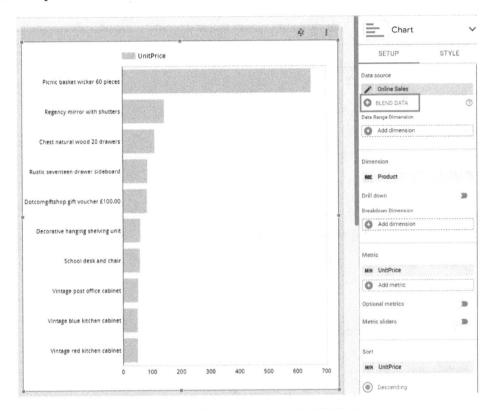

Figure 7.21 – Blending data from the SETUP tab

4. This opens up the **Blend data** pane with **Table 1** dimensions and metrics that have already been chosen based on the selected chart. Click **Join another table** and select the *Product Info* data source. So, each table in a blend is based on a data source and typically contains a subset of fields and metrics.

5. Set **Dimension** to **ProductName** and **Metric** to **UnitCost** for **Table 2**.

6. Click **Configure join** between the two tables. You can choose between the different types of join operators that determine how the matching rows are returned. The options include the full spectrum of possibilities:

    • **Left outer** join – returns all rows from the left table and only the matching rows from the right table

- **Right outer** join – returns all rows from the right table and only the matching rows from the left table

- **Inner** join – only returns the matching rows from both tables

- **Full outer** join – returns all rows from both the left and right tables irrespective of the match

- **Cross** join – no match happens in this type of join and returns every possible combination of rows from both tables

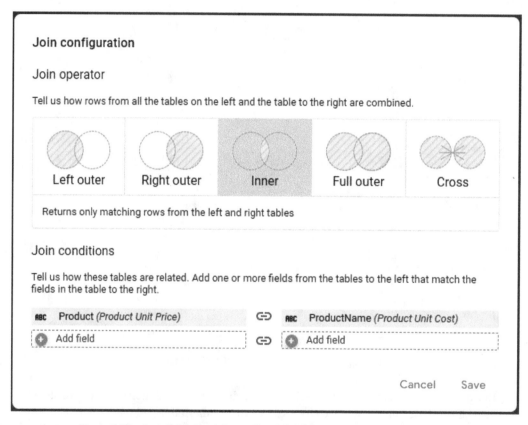

Figure 7.22 – Specifying the join configuration between two tables in a blend

Left outer is the default selection. Choose the **Inner** join for this example. You then need to specify the join conditions. You can match the tables on one or more fields. The multiple conditions are applied together with a logical AND operation. Blending only supports equality conditions at the time of writing. If your join logic needs are complex and cannot be met by blending, you need to combine the data appropriately outside Looker Studio or use custom SQL for supported data sources.

7.   Provide names to each of the tables and the blend itself as shown in the following image:

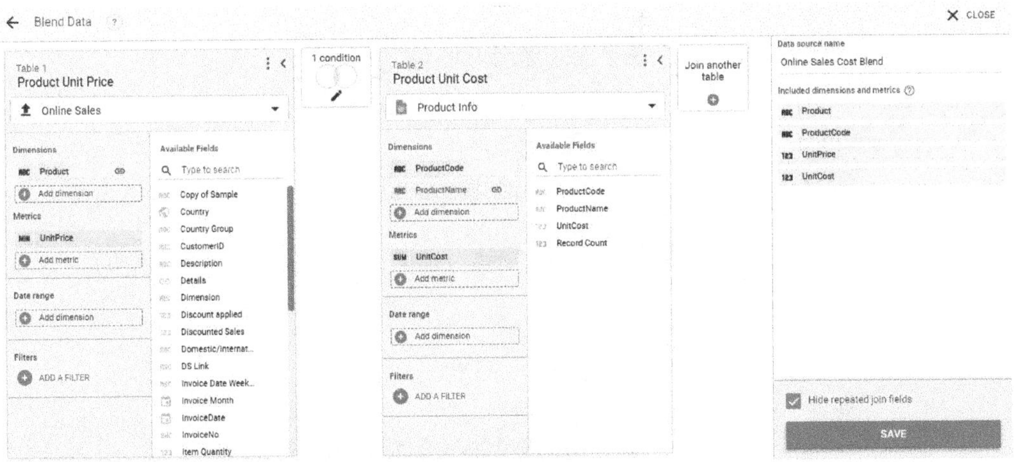

Figure 7.23 – Blending two data sources

Notice that the blended data source lists all fields, including the metrics from the constituent tables, as dimensions. These dimensions can be aggregated appropriately within the charts.

8.   Save the blend. The blend is now set as the data source for the chart. In this example, **UnitCost** is added as a metric to the chart automatically, as it's the only numeric field from the joined table in the blend. Add the desired fields and modify the chart configurations appropriately to visualize this combined information in a meaningful way. Refer to *Chapter 6, Looker Studio Built-in Charts,* for further details on the appropriate chart types in Looker Studio and how to configure them:

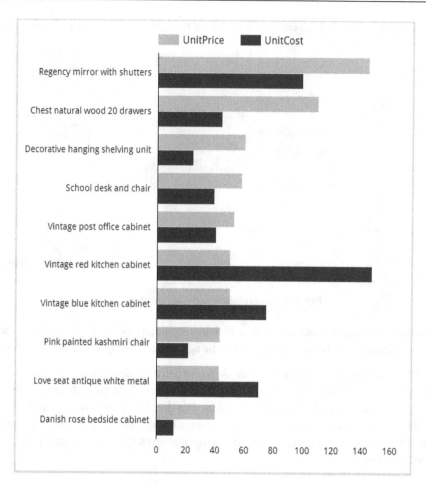

Figure 7.24 – A chart based on a blend depicting the metrics from two different underlying data sources

Once a blend is created, you can rename the tables or the blend itself, and add or remove fields from the blend by editing it. You can edit a blend by clicking on the pencil icon from the data source field in the **SETUP** tab or from the **Manage blends** page under the **Resource** menu.

It is not possible to create calculated fields within the blend itself. However, you can create chart-specific calculated fields using the fields from the blend. In the current example, to display the top products with the highest profit, you need to create a calculated field within the chart configuration as shown in the following image:

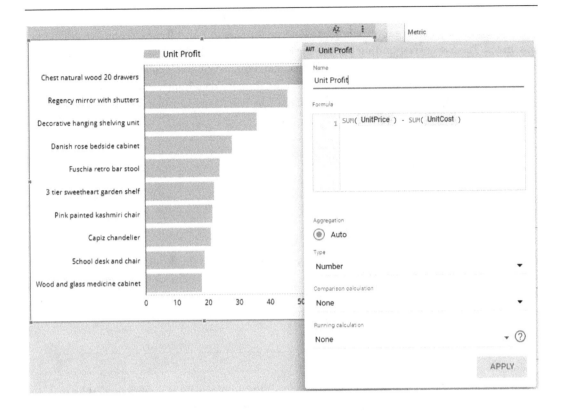

Figure 7.25 – Creating calculated fields when using a blend as the data source

At the time of writing, you can join up to five tables in a single blend. You can specify different configurations for each join, which means that all the tables need not be joined by the same set of fields or use the same join type. Joins are evaluated in the blend from left to right and you can join a table with any of the preceding tables on its left. The utmost care should be taken when specifying the correct join conditions and operators – otherwise, the blend can result in a large number of duplicate rows and can lead to a "too much data requested" error in the chart.

While the current limit of five tables per blend may be increased in the future, it does prevent us from abusing data blending. Blending is computationally intensive and can slow down your report considerably if overly used. As a best practice, limit the use of blending to a few individual charts and only with a handful of fields. Do not attempt to build blends to power an entire report with a large number of fields from all the constituent data sources. Perform any complex or large-scale operations outside Looker Studio in platforms such as databases and data warehouses. Also, Looker Studio currently allows you to choose only up to 10 dimensions and 20 metrics from each of the tables in the blend. This limitation also helps in not going too far with blending and easing the computational burden on Looker Studio.

The next example showcases a more complex blending use case that involves blending five different data sources. The five corresponding underlying datasets belong to the BigQuery public dataset – `epa_historical_air_quality` (in BigQuery parlance, a dataset is a collection of tables). This BigQuery dataset contains several tables that provide summary data hourly and daily for locations across the United States on various air pollutant levels. The following five tables are added as separate data sources for this example:

- `co_daily_summary`
- `no2_daily_summary`
- `o3_daily_summary`
- `pm25_frm_daily_summary`
- `so2_daily_summary`

These five tables provide the daily average measurements of carbon monoxide, nitrogen dioxide, ozone, fine particulate matter, and sulfur dioxide levels respectively. These tables are huge and contain the pollutant levels data for each day from the year 1990 to 2019 across different locations in the United States. Also, some of these pollutants are measured for different sample durations such as 1 hour, 8 hours, and so on.

> **Note**
>
> It is preferable to use a custom query with BigQuery to combine data from different tables or views into a single data source rather than resorting to blending within the report. However, a couple of scenarios where this may not be feasible include 1) when there is a lack of sufficient SQL skills and 2) when the underlying datasets reside in different locations and cannot be queried together.

For this example, let's visualize the median daily values for all five pollutants across different states in a single chart using data blending. Given the complexity and the large size of the datasets, care must be taken to configure blends with the right fields, filters, and join configurations. The steps are as follows:

1. Add the five pollutant BigQuery tables as separate data sources to the report.

2. Open **Report settings** from the **File** menu and set **Data source** to `co_daily_summary` (you could choose any of the five data sources). Set the **Default date range** to `Dec 1, 2019` to `Dec 31, 2019`. One month of data is sufficient for our purpose and setting this report property limits the amount of data queried from BigQuery for this report.

3. Select **Resource | Manage blends** from the menu and click **ADD A BLEND**.

4. Choose `co_daily_summary` as the data source (or whichever data source you set at the report level in *step 2*) for **Table 1**:

   A. Add **date_local**, **state_code**, **state_name** (rename it `State`), and **sample_duration** as the dimension fields.

   B. Add **first_max_value** as the metric, which represents the highest pollutant measurement value for the day. Rename it `co` and set the aggregation to **Median**. The underlying dataset is highly granular with data provided for different locations identified by latitude and longitude. In this table, we are computing the median pollutant level for each state across all its locations.

   C. Select **date_local** as the date range dimension. This applies the report level date range selection to this table.

   D. Add a filter for **Sample Duration** equal to **1 HOUR**. The `co_daily_summary` data source provides measurements for more than one sample duration. We need to choose one specific measurement type to accurately aggregate and analyze the data.

5. Click **Join another table** and select `no2_daily_summary` as the data source. Add **date_local** and **state_code** as the dimensions. Select **first_max_value** as the metric and rename it `no2`. Configure the join by selecting the **Inner** join operator and setting the join fields to **date_local** and **state_code**. There is no need to join **sample_duration** for this table because the `no2` data source only has measurements for one sample duration.

6. Add **Table 3** by joining `o3_daily_summary` to **Table 1** with a similar configuration as **Table 2**.

7. Add **Table 4** and **Table 5** using the `pm2.5` and `so2` data sources respectively. The join conditions for these tables should include **sample_duration** besides **date_local** and **state_code**. These tables are directly joined to **Table 1** as well.

8. Give the individual tables and the blend itself user-friendly names. The final blend configuration looks as follows:

Figure 7.26 – Blending the five BigQuery tables

9.   Add a table chart to the report canvas and choose the blend as the data source. Select **State** as the dimension and **co, no2, o3, pm25**, and **so2** as the metrics. Set the aggregation to **Average**. This calculates the average of the median pollutant level for each state for December 2019. You can configure the chart as needed:

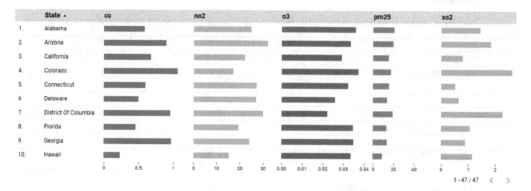

Figure 7.27 – A chart visualizing the data from five different data sources using blending

For the representation depicted in the preceding image, I've sorted the table by **State** and turned-on axis for all metrics.

Blending charts

You can also use the preceding blend to visualize the pollutant measurements for each date. However, if you would like to see the data at a higher granularity of date, such as by week, the current blend results in duplicate data, as shown in the following image:

	Week ▾	co	no2	o3	pm25	so2
1.	Dec 30, 2019…	0.46	17.21	0.03	14.58	1.04
2.	Dec 30, 2019…	0.37	13.96	0.03	10.05	0.79
3.	Dec 23, 2019…	0.44	15.52	0.03	14.45	0.84
4.	Dec 23, 2019…	0.53	17.32	0.03	18.79	0.86
5.	Dec 23, 2019…	0.56	20.75	0.03	19.12	1.01
6.	Dec 23, 2019…	0.57	21.3	0.03	20.25	1.09
7.	Dec 23, 2019…	0.69	19.9	0.03	20.26	1.12
8.	Dec 23, 2019…	0.74	22.71	0.03	19.99	1.42
9.	Dec 23, 2019…	0.84	26.81	0.03	21.72	1.69
10.	Dec 16, 2019…	0.75	21.72	0.03	22.59	1.56
11.	Dec 16, 2019…	0.74	23.32	0.03	23.08	1.53

1 - 31 / 31   < >

Figure 7.28 – Blends can result in duplicate data if not appropriately configured

This is because the tables are combined based on the date rather than the week. A different blend that is based on week needs to be created specifically for this purpose. At the time of this writing, you cannot change the granularity of the date fields in the tables of the blend directly. What you can do instead is build individual charts for each of the data sources with the following configuration and select **Blend data** from the right-click menu:

1. Add a table chart to the canvas.

2. Add **state_code**, **state_name** (needed only for the first chart), and **date_local** as the dimensions. Change the type of the **date_local** field to **ISO Year Week** and rename it Week.

3. Add **first_max_value** as the metric and set the aggregation to **MAX** (to get the maximum value of the measurement for the week). Rename the metric to the appropriate pollutant name.

4. Add a **Sample Duration** filter equal to **1 HOUR** for charts using the co, pm25, and so2 data sources.

The five table charts are shown in the following image:

	Week ▲	state_code	state_name	co
1.	Nov 25, 2019 ...	26	Michigan	0.7
2.	Nov 25, 2019 ...	36	New York	0.4
3.	Nov 25, 2019 ...	17	Illinois	0.54

1 - 100 / 312   ‹   ›

	Week ▲	state_code	no2
1.	Nov 25, 2019 ...	18	13.5
2.	Nov 25, 2019 ...	39	33
3.	Nov 25, 2019 ...	56	31.2

1 - 100 / 293   ‹   ›

	Week ▲	state_code	o3
1.	Nov 25, 2019...	50	0.04
2.	Nov 25, 2019...	26	0.04
3.	Nov 25, 2019...	80	0.04

1 - 100 / 318   ‹   ›

	Week ▲	state_code	pm25
1.	Nov 25, 2019 to De...	06	64.9
2.	Nov 25, 2019 to De...	25	36
3.	Nov 25, 2019 to De...	16	7

1 - 100 / 299   ‹   ›

	Week ▲	state_code	so2
1.	Nov 25, 2019 to De...	04	2
2.	Nov 25, 2019 to De...	50	0.8
3.	Nov 25, 2019 to De...	20	2.1

1 - 100 / 312   ‹   ›

Figure 7.29 – The individual charts to be blended

A blend is created automatically and a new table chart using the blend as the data source is added to the canvas:

	state_code	state_name	Week	co ▼	no2	o3	pm25	so2
1.	06	California	Dec 23, 2019	35	48.9	0.05	90.9	6.6
2.	72	Puerto Rico	Dec 9, 2019	6.3	26.1	0.03	null	2.2
3.	06	California	Dec 2, 2019	4.5	86	0.05	72	4.1
4.	48	Texas	Dec 9, 2019	4.2	53.2	0.06	108	129.6
5.	06	California	Dec 16, 2019	4.1	64.3	0.05	142	5.8
6.	48	Texas	Dec 23, 2019	3.79	56.5	0.06	100	95.6

1 - 100 / 312   ‹   ›

Figure 7.30 – The resultant blended chart

Edit the resultant blend to verify the join and other configurations. Tables are ordered in the order in which the charts are selected. The tables are joined using the default join operator, the **Left outer** join. Change the configurations as needed. Remove **state_code** from the blended chart. Change the chart type to a **Pivot** table with a heatmap and specify **Week** as the column dimension. Sort the columns by **Week**. The resultant visual looks as follows:

										Week / co / no2 / o3 / pm25 / so2	
			Nov 25, 2019							Dec 2, 2019	De...
state_name	co	no2	o3	pm25	so2	co	no2	o3	pm25	so2	
California	1.7	39.8	0.04	64.9	2.5	4.5	86	0.05	72	4.1	
Texas	1.51	47.1	0.04	61.3	11.6	2.3	65.1	0.06	146	93	
Colorado	2.49	65.1	0.05	30.5	8.1	2.77	84.4	0.05	48.9	9	
Arizona	2	43	0.05	48	2	2.9	43	0.04	141	126.5	
Puerto Rico	1.1	19.6	0.03	-	0.8	1.6	22	0.02	-	4.5	
Alaska	0.42	-	0.03	12	5.4	1.59	-	0.05	21	25.2	
Nevada	1.2	38	0.04	29.5	1	2.3	47.6	0.05	44.4	3	
Pennsylvania	0.9	31.1	0.04	38.1	3.2	1.38	37.4	0.04	79	30	
Rhode Island	0.79	-	0.04	14	0.6	1.49	33.7	0.04	20	1.2	
Michigan	0.7	21.1	0.04	23.7	42.5	1.2	37.8	0.04	51.8	32.1	
New Jersey	0.6	37.9	0.04	26.8	3.4	1.7	47.7	0.04	30.9	2.3	
Ohio	0.8	33	0.04	13.8	4	1.37	38	0.04	43.2	29	
Utah	0.7	48	0.04	21.5	9.4	1.7	53.9	0.04	66.7	16.2	
Maryland	0.34	18.3	0.03	25	1.5	1.24	40.2	0.04	70	3.5	
Oklahoma	0.33	6.9	0.04	4.5	4	1.7	47.3	0.06	91	47	

Figure 7.31 – Modifying the blended chart to visualize the data appropriately

When charts of different types are blended, the resultant chart type is usually based on the first individual chart selected. This is true when all the individual chart types are compatible with each other (for example, vertical and horizontal bar charts, or pie and donut charts). For incompatible chart types, the blended chart is created as a table by default.

When multiple charts are blended, the resulting blended chart typically includes all the fields from the blend. With the exception of only blending scorecards, all other blends simply add the additional metrics from the blend as appropriate. When two scorecard charts are blended, the resultant scorecard shows the ratio of two metrics from the individual charts based on two different data sources (*Online Sales* and *Product Info*) as the metric, as shown in the following figure:

Figure 7.32 – Blending scorecards

By default, the resultant scorecard displays the metric as a percentage. For this example, the type is changed to **Number** and the format is updated to display compact numbers. This is an easy way to display KPIs without having to create blends and calculated fields manually.

Note that these types of blends can also be created from the charts using the same data source. However, it is always preferable to create the required calculated field directly within the data source when possible and use blends only when absolutely necessary.

Next, you will learn about another common scenario where blends are useful.

Reaggregating metrics using blending

You can see how we aggregated an already aggregated value in the preceding example – we calculated the average of the median pollutant levels. This is a powerful application of data blending. In a blend, the individual tables are created first and then combined based on the join configurations. You perform the first level of aggregation within the table. The resulting blend fields are all non-aggregated dimensional fields, which can then be aggregated as desired in the charts.

If you want to reaggregate a field within a data source, create a blend with itself. For example, you can find the maximum weekly sales of each country as follows. Use the *Online Sales* dataset for this example:

1. Add a table chart to the report with **Country** and **InvoiceDate** as the dimensions. Change the format of the **InvoiceDate** field to **ISO Year Week**. Add **Sales** as the metric.

2. Click **BLEND DATA** in the **SETUP** tab. Add the same data source as **Table 2** with only **Country** selected as a dimension. Specify the join condition on the **Country** field and save the blend:

Figure 7.33 – Blending a data source with itself allows the reaggregation of data

3.   In the chart, remove the **InvoiceDate** field and change the aggregation of the **Sales** metric to **MAX**. Update the display name to Max Weekly Sales. The chart now displays the maximum weekly sales for each country. The resulting chart and its configuration look as follows. You can change the chart to a different type as desired:

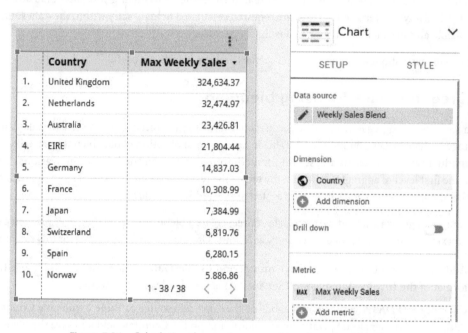

Figure 7.34 – Calculating the maximum weekly sales using blending

Blending is a powerful capability that allows you to visualize data from multiple data sources together and implement reaggregation. Beware of the pitfalls though, as blends can lead to slower reports and data inaccuracies. Effective blending involves choosing the right join conditions and a limited number of fields from the original data sources.

Adding community visualizations

Community visualizations are custom visualizations developed by third-party developers and partners. They are available from the Looker Studio Report Gallery, as well as in the report designer. To display data using community visualizations in a report, they need to be allowed access to the associated data source(s). This option is enabled by default for any data source that uses **Owner's credentials**. It can be turned off from the data source editor page. Community visualizations cannot be used with data sources that use **Viewer's credentials**.

From the toolbar, select the **Community visualizations and components** icon. You can choose from the featured visualizations or click on **+ Explore more** to select from the full collection in the gallery:

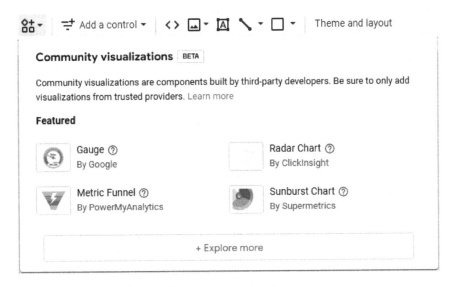

Figure 7.35 – Adding community visualizations to the report

You are then prompted to grant consent for the report to display the data in the visualization. When consent is not provided, the visualization is not rendered. You can configure the community visualization chart using the **DATA** and **STYLE** tabs just as with the built-in charts. Any community visualization types added to the report are marked as **Added report resources**. You can view the number of instances of each added visualization type in the **Manage visualization resources** page reached from the toolbar icon, as well as from the **Resource | Manage community visualizations** menu:

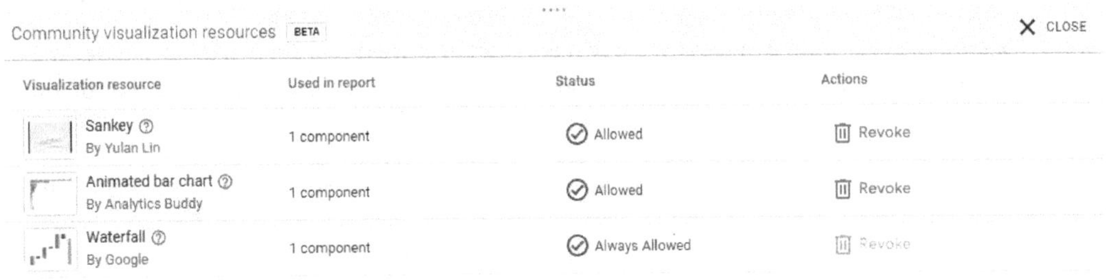

Visualization resource	Used in report	Status	Actions
Sankey ⑦ By Yulan Lin	1 component	⊘ Allowed	🗑 Revoke
Animated bar chart ⑦ By Analytics Buddy	1 component	⊘ Allowed	🗑 Revoke
Waterfall ⑦ By Google	1 component	⊘ Always Allowed	🗑 Revoke

Community visualization resources BETA   ✕ CLOSE

Figure 7.36 – Managing community visualization resources

You can also revoke consent to any visualization resources from this page. If any report components are based on this resource, revoking consent will break those components.

Community visualizations enable you to leverage new and different visual representations beyond the built-in chart types available, as well as implement custom functionality. You can also build your own custom visualizations using the Google developer resources (`https://developers.google.com/lookerstudio/visualization`) and use these visualizations in your reports. You can choose to publish your community visualization to Looker Studio Gallery and make a submission to Google for review. This allows you to share your creation with the wider Looker Studio community.

A key concern for many using community visualizations is how secure they are. While the visualization needs access to your data to render it, all community visualizations are subject to a **content security policy (CSP)** that restricts these visualizations from talking to any external resources. This mitigates the risk of a community visualization sending data to an external server. Moreover, the review process mandates third parties to link to their own terms of service and privacy policies from the visualization. Review these carefully before using any published partner community visualizations.

At the time of writing, even the unpublished visualizations that you have developed yourself are enforced by the CSP and cannot make requests for external resources. Some community visualizations may be built and provided by Google using the same process as other community visualizations. These are directly covered by Looker Studio's terms of service and privacy policy. They also do not need explicit user consent to render the data. In the preceding figure, you can see that the **Waterfall** visualization resource built by Google is **Always Allowed**.

Creating report templates

Report templates allow you to share your reports widely, outside your organization, and with the public. Templates allow others to use your reports with their own data. In *Chapter 4, Google Looker Studio Overview*, you learned about what report templates are, where to find them, and how to create reports from a template. In this section, you will learn how to create and share a report template.

Template creation is a very simple process and any report can be turned into a template just by adding `/preview` to the end of its URL. However, there are a few things that need to be kept in mind and followed through to ensure its wider utility.

First and foremost, templates should be based on standard schema data sources or connectors. This makes sure that others will be able to use their own data with the template and create reports from it as needed. Templates made out of non-standard and custom data sources have limited use, if any. You can either share your templates with specific users and groups or publicly with anyone.

The steps to create a report template are as follows:

1. Create and design a Looker Studio report using a data source with a standard schema. Make sure this is a schema that your intended target users can access. You can use connectors with fixed schemas such as Google Ads, Google Analytics, Facebook Ads, and Salesforce, or standard open datasets. Do not use your own personal or confidential data to build the report. Make sure only sample data sources or publicly available data are used. If you would like to use an existing report to create a template, make a copy of the report and replace the data sources with sample data.

2. Use **Owner's Credentials** for the data sources used in the report.

3. Name the report appropriately (for example, `Sales Performance Analysis Template`).

4. Enable **Link sharing** by selecting the **Anyone with the link can view** option from the report sharing settings.

5. Add `/preview` to the end of the report URL and share this link with others.

6. You can also submit your template to the Looker Studio Report Gallery (`https://lookerstudio.google.com/gallery`). Google periodically reviews all these submissions and publishes a handful of them to the gallery.

So far in this chapter, we have explored various advanced features, their applications, and how to use them. We have seen how calculated fields, parameters, and data blending capabilities help build more powerful and useful reports. We have looked at community visualizations and how they provide additional chart types and enhanced functionality. We have also learned about how to create report templates that enable us to share our reports widely. Next up is the final major topic in this chapter, which talks about ways to optimize Looker Studio report performance.

Optimizing reports for performance

Fast report load times and responsiveness are paramount for a good user experience in any visualization tool. Certain design and implementation choices may adversely impact report efficiency. In this section, you will learn about several techniques that will help you optimize Looker Studio reports performance-wise. Some of the considerations here may only be relevant when dealing with truly large volumes of data.

Optimizing data sources

A major reason for lag in Looker Studio is the volume or size of the data being queried. Hence, the first place you can look to for improving the performance of your reports is the data sources.

Modeling the data source

Data sources in Looker Studio are logical constructs and do not pull data from underlying datasets unless this is requested from reports and explorations. Typically, date ranges and other filters defined at the report level determine the maximum volume of data the report can retrieve and visualize – for example, filtering the report on a specific product to analyze the corresponding sales performance, or setting the default date range of the report to the past 6 months of sales transactions.

However, report editors can override report filters at the individual page or component level by disabling filter inheritance. Whenever possible, it's a good practice to limit data at the data source level itself to ensure report queries will not retrieve large result sets inadvertently. Not all connectors have this provision though.

Some connectors allow you to limit the number of rows for a data source through parameters. Earlier in this chapter, you may have seen that the Twitter Public Data connector provides a parameter – **# tweets per keyword** – to limit the data that you can connect to. Not allowing this parameter to be overridden in the report ensures that more data cannot be retrieved. For SQL-based datasets, you can use the **Custom SQL Query** option with a WHERE clause to filter the data as needed by date or other attributes.

Aggregating the data appropriately either using a custom SQL query in the connector settings or in the underlying platform itself also helps optimize the data source by limiting the dataset size. For example, if your analysis is only based on weekly or higher date granularity, there is no need to connect to data that is at a daily or hourly granularity.

The number of fields in the data source does not typically affect the report performance, owing to the logical nature of the data source. However, defining data sources with only the fields that are required and used in the reports has its benefits. First of all, a smaller data source is more manageable, easier to work with, and reduces overhead. When the underlying dataset is SQL-based, such as databases (MySQL or Postgres) and data warehouses (BigQuery or RedShift), you can use a custom SQL query to select only the fields that are needed. While connecting to data in Google Sheets, you can choose a range instead of the entire worksheet. The range has to be continuous though. Equally, depending on the connector, there may be certain connection properties that will help you choose a limited number of fields from the underlying datasets.

Secondly, the ability of the underlying data platform to efficiently query a handful of fields from a very wide dataset can affect report performance. Data warehouse systems that use column-oriented storage can query datasets with hundreds of fields and retrieve one or a few columns very efficiently compared to database platforms that use row-oriented storage. Other kinds of platforms may have their own quirks. So, designing the dataset with an appropriate number of fields becomes key for certain data platforms.

Extracting a data source

There may be some situations when you are not able to limit the data (the fields and rows) in a data source as desired and therefore experience poor performance in the associated reports. This can include the following:

- The connector does not provide options to choose the fields or limit the rows
- No access to the underlying platform to create the dataset with the desired aggregation, fields, and filters

In such cases, you can leverage the **Extract data** capability to extract a subset of data from an existing data source. **Extract data** retrieves a copy of the data and creates a snapshot in Looker Studio. This provides higher performance benefits compared to an equivalent data source based on a live connection. It can be leveraged for any existing data source that is slow so that the associated reports and explorations can be made more responsive and faster to load.

The extracted data is created as a separate data source in Looker Studio and can be used with reports and explorations just as with regular data sources. The following are the steps to create and use extracted data:

1. Select **Create | Data source** from the home page or **Add data** from within a report.
2. Choose **Extract Data** from the connectors list.
3. Select the data source from which to extract the data. When creating the extracted data source from the home page as a reusable data source, only other reusable data sources are available to choose from. Equally, when extracting data from within a report, the extracted data source is created as an embedded data source and it can only be based on the data sources added to the report. You can add any available reusable data source to the report on this screen and use it for extraction as well:

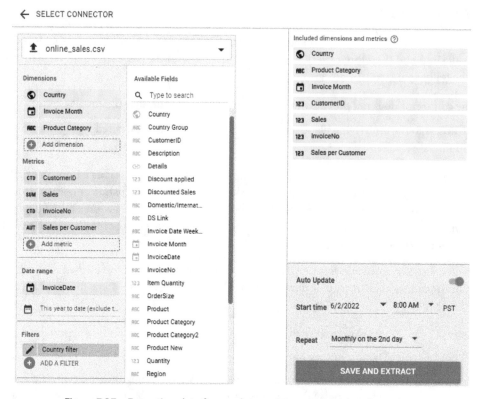

Figure 7.37 – Extracting data from a data source to improve performance

4.   Choose the fields to extract as dimensions and metrics, add filters, and set the date range as needed for your purpose. Selecting only a handful of fields from the chosen data source creates an aggregated result set. It can be customized and reduced in size further by defining the filters and the date range. You cannot create calculated fields here. Create them in the base data source if you want to aggregate them on a derived field. For any calculations needed for reporting based on the extracted data, create them within the extracted data source itself.

5.   The extracted data source creates a snapshot of data and is not updated by default. You need to explicitly enable **Auto Update** and set a schedule to refresh it regularly.

6.   Click **SAVE AND EXTRACT** to create the extracted data source.

7.   You can now create new reports and explorations using this data source. You can also replace the corresponding live-connection-based data source with the extracted one in existing reports to speed them up.

Extracted data sources can only contain up to 100 MB of data. So, they cannot be used for reporting on really large datasets. Extracting data for specific reporting needs rather than serving a wide range of use cases is a good approach.

Setting the optimal data freshness frequency

Each chart and control in a Looker Studio report issues a separate query to the underlying dataset. Looker Studio stores the query result of each chart in its own cache. Any change in the filter selections or the date range for new values triggers new queries, for which data is retrieved directly from the dataset. Looker Studio remembers the previous queries for each report component and stores the result sets in the component cache.

Looker Studio also refreshes the data source periodically even if no queries are generated from the report to ensure the report reflects up-to-date data automatically. All data sources have a data freshness setting that determines how often the cache is refreshed by directly querying the underlying dataset at regular intervals. It could be every 15 minutes, every hour, 12 hours, or daily. The default refresh rate and the frequency options available depend on the data source connector type. Between the refresh intervals, data is fetched from the cache for all repetitive queries.

A data source refresh clears the cache and all the previous queries are forgotten. So, after each refresh interval, all the queries from the report components go directly to the dataset. If the underlying data is not updated frequently or the report does not need to reflect the most up-to-date data, you can choose a longer refresh interval for your data sources that suits your needs. For example, when the underlying dataset only gets updated twice a day, the corresponding Looker Studio data source need not be refreshed more than every 12 hours. Moreover, for a sales performance dashboard built using this data source, daily updates may suffice.

It is always faster to get data from the cache compared to querying the dataset directly. A Looker Studio report slows down considerably when a lot of queries are sent to the dataset. Setting the refresh interval as too frequent generates new queries for all the components too often. This can also sometimes overload the underlying platform and further degrade performance.

Performing data manipulation outside Looker Studio

Looker Studio allows you to transform your data and manipulate it via calculated fields and blending. You can create derived fields to create custom groupings of dimension values, perform arithmetic and mathematical operations, and manipulate text. However, it is not the best place to do any considerable data transformations due to the following reasons:

- Looker Studio is not built for robust data preparation
- Looker Studio has a limited breadth of data manipulation capabilities
- Performing any significant data preparation within Looker Studio slows down the reports

It's always preferable to transform and prepare data outside Looker Studio in Google Sheets or underlying databases, for example. Limit the number of calculated fields within a data source to a handful and keep them simple (as opposed to complex multi-level branching logic).

Use blending with caution. Data blending is also a form of data manipulation. Using blends heavily on a number of charts in a report affects the performance considerably. Keep the columns and tables in a blend to a minimum, and specific to one or a few charts and controls for the best experience.

Optimizing reports

There are a couple of things you can consider while designing and building the report to avoid slower load times and response times. You want to keep the report as light as possible, with fewer components and computations, to ensure the best performance. These aspects are described in detail in the following subsections.

Refraining from overloading the report

As the number of charts and controls within a report increases, the responsiveness and load times tend to suffer. This is because Looker Studio generates individual queries for each component.

Consider consolidating information into a small number of charts with clever design choices – for example, displaying multiple measures in a single bar or line chart rather than in separate charts when appropriate (this only works when the metrics are on the same or similar scale), or using tables or pivot tables to represent multiple dimensions and metrics together. Limiting the level of detail in a chart also helps, as the query returns a much smaller result set with fewer dimensions used. Also, use drill-through purposefully. Choosing the right chart type also impacts the performance in certain cases. For example, when you are interested in total metric values, use scorecards rather than time series or tables. Enabling chart cross-filtering for all charts also contributes to performance degradation, as each chart interaction can result in new queries for all the affected charts on the report page. Regulate cross-filtering by limiting the affected scope (for example, using groups), as well as only enabling this capability for a handful of charts, to support carefully planned user interaction flows.

A report with a lot of charts, especially when coupled with large datasets, makes the report interactions and thereby the user experience cumbersome and less than ideal. In such scenarios, organize your visualizations and controls into multiple pages that provide a logical grouping around different business questions or themes. This kind of report layout results in better report performance, besides making it easier for the users to consume all the information. You may also want to limit the number of pages in a report for better manageability. It's a best practice to keep each report lightweight and focused on a limited scope.

Using fewer calculated fields

Following the same theme of keeping a report lightweight, do not create too many calculated fields within the chart configurations. Both the number and complexity of calculated fields contribute to increased load times. Looker Studio tries to push down computations to the underlying dataset as much as possible. However, it cannot always be done, especially with platforms with limited or no processing capabilities.

Try to perform the majority of calculations in the underlying dataset itself and keep the derived fields in Looker Studio to a minimum. Examples of valid scenarios include data conversions that are not possible in the underlying platform, and ratios and rate calculations that are not cumulative and that change based on the granularity of the chart query.

A non-performance-related reason to limit calculations in Looker Studio concerns business logic and rules. It's almost always not a good idea to implement business logic in a reporting tool. This is because it limits accessibility and the consistent implementation of said logic across multiple visualization tools used in an organization. Key metric computations and business logic are better served by managing them in a more centralized backend system.

Underlying dataset performance

A key external factor that affects Looker Studio performance is the platform or system where the underlying dataset resides. Looker Studio connects to the underlying dataset through a live connection. This means that Looker Studio queries the underlying dataset to render visualizations and controls within a report or exploration. The performance of the underlying platform is a critical factor that impacts Looker Studio load times and responsiveness. Data platforms differ in their capability and efficiency when processing data and supporting analytical queries. Most do well for small datasets and simple queries.

When the data volume or query complexity increases, many suffer from low performance. For example, platforms such as Google Sheets have limited processing capabilities. Meanwhile, data warehouse systems such as BigQuery are purpose-built for large analytical use cases and can handle massive volumes of data (think terabytes and petabytes) and complex processing very efficiently. While relational databases such as MySQL can also provide great performance, they are not ideal for large-scale reporting use cases due to their physical architecture. However, with reasonable volumes (think 100s of megabytes to gigabytes) and an appropriate, logical data design, they serve analytical and reporting needs well.

In addition to the platform itself, the way the data is organized is also important,   as in, whether it is normalized into multiple underlying tables or denormalized into a single flat table, the latter being more performant for reporting use cases. Often, you will not have a choice about where your dataset is hosted or how it is designed. If you do, choose an appropriate platform and data model that can support your data volumes and analytical complexity.

You may also run into performance issues when a large number of users are interacting with the report at the same time. The generated individual queries from all these users can easily overload the underlying dataset platform if it cannot support such a workload. This invariably increases the query response times and leads to further degradation of the report performance.

BigQuery provides an in-memory analysis service called BI Engine that provides sub-second query response time and allows a high number of concurrent queries. This allows you to build faster, more responsive dashboards and explorations in Looker Studio without having to worry about scale or complexity.

Summary

In this chapter, you gained an understanding of several advanced concepts in Looker Studio. We explored the corresponding features and looked into some interesting ways to use them. Calculated fields enable you to enrich the data source and manipulate the data to meet your reporting and analytical needs. Parameters allow you to capture user input and use it to perform dynamic calculations, limit the data retrieved from the dataset, and even drive the content displayed in a visual.

Data blending helps you visualize data from multiple data sources together or perform reaggregations. You learned about how to use community chart types and create report templates easily. A report that loads quickly and responsively is important for a good user experience. In this chapter, you also learned about several factors that affect report performance and optimization strategies to address them. This concludes *Part 2* of the book, which described the many useful features and capabilities of this tool. From the next chapter onward, we will now go through a few examples of building dashboards step by step from start to finish using various datasets.

Part 3 – Building Data Stories with Looker Studio

Part 3 presents three end-to-end examples from various domains to illustrate how to build data stories with Looker Studio. Each chapter takes you through the data storytelling methodology from *Part 1* for a different use case and scenario. The final chapter discusses how to track and monitor Looker Studio report usage using Google Analytics.

This part comprises the following chapters:

- *Chapter 8, Employee Turnover Analysis*
- *Chapter 9, Mortgage Complaints Analysis*
- *Chapter 10, Customer Churn Analysis*
- *Chapter 11, Monitoring Looker Studio Report Usage*

8
Employee Turnover Analysis

In *Part 1, Data Storytelling Concepts*, you learned about the theory and principles of data storytelling. In *Part 2, Looker Studio Features and Capabilities*, you familiarized yourself with Looker Studio. This chapter is the first of *Part 3, Building Data Stories with Looker Studio*, which demonstrates how to apply what you've learned to build effective Looker Studio reports through a series of examples. This chapter will walk you through the process of building a detailed multi-page report for analyzing the employee turnover of a fictitious company. The report will highlight various factors affecting employee turnover in a particular year. We will be following **the 3-D approach to data storytelling** defined in *Chapter 1, Introduction to Data Storytelling*, to build the report: determine, design, and develop. First, you will understand the example scenario and the importance of analyzing employee turnover in a company. Then, you will build the report step by step while following the aforementioned three stages. You will determine the audience and objectives of the report and then design the relevant metrics, visualizations, and layout of the report at a high level. Finally, based on the report objectives and the high-level design, you will develop the report by configuring the charts and other components as needed.

In this chapter, we are going to cover the following topics:

- Describing the example scenario
- Building the report - Stage 1: Determine
- Building the report - Stage 2: Design
- Building the report - Stage 3: Develop

Technical requirements

To follow the implementation steps for building the example report in this chapter, you need to have a Google account so that you can create reports with Looker Studio. It is recommended that you use Chrome, Safari, or Firefox as your browser. Finally, make sure Looker Studio is supported in your country (https://support.google.com/looker-studio/answer/7657679?hl=en#zippy=%2Clist-of-unsupported-countries).

You can access the example report at `https://lookerstudio.google.com/reporting/c54a3754-0300-4661-9dd6-e3c46627adf9/preview`, which you can copy and make your own. The data source for the report can be viewed at `https://lookerstudio.google.com/datasources/6bbc47b8-fe1d-4a53-80f0-318d6c90525c`.

Describing the example scenario

Employee turnover refers to the number of employees who leave a company in a given period. Employees leave an organization either voluntarily through resignation or retirement or involuntarily through layoffs, firings, removal of their position, and so on. Employee turnover is sometimes interchangeably discussed with employee attrition or churn. However, these two phenomena are distinct in a key way. With turnover, the employer intends to replace the employees who left. On the other hand, attrition refers to a scenario where the employees who left will not be replaced by the company. In addition, attrition occurs only when employees leave voluntarily to retire, go to school, work for a new company, and so on. On the other hand, turnover encompasses both voluntary and involuntary loss of employees.

Employee turnover results in heavy costs. Hiring new talent and onboarding them effectively is expensive. Research by Allied HR shows that, on average, it takes up to 8 months for a new employee to be fully effective. The **Society for Human Resource Management (SHRM)** reports (`https://1rshrm.shrm.org/blog/2017/10/essential-elements-employee-retention`) that replacing an employee can cost the company an amount equivalent to 6 to 9 months' salary for the employee. Beyond these direct costs, high employee turnover results in low morale and decreases the overall productivity of the remaining employees. All of these can have a significant impact on the company's bottom line.

High employee turnover may indicate problems such as employee disengagement, mismanagement, poor onboarding, burnout, limited growth opportunities, lack of purpose, poor recognition, and more. Organizations must measure and benchmark employee turnover rates and understand the contributing factors and root causes so that appropriate measures can be taken to increase employee retention levels.

In this chapter, we are going to work with a custom dataset based on the fictional employee attrition dataset created by IBM data scientists. It provides a snapshot of employee data on various attributes related to job characteristics, work environment, employee demographics, and more and whether the employee is active or terminated. For this example, we can assume that the fictitious company belongs to the life sciences industry and that the dataset represents a snapshot as of the end of 2018. Based on these assumptions, we can identify the industry global employee turnover benchmark as 13.2% from the 2018 Workforce Trends Report by Radford.

This original dataset is available for public use through *Kaggle* and *data.world*. Kaggle is a machine learning and data science community, which allows the public to find and publish datasets, among other things. data.world is a cloud-native enterprise data catalog and it hosts the world's largest collaborative data community. Anyone can leverage these two communities by creating free accounts. For this example, I've enhanced the dataset with a few additional data points and also cleaned it up a little bit to serve the current purpose of reporting. I've hosted this dataset on *data.world* to walk you through the steps of creating a Looker Studio data source using the *data.world* community connector. You can access the dataset at `https://data.world/sireeshapulipat/employee-turnover-analysis`. You can find the dataset as a CSV file at `https://github.com/PacktPublishing/Data-Storytelling-with-Google-Data-Studio/blob/a31bf2de1ca10db433cf9d0ecb15c3cf4fa882d2/employee_turnover.csv`. You can use the File Upload connector to create the data source in Looker Studio using this CSV file.

The company's **Human Resources (HR)** department works toward the goals of increasing employee engagement and productivity and reducing undesirable attrition. Employee turnover analysis enables them to understand the reasons why employees leave the company and identify attrition risk factors. The HR department wants to understand the extent of employee turnover during the year and identify factors causing the employees to leave the company for various reasons. They want to look at relevant employee surveys, demographics, and job characteristics data to identify problem areas. The objective is to generate actionable insights that can help reduce the employee turnover rate in the future. To serve this purpose, the data story takes the form of a report with a detailed analysis of various attributes.

As a recap, the 3-D approach to data storytelling consists of three stages:

1. Determine
2. Design
3. Develop

Let's look at each of these stages in detail.

Building the report - Stage 1: Determine

The first stage of the data storytelling approach involves determining the business questions to answer, identifying the target audience, and finding and understanding the data needed to build the report.

The target audience of the report is primarily the HR leaders, who like to delve into the employee turnover patterns and how various employee and job attributes are associated with and influence voluntary attrition and involuntary turnover. The target audience primarily wants to understand the who, when, and why of the employee turnover phenomenon. The key business questions that the HR executives like to answer include the following:

- How do we compare against the industry benchmark?
- What are the cost and productivity implications of employee turnover?
- At what rate did we lose our star employees compared to others?
- When did employees leave the company regarding their association with the company?
- What are the top reasons for employees leaving the company voluntarily?

- What types of jobs, departments, and office locations suffer from the highest turnover?
- How do employee satisfaction and involvement levels impact the turnover rate?
- Which employee gender and age demographic group(s) are more susceptible to leaving the company voluntarily?
- How do job conditions such as overtime, work-life balance, commute distance, current manager, and so on affect employee attrition?

The available data includes 32 data points for all 1,470 employees, as follows:

Demographics	Job Characteristics		Work Conditions
Employee Number	Department	Distance From Home	Job Satisfaction
Age	Job Role	Overtime	Job Involvement
Gender	Job Level	Training Times Last Year	Environment Satisfaction
Marital Status	Location	Performance Rating	Relationship Satisfaction
Education	Business Travel	Percent Salary Hike	Work-Life Balance
Education Field	Stock Option Level	Years since Last Promotion	
Total Working Years	Status	Years in Current Role	
Number of Companies Worked	Turnover Type	Years with Current Manager	
	Turnover Reason	Years at Company	
	Monthly Income		

Table 8.1 – List of dataset fields

Data is not available on costs associated with employee turnover. Specific reasons for voluntarily leaving the job beyond resignation versus retirement are also not captured in the dataset. Hence, the report will not be able to address these aspects. Based on the business questions that the target audience wishes to be answered and inputs from the subject matter experts, a subset of the aforementioned attributes is chosen to be included in the report. Initial exploration of the data also suggested that some of the attributes are correlated with others, so they can be excluded as they do not provide any additional information. For example, **Years in Current Role** is highly correlated with **Years with Current Manager**, where the latter is deemed more useful to identify whether turnover indicates poor management. The following table lists the attributes that will be included in the report:

Demographics		Job Characteristics	Work Conditions
Age	Department	Distance from Home	Job Satisfaction
Gender	Job Role	Overtime	Job Involvement
Number of Companies Worked	Job Level	Training Times Last Year	Environment Satisfaction
	Location	Performance Rating	Relationship Satisfaction
	Department	Years since Last Promotion	Work-Life Balance
	Monthly Income	Years with Current Manager	
		Years at Company	

Table 8.2 – List of attributes to be analyzed in the report

Given the open-ended nature of the report's purpose, the report should allow the users to interact with the visualizations and enable meaningful comparisons.

In practice, as a report developer, you will be conducting a thorough requirements gathering process in the determine stage to identify precise comparisons, slices, filters, interactions, and more that the report needs to include. In some cases, the target users may also provide specific visualization requirements such as chart types, report navigation, and more. The current approach works out many of these details during the design stage based on an understanding of the target audience and their objectives. Best practices are applied while designing and developing the report and some of the details may be refined iteratively based on user feedback.

Building the report - Stage 2: Design

In the design stage, you identify and define the key metrics needed to perform the analysis. You choose the right visualization types to present the data effectively. Then, you design the layout of the report and determine key interactive elements that may be needed. The idea is not to flush out every single detail in this phase; instead, it is to create the overall narrative and identify key elements, making sure the high-level design meets the needs of target users. It also often happens that some of the design decisions made in this stage may have to be modified or adapted during development, to improve their overall effectiveness and visual appeal. The extent of changes usually depends on both the level of thoroughness of the design process, as well as unforeseen technical challenges that arise during development. It is in this phase that you may also look at the data more closely and identify any data preparation and cleansing needs.

> **Note**
>
> Looker Studio is not built for robust data manipulation, so it is recommended to prepare the data outside the tool. The underlying dataset platform can be leveraged for this purpose, if possible. For flat files, you can use applications such as Google Sheets for data manipulation.

In Looker Studio, the data source is the logical abstraction of the underlying dataset. You can enrich the data source by defining appropriate data types for the fields and adding new derived fields and metrics.

Defining the metrics

The following key metrics help analyze employee turnover in useful ways:

$$Turnover\ rate = \frac{No.\ of\ employees\ terminated\ (during\ the\ year)}{Average\ total\ number\ of\ employees\ (for\ the\ year)}$$

The average total number of employees (for the year) is calculated as the average of the number of employees at the beginning of the year and the number of employees at the end of the year:

$$Average\ total\ number\ of\ employees$$
$$= \frac{No.\ of\ employees\ at\ the\ beginning\ of\ the\ year + No.\ of\ employees\ at\ the\ end\ of\ the\ year}{2}$$

The overall turnover rate is the basic metric that needs to be measured and tracked against benchmarks and targets. Turnover can be either voluntary or involuntary and it helps to look at this metric for each type of turnover to identify patterns and determine the right strategies to address issues:

$$Voluntary\ Turnover\ rate = \frac{No.\ of\ employees\ who\ left\ the\ company\ voluntarily}{Average\ total\ number\ of\ employees}$$

$$Voluntary\ Turnover\ through\ resignation\ rate = \frac{No.\ of\ employees\ who\ resigned}{Average\ total\ number\ of\ employees}$$

$$Voluntary\ Turnover\ through\ retirement\ rate = \frac{No.\ of\ employees\ who\ retired}{Average\ total\ number\ of\ employees}$$

$$Involuntary\ Turnover\ through\ layoffs\ rate = \frac{No.\ of\ employees\ who\ were\ laid\ off}{Average\ total\ number\ of\ employees}$$

If the voluntary turnover rate through resignation is high, this usually means employees are leaving for better opportunities. Changes to recruiting, hiring, and career growth practices can be considered to address this. Similarly, if the turnover through retirement seems high, proper succession planning could be implemented in time. A high involuntary turnover rate may indicate poor hiring decisions:

$$Average\ length\ of\ employment\ (Avg.\ tenure)$$
$$= \frac{Total\ number\ of\ years\ at\ company\ for\ all\ employees}{Total\ number\ of\ employees}$$

Understanding the average length of employment for all employees, as well as for those who leave the company, enables HR professionals to plan for timely interventions to increase retention. The turnover of recently hired employees results in sunk costs as they leave before they become fully productive. A very high new hire turnover rate also affects the company's reputation. A better recruiting process is key to making sure the right people are sourced and hired. The onboarding experience also often plays a key role in new employees leaving the company:

$$New\ hire\ turnover\ rate = \frac{No.\ of\ employees\ who\ left\ the\ company\ within\ their\ first\ year}{Total\ number\ of\ employees\ who\ left}$$

A high turnover rate of low-performing employees, whether voluntarily or involuntarily, is a good sign. The costs usually outweigh the gains from these employees, so losing them is a benefit. Higher retention rates of low-performing employees may also impact others' morale and productivity adversely. However, you need to keep the overall proportion of low-performing employees low in the company:

$$Low - performing\ employees\ turnover\ rate$$
$$= \frac{No.\ of\ employees\ with\ the\ lowest\ performance\ rating\ who\ left\ the\ company}{Total\ number\ of\ employees\ who\ left}$$

On the other hand, you want the high-performing – that is, star – employees to stay with the company as long as possible and keep their turnover rate as low as possible:

$$Star\ employees\ turnover\ rate$$
$$= \frac{No.\ of\ employees\ with\ outstanding\ performance\ rating\ who\ left\ the\ company}{Total\ number\ of\ employees\ who\ left}$$

A composite employee satisfaction score can be calculated for each employee based on job satisfaction, environment satisfaction, and relationship satisfaction levels, as follows:

$$Composite\ employee\ satisfaction\ score$$
$$= \frac{Job\ satisfaction + Environment\ Satisfaction + Relationship\ satisfaction}{3}$$

This composite score offers simplicity by allowing you to balance the individual satisfaction scores and providing a single value to measure the employee turnover against overall employee satisfaction in the job and work environment.

Choosing the visualization types

The **Key Performance Indicators** (**KPIs**) can be depicted as single numbers. Scorecards serve this purpose well. To compare the turnover rate against the industry benchmark (and company target), a bullet chart is a fine choice. Gauges can also be used for actual versus target comparisons.

The report needs to present the turnover rate metric for various attributes and allow effective comparison and pattern identification. Except for monthly income, all the other attributes are categorical. Bar charts can be used to compare the turnover rate by job roles, departments, and even office locations. The office location cities can be represented on a geographical map. However, only three cities are spread across different continents in the dataset. Plotting those three data points on a world map, while feasible, may not provide any additional utility. A bar chart, on the other hand, can visualize this data more effectively. Another aspect to keep in mind is not to use too many chart types in a report just for variety's sake.

Dimensions such as **Years at Company, Years since Last Promotion, Job Satisfaction**, and others are ordinal. Hence, line charts can be leveraged to visualize those attributes. Combination charts with both bars and lines help depict multiple metrics along the same dimension effectively.

Donut (or pie) charts help show the proportion of turnover across categorial dimension values, especially those with only a few values. Examples include **Gender** and **Overtime** (whether or not an employee did overtime).

Considering the filters and their interactions

The report includes a detailed analysis of employee turnover while considering several attributes depicting patterns, comparisons, proportions, and more. This helps provide the maximum flexibility possible for users to interactively look at different cross-sections and slices of data. This can be achieved through cross-filtering, which allows users to understand the impact of different combinations of attribute values on turnover. With cross-filtering enabled for a chart, any user selections of data in the chart are applied as filters to all other charts on the report page.

Cross-filtering is more intuitive and offers greater flexibility in analyzing how specific dimensions and metrics affect each other than providing a bunch of explicit filter controls. Cross-filtering doesn't provide any visual cues for users to filter in particular ways as opposed to filter controls, so it is not intrusive. Interactive filter controls, however, are useful for filtering the components by attributes that are not visualized on the page. These can be added as needed based on how the report is organized.

As a good practice, filter controls and cross-filtering should be added minimally to the reports. They should ideally only allow the desired and useful analytical journeys to meet the purpose of the report and not attempt to provide every possible way of slicing the data. Offering too many pathways may distract the users and make the report less effective. Furthermore, a large number of filters overloads the report and affects its performance.

For our current report, which presents a detailed analysis, enabling cross-filtering makes sense, as the users need the greatest flexibility in interactively analyzing various factors that influence employee turnover. In Looker Studio, cross-filtering is configured at the visual level and is enabled by default.

Designing the layout

Given that the report needs to include a detailed analysis of a large number of attributes, it can span multiple pages. It is important to ensure the report doesn't look cluttered while at the same time providing a cohesive picture. The specific number of pages can be determined based on logically grouping the attributes either related to each other or providing interesting insights when they're analyzed together. So, the layout largely depends on the scope, level of detail, and logical flow of the analysis.

The current report's narrative can be organized into three pages:

- **Overview**: This depicts the overall key metrics and basic attributes such as department, job role, job level, location, and more
- **Job characteristics**: This depicts the turnover rate and its distribution across job attributes such as overtime, commute distance, years since last promotion, years with current manager, income, and more
- **Employee demographics & perceptions**: This depicts the metrics by key employee demographics such as gender and age group, as well as employee perceptions on satisfaction and work conditions

On each page, you can allow users to choose to visualize either overall or specific types of turnover – resignation, retirement, layoff (involuntary), and so on – dynamically. Interesting insights gleaned from the analysis can be called out on each page for the user's benefit.

The next step is to create a wireframe of the report that depicts how various visuals and report components can be arranged on the canvas. On the **Overview** page, the key metrics are displayed at the top and the turnover rate by department, job role, job level, tenure at the company, and office location are arranged at the bottom, as shown in the following diagram. The insights are also placed in a relatively prominent place to capture the user's attention:

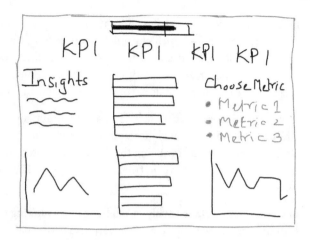

Figure 8.1 – Handdrawn sketch demonstrating the wireframe of the Overview page

The **Job characteristics** page presents a series of charts visualizing turnover metrics for the job attributes – overtime, commute distance, years with current manager, years since last promotion, income, and amount of training in the past year. The insights are placed at the top:

Figure 8.2 – Handdrawn sketch demonstrating the wireframe of the Job characteristics page

Likewise, the **Employee demographics & perceptions** page shows various charts that visualize the turnover metrics for employee demographics such as gender, age, and the total number of companies worked at, as well as employee perceptions of overall satisfaction, job involvement, and work-life balance:

Figure 8.3 – Handdrawn sketch demonstrating the wireframe of
the Employee demographics and perceptions page

The design decisions that are made during this phase inform and guide the development of the report, which is the final stage in the process.

Building the report - Stage 3: Develop

Beyond the high-level design considerations made in the previous stage, implementing the report involves deliberations on details such as report theme and styling configurations, additional user interactions, calculated fields needed, and so on.

Setting up the data source

First, we must connect to the dataset using the *data.world* community connector and create the data source. Follow these steps:

1. From the Looker Studio home page, select **Create | Data source**.

2. On the **Connectors** page, search for and select the *data.world* partner connector and rename the data source **Employee Turnover**.

3. If this is the first time you are using this connector, you need to authorize Looker Studio to use it:

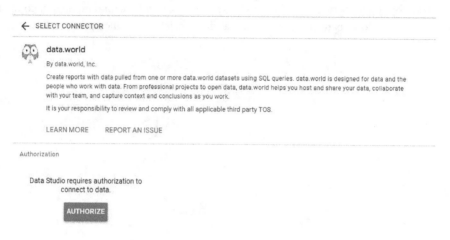

Figure 8.4 – Authorizing Looker Studio to use the partner connector

4. Clicking the **Authorize** button prompts you to allow the *data.world* connector to access your Google account (used with Looker Studio):

Figure 8.5 – Allow data.world connector to access your Google account

5. Then, you must authorize *data.world* to connect to the data:

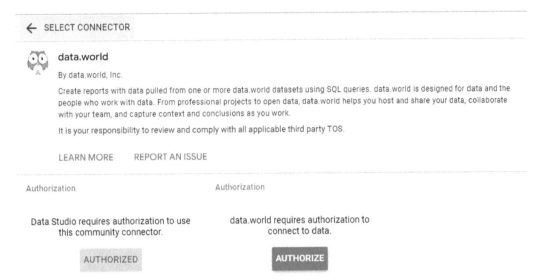

Figure 8.6 – Authorizing data.world

6. Sign in to *data.world*:

Figure 8.7 – Signing into data.world

7. Provide the dataset details as follows and click **CONNECT**:

    A. **Dataset or Project URL**: `https://data.world/sireeshapulipat/employee-turnover-analysis`

    B. **SQL Query**: `SELECT * FROM hr_employee_turnover_employeeturnover_tsv`:

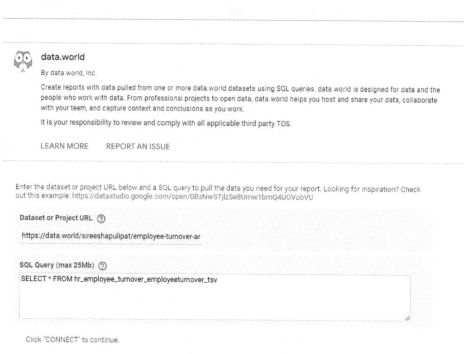

Figure 8.8 – Providing the dataset details

With that, the data source has been created.

Another way to add the *data.world* dataset to Looker Studio is by selecting **Open with Google Looker Studio** directly from the dataset page. This auto-populates the **Project URL** and **SQL Query** fields once the necessary authorization is in place:

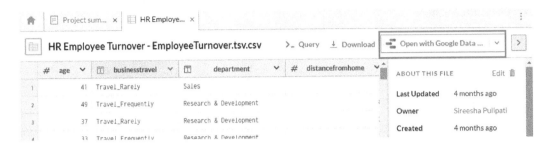

Figure 8.9 – Looker Studio integration in data.world

In the data source editor, review the list of fields, their data types, and default aggregation methods to make sure they are appropriate. Make the following edits to the fields:

- Change the data type for **monthlyincome** to **Currency (USD – US Dollar ($))**

- Update the default aggregation for **employeenumber** to **Count**

Some fields in the dataset contain numerical encoded values that correspond to actual text values, as per the mappings provided on the *data.world* project page at `https://data.world/sireeshapulipat/employee-turnover-analysis`. You must add new derived fields with the decoded values to the data source to facilitate user reporting, as follows:

- **Job involvement**:

```
CASE jobinvolvement
    WHEN 1 THEN 'Low'
    WHEN 2 THEN 'Medium'
    WHEN 3 THEN 'High'
    WHEN 4 THEN 'Very High'
END
```

- **Performance rating**:

```
CASE performancerating
    WHEN 1 THEN 'Low'
    WHEN 2 THEN 'Good'
    WHEN 3 THEN 'Excellent'
    WHEN 4 THEN 'Outstanding'
END
```

- **Work-life balance**:

```
CASE worklifebalance
  WHEN 1 THEN 'Bad'
  WHEN 2 THEN 'Good'
  WHEN 3 THEN 'Excellent'
  WHEN 4 THEN 'Outstanding'
END
```

Now, you must create a new composite employee satisfaction score based on individual scores of job satisfaction, environment satisfaction, and relationship satisfaction.

- **Composite satisfaction score**:

```
ROUND((jobsatisfaction + environmentsatisfaction +
relationshipsatisfaction) / 3, 0)
```

Now, you must map the scores to meaningful text values with an additional field.

- **Overall employee satisfaction**:

```
CASE Composite satisfaction score
  WHEN 1 THEN 'Low'
  WHEN 2 THEN 'Medium'
  WHEN 3 THEN 'High'
  WHEN 4 THEN 'Very High'
END
```

A common way to analyze age is by defining generations.

- **Generation**:

```
CASE
  WHEN age <= 25 THEN 'Gen Z'
  WHEN age <= 41 THEN 'Millennials'
  WHEN age <= 57 THEN 'Gen X'
  WHEN age <= 67 THEN 'Boomers II'
  WHEN age <= 76 THEN 'Boomers I'
  WHEN age <= 94 THEN 'Post War'
END
```

Generational analysis relies on the common formative events and experiences that shape each cohort while interpreting their attitudes and behaviors. The generational beliefs and behaviors may vary based on geography and are not truly global. For this reason, given that the current company has a global workforce, using a more generic age group categorization to define the cohorts of employees makes more sense. An added advantage to using age groups is that they are easier to interpret and understand compared to generational cohorts, which requires some mental processing and contextual knowledge of the users. Bucketing the age attribute allows you to analyze turnover by different age groups.

- **Age group**:

```
CASE
    WHEN age < 25 THEN '24 and under'
    WHEN age < 35 THEN '25-34'
    WHEN age < 45 THEN '35-44'
    WHEN age < 55 THEN '45-54'
    ELSE '55 and above'
END
```

Now, you must create the various turnover metric fields needed for use throughout the report. These formulas are based on the definitions we determined in stage 1. To calculate the average total number of employees in the year, we must create a dimension field that identifies whether an employee is a new hire or not.

- **Is new hire**:

```
CASE yearsatcompany
    WHEN 0 THEN 1
    ELSE 0
END)
```

- **Average number of employees**:

```
((COUNT(employeenumber) - IFNULL(SUM(Is new hire), 0)) +
COUNT(employeenumber)) / 2
```

Similar to the calculation of the **Average number of employees** metric, for calculating the turnover rate metric, we must compute the number of employees who left the company during the year as a separate field.

> **Note**
>
> Breaking down the components of a complex calculation into separate derived fields means easily interpretable and simpler formulas. It also allows reusability of the individual components and makes it easier to make changes to the logic when needed.

- **Is employee terminated**:

```
IF(status = 'Terminated', 1, 0)
```

- **Turnover rate**:

```
SUM(Is employee terminated)/ Average number of employees
```

- **Voluntary turnover rate**:

```
SUM(IF(turnovertype = 'Voluntary', 1, 0)) / Average number of
employees
```

- **Resignation turnover rate**:

```
SUM(IF(turnoverreason = 'Resignation', 1, 0)) / Average number
of employees
```

- **Retirement turnover rate**:

```
SUM(IF(turnoverreason = 'Retirement', 1, 0)) / Average number
of employees
```

- **Involuntary turnover rate**:

```
SUM(IF(turnovertype = 'Involuntary', 1, 0)) / Average number of
employees
```

- **New hire turnover rate**:

```
SUM(CASE
    WHEN Is new hire = 1
  AND Is employee terminated = 1 THEN 1 END) / SUM(Is employee
terminated)
```

- **Star employees terminated**:

```
SUM(IF(performancerating = 4,Is employee terminated, 0))
```

- **Star employees turnover rate**:

```
Star employees terminated / SUM(Is employee terminated)
```

- **Low-performing employees terminated**:

```
SUM(IF(performancerating = 1,Is employee terminated, 0))
```

- **Low-performing employees turnover rate**:

```
Low-performing employees terminated / SUM(Is employee
terminated)
```

- **Terminated average tenure**:

```
AVG(CASE
    WHEN status = 'Terminated' THEN yearsatcompany END)
```

Update the data type of all the "rate" metrics from **Number** to **Percent** in the data source. These are the basic calculated fields that you can create up front. Any additional fields that are needed during the report development can be added at that point.

Creating the report

From the data source page, select **CREATE REPORT** to create a new report and provide confirmation for adding the data to the report. Name the report **Employee Turnover Analysis**. Choose any desired report theme. I've chosen a custom theme generated from an image. In the **LAYOUT** tab of the **Theme and Layout** panel, choose the desired **navigation type**. I chose **Tab** navigation. Also, increase the height of the canvas to **1200** px to accommodate all the planned components on a page. These layout settings are shown in the following screenshot:

Figure 8.10 – Report layout settings

Build the pages using the wireframe that we sketched during the design phase as guidance. Prepare to adjust, modify, and fine-tune it as needed.

Page 1 – Overview

The first page of the report is the **Overview** page, which provides the list of key metrics and visualizes basic attributes. The finished page looks as follows. Let's go through the development process and design choices for each component on this page:

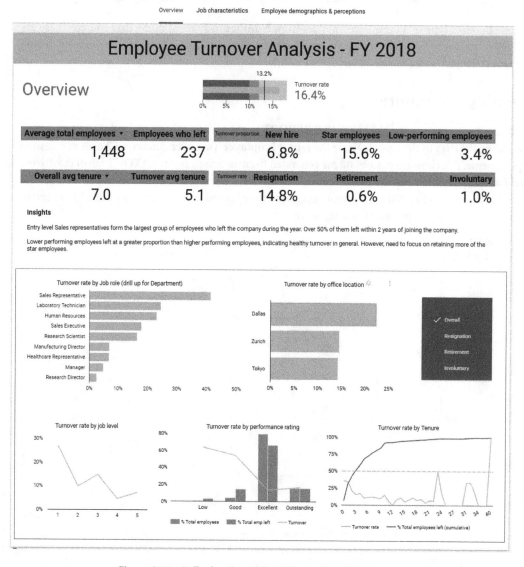

Figure 8.11 – Fully developed Overview page of the report

To show the overall turnover rate against the industry benchmark of 13.2%, you can use a combination of bullet charts and scorecards. A bullet chart enables you to visually compare the actual value, not only against the target but also against defined ranges. The goal of the company is to keep the employee turnover below 12%, which you can use as one of the ranges. The **Bullet** chart type in Looker Studio does not allow you to display the actual and target values. The actual employee turnover value can be shown by using a scorecard and placing it near the bullet chart. Similarly, you can use the **Text** control to display the target value. The bullet chart data configurations are as follows:

1. Set **Turnover rate** to **Metric**. **Turnover rate** is a calculated field that you created earlier in the data source.

2. For the **Range Limits** values set **0.1** for **Range 1**, **0.12** for **Range 2**, and **0.18** for **Range 3**.

3. Select **Show Target** and set **Target value** to **0.132**.

You can retain the default styling settings.

The scorecard is created by selecting the **Turnover rate** metric in the **SETUP** tab. In the **STYLE** tab, set the decimal precision to **1** and apply a conditional formatting rule to display the metric value in red font if it exceeds 12%. Under **Conditional formatting**, click **Add** and define the rule, as shown in the following screenshot:

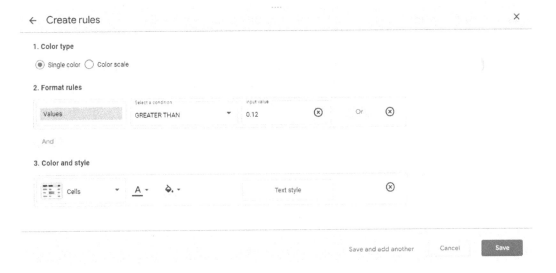

Figure 8.12 – Conditional formatting rule for the KPI scorecard

Show the other KPIs using four table charts, with each table presenting a set of related metrics. Tables are used instead of the obvious choice of scorecards to display these metrics, but only to achieve this specific look and feel. For each table, define the following configurations:

- The **SETUP** tab:

  - Add the desired metrics

  - Remove the default dimension that gets added to the table

- The **STYLE** tab:

  - Increase the font sizes for **Table Header** to **20px** and **Table Labels** to **36px**

  - Choose the appropriate color for the header background

  - Uncheck **Row numbers** and **Show pagination**

  - Set **Decimal precision** for each metric to **1**

  - Select **Do not show** for **Chart Header**

For the rest of the visuals, plot the turnover rate by job role, department, job level, performance rating, and length of employment, also known as tenure. The user can choose the type of turnover rate to view in these charts by selecting one from the list on the right. This can be achieved using parameters and calculated fields, as follows:

1. Click **ADD A PARAMETER** from the data source editor (or the **Available Fields** pane of the report designer) and create the **Turnover Type** parameter with four values, as shown in the following screenshot. Choose **Overall** as the default value:

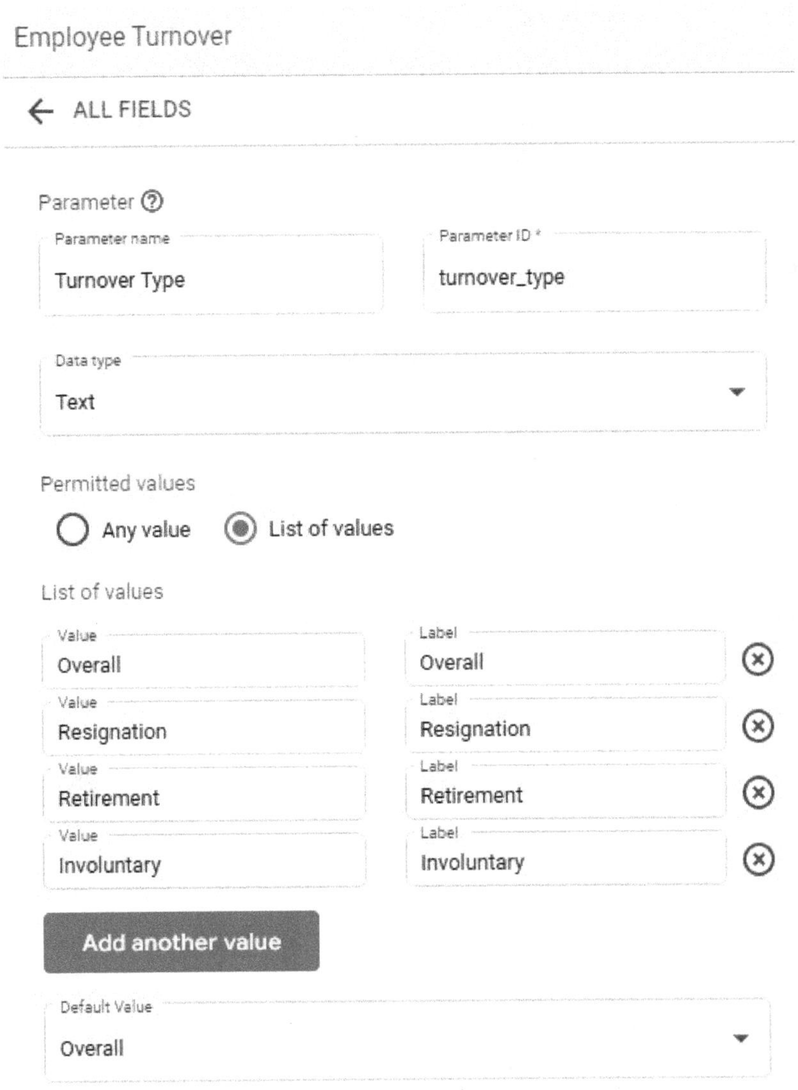

Employee Turnover

← ALL FIELDS

Parameter ⑦

Parameter name
Turnover Type

Parameter ID *
turnover_type

Data type
Text ▼

Permitted values

○ Any value   ◉ List of values

List of values

Value	Label	
Overall	Overall	⊗
Resignation	Resignation	⊗
Retirement	Retirement	⊗
Involuntary	Involuntary	⊗

Add another value

Default Value
Overall ▼

Figure 8.13 – Creating the Turnover Type parameter

2. Create a calculated field called **Turnover metric** in the data source by clicking **ADD A FIELD** and using the following formula:

```
CASE Turnover Type
    WHEN 'Resignation' THEN Resignation turnover rate
    WHEN 'Retirement' THEN Retirement turnover rate
    WHEN 'Involuntary' THEN Involuntary turnover rate
```

```
        WHEN 'Overall' THEN Turnover rate
    END
```

3. Add a fixed list control to the canvas and choose the **Turnover Type** parameter as the control field. Choose an appropriate background color and text color. For both the header background and text, choose the same color that you chose for the control background. This hides the header text.

4. The charts on the page, which are built using the new **Turnover metric** field, display the appropriate turnover metric based on the parameter selection.

You should visualize job roles, departments, and office locations using horizontal bar charts instead of vertical bar charts to allow the long attribute values to be displayed properly. Job roles and departments can be depicted within the same chart using the drill-down/up capability. The roles in each department are mutually exclusive except for the manager role, which exists in all three departments. So, it's not a strict hierarchy. You must choose **jobrole** as the default dimension to display as there are only nine roles in total; this provides a more useful view of the data. The following configurations must be made for this:

-   The **SETUP** tab:

    -   Choose **department** and **jobrole** as dimensions

    -   Enable **Drill down** and set **Default drill down level** to **jobrole**

    -   Add **Turnover metric** (which is driven by the parameter defined previously) as the metric field and rename it **Turnover rate**

    -   Sort the chart by **Turnover metric** in **Descending** order

-   The **STYLE** tab:

    -   Remove the gridlines by setting **Grid color** to **Transparent**

    -   Hide **Legend** by choosing **None**

Build the chart for presenting the turnover rate by office location in the same way, using **Turnover metric** and just a single dimension with no drilldown. Once you have configured the data settings, you can copy and paste the styling from the previous chart you built. To do this, first, copy the job role chart. Then, select the office location chart, right-click, and choose **Paste special | Paste style only**. This is a quicker way to apply the same styling to different charts.

You can visualize the job level as a line chart since it is an ordinal dimension. Similar to the previous charts, build this chart with the parameter-driven **Turnover metric** field. Make sure that you sort the chart by the job level instead of the metric.

To analyze turnover by employee performance, in addition to looking at the turnover rate, it is useful to compare the proportions of total employees and those who left for each performance group. For top-performing groups, it is desirable to have the proportion of employees who left much lower than the proportion of all employees. Losing a star or high-potential employee has greater financial and reputational impacts than losing a non-star employee. You can use a combination chart to present this analysis. The following configurations must be made for this:

- The **SETUP** tab:

  - Add the calculated **Performance rating** field as the dimension.

  - Add **employeenumber** as a **metric** with **Count** or **Count Distinct** as the method of aggregation. Set **Comparison calculation** to **Percent of total**. Rename the field **% Total employees**.

  - The next metric is based on the number of employees who left. To compute this number based on the **Turnover Type** parameter selection, a new calculated field is needed. Create it in the data source (rather than within the chart) as follows:

Is employee terminated – Turnover Type:

```
CASE Turnover Type
    WHEN 'Overall' THEN Is employee terminated
    WHEN 'Resignation' THEN Has employee resigned
    WHEN 'Retirement' THEN Has employee retired
    WHEN 'Involuntary' THEN Is employee laid off
END
```

Has employee resigned, **Has employee retired**, and **Is employee laid off** are derived fields that can be calculated as follows, respectively:

- `IF(turnoverreason = 'Resignation', 1, 0)`
- `IF(turnoverreason = 'Retirement', 1, 0)`
- `IF(turnoverreason = 'Layoff', 1, 0)`

Add this metric as the second metric field in the chart configuration with **Sum** as the method of aggregation. Set **Comparison calculation** to **Percent of total** and rename the field **% Total employees left**.

  - Add **Turnover metric** (a dynamic metric driven by the **Turnover Type** parameter) as the third metric field and rename it **Turnover rate**.

  - To sort the axis by performance rating, use the numerical **performancerating** field with **Average** as the method of aggregation. This ensures that the axis is sorted by the rating scores instead of the displayed textual values.

- The **STYLE** tab:

  - Select **Bars** for the first two series and **Line** for the third series. Choose appropriate colors for all the series.

  - Change the position of the legend to **Bottom**.

The final chart on this page is a line chart that represents the turnover rate by length of employment. A cumulative line is also added to depict the proportion of employees who left with each increasing year at the company. This shows that over 50% of the employees who left did so within 4 years of their tenure at the company. It's also interesting to see that over one-third of new hires left the company within their first year. The following configurations must be made for this:

- The **SETUP** tab:

  - Add **yearsatcompany** as the dimension.

  - Add the **Turnover metric** field as a metric and rename it **Turnover rate**. Immediately, you will notice that the turnover rate value for 0 years tenure is high at 73%. Inspecting the data and calculations reveals that **Average number of employees** with 0 years at the company returns 22, whereas 44 employees are hired during the year. In this case, you should consider all the new employees to accurately compute the turnover rate. Hence, the turnover rate's calculated metrics need to be modified as follows:

  - **Turnover rate:**

    ```
    SUM(Is employee terminated) /
    CASE
      WHEN SUM(yearsatcompany) = 0 THEN SUM(Is new hire)
      ELSE Average number of employees
    END
    ```

  - In all the calculated fields where **Average number of employees** is used as the denominator, replace it with the following:

    ```
    CASE
      WHEN SUM(yearsatcompany) = 0 THEN SUM(Is new hire)
      ELSE Average number of employees
    END
    ```

  - The following calculated fields need to be modified:

    - Turnover rate

    - Involuntary turnover rate

- Voluntary turnover rate

- Resignation turnover rate

- Retirement turnover rate

This change doesn't impact any other charts.

- Sort the chart by **yearsatcompany** in ascending order.

- The **STYLE** tab:

  - Set **Cumulative** to **Series #2**.

  - Add a reference line of the **Constant value** type and set the value to **0.5** to represent the 50% line. Choose an appropriate color and label text.

  - Change the position of the legend to **Bottom**.

Add a rectangle shape to the page to enclose the bottom charts. Send the rectangle back from the **Arrange** menu. This rectangle provides a visual cue to the users that the turnover type selected from the list applies to only these charts.

Add titles to all the charts using **Text** control. Also, add insights in a text box under the **KPIs** section. If needed, adjust the canvas size from the **Current Page Settings** panel's **STYLE** tab to make sure all the charts can be arranged properly with enough whitespace for an uncluttered look.

Page 2 – Job characteristics

The second page of the report includes an analysis of various job characteristics, including overtime, commute distance, years with the current manager, years since the last promotion, monthly income, and the amount of training in the past year:

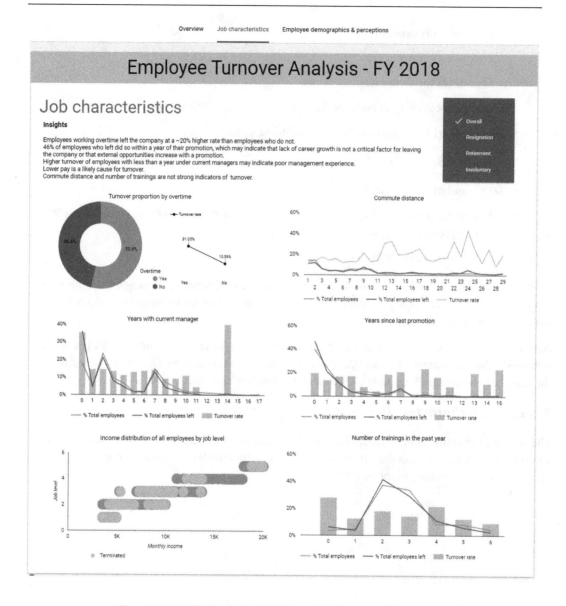

Figure 8.14 – Fully developed Job characteristics page of the report

The turnover metrics depicted in all the charts on this page are determined by the turnover type that the user selects. Copy the fixed control list from the previous page and paste it into the top right on the second page.

A donut chart is used to visualize the proportion of employees who left according to whether they did overtime or not. To create this chart, you need a new dynamic field that is driven by the **Turnover Type** parameter. Create the field as follows:

Is employee terminated – Turnover type:

```
CASE Turnover Type
    WHEN 'Overall' THEN Is employee terminated
    WHEN 'Resignation' THEN Has employee resigned
    WHEN 'Retirement' THEN Has employee retired
    WHEN 'Involuntary' THEN Is employee laid off
END
```

Choose this field as the metric for the donut chart. While this is useful information, the users may also need to look at the actual turnover rate for each category to understand the impact overtime has on turnover. A simple line chart can be used to represent the turnover rate. Since there are only two values, you must make it look like a slope graph by hiding the axes and other chart elements. Then, you must add category labels using text controls. The following configurations must be made for the **Overtime** line chart:

- The **SETUP** tab:

    - Add **overtime** as a **dimension** and **Turnover metric** as a **metric**. Rename the **Metric** field **Turnover rate**.

    - Sort by **overtime** in **Descending** order. This ensures that the order of categories does not change based on the metric value and that we can use static text labels for the categories.

- The **STYLE** tab:

    - Set the line color to black (so that it matches the text color).

    - Select **Show Points** and **Show data labels**.

    - Unselect **Show axes**. For **Y-Axis**, set **Axis Max** to **0.6** to reduce the slope of the line. This limit works with our data as the turnover rate doesn't exceed this value for any combination of attribute selections.

    - Hide the gridlines by making the color transparent. Keep the legend in the default **Top** position.

Commute distance, **Years with current manager**, **Years since last promotion**, and **Number of trainings in the past year** can be analyzed by visualizing three metrics:

- Turnover rate
- Percent total employees
- Percent total terminated employees

Comparing the percent total terminated employees against the percent total employees for different values of the attribute allows users to identify any significant differences in proportions that may indicate a problem area.

You can use combination charts to visualize **Years with current manager**, **Years since last promotion**, and **Number of trainings in the past year**. For **Commute distance**, use lines for all the series as it is not preferable to use bars for a large number of categories. These four charts use the same configurations, as follows:

- The **SETUP** tab:

  - Use the appropriate field as a **dimension** (**distancefromhome, yearswithcurrmanager, yearssincelastpromotion**, or **trainingtimeslastyear**).

  - Add the **employeenumber** field as a **metric**, set **Comparison calculation** to **Percent of total**, and rename it **%Total employees**.

  - Add **Is employee terminated – Turnover Type** as the second metric. Set **Comparison calculation** to **Percent of total** and rename it **% Total employees left**.

  - Add **Turnover metric** as the third metric and rename it **Turnover rate**.

  - Sort by the **Dimension** field in **Ascending** order.

- The **STYLE** tab:

  - Except for the commute distance chart, select **Bars** for **Series #3**, which represents **Turnover rate**.

  - Hide the gridlines and change the position of the legend to **Bottom**.

Since the monthly income is a continuous value, you must use a scatterplot to visualize it. Since income is correlated to the job level, it can be used as the second metric on the y axis. Each bubble represents an individual employee and the color of the bubble indicates which employees are no longer with the company. To identify only the employees who left by the user-selected turnover type, a new calculated field needs to be created, as follows:

Status – Turnover Type:

```
CASE Is employee terminated - Turnover type
  WHEN 1 THEN 'Terminated'
  ELSE ' '
END
```

The following configurations need to be made for the scatterplot:

- The **SETUP** tab:

  - Add **employeenumber** to the **Dimension** field.

  - Add the newly created **Status – Turnover Type** field as the second dimension.

  - Choose **monthlyincome** for **Metric X** and rename it **Monthly income**. Use **Sum** as the method of aggregation.

  - Choose **joblevel** for **Metric Y** and rename the field **Job level**. Use **Average** as the method of aggregation.

  - Choose **employeenumber** with **Count** aggregation for **Bubble Size Metric**. This returns the same value for each data point, so the bubble size doesn't vary. However, choosing a bubble size metric field enables you to adjust the bubble size in the **STYLE** tab. By doing so, you can make the bubble bigger or smaller.

- The **STYLE** tab:

  - Adjust the bubble size on the slider

  - Choose **Status – Turnover Type** for **Bubble Color** and select the appropriate colors

  - Select **Show axis title** for both axes

  - Set the position of the legend to **Bottom**

> **Note**
> In the chart legend, I've hidden the bubble associated with the empty value by overlaying a circle shape with a white background (so that it matches the chart's background) on top of it.

Add appropriate titles for the charts using **Text** controls. Also, add the identified key insights at the top.

Page 3 – Employee demographics & perceptions

The final page of the report provides information on how turnover may be affected by employee age, gender, and the total number of companies that employees worked for in their careers. It also visualizes the turnover rate by employee perceptions of work-life balance, job involvement, and overall work satisfaction. Similar to the other pages, the users can select the type of turnover metric to look at on this page as well by selecting the parameter value from the fixed list control:

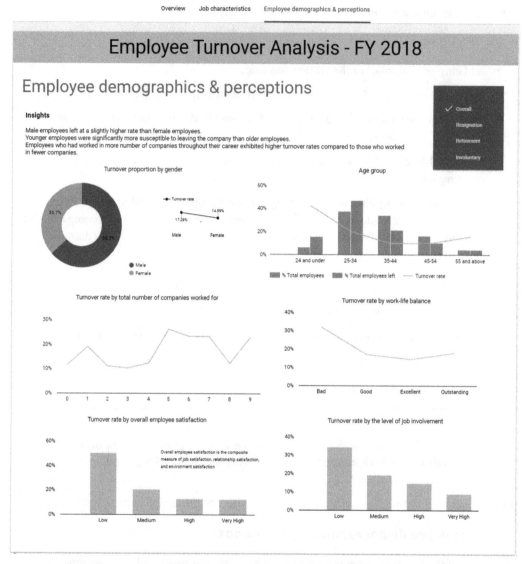

Figure 8.15 – Fully developed Employee demographics & perceptions page of the report

For analyzing turnover by gender, use a donut chart and minimal line chart, similar to what we did for the **Overtime** attribute analysis. The donut chart displays the proportion of male and female employees who left the company during the year, while the line chart shows the turnover rate for each gender type. Use the calculated **Is employee terminated – Turnover Type** field for the donut chart and the **Turnover metric** field for the line chart. Refer to the previous section for detailed configurations for these two charts.

To understand patterns of turnover by employee age, the turnover metrics must be plotted for different age groups. A pie or donut chart can be used, as originally envisioned in the wireframe or mockup, to depict the proportional breakdown of the turnover metric by different age groups. However, upon working with the data during the development process, providing additional context is deemed to help with effectively analyzing this attribute. A bar and line combination chart is the appropriate choice here. The proportion of total employees and the terminated employees for each age group are visualized to help users understand variations in the distributions, along with the turnover rate. The following configurations must be made for this combo chart:

- The **SETUP** tab:

  - Add the calculated **Age group** field as a **dimension**.

  - Add **employeenumber** as a **metric** with **Count** as the method of aggregation. Set **Comparison calculation** to **Percent of total** and rename the field **% Total employees**.

  - Add **Is employee terminated – Turnover Type** as the second metric with **Sum** as the method of aggregation. Set **Comparison calculation** to **Percent of total** and rename the field **% Total employees left**.

  - Add **Turnover metric** as the third metric field and rename it **Turnover rate**.

  - Sort by **Age group** in ascending order.

- The **STYLE** tab:

  - Select **Bars** for the first two series and **Line** for the third series (turnover rate). Choose appropriate colors for all the series.

  - Change the position of the legend position to **Bottom**.

Analyzing the remaining attributes while visualizing only the turnover metric is sufficient and provides the necessary insights. Use the parameter-driven **Turnover metric** field as a **metric** in each of these charts. Plot **Employee satisfaction** and **Job involvement** as bar charts, and the remaining two attributes as line charts. The following configurations need to be made for this:

- The **SETUP** tab:

  - Use the appropriate field as a **dimension** for each chart – that is, **numcompaniesworked**, **Work-life balance**, **Overall employee satisfaction**, and **Job involvement**.

  - Add **Turnover metric** as a **metric** and rename it **Turnover rate**.

  - Sort by the **Dimension** field in **Ascending** order. For **Work-life balance, Overall employee satisfaction, and Job involvement**, use the respective numerical encoded fields – that is, **worklifebalance, Composite satisfaction score**, and **jobinvolvement** – to appropriately sort the attribute values along the axis. The following screenshot shows the data settings for the **Work-life balance** chart:

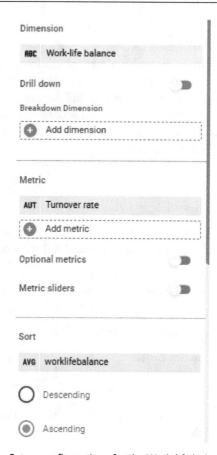

Figure 8.16 – Setup configurations for the Work-life balance line chart

- The **STYLE** tab:

  - Hide the gridlines and legend

Add the appropriate titles to all the charts using **Text** controls. Then, display the identified insights at the top. Adding a description of the overall employee satisfaction attribute for the corresponding chart is helpful.

Cross-filtering is enabled by default for all charts. In this report, just leave the default behavior as is to allow the users to interact with the charts flexibly.

Throughout this report, care has been taken in the following areas:

- Colors were used consistently and sparingly. This mainly means not using too many different hues, using color purposefully, and using the same color to represent the same dimension or metric across various charts.

- The report components were organized, aligned, and formatted properly. This includes using consistent text and other forms of styling, aligning charts and axes uniformly, arranging the components intelligently to improve readability, and more.

- Enough whitespace was left to avoid clutter. This avoids or minimizes chart junk (any design elements that do not add information).

Now, let's summarize what we've learned in this chapter.

Summary

In this chapter, you developed a detailed report for analyzing a fictitious company's employee turnover to address the HR department's business questions. You used a public dataset available on the open data community called *data.world*. You followed the three-step approach to building data stories. First, you determined the target audience, their objectives, the questions they want to get answered, and the data available and needed for the analysis. Next, you defined the key metrics, chose the right visualizations to present data effectively, identified the filters and interactions needed to meet the objectives, and created wireframes for the report pages. Finally, you went through the report development process and reviewed many of the implementation considerations, including creating calculated fields and parameters, chart configurations, and other report elements. In the next chapter, we will work on a different example and use a dataset from Google BigQuery.

9
Mortgage Complaints Analysis

The example dashboard in this chapter pertains to the analysis of American consumer complaints about mortgage products and services using the data provided by the **Consumer Financial Protection Bureau (CFPB)**. This chapter will guide you through the process of building an operational dashboard that helps CFPB to monitor and analyze complaints data. While CFPB and the complaints data are real, the premise of the dashboard is made-up and rests on assumptions about the target audience and their objectives. The complaints database is available as a public dataset on BigQuery, Google's Cloud data warehouse. A short primer on BigQuery is provided, which highlights its key features and how to use it for analytics. The dashboard building process involves three main stages – Determine, Design, and Develop.

In this chapter, we are going to cover the following topics:

- Describing the example scenario
- Introducing BigQuery
- Building the dashboard - Stage 1: Determine
- Building the dashboard - Stage 2: Design
- Building the dashboard - Stage 3: Develop

Technical requirements

To follow along with the implementation steps for building the example dashboard in this chapter, you need to have a Google account that allows you to create reports with Looker Studio. Use one of the recommended browsers – Chrome, Safari, or Firefox. Make sure Looker Studio is supported in your country (https://support.google.com/looker-studio/answer/7657679?hl=en#zippy=%2Clist-of-unsupported-countries).

You will need access to Google BigQuery, where the dataset used for this example lives. The BigQuery sandbox is available to anyone with a Google Account. Using the sandbox does not require a billing account and is free to use. The usage is subject to a few limitations though, in terms of storage and compute capacity, and table expiration time. The sandbox serves the purpose of this chapter, however. Another option is to sign up for the 90-day free trial of **Google Cloud Platform (GCP)**, which offers the full breadth of capabilities and features. While some level of prior knowledge of **Structured Query Language (SQL)** for querying data from BigQuery is helpful, it is not mandatory for following this chapter. For those who cannot access Google BigQuery for some reason, I've made the dataset needed to build the dashboard available as a CSV file at `https://github.com/PacktPublishing/Data-Storytelling-with-Google-Data-Studio/blob/master/cfpb_mortgage_complaints_dataset.csv`. The CSV file contains 6 months of mortgage complaints data.

You can access the example dashboard at `https://lookerstudio.google.com/reporting/0130033c-e1eb-4aff-b61f-a8d52be675c3/preview`, which you can copy and make your own. The enriched Looker Studio data source used for the report is available to view at `https://lookerstudio.google.com/datasources/390f38b5-2f83-497e-898c-5fa3a68c01de`.

Describing the example scenario

The CFPB is a U.S. government agency that implements and enforces federal consumer financial law. It empowers consumers by providing useful information and educational materials. It supervises financial institutions and companies to ensure that markets for consumer financial products are fair, transparent, and competitive. It also accepts complaints from consumers and helps connect them with financial companies to get direct responses about their problems. The CFPB regularly shares this data with state and federal agencies and presents reports to Congress. Accordingly, the CFPB closely monitors the incoming complaints data and their responses to identify key patterns in the problems that consumers are facing.

The CFPB makes complaint data available for public use by publishing complaints to the Consumer Complaint Database (`https://www.consumerfinance.gov/data-research/consumer-complaints/`). Complaints that are sent to companies are only included in the database after the company confirms a commercial relationship with the consumer, or after 15 days, whichever comes first. This data is by no means a truly representative sample of the overall experiences of consumers in the marketplace.

The complaints database includes complaints made since 2011, when the agency was established, on various products such as credit cards, prepaid cards, consumer loans, student loans, debt collection, mortgages, money transfers, and bank accounts, among other things. The complaint process works as follows:

1. A complaint is submitted by the consumer or gets forwarded by another government agency to the CFPB.

2. The CFPB sends the complaint to the concerned company for its review.

3. The company communicates with the consumer as needed and generally responds within 15 days. In some cases, the company can set the response as "in progress" and provide a final response within 60 days.

4. The CFPB publishes the complaint to the database after removing any identifiable information.

5. The CFPB lets the consumer know when the company responds. The consumer can review the company response and provide feedback within 60 days.

Google hosts the complaints database on BigQuery and makes it available to the general public for easy access and use. This enables us to readily analyze this data using SQL and integrated applications such as Sheets and Looker Studio.

There are three major types of dashboards based on their purpose – operational, tactical or analytical, and strategic:

- An **operational dashboard** helps us understand what is happening now and provides a snapshot over a short time period – for example, the last 7 days, the last 30 days, the current month, or the last 90 days. The appropriate time period varies based on the underlying processes. The scope of operational dashboards is usually narrow, often depicting only a single process or a few related processes. This type of dashboard focuses on monitoring operational processes and measuring performance against targets and helps with daily decision-making.

- **Tactical** or **analytical dashboards** provide a much broader perspective at the department or business unit level and generally include a larger volume of data. The objective here is to generate insights from historical data and investigate trends. Analytical dashboards help perform deeper and broader analyses to aid problem-solving and medium-term decision-making.

- **Strategic dashboards** serve executives and higher leadership by providing an at-a-glance view of the organization's performance measured against its strategic long-term goals. These typically include high-level metrics, aggregations, and summary data. Strategic dashboards also often provide multi-year analyses to understand long-term trends and patterns.

For this chapter, we assume that the CFPB has small individual teams for each product type responsible for managing the respective incoming complaints, communicating with the companies concerned, and other operations. In the current example, we will be building an operational dashboard that can be leveraged by the mortgage analysis team within the CFPB. This dashboard monitors mortgage complaints data for the last 30 days, helping the mortgage team track operational processes and related metrics.

In the next section, a brief overview of BigQuery is provided. As a Looker Studio developer, learning about BigQuery helps you maximize the effectiveness of Looker Studio due to its deep integration with BigQuery. BigQuery is easy to use and powerful. It helps you examine complex and large datasets effortlessly.

Introducing BigQuery

BigQuery is a highly scalable distributed cloud data warehouse from Google that is purpose-built for running analytics. It is fully managed by Google and serverless, allowing users to use the service without worrying about setting up and managing infrastructure.

BigQuery is optimized for **Online Analytical Processing (OLAP)** workloads that perform ad-hoc analysis over large data volumes. This is in contrast to relational databases such as MySQL and PostgreSQL, which are built for **Online Transactional Processing (OLTP)**. OLTP systems are optimized for capturing, storing, and processing transactions in real time.

BigQuery is highly performant and can process terabytes of data in seconds and petabytes of data within a few minutes. This is possible due to the decoupling of the storage and compute in its architecture, which allows BigQuery to scale them independently on demand. BigQuery charges you separately for storage and processing. Storage pricing is based on the total volume of data stored. Compute charges, on the other hand, are based on the amount of data scanned by a process or query, not the size of the result set. For the compute, you can either use the on-demand model and pay for use or purchase a specific capacity for unlimited use.

Getting started with BigQuery

To get started with BigQuery, you need a GCP account. You can use an existing Google Account (Gmail or any email registered as a Google Account) or create a new one. A valid credit card is required to complete the setup. If you are eligible for a free trial, the card will not be charged during the 90-day trial period. At the end of the trial, the resources are paused and you have 30 days to upgrade to a paid account and resume your work. Whether part of the GCP trial or a regular account, BigQuery always has a free tier, which allows you to query the first terabyte of data per month free of charge. The steps to create a GCP account are as follows:

1. Go to `https://cloud.google.com/` and click **Get started for free.**
2. Provide a Google Account email address or create a new one.
3. Fill in the name, address, credit card, and other details.
4. Click **Start my free trial.**

The free trial offers a credit of $300 and you will be prompted to upgrade to a regular account when the credit runs out or the trial period ends, whichever happens first. The free trial provides the full breadth of GCP services and capabilities and helps you evaluate any and all Google Cloud products.

In addition to broader GCP access, BigQuery provides a sandbox environment for users to try out the service without requiring a credit card and billing enabled. However, only a limited set of features (`https://cloud.google.com/bigquery/docs/sandbox#limitations`) are supported in the sandbox. The BigQuery sandbox is available to anyone with a Google Account. It doesn't require you to create a GCP account first. You can open the sandbox directly using the following URL: `https://console.cloud.google.com/bigquery`.

To use any Google Cloud resource, including BigQuery, you need to create a **Google Cloud Project** first. If it's a brand-new account, the home page shows the **Create project** link for you to get started. In an existing account, a new project can be created from the project selection dropdown displayed in the blue header at the top.

In Google Cloud, a **Project** is a logical container that organizes cloud resources and helps define configurations for them. A resource can belong to only one Google Cloud Project. BigQuery resources follow a hierarchy as follows:

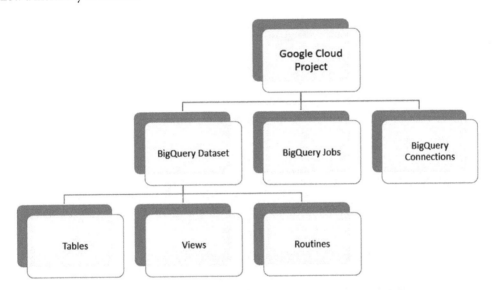

Figure 9.1 – The hierarchy of BigQuery resources

BigQuery datasets are logical containers that are created in a specific Google Cloud location such as *us* (multiple regions in the United States), *us-west-1* (Oregon), *europe-north1* (Finland), or *asia-south2* (Delhi). At the time of writing, Google Cloud is available in 334 regions around the globe. BigQuery datasets are akin to databases or schemas in other database systems. You create tables, views, and routines such as functions and procedures inside a dataset.

BigQuery is SQL-based and supports the ANSI SQL 2011 standard. You can interact with BigQuery through a web console, a command line, and client libraries in Java, Python, or C#, as well as REST APIs. In general, feature parity exists between all these methods. The rest of this section focuses only on the web UI and SQL interaction methods.

The web UI looks similar to the following image. Explorer lists the datasets, tables, and other BigQuery resources that you have access to. The Query editor allows you to write SQL queries and scripts. The query results, execution details, and other outputs are shown below the editor. BigQuery automatically stores the history of all executions and displays them in the bottom panel, which you can expand and collapse as needed:

Figure 9.2 – The BigQuery web user interface

Before running the query, the editor indicates how much data will be processed by the query. This helps us understand the billing implications and provides an opportunity for us to optimize the query to scan a lesser volume of data, if possible. You can query data across multiple datasets, as well as projects, as long as the concerned datasets share the same location.

> **Note**
>
> In Google Cloud, different projects can be set up with different billing accounts and methods. Compute charges will be made against the project that is executing the query. In the UI, the project in use is displayed in the top blue header bar. Storage charges will be incurred by the projects under which the datasets and tables are defined.

Getting data into BigQuery

One way to get data into BigQuery is using the **Create table** option from the dataset. To create a dataset first, click on the project from the **Explorer** panel and select **Create dataset** from the ellipses. The steps to create a new table are as follows:

1. Click on the dataset name from **Explorer** to open it in the right pane. Select **CREATE TABLE**. This opens the **Create table** pane.

2. Set **Source** to one of the following

    A. `Empty table` - To create an empty table.

    B. `Google Cloud Storage` - Google Cloud's object storage system.

    C. `Upload` - To upload files from your local machine.

    D. `Drive` - The files stored in Google Drive. The file can be in a CSV, JSON, Avro, or Google Sheet format.

    E. `Google BigTable` - A wide-column NoSQL database.

    F. `Amazon S3` - AWS' object storage system.

    G. `Azure Blob Storage` - Azure's object storage system.

3. Depending on the source type selected, provide the source file or data details.

4. Specify the destination table name. You can keep the auto-populated project and dataset details or choose a different destination if you change your mind.

5. Check the **Auto detect** checkbox to let BigQuery automatically detect the schema of the source. Alternatively, you can define the list of fields and corresponding data types.

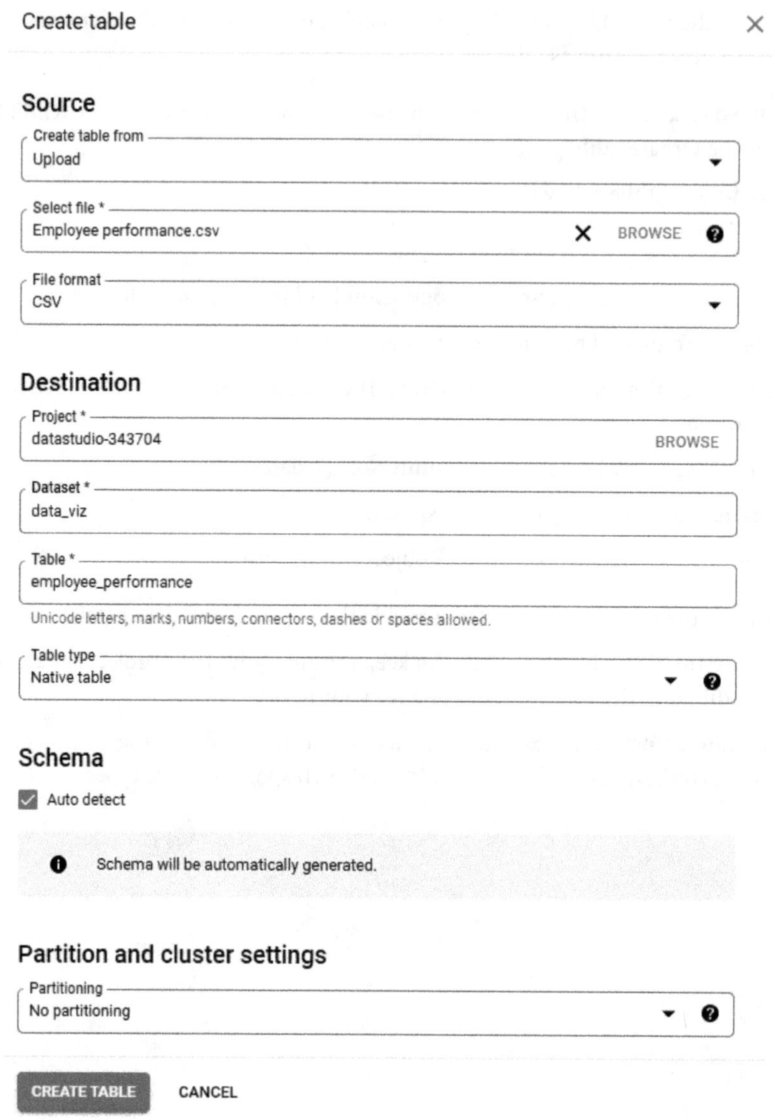

Create table   ×

Source

Create table from
Upload   ▼

Select file *
Employee performance.csv   ✕   BROWSE   ❷

File format
CSV   ▼

Destination

Project *
datastudio-343704   BROWSE

Dataset *
data_viz

Table *
employee_performance

Unicode letters, marks, numbers, connectors, dashes or spaces allowed.

Table type
Native table   ▼   ❷

Schema

☑ Auto detect

ⓘ   Schema will be automatically generated.

Partition and cluster settings

Partitioning
No partitioning   ▼   ❷

[CREATE TABLE]   CANCEL

Figure 9.3 – Creating a table from the web UI

There are two types of tables that BigQuery can create for you:

- A native table

- An external table

A native table is where data gets transferred from the source and is stored in BigQuery. Creating an external table, on the other hand, does not involve any data movement. The data remains in the source. Instead, BigQuery just creates and stores the schema and other metadata. You can query an external table just as you would a native table using SQL. Certain source types such as Drive and Amazon S3 only allow you to create an external table from the **Create table** form.

You can also get data into a new table by copying it from another dataset or project. To copy the baseball games data from the public datasets project, the following steps can be used:

1. Search for "baseball" in **Explorer**. Click **Broaden search to all projects** to view the results from the **bigquery-public-data** project.

2. Expand the baseball dataset and click on a table. This opens the table details page on the right. Click **COPY**.

3. In the **Copy table** form, provide the destination **Project** and **Dataset** names where the table copy needs to be created. Specify the destination **Table** name, which should be unique within that dataset:

Copy table

Source

Project name	Dataset	Table name
bigquery-public-data	baseball	schedules

Destination

Project *

datastudio-343704   BROWSE

Dataset *

data_viz

Table *

baseball_schedules

Unicode letters, marks, numbers, connectors, dashes or spaces allowed. The job will create the specified destination table if needed.

Advanced options   ∨

COPY   CLOSE

Figure 9.4 – Creating a full copy of a table

Another way to copy data into a new table is using a SQL statement as follows:

```
CREATE TABLE `datastudio-343704.data_viz.baseball_schedule`
AS
SELECT * FROM `bigquery-public-data.baseball.schedules`
```

In BigQuery, the fully qualified table name uses the following notation:

```
`project-name.dataset_name.table_name`
```

You can also move data into BigQuery using any data integration tool that supports the BigQuery destination. Examples include Google Cloud Data Fusion, Fivetran, and Striim.

Analyzing data in BigQuery

In BigQuery, you can run ad-hoc queries on one or more tables to analyze the data on demand. You can also schedule SQL scripts and queries to be executed regularly. This helps perform transformations and move data on a cadence. Standard SQL provides a rich set of commands and built-in functions that help summarize, manipulate, and transform data in the desired ways. The query results can be explored further in Google Sheets and Looker Studio by selecting **EXPLORE DATA** from the **Query results** pane, as shown in the following screenshot:

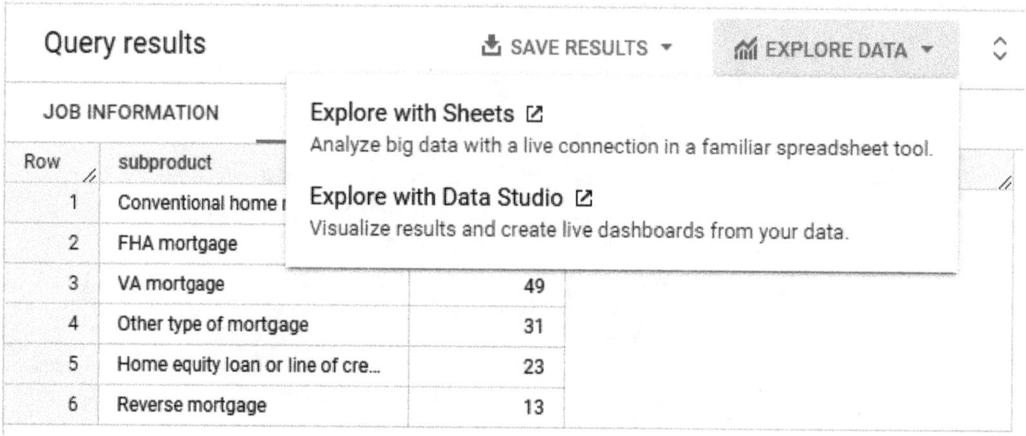

Figure 9.5 – Exploring the query results with Sheets and Looker Studio

Choosing either option creates a live connection to BigQuery using the SQL query that generated the result. This direct integration provides a seamless experience where you can start looking at raw data in BigQuery and then switch to Looker Studio, for example, to visualize data and explore further. When the Looker Studio option is selected, a new report is created with some default visuals as follows:

Figure 9.6 – The default Looker Studio report created from the query results

We have barely scratched the surface of the capabilities and features of BigQuery in this section. BigQuery is beyond just an analytical storage and processing system. Some of its other features include the following:

- BigQuery ML – performs ML with simple SQL statements without the need for advanced data science and programming skills

- BI Engine – an in-memory analysis service that offers the sub-second query response time needed for dashboards and reports

- Geospatial analysis – supports geography data types and provides SQL geography functions

- BigQuery Omni – enables data analysis across different clouds (Google, AWS, and Azure)

The rest of this chapter is about building a dashboard in Looker Studio by connecting to the CFPB complaints data stored in BigQuery. The **3D approach** to building effective dashboards consists of three stages:

- Determine

- Design

- Develop

Let's go through each of these stages in detail in the following sections.

Building the dashboard- Stage 1: Determine

In the first stage of the data storytelling approach, you determine the target audience, the purpose, and the objectives of the dashboard, as well as identify the data needed to meet the user needs. The mortgage operational team of the CFPB is the target audience of this dashboard. The team wants to understand current patterns within the issues that the complaints are about and company responses to them for various mortgage products and services. A key operational metric they would like to monitor is the time taken to triage the received complaints and send them to respective companies. The goal is to send the complaints within a day of receiving them. Another aspect the team is responsible for monitoring is the number and rate of untimely responses from the company. Once the company receives the complaint from the CFPB, it should respond within 15 days. Otherwise, it is marked as an untimely response. A higher number or percentage of complaints with untimely responses for a company or an issue type may signify the need for CFPB intervention in terms of imposing penalties or reviewing regulations and laws. Operationally, the mortgage team like to understand the following for the last 30 days:

- What's the overall complaint volume?

- What's the proportion of complaints with untimely responses and is it below the acceptable rate of 2%?

- What's the mean duration taken for the CFPB to process the received complaints and send them to the companies? How does it compare with the desired duration of 1 day?

- Which issue types are the most common and how do companies respond to various issue types?

- What proportion of complaints comes from older Americans and service members?

- Which geographical locations have a higher density of complaints and how does that vary between high-income and low-income geographies?

- What are the top companies by overall complaint volume, untimely responses, and in-progress responses?

- The daily trends for the volume of complaints and other metrics

The database includes 18 fields and over 2 million complaints at the time of writing (https://cfpb.github.io/api/ccdb/fields.html):

Field	Description
Date received	The date the CFPB received the complaint.
Product	The type of product the consumer identified in the complaint.
Sub-product	The type of sub-product the consumer identified in the complaint.
Issue	The issue that the consumer identified in the complaint.
Sub-issue	The sub-issue that the consumer identified in the complaint.
Consumer complaint narrative	A consumer complaint narrative is the consumer-submitted description of "what happened" in the complaint.
Company public response	The company's optional, public-facing response to a consumer's complaint.
Company	The company the complaint is about.
State	The state of the mailing address provided by the consumer.
ZIP code	The mailing ZIP code provided by the consumer.
Tags	Data that supports easier searching and sorting of complaints submitted by or on behalf of consumers. Indicates whether the consumer is a service member, older American, or both.
Consumer consent provided?	Identifies whether the consumer opted in to publish their complaint narrative. We do not publish the narrative unless the consumer consents and consumers can opt out at any time.
Submitted via	How the complaint was submitted to the CFPB.
Date sent to the company	The date the CFPB sent the complaint to the company.
Company response to consumer	This is how the company responded. For example, "closed with an explanation."
Timely response?	Whether the company gave a timely response.

Table 9.1 – A list of dataset fields

Most of these data points are useful in addressing the questions that the mortgage team is looking to answer. The Bureau discontinued the consumer dispute option on April 24, 2017. Hence the **Consumer disputed?** field is not used in the analysis.

Additional information about the geography and census information such as population and income are required to address the question regarding the geographical distribution of complaints. BigQuery provides this information as part of the census_bureau_acs public dataset. Moreover, the *State* field in the complaints database only holds the state abbreviation. It would be more user-friendly to display state names on the dashboard instead. The BigQuery tables needed to construct the data source include the following:

- The complaint_database table from the cfpb_complaints dataset
- The zip_codes_2018_5yr table from the census_bureau_acs dataset
- The state_2018_5yr table from the census_bureau_acs dataset
- The zip_codes table from the geo_us_boundaries dataset

A combined data source from different tables in BigQuery can be created using a custom query based on the following data relationships:

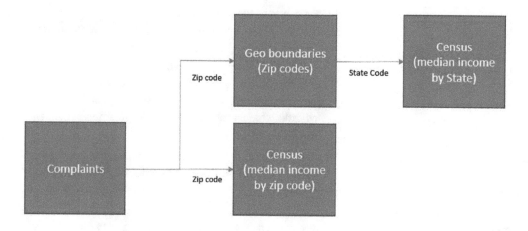

Figure 9.7 – The data model to use for the data source custom query

At the time of writing (June 2022), only the 2018 census information is available in BigQuery. The **American Community Survey (ACS)** released the 2020 data on March 31, 2022. But this data hasn't been made available in BigQuery yet. You can download more recent population and income estimates from https://data.census.gov and upload them to your BigQuery project.

Building the dashboard- Stage 2: Design

In this next stage of the process, you define any key metrics needed, assess the data preparation needs, select the appropriate visualizations, and design the dashboard layout at a high level. The current analysis only requires simple aggregations such as counts and calculating the percentage of total counts for specific attribute values as key metrics. Turnaround time, which helps measure the efficiency of the CFPB, can be defined as follows:

$$Average\ Turnover\ time = \frac{Total\ duration\ in\ days\ between\ the\ date\ of\ complaint\ received\ and\ date\ of\ complaint\ sent\ for\ all\ complaints}{Total\ number\ of\ complaints}$$

The other key metrics include the volume of complaints, the percentage and volume of untimely responses, and the percentage and volume of in-progress responses.

The complaints database contains most of the required data in usable form. On closer inspection, you discover that the ZIP code data is not clean – with non-digit and extra characters.

Analyzing complaints at both the state and ZIP code level provides a zoomed-in and zoomed-out view of the distribution of the consumers who log complaints for various mortgage issues. This helps in identifying any population concentration concerning general and specific types of issues.

Choosing visualization types

Key metrics can be represented as scorecards, showing the rate of change compared to the previous period. For metrics that have benchmarks to be tracked against – untimely responses and turnaround time, gauges can be used to depict the actual versus target comparison.

The number of complaints for different issue types is best presented as a horizontal bar chart to properly display lengthy text labels. A Sankey chart is perhaps ideal to show the relationship between different types of issues that consumers are complaining about and the response categories that companies provide. This chart type is available as a community visualization in Looker Studio. This community visualization has a few limitations though. It doesn't show any tooltips or allow cross-filtering. While this limits its utility in the dashboard, it provides a very useful representation of the flow and patterns of company responses to complaints on specific types of issues. The Sankey community visualization will inherit any filters applied to the dashboard through filter controls or cross-filtering from other charts.

Geographical distributions of complaints by state and ZIP code can be displayed as maps. Viewing the proportion of complaints based on population for different states and the ability to drill down into individual ZIP codes would be helpful. The Geo chart type in Looker Studio offers drill-down capability. However, the Geo chart does not support a postal code geo-dimension. Postal codes can be plotted using the Google Maps chart type but this doesn't support drill-down. One approach could be to show the volume of complaints by state as bars and by zip code on a Google Maps chart. Alternatively, the distribution of states can be displayed in its own geographical map chart. Cross-filtering will allow the users to select a state in one chart and only view the corresponding ZIP codes in the other chart.

Consumers are tagged as being either an older American, a service member, or both. The proportion of complaints by consumer type can be visualized as a pie chart or donut chart. A table works best to present multiple measures and a large number of dimension values. Hence, the number of complaints, in-progress responses, and untimely responses associated with various companies can be displayed using a table chart.

Finally, the trends of key metrics over time really help the target audience quickly identify any interesting patterns in the processing of received complaints. A time series chart is apt for this purpose. However, a combination chart with both bars and lines can be used to display multiple measures effectively in a single chart.

Considering filters and interactions

The dashboard will be built for monitoring the last 30 days of data as per the requirement of the target users. Having a date range control filter will enable users to choose a longer time frame to understand broader trends and patterns as needed. The mortgage financial product comprises several sub-products and a drop-down filter can allow users to choose one or a few sub-products at a time in the dashboard.

The ability to cross-filter charts so that metrics can be viewed for one or more slices of issue types, companies, geographies, or consumer types is beneficial. As noted earlier, you cannot cross-filter using the Sankey community visualization chart.

Designing the layout

For this example, I'm going to build a one-page dashboard. Given the level of detail and breadth of information to be visualized, the page may extend beyond the typical desktop screen size. The choice of the number of pages and the page size required usually depends on various factors, such as the amount of information and charts, the number of distinct topics or focus areas, and the ease of navigation and filtering.

The arrangement of report components on the canvas should allow users to effortlessly consume the most important information, easily make comparisons, and intuitively enable interactions. High-level KPIs can be placed at the top of the dashboard with the analysis of different attributes spread below them.

The following image shows the wireframe of the dashboard:

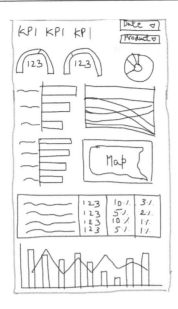

Figure 9.8 – Handdrawn sketch demonstrating the wireframe of the Overview page

The filter controls are placed at the top to indicate that the selections apply to the entire dashboard. Despite being prominently positioned on the canvas, filters can be made as unobtrusive as possible. The charts depicting issue types and company responses are placed side by side. Similarly, visualizations representing geographical dimensions are located together. The most detailed company-related metrics and trends over time are arranged at the bottom of the page. The donut chart showing the proportion of complaints volume by different consumer groups is placed at the top beside the KPIs, more as a convenience than anything else.

The development of the dashboard uses this wireframe and any other design decisions made during this phase as guidelines.

Building the dashboard- Stage 3: Develop

Now, it's time to start implementing the dashboard. Creating the data source to power the dashboard is the first step.

Setting up the data source

You need to use Google's BigQuery connector to create the data source. Since the required data resides in different BigQuery public datasets, using a custom query in the connection settings is the best option. Alternatively, if it's possible for you, you can create a view (as in, a saved query) or table with the required data fields within BigQuery in your own Google Cloud Project and use this view or table as the dataset to connect to from Looker Studio. The BigQuery sandbox or a GCP free trial will allow you to create tables and views, subject to quotas and other limitations.

> **Note**
>
> The BigQuery public datasets project is read-only and you cannot create tables or views in it.

The custom SQL query to use for defining the data source is as follows:

```
SELECT
    date_received,
    product,
    subproduct,
    issue,
    subissue,
    company_public_response,
    company_name,
    complaints.state,
    cen_zip.geo_id AS zip_code,
    tags,
    submitted_via,
    date_sent_to_company,
    company_response_to_consumer,
    timely_response,
    complaint_id,
    zip.state_name,
    cen_zip.total_pop zip_code_population,
    cen_state.total_pop state_population,
    ROUND(cen_zip.median_income,0) median_income_zip_code,
    ROUND(cen_state.median_income,0) median_income_state
FROM (
    SELECT
      *,
      LEFT(REGEXP_REPLACE(zip_code, r'[^0-9]', ''), 5) zip_code_
clean
    FROM
      `bigquery-public-data.cfpb_complaints.complaint_database` )
complaints
LEFT JOIN
    `bigquery-public-data.census_bureau_acs.zip_codes_2018_5yr`
cen_zip
ON
    complaints.zip_code_clean = cen_zip.geo_id
```

```
LEFT JOIN
  `bigquery-public-data.geo_us_boundaries.zip_codes` zip
ON
  complaints.zip_code_clean = zip.zip_code
LEFT JOIN
  `bigquery-public-data.census_bureau_acs.state_2018_5yr` cen_
state
ON
  zip.state_fips_code = cen_state.geo_id;
```

Using a custom SQL query for the data source connection allows you to perform data transformations and create derived fields beyond just combining data from multiple tables. The first source table in the FROM clause is the complaints database table, with the cleaned-up and transformed ZIP code as an additional field. Any characters other than numerical digits are removed from the original ZIP code field and only the first five characters are selected. This ensures an accurate and consistent format to allow appropriate mapping with the data in other tables. The correct representation of the ZIP codes is also important to make sure it can be defined as a geo-dimension and visualized via Maps in Looker Studio.

This transformed ZIP code field is used to connect the ZIP-code-level census table and extract the population and median household income fields from it. It is also used to connect the geo-boundary table to get the corresponding state name and code. Finally, the state code is used to connect the state-level census data to obtain the total state population and the corresponding median household income.

In the SELECT clause, only a limited number of fields needed for the analysis are included. A ZIP code is chosen from the geo-boundary table instead of from the complaints table to ensure only the standard US geographical information is included. The income fields are rounded to zero decimal places, as we do not need further precision than that. Certain columns are given appropriate aliases.

You can add a WHERE clause to the query to restrict the result set, say, to only mortgage-related complaints received in the last 12 months. In this example, we will leverage date range parameters to dynamically query the underlying data and configure a **Product** filter at the report level to restrict it to mortgage complaints. This way, the data source is generic enough and can be reused for other reporting purposes.

For any complex data manipulation needs, it is desirable to perform those operations within BigQuery using SQL queries and scripts. For our dashboard, we just need a few simple enhancements, which can be made within the Looker Studio data source.

The steps to create the data source are as follows:

1. From the Looker Studio homepage, select **Create | Data source**.

2. On the **Connectors** page, search for and select the BigQuery connector and rename the data source CFPB Complaints.

3. Select the **CUSTOM QUERY** option from the left-hand pane and choose **Billing Project**. This is your own Google Cloud Project that gets billed for the queries executed. BigQuery has a free tier, which allows you to process up to 1 TB of data per month.

4. Enter the custom SQL query and enable the date range parameters. This enables report users to only query the complaints for a specific time period dynamically through date range control selection. Pass these parameters in the WHERE clause as follows:

```
WHERE date_received BETWEEN PARSE_DATE('%Y%m%d', @DS_
START_DATE) AND PARSE_DATE('%Y%m%d', @DS_END_DATE)
```

5. Click the **CONNECT** button to create the data source:

Figure 9.9 – The BigQuery data source connection settings

Enrich the data source by modifying the data types for the following fields:

- `median_income_state` - Currency (USD – US Dollar ($))
- `median_income_zip_code` - Currency (USD – US Dollar ($))
- `state` - Country subdivision (1st level)
- `state_name` - Country subdivision (1st level)
- `zip_code` - Postal code

Create the following derived fields to help facilitate the dashboard development:

See the following for **is_in_progress**:

```
CASE WHEN REGEXP_CONTAINS(company_response_to_
consumer,'.*progress.*') THEN 1 ELSE 0 END
```

This derived field indicates whether the company responded to the consumer with an "in progress" status to signify that the additional time period, up to 60 days, is needed to provide a valid response.

The accompanying metric field, **pct_in_progress**, is as follows:

```
SUM(is_in_progress) / COUNT(complaint_id)
```

See the following for **is_untimely_response**:

```
IF(timely_response = FALSE, 1, 0)
```

This field simply denotes an untimely response as 1 to allow easy aggregations.

The corresponding calculated metric, **pct_untimely_response**, is as follows:

```
SUM(is_untimely_response) / COUNT(complaint_id)
```

Update the data type as **Number** à **Percent** for both the percentage fields.

See the following for **turnaround_time**:

```
DATE_DIFF(date_sent_to_company, date_received)
```

The turnaround time is the time taken in days from the date a complaint is received and the date when it is sent to the concerned company. Update the default method of aggregation for this field to **Average**.

Individual company responses to a consumer can be summarized into three categories for easier analysis: **Closed with relief**, **Closed with explanation**, and **Other**. The **Other** category includes untimely responses and in-progress complaints.

See **company_response_category:**

```
CASE
  WHEN CONTAINS_TEXT(company_response_to_consumer, "relief")
THEN "Closed with relief"
  WHEN CONTAINS_TEXT(company_response_to_consumer,
"explanation") THEN "Closed with explanation"
  ELSE "Other"
END
```

Similarly, issue types can also be grouped into a few meaningful categories as follows.

See **issue_category:**

```
CASE
  WHEN CONTAINS_TEXT(issue, "Credit") THEN "Credit report and
monitoring"
  WHEN CONTAINS_TEXT(issue, "report") THEN "Credit report and
monitoring"
  ELSE issue
END
```

The **tags** field provides information on whether the consumer is an older American, a service member, or both. If the consumer is none of these, it shows a NULL value. The following calculated field can be created to display **Other** when the **tags** field has no value.

See **consumer_type:**

```
IFNULL(tags, 'Other')
```

Designating states and ZIP codes as either lower income or higher income geographies compared to the national median helps with understanding the patterns in complaints data from the consumers based on household income. We need two derived fields, one each for state and ZIP code. Since the census information is from 2018, we need to use the national median income for 2018 for comparison, which is $61,937.

See **state_income_category:**

```
IF(median_income_state <= 61937, "Lower income", IF(median_
income_state > 61937, "Higher income", ""))
```

See **zip_income_category**:

```
IF(median_income_zip_code <= 61937, "Lower income", IF(median_
income_zip_code > 61937, "Higher income", ""))
```

Another way to implement these calculated fields is to use a parameter to hold the value of the national median income and reference the parameter in the formulas. This approach allows you to define and manage the value in one place:

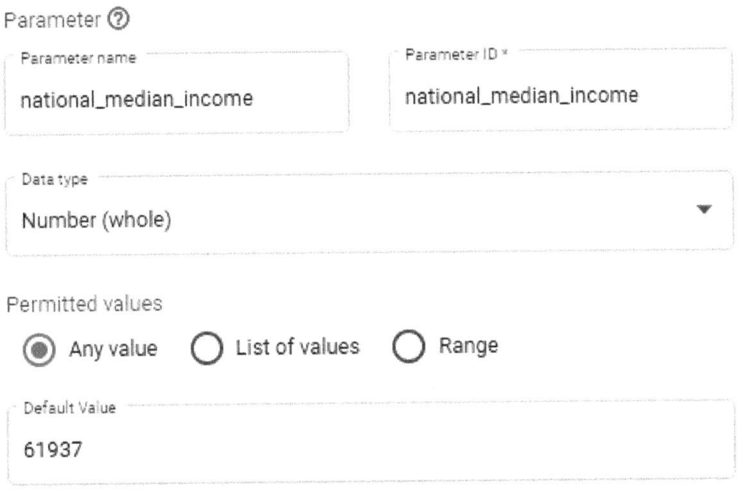

Parameter ⑦

Parameter name	Parameter ID *
national_median_income	national_median_income

Data type

Number (whole) ▼

Permitted values

◉ Any value   ○ List of values   ○ Range

Default Value

61937

Figure 9.10 – Creating a parameter to hold the national median income value

The formula using the parameter looks as follows:

```
IF(median_income_zip_code <= national_median_income, "Lower
income", IF(median_income_zip_code > national_median_income,
"Higher income", ""))
```

To properly compare the volume of complaints between different geographic locations, you need to consider the per capita volume. To be able to visualize the per capita volumes properly, I used the population in millions for states and the population in thousands for ZIP codes.

See **complaints_per_state_population_millions**:

```
COUNT(complaint_id) * 1000000 / MIN(state_population)
```

A state population is repeated for each complaint originating from that state and we need to select just one value per state. This is achieved by using the MIN aggregation, but you can also use MAX or AVG.

See **complaints_per_zip_population_thousands**:

```
COUNT(complaint_id) * 1000 / MIN(zip_code_population)
```

Creating a report

Create a new report from the newly created data source page by selecting **CREATE REPORT**. Update the report name to **Mortgage Complaints Dashboard**. From the **Theme and Layout** panel, choose any report theme of your choice. I've used a custom theme generated from an image.

In the **Report Settings (File à Report settings)** panel, configure the following settings:

- **Data source**: CFPB Complaints
- **Date Range Dimension** : date_received
- **Default date range**: Use the **Advanced** option to choose the last 12 months:

  - **Start Date: Today Minus 12 Months**

  - **End Date: Today Minus 0 Days**

- Select **ADD A FILTER** to define a report filter on **Product (Mortgage)**

These settings ensure that only limited and appropriate data is queried from BigQuery and used in the report. Configuring the default date range at the report level, in addition to the date range parameters in the query, makes sure that users cannot query complaints that are older than 1 year.

Choose **Current page settings** from the **Page** menu to open the panel on the right. From the **STYLE** tab, set the **Height** field of the canvas to 2100.

Now, build the report components based on the wireframe and other high-level design considerations made in the earlier stage. Styling, colors, labeling, and other implementation details will be worked out and addressed in this stage.

The following image shows how my implementation of the dashboard looks:

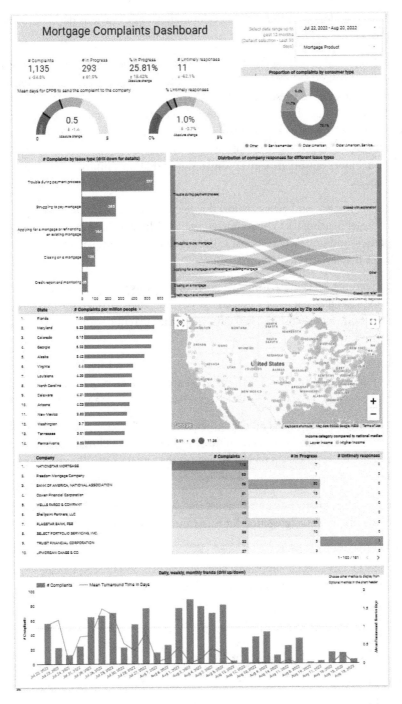

Figure 9.11 – A fully developed dashboard for monitoring mortgage complaints

In the rest of this section, let's go through the development steps of various dashboard components and their configurations.

Add a Text control to provide a title on the top-right-hand side of the dashboard. Place the date range control on the top-right-hand side and configure **Default date range** to **Last 30 days**. To let users readily know that the dashboard presents the last 30 days of data with the ability to extend the date range up to the last 12 months, place a helpful note right beside the filter component. Add the drop-down filter control below the date range control and set **Control field** to **subproduct**. Rename the control field `Mortgage Product`. Use the count of `complaint_id` as the metric and rename it `# Complaints`. Filter controls are a great way to show additional information without requiring any extra canvas space.

Create KPI charts, scorecards, and gauges below the dashboard title. Use scorecards for the metrics that do not have a target benchmark to be compared against. These include the volume of complaints, in-progress responses, and untimely responses. The percentage of complaints with an **in-progress** response can also be displayed as a scorecard.

For each of these scorecards, set **Comparison date range** to **Previous period**. This allows the comparison metric to display the absolute change or a percentage of the change between the metric value for the last 30 days and the value for the last 31 to 60 days when the current period is set to the last 30 days using the date range control filter.

For all these metrics, positive growth is undesirable and vice versa. Accordingly, update the comparison metric colors from the **STYLE** tab. For a **% In Progress** scorecard, display the comparison metric as an absolute change, as it would be confusing to interpret a percentage change in a percentage metric.

The CFPB mortgage team strives to send consumer complaints to companies promptly, within a single day. Hence, the turnaround time is monitored against this benchmark in a gauge. Similarly, the percentage of untimely responses is measured against the target of 2%. The configurations for the gauges are as follows:

1. Set the **Metric** values to `turnaround_time` and `pct_untimely_responses` respectively. Make sure the method of aggregation for turnaround time is set to `Average`.

2. Set **Comparison date range** to `Previous period`.

3. From the **STYLE** tab, select appropriate colors for the bars and the comparison metric. Choose red for a positive change and green for a negative change.

4. Enable **Show Absolute Change**.

5. Define the range limits:

    A. Turnaround time: **Range #1** to 1, **Range #2** to 2, and **Range #3** to 3

    B. % Untimely responses: **Range #1** to 0.01, **Range #2** to 0.02, and **Range #3** to 0.03

6. Set the axis limits:

    A. Turnaround time: **Axis Min** to 0 and **Axis Max** to 5

    B. % Untimely responses: **Axis Min** to 0 and **Axis Max** to 0.05

7. Enable **Show Target** and provide the value:

    A. Turnaround time: 1

    B. % Untimely responses: 0.02

8. Select **Hide Metric Name**. Use text controls instead at the top to display the desired name.

9. Select the **Do not show** option for **Chart Header.**

Wherever the comparison metric shows the absolute change value instead of the percent change, add a custom label to that effect using text control.

Visualize the breakdown of the volume of complaints by consumer type as a donut chart and place it to the right of the KPIs. A pie chart can also be used for this purpose, as a donut chart and a pie chart are perfectly interchangeable. Understanding the proportion of complaints from different groups of consumers helps the CFPB to identify any need for intervention to support the affected groups. Using a monochromatic color scheme for the donut chart helps limit the overall number of disparate colors on the dashboard. This helps reduce distraction and creates an elegant look. All effective data stories, whether business-related or otherwise, lend to this principle of minimizing the number of colours to reduce visual clutter.

The next set of visualizations is related to the issue types and company responses. Use a horizontal bar chart to display the volume of complaints by issue category, which is a derived field, and add the **issue** regular field as the drill-down dimension. The mortgage product doesn't have any sub-issue types to analyze. Hence, it is not included in the chart. Either use **Record Count** or the count of **complaint_id** as the metric to represent the number of complaints. Make sure the chart is sorted by the metric in descending order. Adjust the *y*-axis to display the label properly. Enable data labels from the **STYLE** tab. Make sure **Show axis title** is unchecked. Hide the legend by choosing **None**. Add a chart title using text control to indicate what the chart is about. I chose to use appropriate chart titles that describe the chart data in lieu of showing axes labels in this dashboard. You can choose either based on your design. You do not need to add both if they provide the same information.

A Sankey chart helps visualize the flow between the type of complaint issue and the company responses. Create the Sankey chart using the following configurations:

1. Select the community visualizations and components icon from the toolbar, click **Explore more**, and choose **Sankey** from the list.

2. Grant consent to allow this community visualization to render the data:

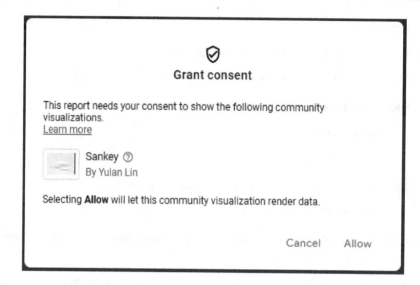

Figure 9.12 – Granting consent to the community visualization

3. Select **issue_category** and **company_response_category** as the dimensions.

4. Set **Metric** to **Record Count** or **complaint_id**. Sort by the metric in descending order.

5. From the **STYLE** tab, choose **Node color** and **Link color**. Adjust the opacity as needed. I've increased it to **40%**.

6. Select **Show node labels?** and set the **Node label** font size to **10px**. Provide appropriate values to **Left label offset** and **Right label offset** to make sure the node labels are easy to read. I've provided the values 10 and 3 respectively.

7. Select the **Do not show** option for **Chart Header**.

The generated visualization is as follows:

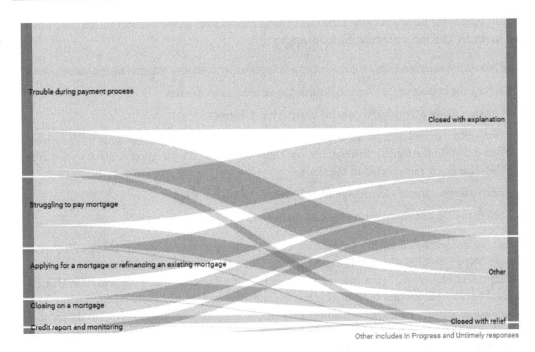

Other includes In Progress and Untimely responses

Figure 9.13 – A Sankey chart to visualize the distribution of company responses for different issue types

The width of the link represents the volume of complaints. As noted in the earlier section, the current implementation of the Sankey community visualization is limited in its functionality. It would have been great to see the complaint volume and proportion values in the tooltip.

Create a Google Maps bubble chart to visualize complaints volume by ZIP code. Set **Size metric** to the **complaints_per_zip_populatpon_thousands** derived field and rename it `# Complaints per thousand people`. Set **Color dimension** to **zip_income_category**. Rename it `Income category compared to national median`. These user-friendly names are displayed in the tooltip and legend. At this point, you might notice that the bubbles appear in other countries and continents even though the ZIP codes are US-specific. This is because the ZIP code alone is not enough to identify the geography uniquely. A new derived field combining the ZIP code and state is needed here. Create the new field as follows.

See **zip_code_us**:

```
CONCAT(zip_code, ", ", state_name)
```

Using this field as the **Location** field in the chart configuration plots all the bubbles within the United States. In the **STYLE** tab, configure the following:

1. Choose appropriate colors for the income categories by updating the dimension value colors.

2. Adjust the bubble size under the **Bubble Layer** settings as desired.

3. Unselect **Show Street View control** under **Map Controls**.

4. Leave **Size Legend** as **Bottom** and align it **Left**. Unselect **Show legend title**, as the long label gets cut off in the legend. Instead, use the chart title, created with a text control, to describe the value being represented in the chart.

5. Leave the position of **Color Legend** as **Bottom** and align it **Right**.

6. Select the **Do not show** option for **Chart Header**.

Different options work well for displaying complaints volume for different states. Using a Geo chart of Google Maps with filled-in areas is a good choice. Using bubbles instead of filled-in areas allows you to represent higher and lower income states, as with the ZIP code map built just now. Using a horizontal bar chart is another option. This has the added advantage of a more precise comparison of values across states, as humans can detect variation in lengths more accurately than differences in color intensities or areas. As with the map chart, the bars can be colored based on state income category, using the stacked bars option:

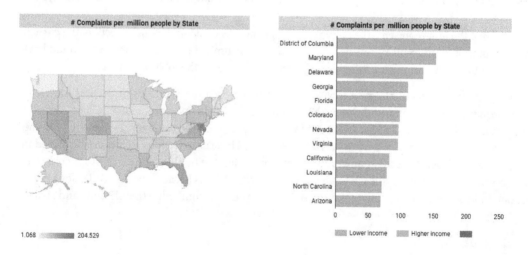

Figure 9.14 – A couple of ways to visualize the volume of complaints by state

The downside of using a bar chart is that only a limited number of states can be displayed clearly within the confined space without the necessity to scroll through a long list of dimension values. A table chart with bars can present all the states and enables users to scroll through all the values. However, depicting higher and lower income states using color becomes tricky without actually displaying the income category in the table. In the end, it's a trade-off between precision and clarity. I've opted for the table chart and displayed the metrics as bars.

Next, use a table chart with a heatmap to display the volume of complaints, in-progress responses, and untimely responses for various companies. Sort the table by the volume of complaints to display the companies with the most complaints at the top. Enable **Metric sliders**. This allows users to filter the companies by the metric values depicted in the chart.

Display the daily trends in the volume of complaints and other metrics with a combination chart. A time series chart also can handle multiple metrics and display them on both the *y*-axes. However, using bars and lines to represent metrics on different axes is maybe easier to interpret. Dual axis charts work best only when the units and scale of the two axes are very different from each other. The volume of complaints is represented as bars on the left *y*-axis. The mean turnaround time, % in progress, and % of untimely responses can be plotted as lines using the right-hand *y*-axis. Enable the **Optional metrics** setting to allow users to see only one or more metrics at a time in the chart. The configurations are as follows:

This is the configuration for **SETUP**:

1. Set **Dimension** to **date_received** and set **Type** to **Year Month**. The monthly view is helpful when the user extends the date range of the dashboard beyond the default 30 days using the date range filter control.

2. Add the **date_received** field again and set **Type** to **ISO Year Week**.

3. Add **date_received** one more time and leave **Type** as **Date**.

4. Enable **Drill down** and set **Default drill down level** to **date_received (Date)**.

5. Add the following as **Metrics** and rename them appropriately:

   A. **Record Count - # Complaints**

   B. Average of **turnaround_time - Mean Turnaround Time in Days**

   C. **pct_in_progress - % In Progress**

   D. **pct_untimely_responses - % Untimely responses**

6. Enable **Optional metrics**.

7. Sort by **date_received (Date)** in ascending order.

8. Disable the **Cross-filtering** and **Change sorting** options. The target users do not necessarily want to use this chart to slice the rest of the charts based on date, week, or month. The date range control helps them to focus on a specific time frame.

This is the configuration for **STYLE**:

1. Choose **Bars** for **Series #1** and **Line** for the rest of the series. Set **Axis** to **Right** for the second, third, and fourth series.

2. Choose appropriate colors for all the series.

3. Add a **Reference Line** with a **Value** of 1 on **Right Y-axis**. Uncheck **Show label**. Choose the same color as **Mean Turnaround Time** for the line. Choose a **Dotted** line type with a weight of 2. This line helps to compare the trend of turnaround time against the benchmark of 1 day.

4. Show the axis titles for both the *y*-axes.

5. Switch back to the **SETUP** tab and move the **% In Progress** and **% Untimely responses** metrics under **Optional metrics**. This ensures that only **# Complaints** and **Turnaround Time** are displayed in the chart by default.

Add a note over the chart to inform users about optional metrics. Add chart title on the top similar to other charts.

This completes the creation of the mortgage complaints dashboard that the mortgage team of the CFPB can use to monitor the metrics on a daily or weekly basis. For most of the charts in this dashboard, the chart header is disabled to minimize the overlap of the header with the chart titles. Most of the options available from the header, such as drilling up or down and exporting, are also accessible via the right-click context menu. The exceptions include the **Optional metrics** and **Metric sliders** features, which are leveraged in the bottom two charts. Hence, **Chart header** is set to the default **Show on hover** for the bottom two charts.

Summary

In this chapter, you learned about the American consumer complaints data on financial products and services from the CFPB, the US government agency that receives these complaints. You walked through the process of building an operational dashboard for a fictional team within the CFPB to monitor the volume of complaints and other related metrics for mortgage products. The complaints database is available as a Google BigQuery public dataset, which we used to create the data source for the dashboard. You were also introduced to BigQuery and its features briefly. In the next chapter, we will go through one more example and create a dashboard using customer churn data.

10
Customer Churn Analysis

Customer churn is a vital problem for any subscription business. The example dashboard in this chapter presents an analysis of the customer churn phenomenon for a broadband service provider. This chapter will walk you through the process of building the dashboard using the **3-D approach**: **Determine**, **Design**, and **Develop**. You will understand the relevant churn metrics and how blending can be used to calculate them in Looker Studio.

In this chapter, we are going to cover the following topics:

- Describing the example scenario
- Building the dashboard – Stage 1: Determine
- Building the dashboard – Stage 2: Design
- Building the dashboard – Stage 3: Develop

Technical requirements

To follow the implementation steps for building the example dashboard in this chapter, you need to have a Google account that allows you to create reports with Looker Studio. It is recommended that you use Chrome, Safari, or Firefox as your browser. Also, make sure Looker Studio is supported in your country (https://support.google.com/looker-studio/answer/7657679?hl=en#zippy=%2Clist-of-unsupported-countries). The dataset is a CSV file and is available to download in compressed form at https://github.com/PacktPublishing/Data-Storytelling-with-Google-Data-Studio/blob/master/customer_churn_data.zip.

You can access the example dashboard at https://lookerstudio.google.com/u/0/reporting/a02f5dd9-1070-42a6-8ebb-93d89947e666/preview, which you can copy and make your own. The enriched Looker Studio data source that's used for the report can be viewed at https://lookerstudio.google.com/datasources/99469508-0cd4-4269-9522-0f95bf3de996.

Describing the example scenario

Customer churn is a phenomenon where customers voluntarily or involuntarily stop doing business with a company. It affects subscription-based businesses such as **Software-as-a-Service (SaaS)**, media streaming, telecom, and others as well as non-subscription-based businesses such as retail, hospitality, travel, and others. A non-subscription-based business relies on new customers and repeat purchases from existing customers to generate revenue. Their business model is transaction-based, where repeat purchases are not guaranteed.

In contrast, a subscription business has a customer generating a steady stream of revenue for the duration of the subscription. Losing customers implies lost revenue. Measuring and reducing customer churn is more critical to a subscription-based company as its business model is highly dependent on the long-term relationship with its customers.

It is more expensive to acquire new customers than to retain existing ones. The new customer acquisition costs can be up to five times those of retaining current customers (`https://www.invespcro.com/blog/customer-acquisition-retention/`). It is very important to measure customer churn and minimize it as losing a customer base is detrimental to a company's bottom line.

The extent to which customers typically churn varies widely across different industries. As per **Recurly Research** (`https://recurly.com/research/churn-rate-benchmarks/`), the annual churn rate for subscription businesses varies between 5% and 7%. In general, **Business-to-Consumer (B2C)** businesses experience a higher churn rate compared to **Business-to-Business (B2B)**. B2B services are usually at a higher price point and involve a more complex purchase process compared to B2C offerings, causing B2B customers to be more thorough in their purchase decisions.

Customer churn can occur as a result of the following issues:

- Cancellations

- Expirations (non-renewals)

- Payment failures

Customers may leave a business by canceling an active subscription for reasons such as not requiring the service anymore, not being happy with the price, issues with the product, not being satisfied with customer service, and so on. Subscriptions can be ongoing or time-bound, such as 1 year, 3 years, and so on. Customers may also voluntarily leave the company by not renewing a time-bound subscription when it expires due to one or more of the same reasons mentioned earlier for active cancellations. If a significant proportion of the churn is due to non-renewals, this may indicate higher termination costs of active subscriptions, which discourage unhappy customers to leave midway. It also signifies an opportunity to provide attractive deals to customers with upcoming renewals.

While voluntary churn is the major component of the overall customer churn, involuntary churn due to payment failures and delinquency is not insignificant and can typically range from 20% to 40% (`https://www.profitwell.com/recur/all/involuntary-delinquent-churn-failed-payments-recovery`). Some strategies organizations can use to combat involuntary churn include sending timely reminder messages and emails, offering debit and auto payment options, prompting users to verify and update payment information periodically, and so on.

The dataset used in this chapter is available as a compressed CSV file in the GitHub repository associated with this book at `https://github.com/PacktPublishing/Data-Storytelling-with-Google-Data-Studio/blob/master/customer_churn_data.zip`.

The dataset includes 2 years' worth of billing, contract, churn, and other information for over 20K customers. In the remainder of this chapter, you will build a dashboard that depicts the customer churn metrics and trends based on this dataset.

Building the dashboard- Stage 1: Determine

In the Determine stage of the dashboard building approach, you determine the target users and objectives of the dashboard. You also identify the data needed to build the dashboard in this stage.

The target audience of this dashboard is the customer success teams in the company. Customer churn is an organizational problem and various departments such as marketing, sales, production, and support have a stake in it. However, the central customer success department is responsible for increasing customer satisfaction, decreasing churn, and driving product adoption.

The purpose of the dashboard is to depict the churn metrics for the last 24 months and help identify potential causes of customer loss. The questions that the target audience aims to answer with this dashboard include the following:

- At what rate do customers leave the company?
- What revenue loss has been incurred?
- When do customers leave the company concerning contract status and overall tenure?
- What are the top reasons for customers to stop using the service?
- Do customers complain before leaving?
- Do customers who use the phone service in addition to broadband leave at a higher or lower rate than those using only broadband?
- How does customer churn vary for various broadband bandwidths?

These questions can be answered using the broadband customer monthly billing dataset, which includes the following information:

Field	Description
Month	Billing month and year
Account No.	Unique customer account number
Tenure	No. of months the customer is using the service
Effective start date	Contract start date
Effective end date	Contract end date
Contract length	Contract duration in months
Bill amount	Monthly revenue from the customer
Bandwidth	Bandwidth of the broadband service
Termination reason code	Reason (code) provided by the customer when leaving
Termination reason description	Description of the reason provided by the customer when leaving
Complaint count	No. of complaints made by the customer in the month
With phone service	Whether the customer is using phone service in addition to broadband in the current month or not
Current month churn	Has the customer left the company in the current month
Is new customer account	Whether the customer account is new in the current month or not

Table 10.1 – List of dataset fields

No other data will be considered for this dashboard. However, in the real world, additional information such as the following will help in providing a more comprehensive analysis of customer churn and retention:

- Customer acquisition cost

- Customer demographics

- Net promotor score (this measures the loyalty of the customers)

- Usage patterns (upload, download bandwidth, and so on)

For this dashboard, you can assume that the company aims for a 10% annual customer churn rate, which amounts to a 0.87% monthly churn rate. The target users do not expect to interact with the dashboard to perform any ad hoc analysis.

Building the dashboard- Stage 2: Design

In the Design stage, you define the key metrics to be monitored, evaluate the need for any data manipulation, choose the right visualizations and filters needed, and create a wireframe of the dashboard to organize the various components.

Defining the metrics

The primary metrics relevant for measuring customer churn are the customer churn rate and revenue churn rate. You want the customer churn rate to be as low as possible and the revenue churn rate to be a negative value. A negative revenue churn implies a gain in revenue despite a non-zero customer churn owing to new customer acquisitions and upgrades from existing customers.

A simple way to compute customer churn at a monthly level is as follows:

$$Monthly\ Customer\ Churn\ Rate = \frac{Number\ of\ customers\ lost\ during\ the\ month}{Total\ number\ of\ customers\ in\ the\ month}$$

The monthly churn rate can be extrapolated to an annual or longer period using the following formula:

$$Overall\ Customer\ Churn\ Rate = 1 - (1 - Average\ Monthly\ Churn\ Rate)^N$$

Here, N = the number of months

Revenue churn provides another lens to look at the health of the customer base. You can consider both Gross Revenue Churn and Net Revenue Churn.

Gross Revenue Churn measures the revenue lost in the current period due to churned customers from the previous period. It does not consider the revenue generated from new customers gained in the current period:

$$Monthly\ Gross\ Revenue\ Churn$$
$$= Previous\ month\ revenue$$
$$- Current\ month\ revenue\ from\ existing\ customers$$

The average monthly Gross Revenue Churn is calculated for the period of interest, as follows:

$$Average\ Monthly\ Gross\ Revenue\ Churn = \frac{Monthly\ Gross\ Revenue\ Churn}{Number\ of\ months}$$

The revenue churn rate is determined by looking at the current month's revenue churn versus the previous month's revenue:

$$Monthly\ Gross\ Revenue\ Churn\ Rate = \frac{Monthly\ Gross\ Revenue\ Churn}{Previous\ month's\ revenue}$$

Net Revenue Churn considers the revenue generated from new customers in the current period in addition to the revenue from existing customers:

$$\begin{aligned}Monthly\ &Net\ Revenue\ Churn \\ &= Gross\ Revenue\ Churn \\ &- Current\ month\ revenue\ from\ new\ customers\end{aligned}$$

The monthly average Net Revenue Churn is calculated over time by dividing the Net Revenue Churn by the number of months.

$$Average\ Monthly\ Net\ Revenue\ Churn = \frac{Monthly\ Net\ Revenue\ Churn}{Number\ of\ months}$$

The Net Revenue Churn rate is determined as the ratio of the current month's Net Revenue Churn and the previous month's revenue:

$$Monthly\ Net\ Revenue\ Churn\ Rate = \frac{Monthly\ Net\ Revenue\ Churn}{Previous\ month's\ revenue}$$

Other useful metrics to monitor include the following:

- The average number of customers churned per month:

$$Average\ customers\ churned = \frac{Total\ customers\ lost}{Number\ of\ months}$$

- The average number of new customers acquired per month:

$$Average\ new\ customers\ acquired = \frac{Total\ monthly\ new\ customers\ acquired}{Number\ of\ months}$$

- The average number of net new customers per month:

$$Average\ net\ new\ customers = \frac{Total\ monthly\ new\ customers\ acquired - Total\ customers\ lost}{Number\ of\ months}$$

You can leverage the dataset in its present form and do not need to perform any data manipulation outside Looker Studio.

Choosing visualization types and filters

Scorecards with accompanying sparkline charts work well for displaying key metrics. Time series charts for customer churn and revenue churn rates help in visualizing the monthly trends. The number of lost customers by the termination reason provided and the broadband service bandwidth used are best represented as horizontal bar charts owing to the long dimension labels.

Customers of the broadband service provider can use their service either with or without a contract. A contract signifies the commitment by the customer to use the service for a set length of time, such as 12 months, 24 months, and so on. Benefits to customers by committing to a contract include low cost and better customer support among other things. The proportion of churned customers by whether the customer has an active contract or not at the time of churn can be displayed using a pie or donut chart.

If a customer has ever had a contract with the provider, it is interesting to see when during the contract or since the contract expiry customers typically leave. A line chart or a bar chart is useful to present this data with the number of months to or since the contract expiry on the X-axis. Irrespective of the timing of customer churn concerning the contract, visualizing the proportion of customers leaving based on the total time they have been with the company is helpful. This also can be visualized as a line or bar chart.

A simple way to address the question of whether the customers who left ever filed complaints with the provider is to visualize the proportion of churned customers with and without complaints. A pie or donut chart fits the bill here. It is more useful to understand the difference in the proportion of churned customers with and without complaints, which can be visualized as a stacked bar chart. The same applies to analyzing customer churn for customers with and without phone service in addition to broadband service.

The dashboard will be set to display the entire 24 months of data by default. A date range control allows users to select a different time-frame. The example dataset used here is a static one and never gets updated with the latest data. In a real-world scenario, the dashboard will be based on a live dataset that gets updated regularly. No other filters are necessary for this dashboard. Cross-filtering will be disabled for all charts as users are not expected to interact with the charts and perform any further analysis.

Designing the layout

It takes some experimentation to arrive at a layout that works for the data and visualizations involved. Place the high-level metrics at the top of the dashboard and detail the breakdown below them. A good way to organize the metrics is by grouping customer churn and revenue churn. The detailed charts depicting customer churn can be arranged around the questions of when customers churn, why they churn, and which customers churn.

The following diagram shows the wireframe of the dashboard:

Figure 10.1 – Handdrawn sketch demonstrating the wireframe of the dashboard

The dashboard includes a single filter control, which is placed at the top right. The location indicates that the filter applies to the entire dashboard. The period that applies to the dashboard is an important piece of information to correctly interpret the overall KPI values. Placing this control at the top quickly helps users understand the dashboard timeline.

The next stage involves developing the dashboard based on the wireframe and other design considerations made so far as guidelines. Refinements and adjustments to these design decisions are expected to be made during development as further nuances are uncovered.

Building the dashboard- Stage 3: Develop

To start creating the dashboard, first, you must set up the data source in Looker Studio.

Setting up the data source

The dataset is a CSV file that you can connect to from Looker Studio using the File Upload connector.

The steps to create the data source are as follows:

1. Download the ZIP file from `https://github.com/PacktPublishing/Data-Storytelling-with-Google-Data-Studio/blob/master/customer_churn_data.zip` and unzip it.

2. From the Looker Studio home page, select **Create** | **Data source**.

3. On the **Connectors** page, select **File Upload** and add the `customer_churn_data.csv` file. If you encounter any upload errors, make sure the CSV file is saved as UTF-8 CSV.

4. Name the dataset **Customer churn data**.

5. Once the file has been uploaded, click **CONNECT**.

Now, the data source can be enriched by renaming the fields appropriately, updating the data types, and adding new derived fields:

- Rename the **month** field to **year_month** as it is an integer representation of the billing year and month

- Update the data type of **bill_amount** to **Currency (USD – US Dollar ($))**

Based on the metrics and visualizations identified during the design phase, you can add some calculated fields to the data source upfront. The rest may be added later as needed. Often, a data source is enriched with additional fields in an iterative fashion while building the dashboard as it is not practical to envision all the necessary calculations beforehand.

Create the **billing_month** field to represent the **year_month** data as a **Date**. Use the following formula:

```
PARSE_DATE('%Y%m', CAST(year_month AS STRING))
```

An additional field is required for this purpose as it is not possible to directly change the data type of the **year_month** field from number to date. First, it needs to be converted into **Text**; then, the `PARSE_DATE` function must be applied.

Looker Studio interprets the **effective_start_date** and **effective_end_date** fields as being of the **Text** type. Create new fields to represent these values as dates:

- **contract_start_date**: `PARSE_DATE('%m/%d/%Y', effective_start_date)`

- **contract_end_date**: `PARSE_DATE('%m/%d/%Y', effective_end_date)`

To analyze customer churn concerning contract status, create the **contract_status** field to indicate whether the customer has an active contract or not for each billing period:

```
IF(billing_month BETWEEN DATETIME_TRUNC(contract_start_date,
MONTH)
  AND DATETIME_TRUNC(contract_end_date, MONTH), 'In Contract',
'Out of Contract' )
```

Calculate **months_to_contract_expiry** to help understand how long before or after the contract ends that customers churn:

```
DATETIME_DIFF(contract_end_date, billing_month, MONTH)
```

A negative number for this field indicates the number of months since the contract ended or expired and vice versa.

To calculate and visualize customer churn metrics, the following derived fields will help:

- Create **has_customer_churned** as a numerical field to facilitate easy aggregation using the `IF(current_month_churn = 'TRUE', 1, 0)` formula
- Calculate **churn_rate** as `SUM(has_customer_churned) / COUNT_DISTINCT(account_no)` - Set the data type as **Number | Percent**.

churn_rate, when visualized for each month, displays the monthly customer churn rate. As defined earlier in the Design stage, the annual or overall churn rate is not just a simple aggregation of the monthly churn rate and the calculation takes into consideration the compounding effect. To compute that, the average monthly value needs to be determined first and the compounded overall churn rate is calculated using the average churn rate. This calls for aggregating an aggregated value. This can be achieved by creating a data blend. Each row in this blend represents the aggregated churn value for each billing month, allowing you to perform computations on these aggregated values. This blend can also be used to calculate revenue churn metrics as they also involve computations on various monthly aggregations. You will create the blended data source from the report designer.

Other metric fields you can create in the data source include the following:

- **avg_customers_churned_per_month**: `SUM(has_customer_churned) / COUNT_DISTINCT(year_month)`
- **avg_new_customers_per_month**: `SUM(is_new_customer_account)/COUNT_DISTINCT(year_month)`

It is useful to display the net new customers gained per month in addition to these, which can be calculated as follows:

- **avg_net_new_customers_per_month**: `net_new_customers / COUNT_DISTINCT(year_month)`, where **net_new_customers** is a derived field calculated as `SUM(is_new_customer_account) - SUM(has_customer_churned)`

The data source is now in good shape, which means we can start building the visuals. It can be further enhanced as the needs arise while developing the dashboard.

Creating a report

Create a new report from the just-created data source page by selecting **CREATE REPORT**. Update the report name to **Customer Churn Analysis**. From the **Theme and Layout** panel, choose any report theme of your choice. I've used the default theme for this example.

In the **Report Settings** (the **File | Report Settings** menu) panel, configure the following:

- **Data source: Customer churn data**
- **Date Range Dimension: billing_month**

Choose **Page | Current page settings** from the menu and make sure **Data source** and **Date Range Dimension** are chosen appropriately. Set the **Default date range** as a fixed date range with **Start Date** set to July 1, 2020, and **End Date** set to June 30, 2022. If it is a live dataset, you would have set the date range to the last 24 months using the **Advanced** option:

- **Start Date**: Today minus 24 months
- **End Date**: Today minus 0 months

This ensures that the date range control on the dashboard will show the date range by default instead of **Select date range**. From the **STYLE** tab, increase the canvas size to **1500x1800**. Adjust this as per your needs.

Build the dashboard component by component based on the design considerations we've made so far. As you are developing the dashboard, do not lose sight of the dashboard's purpose and adjust the design appropriately. The following screenshot shows what my implementation of the dashboard looks like. Yours may vary with regards to layout, colors, specific chart types, and so on, and still meet the stated objectives and high-level design elements of the dashboard:

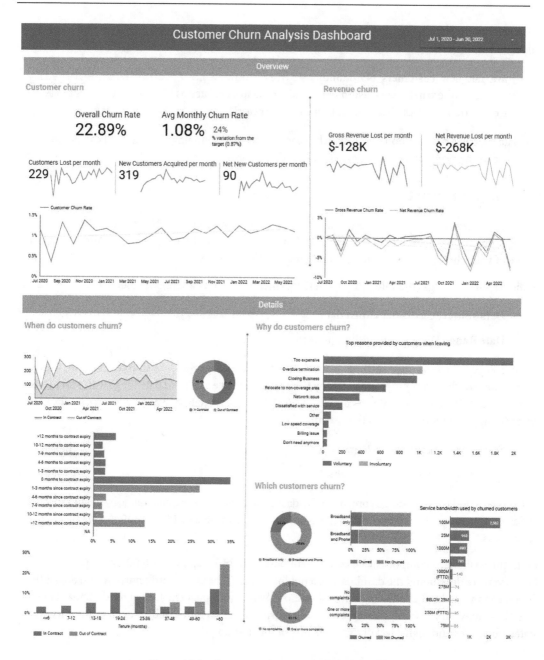

Figure 10.2 – Customer churn analysis dashboard

In the rest of this section, you will go through the implementation process of this example.

Overview section

First, to implement the key metrics, you must create a blended data source. To create a blend that provides monthly aggregation values for churn rate, follow these steps:

1. Select **Resource | Manage blends** from the menu.

2. Select **ADD A BLEND**.

3. Under **Table 1**, set **billing_month** to **Dimension** and **churn_rate** to **Metric**. Rename the metric **monthly_churn_rate**.

4. Set **Data source name** to **Monthly churn** and click **SAVE**:

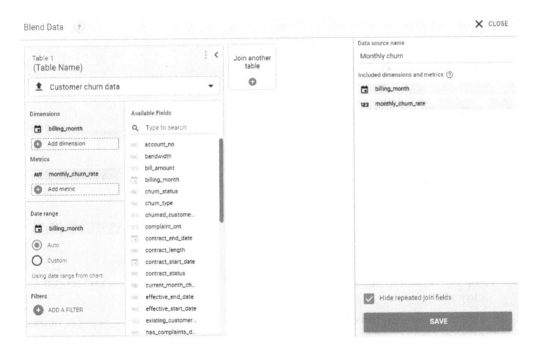

Figure 10.3 – Monthly churn blend to calculate the average monthly churn rate

The overall churn rate for the chosen period, whether it's 6 months, 12 months, or 24 months, can be calculated using the monthly churn rate, as follows:

```
1-POWER((1-AVG(monthly_churn_rate)), COUNT(billing_month))
```

You cannot create a calculated field within a blend itself, so this has to be defined as part of the chart configuration. Note that this is a simple blend that contains just one table and provides an aggregated view of the original data source at a monthly level.

Computing revenue churn requires you to determine both the current and previous month's revenue for churned and new customers. This can be achieved by modifying the *Monthly churn* blend to include this information. Before that, create the following base-derived fields in the original data source (*Customer churn data*):

- **previous_billing_month**: `CAST(DATETIME_SUB(billing_month, INTERVAL 1 MONTH) AS DATE )`

- **new_customer_revenue**: `IF(is_new_customer_account = 1, bill_amount, NULL)`

- **existing_customer_revenue**: `IF(is_new_customer_account = 0, bill_amount, NULL)`

- **churned_customer_revenue**: `IF(has_customer_churned = 1, bill_amount, NULL)`

- **non_churned_customer_revenue**: `IF(has_customer_churned = 0, bill_amount, NULL)`

To calculate the previous month's revenue, the *Monthly churn* blend needs to be updated so that it joins the *Customer churn data* data source on **previous_billing_month**. Follow these steps:

1. Edit the *Monthly churn* blend either from the **Data** panel or from the **Manage blends** page.

2. Select **Join another table** and choose the *Customer churn data* data source.

3. Make the following updates to **Table 1**:

   A. Add **previous_billing_month** as a **Dimension**

   B. Add **bill_amount** as a **Metric** and rename it **current_month_revenue**

   C. Add **existing_customer_revenue** as a **Metric** and rename it **current_month_existing_customer_revenue**

   D. Add **new_customer_revenue** as a **Metric** and rename it **current_month_new_customer_revenue**

4. Define **Table 2** as follows:

   A. Add **billing_month** as a **Dimension**

   B. Add **bill_amount** as a **Metric** and rename it **previous_month_revenue**

   C. Add **existing_customer_revenue** as a **Metric** and rename it **previous_month_existing_customer_revenue**

   D. Add **churned_customer_revenue** as a **Metric** and rename it **previous_month_churned_customer_revenue**

   E. Add **non_churned_customer_revenue** as a **Metric** and rename it **previous_month_non_churned_customer_revenue**

5. Configure the join condition between *Table 1*'s **previous_billing_month** and *Table 2*'s **billing_month** fields. This ensures that the metrics defined in *Table 2* are calculated for the previous month:

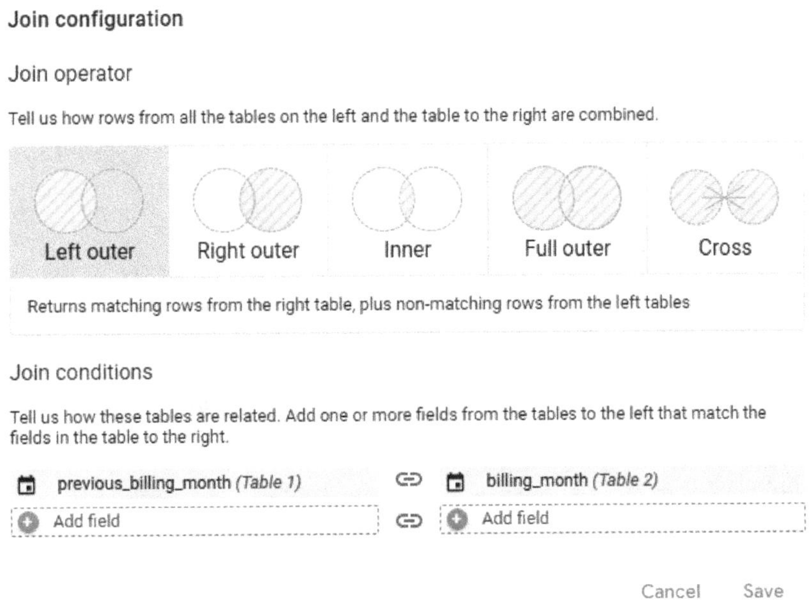

Figure 10.4 – Extending the Monthly churn blend with a join to the
original data source on the previous billing month

6. Make sure **billing_month** is added as the **Date range** field for both tables. This ensures that the date range control filters the charts based on this blend.

The final blend configuration will look as follows:

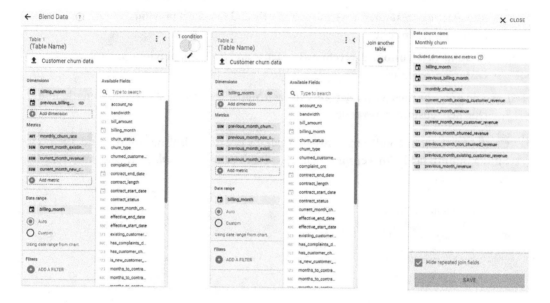

Figure 10.5 – Final Monthly churn blend configuration

Create the overall customer churn rate scorecard chart by following these steps:

1. Choose the **Monthly churn** blend as the **Data source** chart.

2. Click on the default metric that was added and select **CREATE FIELD**.

3. Enter `1-POWER((1-AVG(monthly_churn_rate)), COUNT(billing_month))` as the formula.

4. Rename the field **Overall Churn Rate**.

5. Set **Type** to **Numeric | Percent**.

6. Click **APPLY**.

7. From the **STYLE** tab, increase the font size to **48px** under **Labels**.

For the average monthly churn rate scorecard, use the **monthly_churn_rate** field from the *Monthly churn* blend. Set the aggregation to **Average**. To show the variation from the target value of 0.87%, I've used another scorecard chart and annotated it with the Text control. Arrange these components close to each other to make them look like a single unit:

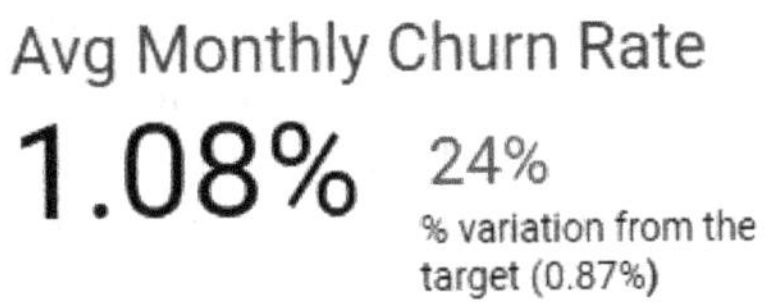

Avg Monthly Churn Rate

1.08% 24%

% variation from the
target (0.87%)

Figure 10.6 – Average monthly churn rate visualization

For the scorecard showing the variation, use the following steps:

1. Create a calculated field in the chart as:

   - **Diff from target**: (AVG(monthly_churn_rate) - 0.0087)/0.0087

2. Set the **Type** as **Number | Percent**
3. In the **STYLE** tab, configure the following:

   A. Set **Decimal precision** as **0**.
   B. Update **label font size** as **24px**.
   C. Select **Hide Metric Name**
   D. Add two conditional formatting rules to show the value in **Red** color when the variation is greater than 0 and in **Green** color when the variation is 0 or negative.

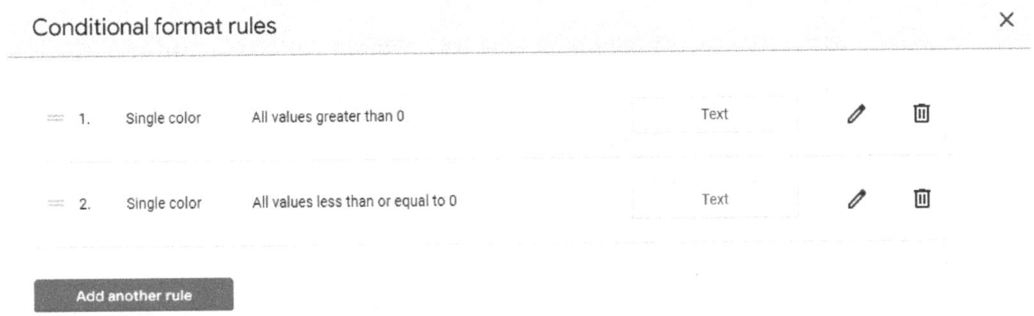

Conditional format rules   ✕

1. Single color   All values greater than 0   Text   ✏ 🗑

2. Single color   All values less than or equal to 0   Text   ✏ 🗑

Add another rule

Figure 10.7 - Conditional formatting rules for the scorecard displaying the variation from the target churn rate

Reminder

As discussed earlier in this book (*Chapter 2, Principles of Data Storytelling*), while green and red are universally associated with good and bad, respectively, they are not completely inclusive. People with color vision deficiency often (depending on the type of deficiency) see these colors differently and may not always be able to differentiate between them. When using any other colors for this purpose, users need additional cues in the form of a legend or notes to help them. A recommended approach is to use icons such as a smile and a frown (in addition to color) to indicate desirability and undesirability. At the time of writing, Looker Studio does not provide this capability out of the box. While using red and green as colors has some caveats, they are not taboo and are still commonly used in visualizations effectively. So, use these colors in your reports and dashboards at your discretion and with due consideration.

Depict the number of customers lost and acquired per month on average for the selected period as scorecards with respective sparklines to provide general trend information. Show the net new customers acquired metric in the same fashion:

Figure 10.8 – Scorecards with accompanying sparkline charts depicting the number of customers lost

For each of these metrics, configure the charts as follows:

- Use **Customer churn data** as a **Data source**
- For each of the scorecards, use the following fields as metrics, respectively:

    - **avg_customers_churned_per_month**; rename it **Customers Lost per month**
    - **avg_new_customers_per_month**; rename it **New Customers Acquired per month**
    - **avg_net_new_customers_per_month**; rename it **Net New Customers per month**

- Update the label size for scorecards to **36px** or as desired from the **STYLE** tab.
- Use the following metrics for each of the sparkline charts:

    - **has_customer_chured** with **Sum** as an aggregation; rename it **Customers churned** (the label appears in the tooltip)
    - **is_new_customer_account** with **Sum** as an aggregation; rename it **New customers acquired**
    - **net_new_customers**; rename it **Net new customers**

- For sparkline charts, make sure **billing_month** is added as a **Dimension** with **Type** set to **Year Month**.

Adjust the chart sizes and arrange them side-by-side, as shown in *Figure 10.7*. Add lines between the three pairs of charts to provide separation and a sense of boundary.

For the Gross Revenue Churn and Net Revenue Churn charts, create the custom metric fields in the respective chart setup configurations. Use scorecards to display the average revenue lost per month, and create the metric fields as follows:

- **Gross Revenue Lost per month**: `(SUM(previous_month_churned_revenue) + SUM(previous_month_non_churned_revenue - current_month_existing_customer_revenue))/(COUNT_DISTINCT(billing_month)-1)`

- **Net Revenue Lost per month**: `(SUM(previous_month_churned_revenue) + SUM(previous_month_non_churned_revenue - current_month_existing_customer_revenue) - SUM(current_month_new_customer_revenue))/ (COUNT_DISTINCT(billing_month)-1)`

You divide the total revenue lost by the number of months minus 1 because the revenue lost for the first month in the range is always 0, and we wouldn't want to dilute the average value by including that month in the denominator.

Net revenue lost is derived by excluding the revenue generated from new customers from the Gross revenue lost. However, when using blends, all calculated metrics are chart-specific and hence cannot be reused:

Figure 10.9 – Scorecards with accompanying sparkline charts depicting the amount of revenue lost

For the corresponding sparkline charts, calculate the revenue churn for each month by just using the numerators from the aforementioned formulas:

- **Gross Revenue Lost**: `(SUM(previous_month_churned_revenue) + SUM(previous_month_non_churned_revenue - current_month_existing_customer_revenue))`

- **Net Revenue Lost per month**: `(SUM(previous_month_churned_revenue) + SUM(previous_month_non_churned_revenue - current_month_existing_ customer_revenue) - SUM(current_month_new_customer_revenue))`

Implement the scorecard and sparkline charts for the revenue churn metrics using the corresponding formulas and make sure you set **Type** to **Currency (USD – US Dollar ($))**:

Figure 10.10 – Setting the data type of the revenue lost metrics to Currency (USD – US Dollar ($))

Similarly, the revenue churn rate can be calculated by dividing the sum of monthly revenue lost by the previous month's revenue. The formulas are as follows:

- **Gross Revenue Churn Rate**: `(SUM(previous_month_churned_revenue) + SUM(previous_month_non_churned_revenue - current_month_existing_ customer_revenue))/SUM(previous_month_revenue)`

- **Net Revenue Churn Rate**: `(SUM(previous_month_churned_revenue) + SUM(previous_month_non_churned_revenue - current_month_existing_ customer_revenue) - SUM(current_month_new_customer_revenue))/ SUM(previous_month_revenue)`

In addition to this high-level representation of key metrics, visualizing customer and revenue churn rates as time series helps in quickly understanding any peaks and valleys over time, as shown in the following screenshot:

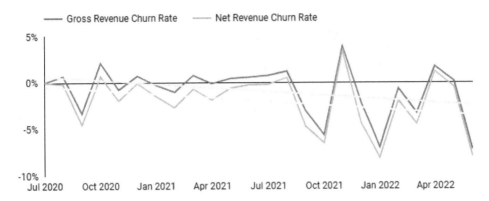

Figure 10.11 – Time series of monthly revenue churn rate

Follow these steps to create the revenue churn rate time series chart:

1. Click **Add a chart** from the toolbar and select **Time series chart**.
2. Choose **Monthly churn** as a **Data source**.
3. Make sure **billing_month** is added as a **Dimension** with **Type** set to **Year Month**.
4. Create the **Gross Revenue Churn Rate** and **Net Revenue Churn Rate** metrics in the **SETUP** tab using the formulas specified earlier. Set **Type** to **Percent** to display the values as a percentage.
5. From the **STYLE** tab, select **Linear** trendlines for both metrics.
6. Choose colors appropriate for the two series. Make sure that you use the same colors for the respective revenue lost sparkline charts.

Build the customer churn rate time series chart with similar configurations but using the original data source – *Customer churn data*. Add trendlines to help users understand the overall trend easily. From these charts, you will notice that the monthly customer churn rate has a slightly increasing trend, while the monthly revenue churn rate has a significantly decreasing trend.

It is interesting to observe that customers churned at the highest rate of 1.39% in Nov 2020, whereas the greatest revenue churn happened in Nov 2021, with a positive revenue loss. As desired, much of the revenue churn is negative, indicating overall revenue gain despite customer churn.

Detail section

The visuals so far provide an overview and trend of the relevant key metrics. The rest of the dashboard will delve into the details regarding when, why, and which customers leave. The overall proportion of customers regarding whether they are in contract or not when they stopped using the service can be visualized using a donut chart. It is also useful to see the actual number of customers churned over time broken down by their contract status when they left. This helps identify whether more or fewer customers churn during any specific period than others. Using the stacked area chart type with a gray color for the out-of-contract status to deemphasize it enables the users to easily perceive the trend of customers who churned while still in an active contract. It also helps them understand the trend of overall customers lost from the top line:

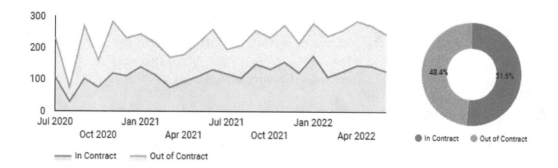

Figure 10.12 – Customer churn by contract status

The configuration steps for the area chart are as follows:

1. From the toolbar, click **Add a chart** and choose **Stacked area chart**.
2. Choose **Customer churn data** as a Data source.
3. Add **billing_month** as a **Dimension** and set **Type** to **Year Month**.
4. Choose **contract_status** as a **Breakdown dimension**.
5. Add **has_customer_churned** as a **Metric** and rename it **Customers churned**.
6. Make sure **Breakdown dimension sort** is set to **contract_status** in **Ascending** order.
7. Choose appropriate colors from the **STYLE** tab.
8. Update the legend's position to **Bottom**.

The donut chart is created using the same fields: **contract_status** and **has_customer_churned**. Make sure that you use the same colors to depict the contract status dimension values and that the legend position also matches for uniformity.

From the preceding charts, we can see that about half of the customers who left were still in a contract. It's helpful to understand how long before or since the contract ends that customers leave. Plotting the number of customers churned by the number of months to contract expiry as a line chart shows that a majority of customers who leave do so right when their contract ends, as shown in the following screenshot:

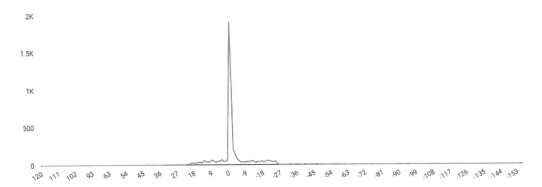

Figure 10.13 – Customers lost by the number of months to contract expiry

This also shows that some customers are on very long contracts and also continue to use the service long after their contract ends. It will be more useful to take a closer look at the proportion of customers leaving during 1 year before and after the contract ends. Depending on the patterns observed, this will signal the need for timely intervention. To build such a visual, it helps to bucket the number of months to contract expiry with user-friendly labels.

To do so, create the field in the data source by selecting **Add a field** from the **Data** panel. Then, Specify the name of the calculated field as **months_to_contract_expiry_buckets** and the formulas as follows:

```
CASE
    WHEN months_to_contract_expiry = 0 THEN '0 months to contract
expiry'
    WHEN months_to_contract_expiry > 0 THEN
CASE
    WHEN months_to_contract_expiry <= 3 THEN '1-3 months to
contract expiry'
    WHEN months_to_contract_expiry <= 6 THEN '4-6 months to
contract expiry'
    WHEN months_to_contract_expiry <= 9 THEN '7-9 months to
contract expiry'
    WHEN months_to_contract_expiry <= 12 THEN '10-12 months to
contract expiry'
    WHEN months_to_contract_expiry > 12 THEN '>12 months to
```

```
contract expiry'
END WHEN months_to_contract_expiry < 0 THEN CASE
   WHEN months_to_contract_expiry >= -3 THEN '1-3 months since
contract expiry'
   WHEN months_to_contract_expiry >= -6 THEN '4-6 months since
contract expiry'
   WHEN months_to_contract_expiry >= -9 THEN '7-9 months since
contract expiry'
   WHEN months_to_contract_expiry >= -12 THEN '10-12 months
since contract expiry'
   WHEN months_to_contract_expiry < -12 THEN '>12 months since
contract expiry'
END
   ELSE 'NA'
END
```

Use a horizontal bar chart to visualize this information. The configurations are as follows:

1. From the toolbar, click **Add a chart** and choose a horizontal **Bar chart**.
2. Choose **Customer churn data** as a **Data source**.
3. Add **months_contract_expiry_buckets** as a **Dimension**.
4. Choose **contract_status** as a **Breakdown dimension**.
5. Add **has_customer_churned** as a **Metric** and rename it **Customers churned**. Select **Comparison calculation** as **Percent of total** to display the proportion of customers churned.
6. From the **STYLE** tab, check the **Stacked bars** option and choose appropriate colors for the contract status dimension values.

You will want to sort the bars from the longest duration to the contract end to the longest duration since the contract ended. Since the buckets defined earlier cannot be naturally arranged in this order based on their labels, you will need another derived field with numerical values to achieve the desired order. Create a field in the data source and name it **months_to_contract_expiry_buckets_sort**. Then, use the following formula:

```
CASE
   WHEN months_to_contract_expiry_buckets = '0 months to
contract expiry' THEN 6
   WHEN months_to_contract_expiry_buckets = '1-3 months to
contract expiry' THEN 7
   WHEN months_to_contract_expiry_buckets = '4-6 months to
contract expiry' THEN 8
```

```
    WHEN months_to_contract_expiry_buckets = '7-9 months to
contract expiry' THEN 9
    WHEN months_to_contract_expiry_buckets = '10-12 months to
contract expiry' THEN 10
    WHEN months_to_contract_expiry_buckets = '>12 months to
contract expiry' THEN 11
    WHEN months_to_contract_expiry_buckets = '1-3 months since
contract expiry' THEN 5
    WHEN months_to_contract_expiry_buckets = '4-6 months since
contract expiry' THEN 4
    WHEN months_to_contract_expiry_buckets = '7-9 months since
contract expiry' THEN 3
    WHEN months_to_contract_expiry_buckets = '10-12 months since
contract expiry' THEN 2
    WHEN months_to_contract_expiry_buckets = '>12 months since
contract expiry' THEN 1
    ELSE 0
END
```

Add this new field to the **Sort** property in the chart configuration and set the aggregation to **Average**. Select **Descending** to see the bars in the desired order:

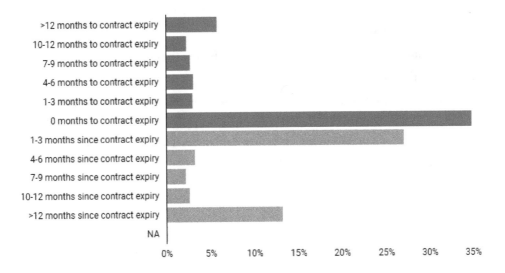

Figure 10.14 – Proportion of customers lost by the number of months to contract expiry (grouped)

The tenure of customers with the company adds another lens to look at the timing of churn. Again, given the broad range of tenure, it is helpful to group the tenure months into buckets. Create a new field called **tenure_buckets** in the data source, as follows:

```
CASE
  WHEN tenure <= 6 THEN '<=6'
  WHEN tenure BETWEEN 7
AND 12 THEN '7-12'
  WHEN tenure BETWEEN 13 AND 18 THEN '13-18'
  WHEN tenure BETWEEN 19
AND 24 THEN '19-24'
  WHEN tenure BETWEEN 25 AND 36 THEN '25-36'
  WHEN tenure BETWEEN 37
AND 48 THEN '37-48'
  WHEN tenure BETWEEN 49 AND 60 THEN '49-60'
  ELSE '>60'
END
```

You can visualize churn for these dimension values in a vertical bar chart, as shown in *Figure 10.14*, as the labels are short and there aren't too many values. The chart configurations are as follows:

1.   From the toolbar, click **Add a chart** and choose **Column chart**.

2.   Choose **Customer churn data** as a **Data source**.

3.   Add **tenure_buckets** as a **Dimension** and rename it **Tenure (months)**.

4.   Choose **contract_status** as a **Breakdown dimension**.

5.   Add **has_customer_churned** as a **Metric**. Set **Comparison calculation** to **Percent of total** to display the proportion of customers churned.

6.   Sort by the **tenure** field in **Ascending** order. Use **Average** as the method of aggregation.

7.   From the **STYLE** tab, select **Show axis title** for **X-axis**:

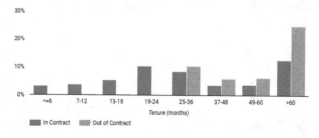

Figure 10.15 – Customers lost by tenure

> **Note**
>
> If you have set the colors for the contract status dimension values in the earlier charts, rather than choosing series order or bar order, the same colors will be applied throughout the dashboard for those values.

To understand why customers are leaving, visualize the top reasons provided by churned customers using a horizontal bar chart. From these reasons, you can deduce that *Overdue termination* refers to involuntary churn, whereas the rest refer to some form of voluntary churn, where customers stopped using the service deliberately. You can use color to differentiate involuntary churn from the rest, as shown in the following chart:

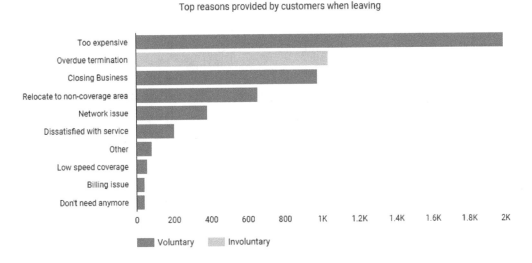

Figure 10.16 – Top termination reasons provided by churned customers

For this, you need to create a new derived field by using **churn_type** and setting the formula to `IF(term_reason_code = 'ODTR', 'Involuntary', 'Voluntary')`.

Follow these steps to configure the chart:

1. From the toolbar, click **Add a chart** and choose a horizontal **Bar chart**.
2. Choose **Customer churn data** as a **Data source**.
3. Add **term_reason_description** as a **Dimension**.
4. Choose **churn_type** as a **Breakdown dimension**.
5. Add **has_customer_churned** as a **Metric**. Set **Comparison calculation** to **Percent of total** to display the proportion of customers churned.

6. **Sort** by the metric field in **Descending** order.

7. From the **STYLE** tab, set the legend position to **Bottom** and choose appropriate colors for the **churn_type** dimension values.

Finally, to understand which customers are leaving, you can consider the broadband bandwidth used by customers, whether customers subscribed for phone service in addition to broadband, and whether customers complained before they stopped using the service. Visualize the number of customers churned concerning the bandwidth they subscribed for when they left using the horizontal bar chart, as follows:

1. From the toolbar, click **Add a chart** and choose **Bar chart**.

2. Choose **Customer churn data** as a **Data source**.

3. Add **bandwidth** as a **Dimension**.

4. **Add has_customer_churned** as a **Metric**. Rename it **Customers churned**.

5. **Sort** by the metric field in **Descending** order.

6. From the **STYLE** tab, select **Show data labels**.

7. Enter a large number such as **10000** for the **Custom Tick Interval** setting for **Bottom X-Axis**. This makes the *X*-axis disappear in the visual.

The resultant bar chart is shown in the following screenshot:

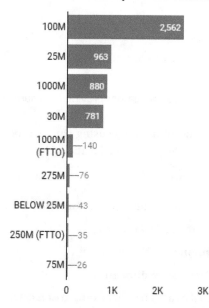

Figure 10.17 – Customers lost by tenure

To represent churned customers by whether they use phone service or not, use the **with_phone_service** field. It has **TRUE** or **FALSE** text values. Create a derived field to provide user-friendly labels by using **with_phone-service_desc** and setting the formula to `IF(with_phone_service = 'TRUE', 'Broadband and Phone', 'Broadband only')`.

Similarly, to understand whether churned customers complained before they left or not, a categorical field can be derived from the **complaint_cnt** field of the dataset. To do so, use **has_complaints_desc** and set the formula to `IF(complaint_cnt > 0, 'One or more complaints', 'No complaints')`.

There are two ways of analyzing churn for these two dimensions:

- Out of all churned customers, what proportion of them use the phone service or had complained?
- Out of all the customers, do customers churn at a higher or lesser proportion between those who use phone service and those who do not, or between those who complained and those who didn't?

The former can be represented simply as a pie or donut chart using existing fields, whereas the latter can be shown as a 100% stacked bar chart and requires a little more complex setup. A simple way to implement these charts is to create a new field to accurately calculate the number of non-churned customers and use it to configure the chart.

To do so, use **non_churned_customers** and set its formula to `COUNT_DISTINCT(IF(has_customer_churned = 0, account_no, NULL))`.

The chart can be set up as follows:

1. From the toolbar, click **Add a chart** and choose **Bar chart.**
2. Choose **Customer churn data** as a **Data source**.
3. Add **with_phone_service_desc** as a **Dimension**.
4. Add **has_customer_churned** as a **Metric**. Rename it **Churned**.
5. Add **non_churned_customers** as another metric and rename it **Not Churned**.
6. From the **STYLE** tab, select **Stacked bars** and **100% Stacking**.
7. Choose appropriate colors and set the legend position to **Bottom**.

The resultant chart will look like this:

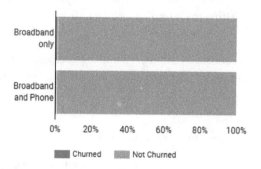

Figure 10.18 – Inaccurate representation of non-churned customers

As you can see, this is incorrect. This is because the **non_churned_customers** calculated field does not count the number of distinct customers correctly. This is a known Looker Studio issue at the time of writing where *COUNT_DISTINCT* does not work well when a date range filter is applied. The current report page is configured for a defined date range, hence the incorrect result. You can verify this by displaying the metric on a separate page without any date range applied; by doing so, you should see the correct count.

An alternate approach to building the desired visuals is to use blending. First, create a new derived field called **churn_status** in the main data source to provide user-friendly labels called *Churned* and *Not Churned*. To do so, set its formula to IF(has_customer_churned = 1, 'Churned', 'Not Churned').

This field will be used in the new blend. Create the blend by following these steps:

1. Select **Resource | Manage blends** from the menu and select **ADD A BLEND**.
2. Choose **Customer churn data** as a data source for **Table 1**.
3. Add **account_no, has_complaints_desc, with_phone_service_desc**, and **churn_status** as **Dimension** properties.
4. Add **billing_month** as a **Date range dimension**.

5. Name the blend **Customers** and click **SAVE**:

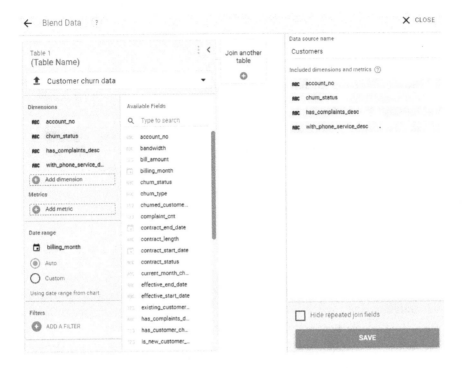

Figure 10.19 – Configuring the Customers blend

This blend provides unique customer information concerning complaints and the phone service dimension. Now, you must build the stacked bar charts correctly so that they look as follows:

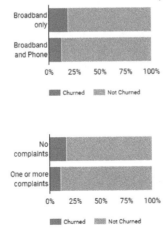

Figure 10.20 – Proportion of churned and non-churned customers

To do this, follow these steps:

1. From the toolbar, click **Add a chart** and choose **Bar chart**.

2. Choose **Customers** blend as a **Data source**.

3. Add **with_phone_service_desc** as a **Dimension** (has_complaints_desc for the respective chart).

4. Choose **churn_status** as a **Breakdown dimension**.

5. Add **account_no** as a **Metric**.

6. **Sort** by the metric in **Descending** order to sort the dimension values along the axis and use **churn_status** in **Ascending** order as the **Secondary sort** field to determine the order in which the stacks inside the bars appear.

7. From the **STYLE** tab, select **Stacked bars** and **100% Stacking**.

8. Choose appropriate colors for the **churn_status** dimension values and set the legend position to **Bottom**.

With that, you have created all the charts. Next, arrange them appropriately using the wireframe as a guide and adjust them as needed. Make sure that you align the boundaries and axes of the charts as much as possible to achieve an orderly look. Use white space, lines, and text labels to add clarity and additional information. Use them sparingly so as not to create a cluttered, disorganized, or busy look. Use fewer colors and use them uniformly. In my implementation, I used blue as the main color for all customer churn metrics. For revenue churn, I used a couple of shades of teal. I've chosen the neutral color gray to emphasize the data displayed in blue.

Disable cross-filtering and sorting for all the charts as the target users do not expect to interact with the dashboard. Given the large volume of data coupled with some complex calculations and blending used, the dashboard may not be very responsive already. Adding further interaction will only lead to a worse user experience. You can disable these options from the **SETUP** tab of the chart configuration.

You can choose to add some cross-filtering in the detail section, especially for the visuals depicting termination reasons, service bandwidth, and time series. This will help users delve into deeper slices of data. Grouping all the components in the detail section limits the scope of the cross-filtering to just the detail charts, leaving the overview charts unaffected.

Summary

In this chapter, you learned about the customer churn problem in subscription businesses and went through the step-by-step process of building a dashboard to monitor key customer churn metrics for a broadband service provider. You used the **3D approach** to dashboard building by first **Determining** the target audience, the business questions that the dashboard needs to address, and the data available to meet the needs. Then, you defined the right metrics, chose the appropriate visualization types, and **Designed** the wireframe of the dashboard. After that, you **Developed** the dashboard by setting up and enriching the data source and then building various visualizations and components based on the dashboard's objectives and the wireframe. You used blending to implement certain complex metrics. In the next chapter, you will learn how to track and monitor Looker Studio report usage using Google Analytics.

11
Monitoring Report Usage

When you have one or more dashboards built and shared with the target audience, you may want to understand how users are engaging with and using these dashboards. After all, when you get a sense of how well the data story you've created is being received, you can then take any actions needed to increase adoption. Looker Studio allows you to monitor report usage through **Google Analytics (GA)**. GA is a web and mobile application Analytics service offered by Google that tracks and reports user traffic. This chapter will examine what tracking report usage involves and walk you through the process of leveraging GA for this purpose. You will learn about relevant GA concepts and its built-in reports for analyzing usage. Alternatively, you can leverage Looker Studio to visualize the usage metrics. Furthermore, you can analyze raw usage data in BigQuery by exporting it from GA.

In this chapter, we are going to cover the following topics:

- Usage monitoring overview
- Google Analytics primer
- Monitoring Looker Studio report usage with GA4
- Exporting GA4 data to BigQuery

Technical requirements

To follow the implementation steps in this chapter, you need to have a Google account that can be used with GA and Looker Studio. It is recommended that you use Chrome, Safari, or Firefox as your browser.

Optionally, you will need access to Google BigQuery if you wish to follow the steps on exporting GA data. BigQuery Sandbox is available to anyone with a Google account. You can learn about getting access to the sandbox at `https://cloud.google.com/bigquery/docs/sandbox`. This does not require a billing account and has limited capabilities. The sandbox serves the purpose of this chapter. Another option is to sign up for a 90-day free trial of **Google Cloud Platform** (**GCP**) at `https://cloud.google.com/free`, which offers a full breadth of capabilities and features.

Usage monitoring overview

Monitoring the usage of reports has several benefits. Knowing how various reports and dashboards are being used helps in both demonstrating your impact and prioritizing your efforts. Even if Looker Studio makes it very easy to create reports, it takes a decent amount of effort and time to build a well-thought-out and properly designed dashboard. You want to invest your efforts where the users will find the results to be most beneficial. Analyzing user traffic data and patterns also helps you identify potential usability issues. Then, you can optimize your reports appropriately to increase their utility. For example, a low engagement rate may indicate that many users do not find the dashboard very useful or find it hard to understand.

Tracking report usage enables you to get answers to questions such as the following:

- How many users are viewing the dashboards?
- How long are they spending on different dashboards?
- How often are they visiting the dashboards?
- Which dashboards are the most popular and show an increasing adoption rate?
- Which dashboards exhibit a decreasing trend of usage?
- Which devices and screen resolutions are being used to view the dashboards?
- Which geographical location do the users belong to?

Dashboard proliferation is a common scenario where a lot of dashboards get created, many of which do not exhibit any sustained use. A lack of or low usage can signify one or more of the following issues:

- The problem or objective that the dashboard addressed isn't relevant anymore
- The dashboard doesn't meet the needs and expectations of the target users
- The dashboard isn't intuitive or is difficult to understand and navigate
- Data is inaccurate or stale
- Users can't find the dashboard easily or do not have access

Upon noticing low or no report usage, follow up with the target audience to uncover specific problems. Then, you can take appropriate action to address the concerns and make the dashboards usable. A common cause of low dashboard adoption is a lack of good requirements understanding and poor design upfront. Improving the design to fit the audience's needs may help in increasing the dashboard's utility. In the case of obsolete or changed needs, you can delete or repurpose the dashboards, respectively.

In addition to the usage or engagement level, understanding user device attributes such as device type and screen resolution helps you adapt dashboard design based on changing patterns. For example, if users are increasingly using mobile devices and other lower-resolution displays to view the dashboards, you may want to reduce the canvas size and reorganize the report layout to provide a better user experience.

Alternatively, you might want to create different versions of the report to provide the best layout for different screen resolutions.

Looker Studio provides a built-in way to track report usage through GA.

Google Analytics primer

This section provides a brief overview of GA concepts and its built-in reports. If you are already familiar with GA, you can skip this section and move on to the next. GA is a web Analytics service that tracks website (and mobile application) traffic and provides tools to analyze it. It is part of the Google Marketing Platform brand and is primarily used for digital marketing and search engine optimization purposes. For instance, it helps you measure site and campaign performance, understand your customer demographics and device attributes, and so on.

GA is a user-friendly and free tool, the latest version of which is called GA 4, or GA4 for short. GA4 supersedes Universal Analytics (that is, GA3), which was introduced in 2012 and will reach end-of-life by June 2023. At the time of writing, Google Universal Analytics is still used by millions of sites and applications. Compared to the Universal Analytics version, GA4 uses a completely new data and measurement model.

The premium or paid version of GA is called GA 360, which provides larger event collection limits, better integrations with marketing tools, advanced customizations and Analytics, **service-level agreements** (**SLAs**), and guaranteed data freshness. Understanding GA and its features and use cases comprehensively is a huge topic by itself. In this chapter, we will focus only on GA4 and touch upon a subset of concepts and features relevant to our current purpose – that is, Looker Studio report usage monitoring.

GA4 comprises the following hierarchy:

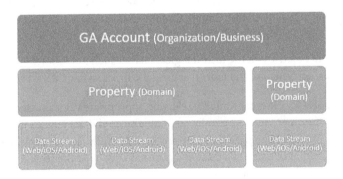

Figure 11.1 – GA4 hierarchy

A GA account is associated with your Google account. As a rule of thumb, you only need a single GA account for a business or an organization. You can create more than one GA account if you are managing multiple organizations.

A property is defined for a domain – that is, a single website or an app. All the subdomains are automatically tracked by the property. This property provides the reporting view of all the data tracked for that site or app. Multiple properties are needed only when you have different logical applications to track. A property receives data through data streams. A data stream can be one of three types – web, iOS, or Android. You can create multiple data streams for a property to track data from different channels – the website, iOS app, or Android app – of a single application. For example, an eCommerce application that has a website and an iOS app will need two corresponding data streams to be created so that you can look at user traffic and engagement across the two and analyze them together. When you want to track two different applications, such as supplier management and customer service, you must create two properties – one for each – and analyze the reports separately.

Understanding GA reports

Out of the box, GA4 provides a rich set of reports and charts under the following categories:

- **Acquisition**: This depicts new and returning users, and channels of acquisition such as direct, organic search, social media, campaigns, and so on.

- **Engagement**: This provides reports on user activity such as events, views, engagement time, and conversions. You can view these metrics for specific web pages or app screens as well.

- **Monetization**: This displays metrics regarding purchasing activity and revenue generated from eCommerce, in-app purchases, subscriptions, and ads.

- **Retention**: This helps you understand returning users through trends, cohort analysis, and lifetime value.

- **User demographics**: This provides user segments based on demographic attributes such as geographic location, age, gender, and interests. This data can be captured through Google Signals for users who have signed into their Google account and turned on Ads Personalization. Having user-level data helps in understanding the cross-device behavior of users.

- **Tech**: This presents metrics on the technological factors such as platforms, devices, operating systems, browsers, app versions, and more that users use to access and interact with the application.

You can view these reports for different times by selecting appropriate values such as **This week, Last 28 days, Last 30 days, This Year**, and so on or by defining a custom date range. You can also compare the metrics for subsets of users to analyze these reports meaningfully. For example, you can compare overall engagement with that of users of a certain age group or look at the trends of new customers acquired in three different countries, and so on.

You can also add additional attributes to tables to further break down the metric values. These attributes are referred to as **secondary dimensions**. Other ways you can interact with and customize the built-in reports include pivoting data, adjusting the sampling size to optimize it for either greater precision or for faster response (sampling is used when the data volume hits the sampling threshold or when advanced analytics are employed), and more.

If you are completely new to GA and haven't set it up for any application yet, you can use the demo account provided by Google to explore and examine the standard reports. The demo account consists of two GA4 properties:

- **Google Merchandise Store** (with a web data stream): Tracks data for the eCommerce website that sells Google-branded merchandise.

- **Flood-It** (with three data streams each corresponding to the web, iOS app, and Android app): Tracks analytics data for the Flood-It strategy puzzle game in which players need to flood the game board with a single color within the allowed number of steps.

These properties can be accessed as a viewer using the following links:

- **GA4 – Google Merchandise Store**: `https://analytics.google.com/analytics/web/#/p213025502`

- **GA4 – Flood-It!**: `https://analytics.google.com/analytics/web/#/p153293282`

You can find these links and details of the demo account in the GA Help documentation here: `https://support.google.com/analytics/answer/6367342`.

The following screenshot shows **Reports snapshot**, which provides an overview based on the detailed reports and acts as the landing page for the **Reports** section. You can customize **Reports snapshot** and determine charts and metrics that are shown as part of it. You can also create an overview report and set it as a **Reports snapshot**:

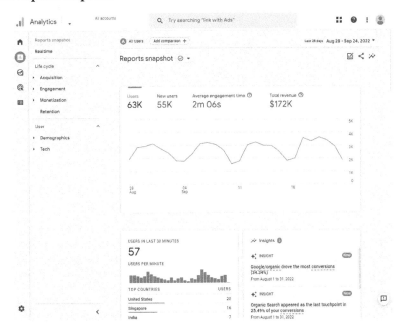

Figure 11.2 – GA4 Reports snapshot provides an overview of all standard reports

In addition to all the built-in reports and the ability to customize them to suit your needs, you can also create new charts and reports based on existing reports using templates or build from scratch.

It takes about 24 to 48 hours for the data to flow into GA. The **Realtime** view enables you to monitor user activity in real time. It shows key metrics such as the number of users, events, conversions, and so on for the last 30 minutes. If there has been no activity in the past 30 minutes, the **Realtime** report shows no data. The following screenshot displays the **Realtime** report for the Flood-It application:

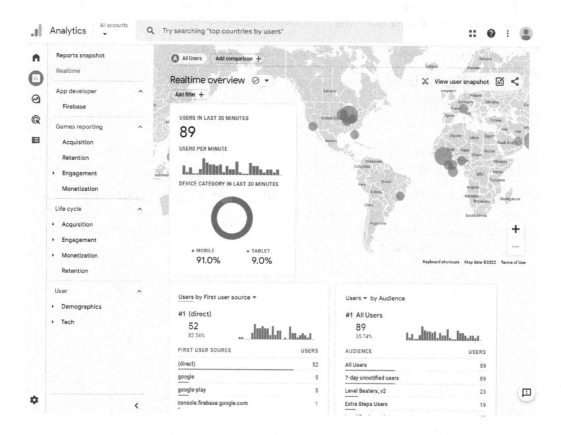

Figure 11.3 – GA4 Realtime report depicts user activity in the last 30 minutes

GA makes it easy for you to analyze and understand this data by providing automated insights. These insights are generated using **machine learning** (**ML**) and other intelligent processes by automatically detecting unusual trends and changes in data. These insights are surfaced as small cards on the **Analytics** home page and **Reports snapshot**. You can click on **View all insights** to view the **Insights** dashboard. Clicking on an insights card shows additional details on the right, as shown in the following screenshot:

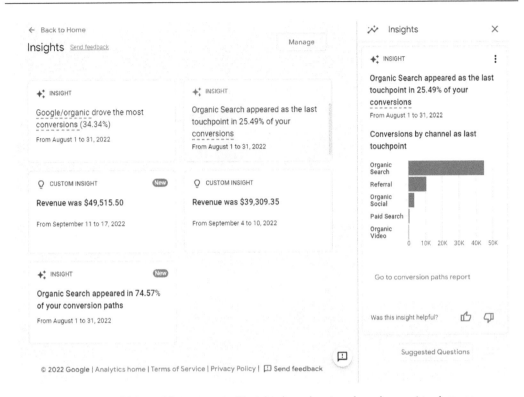

Figure 11.4 – GA4 provides automated insights based on trends and emerging changes

You can create custom insights to detect and alert on conditions that are meaningful to you. You can base your custom insights on suggestions such as anomalies in daily users, daily conversions, daily views, and more, or create them from scratch by defining your own rules. You can access relevant insights from any report by clicking the insights icon at the top right and choosing the desired insight. The following screenshot shows the list of available insights in the form of questions on the **Engagement overview** report, which you can then select and get the answers to:

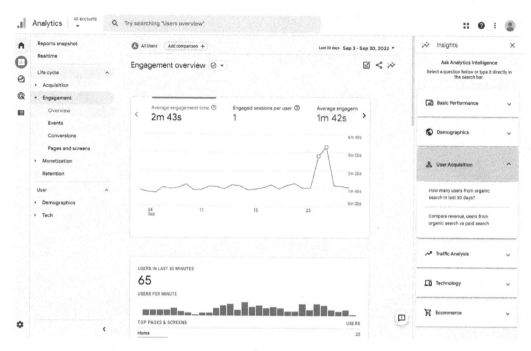

Figure 11.5 – Accessing the relevant insights for each report

Explorations are another feature of GA that enable you to analyze data in more detail and perform ad hoc queries. This provides additional flexibility in interpreting the data and helps in uncovering deeper insights.

> **Note**
>
> Explorations enable you to look at more granular data - at user and event level - but only for a limited timeframe, subject to the data retention settings that GA has in place. You can choose the desired length of retention within the limits. At the time of writing, GA4 allows you to retain the unaggregated granular data for up to 14 months. This restriction applies to only the Explorations reports. All the standard reports show aggregated data, and the data retention setting does not affect them.

To monitor Looker Studio report usage, some metrics and reports are more useful than others. The most applicable and relevant are as follows:

- **No. of users – new and returning**
- **No. of views**
- **Average engagement time**

- **Engaged sessions**
- **Views and users by Pages**

Monetization metrics are not relevant to Looker Studio reports. While you can define events such as scrolls or page views as conversions, it's not meaningful in this context. Analyzing user demographical and technological attributes may be useful in a limited way, especially if the reports are shared with a large user base – either publicly or widely distributed within an organization and/or its clients, partners, and so on.

In such cases, it helps to analyze key metrics by user categories such as location, age group, device, platform, and so on, and identify any interesting patterns. For example, consider a report shared broadly within a global organization. If the usage by users from a particular country or city is steadily decreasing, you may suspect that the needs of the team or business group that is based in that location changed and they do not find the report useful or relevant. Then, you can follow up with that team and determine the next steps. Technology attributes such as operating system and app version are not useful to you as Looker Studio users, as it is a browser-based tool that's managed by Google.

GA enables you to track individual users so that they can be identified across devices, browsers, sessions, and more. This helps in better understanding user journeys and accurately measuring unique users, and it generally helps with attribution. The user ID should be generated by the application and not contain any **personally identifiable information (PII)** in it, such as name, email address, phone number, and so on. Looker Studio does not provide this information at the time of writing.

Monitoring Looker Studio report usage with GA4

You can monitor Looker Studio report usage by adding a GA Measurement ID to each of the reports.

Setting up GA4 for Looker Studio report monitoring

Let's walk through the steps of setting up GA4 for Looker Studio monitoring and tagging the reports for tracking:

1. Visit `https://analytics.google.com`. Log into your Google account if you haven't done so already.

2. If you haven't used GA before, you will see the welcome screen. Clicking the **Start measuring** button will take you to the **Account setup** page. Alternatively, if you have used GA before, you can create a new account from the **Admin** page.

3. Provide the following details:

   A. Account name

   B. Property name

   C. Optionally, account data sharing settings and business information

4. Click **Create** and accept the terms of service and data protection terms.

5. Next, you will see the **ADMIN** page, where you can set up a data stream to collect the data:

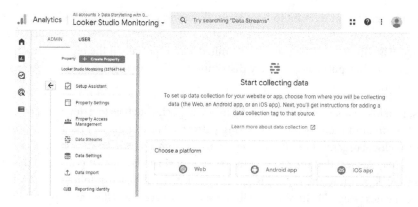

Figure 11.6 – GA4 account admin settings

6. Choose **Web** and set **Website URL** to `https://lookerstudio.google.com`; also, provide an appropriate **Stream name**. Leave **Enhanced measurement** turned on, which tracks events such as page views, scrolls, outbound clicks, and more. Then, click **Create stream**:

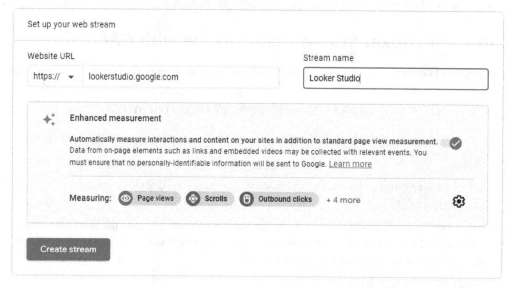

Figure 11.7 – Setting up a web data stream to collect data

7. From the **Web stream details** page, copy the **MEASUREMENT ID** property to add it to Looker Studio reports:

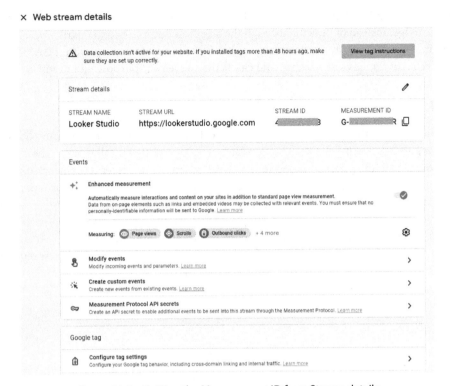

Figure 11.8 – Getting the Measurement ID from Stream details

8. Open your Looker Studio report in **Edit** mode and from the **File** menu, select **Report settings**. Enter the measurement ID from the GA4 web stream. Do this for all the reports that you would like to track usage for:

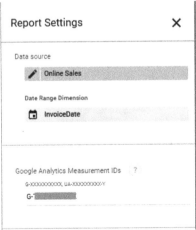

Figure 11.9 – Adding the measurement ID to Looker Studio reports

Data will start flowing into GA within 24 to 48 hours and you can peruse the built-in reports to monitor their usage. Instead of plowing through the significant number of standard reports to find the relevant information and review their usage, you can create custom reports within GA using just a handful of relevant dimensions, metrics, and charts that serve your purpose and needs.

Creating a custom report in GA4

In GA, you can create a detailed report by choosing the dimensions and metrics of your choice and an overview report by choosing the visualization cards from the existing detail reports. These reports can then be organized into collections and topics. A collection is a top-level container that appears as a section in the left navigation panel within **Reports**. A collection can have one or more topics, each of which represents a sub-collection of reports typically organized around a single theme or analysis. Each topic can have, at most, one overview report and one or more detail reports. In the following screenshot, **Life cycle** represents a collection, which contains multiple topics – **Acquisition**, **Engagement**, **Monetization**, and **Retention**. The **Acquisition** topic contains an **Overview** report and two detail reports – **User acquisition** and **Traffic acquisition**:

Figure 11.10 – Reports are organized into collections and topics

Follow these steps to create a collection and topic:

1. From the **Reports** left navigation, select **Library** at the bottom. Select the **Create new collection** tile under the **Collections** section. Then, select **Blank**. You can also create a collection using the templates available.

2. Provide a name for the collection, such as **Looker Studio Report Usage**. Click **Create new topic** and specify the name as, for example, **Report usage**.

3. You can drag and drop detail and overview reports under the topic from the available list on the right. These reports include all the out-of-the-box reports as well as any custom reports you have created. For this collection, we will create custom reports and add them later:

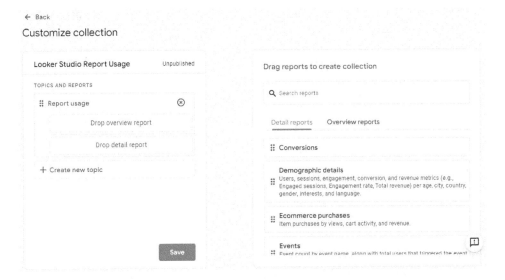

Figure 11.11 – Customizing the collection by adding topics and reports

4. **Save** the collection.

To create a custom detail report, follow these steps:

1. From the **Reports** left navigation, select **Library** at the bottom. Click **Create new report** and choose **Create detail report**:

Figure 11.12 – Create detail report

2. On the **Create new** screen, choose **Blank**. Alternatively, you can choose to start from the templates provided.

3. The detail reports in GA have a standard layout and offer a limited set of options to customize. You can have, at most, two visualization charts on the top and a detailed table below them.

4. Select the desired dimensions and metrics from the right panel. You can set one of the chosen dimensions as the default, which gets depicted in both the top charts and the table below by default. You can view these charts by other dimensions by choosing the desired dimension from the table while viewing the report. You can add up to 12 metrics to a report and they are used in the charts in the order they appear in the list. I've added the following dimensions with **Page title** set as the default:

   A. **Page title**

   B. **Browser**

   C. **City**

D.   **Device category**

E.   **Screen resolution**

F.   **Date _ hour (YYYYMMDDHH)**

The metrics chosen include the following:

G.   **Views**

H.   **Total users**

I.   **Engaged sessions**

J.   **Average engagement time**

5.   The charts can be any of the three types – **Bar Chart**, **Scatter Chart**, or **Line Chart**. You can hide one or both charts by clicking on the eye icon to exclude them from the report. No further customizations are available for these charts. The table below displays all the metrics for the default dimension.

6.   Apply your changes and save the report and provide a name – for instance, **Report usage - detail**. The report will look as follows:

Figure 11.13 – Finished custom detail report

7. You can create summary cards that depict custom charts based on the report metrics and dimensions. These summary cards do not appear within the detail report itself. However, they can be added to an overview report. The summary card can be one of four visualization types: bar, donut, line, or table. Choose the desired dimensions and metrics from the report data and select the appropriate visualization type. The settings for the **Total users by City** summary card are shown in the following screenshot:

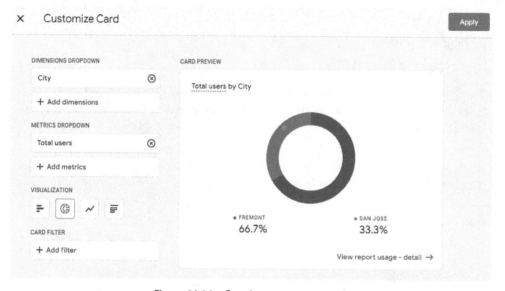

Figure 11.14 – Creating a summary card

8. From the **Library** page, click on **Edit collection** for the **Looker Studio Report Usage** collection you created earlier, and drag and drop the detail report you just created under the collection. Save the collection. Back on the **Library** page, click the ellipses icon for the collection and select **Publish**. Publishing a collection makes it appear in the left navigation.

Now, let's create an overview report using the summary cards from the custom detail report, as well as from the built-in reports:

1. From the **Library** page, click **Create new report** and select **Create overview report**.

2. From the right panel, click **Add Cards** and choose from the available **Summary Cards** and **Other Cards**. You can add up to 16 cards to an overview report:

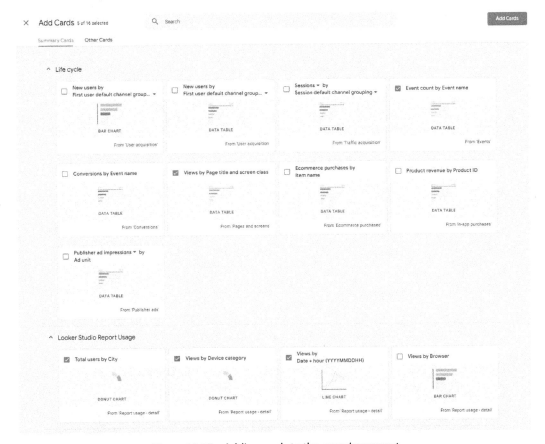

Figure 11.15 – Adding cards to the overview report

3.   Rearrange the order of the cards in the right panel to adjust the layout of the report. Click **Save** and set the report's name to **Report usage overview**. The report will look as follows:

Figure 11.16 – Finished overview report

4.   Add the overview report to the collection by clicking on **Edit collection** from the **Library** page and dragging the newly created overview report under the collection. Then, **Save** the collection.

5.   Back on the Library page, publish the collection from the action menu. This enables GA users can access the custom collection and its associated reports from the left navigation, as shown in the following screenshot:

Figure 11.17 – Custom collection and reports displayed in the left navigation

While GA provides a lot of built-in reporting and enables you to perform fast customizations and explorations, visualizing this data externally in Looker Studio is useful for a few reasons:

- Users can view and access the usage report in a single tool along with all the other reports instead of having to switch to GA. Users may also be unfamiliar with how to navigate and explore GA reports.

- Looker Studio offers more types of visualizations and configuration settings. You can also create more powerful reports in Looker Studio by using advanced features such as calculated fields, parameters, and so on.

- Looker Studio also enables you to better define and manage how users can interact with the report. For example, a user with viewer access to the GA property can modify data that is depicted in the reports by adding secondary dimensions, creating segments, and so on. In Looker Studio, you can determine how little or how much users can change the data that appears in the report through the appropriate use of features such as optional metrics, cross-filtering, filter controls, and more.

GA tracking data, when coupled with Looker Studio's visualization capabilities, enables you to analyze and monitor report usage more effectively.

Visualizing in Looker Studio

You can create a usage dashboard in Looker Studio by connecting to the GA4 property that tracks Looker Studio reports. The following simple dashboard depicts key usage metrics:

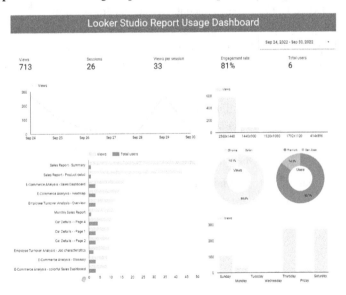

Figure 11.18 – A sample report usage dashboard built in Looker Studio

Follow these steps to build such a dashboard:

1. Create a blank report from the Looker Studio home page. Then, from the **Add data** screen, select **Google Analytics**.

2. Select the appropriate GA account and property defined for the Looker Studio domain:

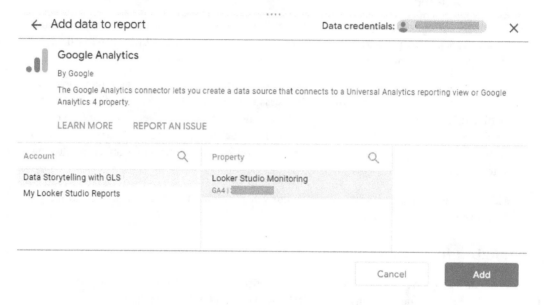

Figure 11.19 – Adding GA4 data to a Looker Studio report

3. From the **Data** panel, use the available list of fields, which includes dimensions and pre-defined metrics, to build the necessary charts. The illustrated sample dashboard comprises the following components:

    A. Scorecards to display the overall metric values. In the sample dashboard, one each is created for **Views**, **Sessions**, **Views per session**, **Engagement rate**, and **Total users**. **Engagement rate** represents the proportion of engaged sessions out of all sessions. An engaged session is one where the user has spent 10 seconds or more or viewed multiple screens/pages.

    B. A horizontal bar chart to display views and users by each report page, which helps in identifying the most popular reports during the selected period.

C. Visualizing views by screen resolution helps users understand the most commonly used screen resolutions to inform any layout changes in the dashboards to improve user experience. A column bar chart serves this purpose quite well as there are only a few dimension values and the labels are short.

D. Donut charts to represent the proportion of views by web browser and the proportion of users by their location. There are just two values for each dimension, so using a donut is apt. As the number of dimension values increases to a much higher number, alternate visualizations such as bar charts, geo maps for location, and more can be considered.

E. It is interesting to view the distribution of page views on different days of the week to understand the patterns of concurrent usage, especially when the report is configured for a longer period spanning multiple weeks. A column chart or even a line chart is a good choice here as the dimension values have a natural order to them.

F. Date range control to allow users to choose different periods. The GA data source defaults to the last 28 days.

The sample dashboard considered here is a simple one using basic visuals and metrics. Depending on your needs, you can augment with additional functionality and data. For instance, you can map user location data with your organizational departments using data blending and monitor the usage for different departments.

Exporting GA4 data to BigQuery

Exporting GA4 data to BigQuery, Google's cloud data warehouse, helps you analyze large volumes of data and perform complex data transformations and queries efficiently. While it may seem like overkill for Looker Studio report usage monitoring, especially at smaller data volumes, exporting raw Analytics data to BigQuery provides benefits such as the following:

- Combining Analytics data with other sources of data easily, either within BigQuery itself or by exporting it to other systems from BigQuery as needed

- Querying and reporting on complete data without any sampling involved

- Manipulating data in ways not easily possible with GA and Looker Studio

- Performing historical analysis beyond the GA limit of 14 months

- Access to more granular data (session-level, event-level, user-level) and additional attributes (for example, geographical hierarchy).

Follow these steps to export GA4 data to BigQuery:

1. From the GA4 **ADMIN** page, select **BigQuery Links** under the **PRODUCT LINKS** section. Select **Link** to create one:

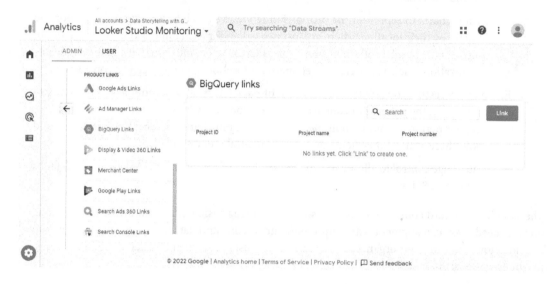

Figure 11.20 – Enabling BigQuery export

Select the BigQuery project that you have access to and that has been set up to be used for this export. If you do not have BigQuery set up yet, you can get access to the free BigQuery sandbox using the instructions provided at `https://cloud.google.com/bigquery/docs/sandbox`. This will suffice to follow along with the current implementation. The project should be configured as follows:

A. The BigQuery API is enabled (it's enabled by default unless explicitly disabled by project admins). Verify this from the **APIs & Services** dashboard in the Google Cloud console, which is accessible from the hamburger menu:

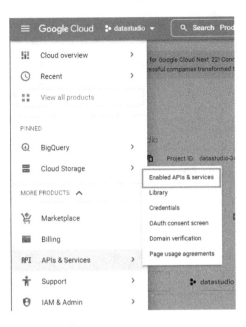

Figure 11.21 – Verifying that the BigQuery API is enabled in the Google Cloud project

B. Add **firebase-measurement@system.gserviceaccount.com** to the project with **Editor** access. From the hamburger menu, select **IAM & Admin | IAM** and click **ADD** at the top. Provide the service account and the role, as shown in the following screenshot:

Figure 11.22 – Adding a service account to the Google Cloud project

2. Choose a location for the BigQuery dataset that will hold the GA data. Once selected, this location cannot be changed.

3. Choose the data streams to export and specify any events to be excluded. Set **Frequency** to **Daily**. If your BigQuery project is enabled with billing (and not just a sandbox), you can enable **Streaming** as well:

Figure 11.23 – Configuring the settings for enabling BigQuery export

4. Review the configuration and click **Submit**.

A separate table is created in BigQuery each day called *events_YYYYMMDD* that contains the full daily export of events data. The following screenshot shows how it appears in the BigQuery console:

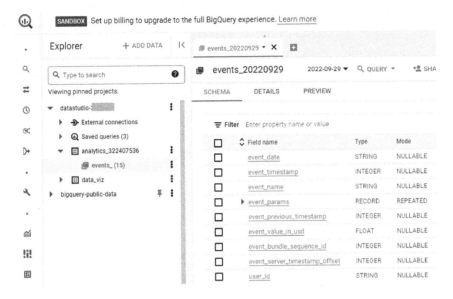

Figure 11.24 – Enabling BigQuery export

Then, you can write SQL queries to look into this data and analyze it within BigQuery. A simple query to find the number of events that occurred by metro area is as follows:

```
SELECT
  geo.metro,
  COUNT(*) AS events
FROM
  'datastudio-xxxxxx.analytics_322407536.events_*'
GROUP BY
  1;
```

You can use wildcard tables to query multiple tables together in a concise way. The preceding query reads the data from the union of all daily events tables. You can also explore and analyze this data in Looker Studio and other integrated tools.

Summary

Monitoring report usage activity is a good way to measure the effectiveness and usefulness of reports. In this chapter, you learned how to monitor Looker Studio reports using Google's web Analytics service, GA. You examined the steps of setting up GA4, the latest version of the service, to track user activity. You also explored the various built-in reports within GA4 and learned how to create custom reports. Visualizing the usage data in Looker Studio allows you to limit the information presented, as well as depict it in more flexible ways than possible within GA4. By doing so, you understood how you can export raw event data to BigQuery so that you can perform advanced and complex analyses on granular and unsampled data.

This was the final chapter of this book. I hope this book helped you learn how to use Looker Studio to build compelling dashboards through a step-by-step approach. I hope it also provided you with foundational knowledge about data storytelling and visualization principles. Looker Studio, as a tool, evolves continuously, and so should your journey as an analyst and data storyteller. Bon voyage!

Index

`Packt.com`

Subscribe to our online digital library for full access to over 7,000 books and videos, as well as industry leading tools to help you plan your personal development and advance your career. For more information, please visit our website.

Why subscribe?

- Spend less time learning and more time coding with practical eBooks and Videos from over 4,000 industry professionals
- Improve your learning with Skill Plans built especially for you
- Get a free eBook or video every month
- Fully searchable for easy access to vital information
- Copy and paste, print, and bookmark content

Did you know that Packt offers eBook versions of every book published, with PDF and ePub files available? You can upgrade to the eBook version at `packt.com` and as a print book customer, you are entitled to a discount on the eBook copy. Get in touch with us at `customercare@packtpub.com` for more details.

At `www.packt.com`, you can also read a collection of free technical articles, sign up for a range of free newsletters, and receive exclusive discounts and offers on Packt books and eBooks.

Other Books You May Enjoy

If you enjoyed this book, you may be interested in these other books by Packt:

Business Intelligence with Databricks SQL

Vihag Gupta

ISBN: 9781803235332

- Understand how Databricks SQL fits into the Databricks Lakehouse Platform
- Perform everyday analytics with Databricks SQL Workbench and business intelligence tools
- Organize and catalog your data assets
- Program the data security model to protect and govern your data
- Tune SQL warehouses (computing clusters) for optimal query experience
- Tune the Delta Lake storage format for maximum query performance
- Deliver extreme performance with the Photon query execution engine
- Implement advanced data ingestion patterns with Databricks SQL

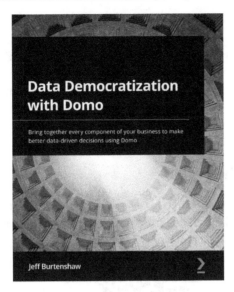

Data Democratization with Domo

Jeff Burtenshaw

ISBN: 9781800568426

- Understand the Domo cloud data warehouse architecture and platform
- Acquire data with Connectors, Workbench, and Federated Queries
- Sculpt data using no-code Magic ETL, Data Views, and Beast Modes
- Profile data with the Data Dictionary, Data Profile, and Usage tools
- Use a storytelling pattern to create dashboards with Domo Stories
- Create, share, and monitor custom alerts activated using webhooks
- Create custom Domo apps, use the Domo CLI, and code with the Python API
- Automate model operations with Python programming and R scripting

Packt is searching for authors like you

If you're interested in becoming an author for Packt, please visit `authors.packtpub.com` and apply today. We have worked with thousands of developers and tech professionals, just like you, to help them share their insight with the global tech community. You can make a general application, apply for a specific hot topic that we are recruiting an author for, or submit your own idea.

Share Your Thoughts

Now you've finished *Data Storytelling with Google Looker Studio*, we'd love to hear your thoughts! Scan the QR code below to go straight to the Amazon review page for this book and share your feedback or leave a review on the site that you purchased it from.

`https://packt.link/r/1-800-56876-2`

Your review is important to us and the tech community and will help us make sure we're delivering excellent quality content.

Printed in the USA
CPSIA information can be obtained
at www.ICGtesting.com
LVHW072245051223
765808LV00048B/1489